Illegal Migrations and
the Huckleberry Finn Problem

John S. W. Park

Illegal Migrations *and*
the Huckleberry Finn Problem

TEMPLE UNIVERSITY PRESS
PHILADELPHIA

TEMPLE UNIVERSITY PRESS
Philadelphia, Pennsylvania 19122
www.temple.edu/tempress

Credit for epigraph on page ix:
A Matter of Time
Written by David Hidalgo and Louis Perez
© 1984 DAVINCE MUSIC (BMI) and NO K.O. MUSIC (BMI)
All Rights Administered by BUG MUSIC, INC., a BMG CHRYSALIS
    COMPANY
All Rights Reserved. Used by Permission.
Reprinted by Permission of Hal Leonard Corporation

Library of Congress Cataloging-in-Publication Data
Park, John S. W.
  Illegal migrations and the Huckleberry Finn problem / John S. W. Park.
    pages cm
  Includes bibliographical references and index.
  ISBN 978-1-4399-1046-7 (alk. paper : cloth) — ISBN 978-1-4399-1047-4
(alk. paper : paperback) — ISBN 978-1-4399-1048-1 (e-book) 1. Minorities—
Legal status, laws, etc.—United States—History. 2. Discrimination—Law and
legislation—United States—History. 3. Law—United States—Public opinion—
History. I. Title.
  KF4755.P368 2013
  342.7308'7—dc23

                                                                    2012042307

Printed in the United States of America

2 4 6 8 9 7 5 3 1

This one is for Edward.

Contents

Speak softly, don't wake the baby,
Come and hold me once more,
Before I have to leave.

I

Status and Illegality in American Public Law and Culture

The Huckleberry Finn Problem

Would You Tell?

I enjoy lecturing off campus, if only because it gives me the opportunity to speak to people quite different from the college-age students I teach every term. When I'm talking to a group of older folks at seven or eight in the evening, they really want to be there, and I know it's less about me than the topic I'm presenting. That topic almost always relates to immigration, race relations, or both, and in southern California, this tends to draw a crowd. During one event, a screaming woman shook her fist at me; during that same evening, another hoped that I would run for public office. It's the kind of thing that tends to draw passionate feelings. And everyone seems to know someone who's illegal, or someone who's hiring "those illegals," or someone who's not doing enough to keep "those Mexicans" out of the country.

On many occasions, though, during the Q & A, I've asked members of my audience whether they *would* report someone who was illegally residing in the United States, knowing that such a person would face deportation. Would they report someone they knew personally, maybe at work or in a more casual setting? Did they ever suspect that the new kid at their kid's school came unlawfully, and would they take the trouble to check? The day laborers at the street corners—did they ever want to check their papers, too? What about their neighbor's maid, her gardener, or his nanny? What about their *own* maid, gardener, or nanny? The varied, textured responses to questions like these were not always what I'd expected, but listening to the conversations made me a better teacher, and I suppose this is why it's a good idea to light out from campus from time to time. If you knew someone who was "illegal," would you tell? This entire book is centered on that last question, and its main point is to show how this kind of dilemma has been a recurring one in American legal history and culture. Many generations of Americans have encountered "illegal" persons of one kind or another.

Thrownness

I've often started many of my classes and lectures by talking about the odd moral and ethical paradox of immigration and citizenship status. It's a paradox I myself learned to appreciate from studying liberal political theory, public law, and modern German philosophers. The most complicated person to read and to understand was Martin Heidegger, and not just because he was once a Nazi, or at least a Nazi sympathizer, nor because his writings were so impenetrable. Heidegger was a deeply flawed German philosopher, but most scholars now acknowledge that his contributions to political philosophy were staggering in their scope and originality. Among many other ideas, Heidegger described the concept of "thrownness," a kind of (self-)awareness of how many of the most important circumstances and aspects of ourselves—our gender, our race, the families into which we're born, and even our core beliefs—are things that describe who we are, but are not the result of conscious choice. We *are* men or women, Catholic or Protestant, Korean or Greek—these adjectives have a social meaning in the real worlds in which we live, and they describe who we are, but I certainly don't recall ever *choosing* those characteristics that define who I am. As Heidegger might say, I was "thrown" into that intersection of Roman Catholic Korean American guy when I was born in Seoul to a devout Roman Catholic migrating Korean mother who, as it turns out, wanted a girl. Now I might be able to change one or two aspects of myself, but not without significant effort.

Like most philosophical concepts, Heidegger's description is both simple and powerful, especially for students of modern political systems that ostensibly value notions of free will, responsibility, choice, and consent. Heidegger's twentieth-century insights helped illuminate a revolution in political thought that had begun with the European Enlightenment, when leading thinkers of the seventeenth, eighteenth, and nineteenth centuries challenged the political authorities of their day. Within liberal political theory, as expressed in the works of John Locke, John Stuart Mill, and Jean-Jacques Rousseau, notions of human equality had a certain, radical shape—these philosophers argued that all persons had free will and the ability to reason, all should be regarded as having equal rights, and so the only legitimate grounds on which to base government was the popular consensus of reasonable, rights-bearing persons within a commonwealth.

In Locke's time, the theory was revolutionary—at a time when kings asserted a "divine right" to rule their subjects, Locke was a prime target for assassination because of his eloquent arguments for consent and choice, against princes who exercised authority based on the circumstances of their birth. Where these princes saw the "hand of God" placing them on their thrones, Locke only saw "thrownness." European princes insisted that God Himself made them kings, and that their subjects must thus obey; men were "blank slates," replied Locke and his supporters, and the sons of princes and kings had no special right to rule over the sons of clerks or of commoners without their consent. Women should have the same rights as men, added Mill, and the sum of electoral majorities—situated from a position of equality, one person, one vote—should drive all governments. Of course, these once radical ideas form the core of representative governments in our day, and they have become in American political thought a "common sense" about how political institutions ought to be designed and operated. The American Constitution validated and protected many obvious inequalities—against African Americans and women and poorer Americans, for example—but in American constitutional history, one is tempted still to see an arc, as various kinds of arbitrary characteristics are no longer defined as distinct legal advantages or disabilities. Popular consensus now (not so much in 1776) tells us that one's ability to enjoy basic constitutional rights should not hinge on the fact that one's father was Kenyan or one's mother was Korean, that one is a man or another a woman, or that one is straight or gay, rich or poor.

Still, "thrownness" continues to shape political life; this is most obvious in the law of citizenship, as most people are born "citizens" because they were born in a particular place or become citizens because their parents were also citizens. The Latin terms *ius sanguinis* (right by blood) and *ius soli* (right by soil) describe how political membership often worked in medieval Europe, and how it still mostly works today. Most American citizens acquire their citizenship because their parents were American citizens (*ius sanguinis*), or because they happened to be born within the territory of the United States (*ius soli*). Under the Fourteenth Amendment, "all persons born or naturalized in the United States, and subject to the jurisdiction thereof, are citizens of the United States and of the State wherein they reside." It is, and has thus far been interpreted as, a birthright citizenship rule. The structural inequality arises because some people are born in better circumstances than others, either to parents from richer nations or just in richer nations. And when people born in poorer countries want to migrate to a wealthier one to change their circumstances, the reaction at the other end is often not neighborly.

Wealthy nations have guarded their borders jealously, and the United States has been no exception; indeed its system of fences, borders, and surveillance has become perhaps the most technologically sophisticated of all. This has functioned to make membership itself, as the political philosopher Joseph Carens has pointed out, more like a feudal privilege, something acquired by accident of birth, capable of greatly amplifying one's rights and opportunities, and yet something not "deserved" or "earned." What did most American citizens *do* to become American citizens? What gives them a moral or legal right to exclude others who were not as lucky? When people fleeing persecution or just looking for a better life try to come here, what gives American citizens the right to say yes or no? No one, after all, deserves in any moral sense to be born on one side of a man-made political boundary rather than another, and yet in our modern world, those boundaries often make all the difference.

Runaway Slaves, Unlawful Migrations

Whatever the moral ambiguities, through concepts like national sovereignty, nations have and do exclude people considered undesirable for one reason or another. And despite the fences, borders, and surveillance that characterize these exercises of national sovereignty, persons have come to industrialized, wealthier countries without inspection over the past several decades, to the point where their numbers are exceeding millions of persons. In response, countries like the United States have spent even more money and resources on enforcement—more fencing, more surveillance, and now more removal. Hundreds of thousands are deported each year, even more people "concede deportability" and "voluntarily depart" when they are discovered or arrested. Yet the numbers have continued to grow, from an estimated three million persons in the late 1980s, to at least six million in the late 1990s, and perhaps more than twelve to fifteen to twenty million at the end of this decade. Terms like "workplace raid" and "detention facility" are common parlance in immigration reporting and scholarship, as the "illegal immigrant" has become a regular fixture of life in the United States, the source of ever greater contention in our politics. Legislative solutions have tended to fail, and in the vacuum created by that failure, there is more enforcement, more removal, and more unlawful migration. Many scholars have discussed at length the geopolitical and economic reasons why this unlawful migration persists, as well as the rationale behind state actions designed, often futilely,

to stem it. Still other scholars have explored the political and material consequences of illegal status on American society, as well as the precarious position of the illegal immigrants themselves.

The point of this book, however, is to take a step back, and to suggest
that problems of "illegality" and illegal status have had a special shape in
the United States, the first of the consent-based modern republics. This is
because the United States was at its founding committed to universal principles of equality even as it denied that same equality to large numbers of people within its borders. This contradiction inspired unique forms of illegality,
often tied to migration, that are instructive for our contemporary dilemmas.

Specifically, for chattel slaves, running away from their masters made
them "illegal"; federal law and state rules both described runaway slaves as a
legal and political problem until they were returned to their rightful place,
their Southern masters. We typically don't consider fugitive slaves as "illegal
immigrants," but in many ways, they were, and their very existence as people—in places where they shouldn't have been—raised questions not unlike
the ones we face today. Slaves often saw themselves in impossible circumstances, faced with a miserable life, with no prospects for change, in a life
trapped by unimaginable daily abuse, and like many, many people who find
themselves in these circumstances, they fled. Their migration, however, was
illegal, and their efforts to escape formed the core of a set of political and
social problems that triggered ever more draconian state and federal rules,
rules so rigid that they precipitated a national crisis and thus endangered the
very Republic itself. Faced with harsher federal mandates to return fugitive
slaves, a great many citizens disobeyed the law.

This work, then, is intended to be corrective: in considering the plight of
contemporary illegal immigrants, many commentators have suggested that
their widespread "illegality" is a rather new phenomenon within the nation-
state system, and I will argue here that this is not entirely true. For runaway slaves and ostensibly "free blacks" in the North, rules governing their
return and denying them the protection of their basic rights were not only
commonplace, they *were* constitutional, the result of consent-based agreement among white property owners. If the Chief Justices John Marshall and
Roger Taney were correct, the formation of the United States did not include
certain kinds of people, namely Native Americans and black slaves, and so
such persons were always like alien bodies within the body of the republic.
These people were the objects of a political agreement made by others, and
if the former had escaped from their masters, they did so beyond the pale
of the law. We live in a moment when national sovereignty, national boundaries, and the right of all nation-states to determine who may or may not

migrate, and thus be "lawfully present" within the United States, are all taken for granted. Yet these consent-based agreements, I shall argue, now tend to enhance the very kinds of structural inequalities that our legal system has rejected over the past two centuries.

As slavery grew in economic value, so did the number of runaway slaves, which in turn generated a range of responses throughout the country. State legislatures like the ones in Illinois and Oregon attempted to ban not just slavery, but also the possibility of "free blacks" and fugitive slaves living among white citizens. In response, abolitionists like the ones at Oberlin College in Ohio openly violated federal and state rules by helping fugitive slaves escape to freedom. Oberlin admitted some as students. The town itself was a kind of "sanctuary city" where a significant number of runaway slaves and free blacks had settled. Angered by such developments, Southern legislators and their sympathizers approved of new fugitive slave rules; these became more severe, culminating in the infamous Fugitive Slave Act of 1850 and the *Dred Scott* decision in 1857. In that decision, the United States Supreme Court attempted to deny the possibility that blacks were, or ever could be, American citizens. Within this literature and history of runaway slaves, we can see the problem of illegality in all of its fullness and terror, and we can see how the problem of illegality is not a new one, but rather a variant of a much older dilemma whose parallels should cause all of us to pause and reflect upon what we are doing, individually and collectively, when we regulate contemporary immigration in the ways we have.

Asians as Illegal Aliens

The problem of unlawful status was not resolved after emancipation or the Thirteenth Amendment. The former slaves and their descendants still lived within white supremacy, an ideology and political movement that became ever more intense after federal troops left the South; racial identity supplanted their identity as slaves, and it became the most significant aspect of their selves within the new law of segregation. African Americans were once slaves, but now they were defined as "Negro" or "colored," and such persons were pushed, threatened, and shoved again into the margins of American society.

Moreover, other people would arrive during that period to add complex dimensions to questions of equality and fairness in American society. As "strangers from a different shore," Asian migrants complicated issues of race, belonging, and illegality even further. Congress' solution was unequivocal: Chinese laborers were not supposed to arrive in the United States under the

Chinese Exclusion Act approved in 1882. Yet many Chinese immigrants continued to come, often illegally, either by helping one another misrepresent themselves or by paying off willing whites to collaborate with them and smuggle them in. Despite the bitterness of immigration detention, despite these new federal laws "harsh as tigers," many Chinese migrants after 1882 evaded the law to live in the United States. To this day, it's still quite interesting to ask a classroom full of college students to evaluate this phenomenon from a moral point of view. Would you have come unlawfully, if you were a Chinese immigrant, to flee a country falling apart, your country "carved like a melon," for the chance at a better life, even within the margins of American society? In short, would it be morally acceptable to evade these race-conscious immigration laws? What if you were a good white Christian in San Francisco, and what if you somehow learned that your Chinese neighbor of ten years was actually not the American son of the Chinese man who himself wasn't really an American citizen? Would you tell?

The problem persisted in other dimensions. New Asian immigrants and their white neighbors, for example, wrestled with analogous dilemmas in the agricultural fields of California in the decades after Exclusion. This state was the first to pass an Alien Land Law, first through its legislature in 1913, and then in 1920 by popular referendum. Asian farmers, particularly Japanese farmers, were not supposed to lease or own land thereafter; other states passed similar rules against these "aliens ineligible for citizenship." Yet these Asian immigrants circumvented these laws, too, sometimes violating them through the willing cooperation of American citizens. Many of the central cases testing the constitutionality of the alien land laws were striking because Asian litigants didn't appear formally at all—*whites* complained that these rules unlawfully restricted their right to lease and sell land to people of their choice. This was all to no avail: by 1925, the United States Supreme Court would uphold the bar against Asians petitioning for American citizenship, and it would also affirm the constitutionality of rules restricting land ownership to American citizens and those eligible for citizenship.

Still, even after 1925, by evading the law, by going around the law, by lying about who actually owned what, Japanese and other Asian immigrants did not obey these laws. Many Asian immigrants thus refused to comply with a set of rules designed to disable them economically. Again, having asked numerous students what they might do in similar circumstances, I've been struck by their willingness to break the law (at least in theory). It's not just the Asian students—many white students freely offered their white identities, so that the Asian kid who wouldn't be able to hold land could "borrow" the whiteness of someone who could. Furthermore, they promised not to tell anyone about their unlawful arrangements and swore that they would never betray their Asian friends, with a passion that reminds us of Peter and Jesus. In Asian American history, as in African American history, problems of illegality, disobedience to law, and moral justifications to avoid the law—these are recurring themes that tell us a great deal about how law might be viewed from the bottom up, from the perspective of people who were *subject* to the law and then resisted it in complex, disquieting ways. Asian Americans may have been framed as a "model minority" in recent decades, but for most of Asian American history, many Asian Americans and Asian immigrants were violating both the letter and spirit of American law, and more than a few of their white neighbors were helping them do it.

One of my students said in class that if his Japanese American neighbors had faced internment, and if they'd asked him to hide them from the authorities for fear of the camps, he would have tried his best to do so. The circumstances reminded him of Anne Frank, he said, and the young man indicated how he would have felt no less an American citizen for having helped his neighbors, even if it was the federal government itself that had ordered the curfew, the evacuation, and then their internment. For many years now, I've thought about his comments and others like them, and it has occurred to me that those of us who study the intersections of legal theory and ethnic studies have not considered sufficiently the profound consequences that might follow from more careful considerations of such reactions. Systemic, recurring disobedience of the law might teach us important lessons about what we mean when we talk about the rule of law, about justice, and about the moral and philosophical consequences of doing—or not doing—what the law requires.

The Huckleberry Finn Problem

Some social dilemmas are best seen small, in the lives and decisions of individuals, and so the next chapter revisits an American classic, *Huckleberry Finn*, originally published in 1884 by Mark Twain, and perhaps the best novel written in the American vernacular. We turn there because this story is familiar to most Americans, and its central moral dilemma lies at the heart of this book that you are holding now. At the center of Twain's story is the relationship between a young boy and a runaway slave, set during a time when slavery was lawful and right (in the eyes of whites), and when all white men knew that runaways should be returned to their lawful masters, no matter the condition of their servitude or the reasons they had for attempting to escape. Twain's novel says volumes about slavery, about the United

States, and about the conflict between a boy's good heart and his country's bad faith.

The law of slavery pervades the novel even though it never appears explicitly. Indeed, much of the story is "lawless," where law is either entirely absent or at best ineffective, and yet the law of slavery governs so much of the life of Jim, the fugitive slave who must rely on Huck to help him to a precarious freedom. The novel is about a runaway slave whose predicament can tell us a great deal about the problem of illegality more generally, through the powerful, enduring narrative of that unique friendship that develops between Huckleberry Finn and Jim. Their close relationship in spite of the law of slavery might say something profound to us now, to those of us who live lawfully in the United States and yet see and interact every day with those who don't. As the two main characters experience their Heideggerian "thrownness" together, on a raft no less, Twain's masterpiece helps us consider more fundamental dilemmas about law, obedience, status, and the troubles of figuring out our common humanity within an ostensibly progressive legal system that has always divided people into problematic categories. These categories at one time seemed so moral, unproblematic, and correct—Huck feels obligated, for example, if he is to be a "good person," to return Jim to slavery—even as we now agree that the very existence of slavery was abhorrent, unjust, and repulsive.

Now, to anticipate at least some of my critics, this book is not about how forms of slavery continue to exist in our current day, nor is it about how illegal immigration is like slavery, or how or if twenty-first-century illegal immigrants have it as badly as nineteenth-century chattel slaves. The two topics are entirely different, and comparing these institutions and people in such a way would tend to become a voluminous and ultimately ridiculous exercise. The forced migration of millions of Africans, their enslavement over several generations, and the many attendant horrors of American slavery are distinct historical realities that militate against any such comparison. Similarly, the condition of contemporary illegal immigrants in the United States is a distinctive twentieth-century phenomenon in terms of its scale and scope. It is the result of postindustrial capitalism, massive revolutions in transportation and communication, and renewed assertions of national sovereignty in an ever-shrinking and much more kinetic world. At any rate, undocumented aliens are not chattel slaves, even though activists and others in recent decades have drawn rhetorical parallels between the two groups. In the late 1980s, for instance, when religious groups and immigrant activists protected Central Americans fleeing from their countries, the activists referred to themselves as a "sanctuary movement," their network of activists as an "underground railroad." This book is not about the strengths or weaknesses of those comparisons per se, as I myself think there are stark differences between nineteenth-century slavery and illegal immigration over the past few decades.

Instead, the primary point of this project is to say something specifically about American public law and its tendency to create "unlawful" people whose status and condition are subject to intense internal political disputes and to garden-variety moral confusion. Since the birth of the Republic, American public law has created categories of people with disparate rights and opportunities, structuring not just disabilities for the people who suffer the law's force, but also dilemmas for people who are often placed in the awkward position of triggering the law's force when they come face to face with an "unlawful" person. Inflicting the law is hard in such circumstances, especially when there's so much evidence of the common humanity of the other. They speak, yearn for freedom, desire an education, and love their children, just like us. Truly, what should we do *now* when we encounter an "unlawful" person? This study looks at that question through a longer lens, to see how the American experience has been full of instructive examples of citizens who've encountered "unlawful people" through a range of circumstances and throughout our common history.

As we shall see from this other perspective, in the fullness of time, those who inflict the law against the other can come off as scoundrels, as morally reprehensible people, while those who do nothing are mostly torn by indecision. Many are ambivalent. And yet the people who disobeyed the law, whether in history or in fiction, are the people we tend to admire the most. Simon Legree had no compunction about beating and abusing slaves, for example, as all of that was lawful, but he is one of the most reviled villains of nineteenth-century American literature, and he is the foil against whom we are meant to see the goodness of Uncle Tom in Harriet Beecher Stowe's novel. Huckleberry Finn, on the other hand, reveals his goodness and decency at that very moment when he chooses to help Jim escape again from bondage, even though Huck believes he will go to hell for it.

When we consider real-life figures from the same era, our judgments remain the same. Roger Taney was a distinguished alumnus of the Harvard Law School, the fifth Chief Justice of the United States Supreme Court, and its first Roman Catholic. Taney's portrait still hangs prominently in the magnificent Harvard Law Library, but as every passing first-year student knows, Taney was the author of *Dred Scott*, the man who said in that case that the American founders never considered persons of African descent to be American citizens nor ever capable of citizenship. Taney deduced from that original understanding the conclusion that persons of African descent should *never* be considered American citizens. Taney remains there in that Library, his portrait an object lesson of an historical error of horrible proportions. On the other hand, Harriet Tubman was a great American hero, at least according to my seven-year old daughter Zoe. She took away that lesson during Black History Month, as she heard the story of how Ms. Tubman had helped people escape from slavery through an Underground Railroad that wasn't really underground. White people helped her, too, Zoe said, and so they were wonderful people as well. Ms. Tubman, I replied, was a law breaker, as were all of her helpful white friends, and other law-abiding white people wanted Ms. Tubman captured or killed for helping slaves escape. Zoe was horrified, as she didn't get that other part of the story in the second grade, and so that was how my reply occupied our family for about a week, as Gowan and I both tried to explain to Zoe and to her sisters, Isabel and Sophie, how someone who had broken American law on a regular basis throughout her life should still now be considered a great American hero.

Living outside the Law

It's instructive to keep these lessons in mind as we discuss contemporary public institutions and their responses to undocumented immigrants in our workplaces, in our schools and at our major universities, and in our towns and cities. We tend to see these types of inversions all over again; showing that, more than anything, is the entire point of this project. Toward that end, Parts II and III of this book focus on labor and on education, as two large-scale areas governed by public law through which we see the evolving discourses of status and illegality working over time. These two areas are distinctive and instructive in unique ways: a close study of labor can tell us a great deal about who was or wasn't a full member of American society, who was or wasn't eligible for the primary benefits of those collaborative, corporate arrangements that became so essential in the United States. Always, access to dignified forms of work has separated citizens from others. In another way, education was once the privilege of a very few until in the late nineteenth and early twentieth centuries, when American educators developed public education systems to provide schooling to more Americans than ever before. Exclusion from this system revealed and reinforced patterns of belonging and citizenship in American public life, and some of the most compelling controversies about equality and fairness in the mid-twentieth century turned on questions of who ought to have access to this important form of public spending. When discussing educational institutions, Americans have spoken of concepts like fairness and equality of opportunity in the most eloquent terms. In our own time, examination of these two areas—labor and education—can still tell us who is and isn't under the full protection of American law.

Indeed, American law once provided no protection whatsoever to many people, and Part II of this book begins by examining the way that labor was organized during and after slavery. Part II shows how American public law structured exploitative relationships between whites and blacks, then restricted the supply of labor through immigration rules, primarily against Asians and now, perhaps unwittingly, still allows for the exploitation of illegal immigrants in a broad range of settings. The last chapter of Part II concerns efforts among labor organizers and their allies to address these trends, primarily by creating new strategies to assist undocumented workers. By insisting that all persons should have dignity in their work and that they ought to be free from abuse and exploitation at the hands of their employers, contemporary labor activists have advocated for people who are an inextricable part of the American economy even though the law says that they should have no place within it nor expect any protection from its provisions. I argue that these circumstances—a law that fails to protect the most vulnerable, and people choosing to help others irrespective of status—are not new in American legal and social history.

Part III deals with the rules that have governed education, that have determined who was and wasn't fit for public resources levied and set aside for that purpose. This part examines the ideal of equal access to educational resources, as they appeared in key federal cases from the early to mid-twentieth century, when public schools and universities became so central to the lives of more and more Americans. Part III also reviews the widespread tendencies toward re-segregation and inequality even in the midst of strident, repeated declarations in favor of desegregation, including solemn commitments to the education of all children. The last chapter in Part III examines how contemporary rules are moving American institutions further away from the ideals of equality expressed in landmark decisions like *Brown v. Board of Education*. That development has been the result of new public laws and common practices that have attempted to control (yet again) the terms under which an education might be offered. Public education has been characterized as a fundamental right that ought to be available to all persons in the United States, not just its citizens; in recent years, in dramatic ways, students without lawful immigration status have made the most compelling appeals in favor of these ideals, and they have thus raised anew *our* moral position as we listen to their pleas for equal treatment, coming as they have, once again, from these persons defined as outside the law.

At work and in our schools, many Americans will have had a variety of "Huckleberry Finn" moments already, times when they've met or discovered someone who was out of status, unlawful, illegal—people defined by some of our current politicians as "nightmares" and singled out as public threats, social problems, or both. Perhaps this unlawful person was a co-worker, an employee, a student, maybe a fellow student, or even a close relative or friend. As we shall see, many public laws require American citizens to check for immigration status across a wide range of circumstances, and some states and local jurisdictions have approved laws to discourage the settlement of "illegals" within their boundaries, whether to protect their public resources or for reasons that may seem to others to reflect a legacy of racism or xenophobia. Whatever the case, public law requires Americans to check and to tell when we've encountered people who shouldn't be here, people who are out of place. Such rules have a sad history in the United States, Jim and Huckleberry Finn would have recognized them, and so we turn first, then, to a careful consideration of that great American story as a way of framing the discussions that follow.

Race, Law, and Personhood
in *Huckleberry Finn*

Huck and Jim

It's an amazing novel. *Huckleberry Finn* works on so many complex levels, and Shelley Fisher Fishkin is right to claim that the work represents for Mark Twain a quantum leap in his art. As other scholars have pointed out, Huck represents a variant of the national ethos, as the restless young man who wishes to be free from the civilizing influences of everyone around him, especially his well-meaning guardians. If Tom Sawyer, Twain's other most famous protagonist, represents the American tendency to be enamored of Old World conventions and romance, Huckleberry Finn is his opposite—untutored, uncivilized, and an outcast among the good people of "St. Petersburg," Missouri. Tom Sawyer draws from a vivid imagination to amuse himself and to trick others; Huck Finn reports events in straightforward terms, revealing both his childishness and his inability to "fit in" to the conventional norms of the frontier South.[1]

There are good reasons for Huck's position as an outsider: his mother is absent and his Pap is a horrible drunk. Pap abuses him to the point where Huck becomes at once accustomed to the abuse and hostile to his father. Huck does receive care from other adults, but they seem unable to reach the boy on a deeper level; Huck's guardians, Judge Thatcher and the Widow Douglas, take turns trying to "sivilize" Huck, the first by trying to discipline his money, and the second by exposing him to religion, school, and conventional manners. None of it takes. Huck doesn't value money, and prayer appears pointless. Huck cannot live easily among people who save, pray, read, study, use utensils, educate themselves and others, and otherwise live within the modernity of the mid-nineteenth century. At the beginning of the novel, he runs away, and at the end, he looks West—indeed, we know he will "light out for the territory," his journey yet another symbol for a restless, young American character not so much interested in living unencumbered rather than just unable to live within civilization and its rules, all of it "dismal regular and decent" like the widow herself. And yet we also know that eventually, civilization will follow Huck, just as it does throughout the story.[2]

If Huck represents the ethos of white men who yearn for a space away from civilization above all else, Jim represents the darker aspects of this same civilization in every sense. He is black, he is a slave, he is unfree. Jim has a wife and children, but they do not belong to one another, and for a profit that she cannot pass over, the Widow Douglas intends to sell him away from all that he loves. Jim is a thing, a "nigger" in the eyes of all the white people around him, even as Jim plans and plots for a freedom that they take for granted and often abuse. Indeed, if we understand by freedom that quintessential human capacity to think and plan and will one's own actions in the world, Jim appears as the most free of all the adults in *Huckleberry Finn*, even though he is the slave. Yet his desire for freedom is the very thing that Huck finds repellent and sympathetic: it is at once a wish he shares, but one that he also immediately recognizes as inappropriate for someone like Jim, a slave who should be with his master. How does Huck know that Jim should not run away? He just does, having grown up in the South, around people who've shared this conception, whether through religion, custom, or law. Even Pap, the alcoholic outcast of white society, knows that it's just wrong for a black man to be free, to "take on airs," even become a professor in a free state where he can *vote*. If Jim had run into Pap instead of Huck, if Pap knew that Jim was a runaway, Jim would surely have ended up taken back for a profit or simply dead. If Mark Twain had written *Pap Finn*, it would have been a shorter novel. But Huckleberry Finn struggles with Jim's condition, as he finds in Jim everything he misses from his own father—nurturing, compassion, and love.

That Jim's fate rests in the hands of this boy, this young man who cannot live within the conventions of civilized society—and yet knows of its conventions—makes for compelling drama. As a rational actor yearning to be free, Jim believes that Huck might not care enough about the rules to turn him in, and when he doesn't, Jim tells Huck that he is the best friend Jim ever had; as a young man constantly "lonesome," which is the heaviest price for all men who gain complete independence, Huck sees Jim as a troublesome and yet wonderful companion, a fugitive like himself, the only adult Huck loves and trusts, a man who does not abuse him but loves and cares for him. But like all slaves, Jim becomes for Huck both a man and a problem. Huck's struggle with this love and anxiety for Jim forms the core of the novel.[3]

"A big stack o' money . . ."

At the beginning of the story, though, Huck cannot recognize Jim's condition as an especially precarious one, even though Huck himself was reduced to a kind of property. When his father reappears and threatens to take him from the widow, Huck becomes a ward over whom the grown-ups fight in court. Pap wants Huck's money, the widow and Judge Thatcher want what they think is in the best interests of the child, and they appear at the mercy of a naive judge. "[It] was a new judge that had just come, and he didn't know the old man; so he said courts mustn't interfere and separate families if they could help it; said he'd druther not take a child away from its father." The new judge gives presumptive custody to Pap, but when Pap drinks and acts himself, the judge and his wife attempt to reform him, though this fails within two paragraphs. Pap is incorrigible, but more importantly, he is unrelenting in pursuit of his son's money, to the point of kidnapping him and removing him altogether from the reach of the law.[4]

Pap possesses Huck in the most brutal way—he holds his own son as a hostage in a remote cabin for over two months, beats him constantly, and tries to undo Huck's education, "no books nor study," but plenty of cursing. Huck explains that although he enjoys a carefree life away from the widow, he can no longer stand the beatings: "I was all over welts." Things get out of hand: Pap chases and almost kills his son in a drunken rage, after which the boy plots his escape.[5] Huck must run away from his father, and so his plan includes an axe, a dead pig, and a canoe floating down the river. He simulates his own murder.

Huck attempts to erase himself from the earth, so that neither his father nor the widow can take custody of him. This strategy is reminiscent of how *slaves* often attempted to escape slavery by staging their own deaths—by drowning, through exposure, and through other forms of violence. Indeed, this is one desperate way that slaves in the South tried to escape their masters, a fact that anyone in the South, and certainly Mark Twain, would have known. That Huck is reduced to a kind of captive property under the control of a homicidal "master" makes his escape reasonable and necessary, even familiar to many of Twain's readers. Huck must escape like a slave in part so that the law cannot reach him, because its officers utterly failed to see that his father should never have had him in the first place.[6]

Despite his similarity to Jim, Huck cannot understand, or rather half-understands, the reason for Jim's escape onto Jackson's Island. Huck learns that Jim has "run-off" after overhearing a conversation between Miss Watson and the Widow Douglas about selling him to a "nigger trader": "I hear old missus tell de widder she gwyne to sell me down to Orleans, but she didn' want to, but she could git eight hund'd dollars for me, en it 'uz sich a big stack o' money she couldn' resis'." Like Huck, Jim planned his escape, and he chose to leave by raft rather than by foot, as a raft leaves no tracks. But even as Jim finishes the story of his escape, Huck's first question reveals his ignorance of Jim's situation: Jim has had nothing to eat, so why didn't he catch "mud turkles"?

Jim's answer draws the distinction between him and this white boy: "How you gwyne to git 'm? You can't slip up on um en grab um; en how's a body gwyne to hit um wid a rock? How could a body do it in de night? En I warn't gwyne to show mysef on de bank in de daytime." Though they are both fugitives, it doesn't occur to Huck that Jim can never appear alone during the day without arousing suspicion. An entire body of federal and state statutes governs Jim's status as a fugitive slave, a fact that starkly separates Jim from Huck. After this explanation, Huck appears to understand why Jim has had nothing to eat, but throughout the remainder of the story, Huck often fails to grasp the danger inherent in Jim's predicament, even as he grows to love and value Jim as a friend. The two grow intertwined by circumstance as well: suspecting that Huck had been murdered, the townspeople look for his body in the river, and Huck learns that Jim is the prime suspect. Huck becomes both the means towards Jim's freedom, but also the very evidence that Jim is not a murderer, and yet as they float down the river together, Huck ponders the thought of turning Jim over to the authorities as a fugitive slave. Will he or won't he do it?[7]

"It's kind of slow, and it takes a long time . . ."

This tension is heightened throughout the novel by the assorted characters that Huck and Jim encounter in their journey. No one appears sympathetic to men like Jim. The law is against the fugitive slave, but a greater danger lies in a "lawlessness" endemic to the frontier in which they find themselves; indeed, much of the environment that Jim and Huck encounter is truly lawless.

For example, the Shepherdsons and Grangerfords hunt and kill one another, and for no other reason that they've always hunted and killed one another. When Huck comes upon Colonel Grangerford, Huck explains that he is "a gentleman, you see." His house is immaculate, his family appears cultivated and well-mannered (though prone to bad poetry), and "each person had their own nigger to wait on them." They host parties, eat well, and otherwise enjoy all the trappings of the Southern aristocracy. And every one of the males is murderous. When Huck asks his new friend Buck Grangerford why he had just attempted to kill Harney Shepherdson, Buck replies that Harney "never done nothing to me," but "it's on account of the feud." Now, none of the Grangerfords, even the "old people," can remember the origins of the feud, and yet it remains the most dangerous fact of their lives. Like the Montagues and Capulets, the two families are quite similar: "[the Shepherdsons] was as high-toned and well born and rich and grand as the tribe of Grangerfords." Both are equally successful and successfully murderous.[8]

For Huck, as a visitor to this place, the Grangerfords and Shepherdsons are confusing: Buck tells the story of how his cousin Bud, "fourteen years old," was hunted down over five miles by "old Baldy Shepherdson," who then killed him. When he knew the old man would catch him, "[Bud] faced around so as to have the bullet holes in front, you know." To Buck, that Bud took the bullet in the chest represents a sign of bravery; to Huck, that an old man would chase and shoot a boy makes the man a "coward." Buck insists that this is not so: "There ain't a coward amongst them Shepherdsons—not a one. And there ain't no cowards amongst the Grangerfords either." That they regularly kill and bleed one another makes them brave, though in a way that Huck cannot understand. The two families attend the same church service, all armed, and "it did seem to me to be one of the roughest Sundays I had run across yet." Even as Sophia Grangerford loves Harley Shepherdson, choosing Huck as her unwitting messenger, their elopement simply leads to more mindless violence, all of it transcending reason or law. As Huck rediscovers Jim and prepares to leave the Grangerfords, a group of older Shepherdson men ambush Buck and his cousin Joe; they are slaughtered as Huck witnesses from a tree.

Throughout this portion of the novel, there is no law. No public authority stopped the first instance of the feud, and Buck assures Huck that "by and by everybody's killed off, and there ain't no more feud. But it's kind of slow, and takes a long time." In other words, no public authority will end the feud—law is entirely absent, legal institutions have no force, there will be blood until they're all dead. Instead of law, "well-born" men like Colonel Grangerford lead their families toward an unthinking, unending predation.[9]

We see this theme again later in the story, at another town, when Huck witnesses Colonel Sherburn, another powerful figure who appears as a kind of Nietzschean Ubermensch on the frontier, a man with no conscience filled only with contempt for the mob that seeks to lynch him for killing Boggs, the town drunk in a small village in Arkansas. Boggs appears loud but harmless. He threatens Huck, but "another one says, 'I wisht old Boggs'd threaten me, 'cuz then I'd know I warn't gwyne to die for a thousan' year.'" Boggs claims a grievance with Sherburn, challenging him "to come out and meet the man you've swindled." Without answering the charge, and with but one warning, at one o'clock, Sherburn shoots Boggs dead. The villagers are shocked, though many have seen it coming. Yet not long after Boggs' corpse is taken from the street, the very witnesses play out the scene of the murder for their own amusement until one of them recommends that "Sherburn ought to be lynched." They soon become a lynch mob, though it's clear that most are just curious to see what will happen when they come upon Sherburn.

Sherburn's reaction is surprising, as he feels no genuine concern for his safety whatsoever from the mob. His reply suggests that there is no rule of law, certainly not in the village, and perhaps nowhere in the world. The mob did not bring a "man" with them—they cannot punish Sherburn according to settled rules, nor can they simply kill him. Without the will of a "man," someone as equally powerful as Sherburn himself, Sherburn says he has nothing to fear from them. His reply speaks both to the powerlessness and the cruelty of the mob: "Because you're brave enough to tar and feather poor friendless cast-out women that come along here, did that make you think you had grit enough to lay your hands on a MAN?" To Sherburn, the mob is "beneath pitifulness." Through his soliloquy, Sherburn puts himself above and beyond the mob, but in a way completely disconcerting to Huck and to anyone reading *Huckleberry Finn*. In this town where people torture animals for their amusement, where they re-enact and congratulate themselves for witnessing a murder, where this Sherburn can kill a person in plain view, there is clearly no law, only power and will. That a man like Sherburn rises to the top of this society suggests a complete absence of the rule of law, and the crowd melts away beneath Sherburn's cold, dangerous stare.

Several of Twain's critics have insisted that Sherburn's monologue in particular, reported verbatim through Huck, was unrealistic as part of the overall narrative within Twain's novel. As literary scholars like Forrest Robinson have suggested, though, this criticism has led many to dismiss the monologue rather than take seriously the argument that Sherburn makes, or rather, the argument that Twain makes through Sherburn. There is no darker view of humanity than that offered in Sherburn's monologue. The idea that at bottom, most men are lacking will, that they are mindless, un-thinking sheep—this idea is at once deeply Biblical as it is pessimistic. In a democracy premised on concepts such as "the will of the people" and "pop-ular sovereignty," Sherburn's monologue acts as a warning that democracy is a cruel joke, that it will tend toward rule by the strong over the weak, where any mob can easily be swayed by men like Sherburn, who is himself unbothered by murder and has nothing but contempt for the very people he rules through terror. He situates himself as a "man," but he is the most dangerous kind of man in this lawless, headless society. The mob retreats in front of Sherburn; they "broke all apart, and went tearing off every which way," and with Huck, many go on to the next amusement, which turns out to be "a real bully circus," including a "clown carried on so it most killed the people."[10]

In Colonels Grangerford and Sherburn, Twain reveals a predemocratic political condition that must have seemed common on the frontier, a con-dition where an aristocracy of hyperviolent men ruled by force rather than settled law. They appear bound by customs and manners, and so are "gen-tlemen," but they are not bound by rules and certainly not by any law cre-ated through democratic, deliberative processes. The customs and manners are themselves problematic, for they reinforce the position of these powerful patriarchs even as they condone and engage in violence and murder. There are no deliberative bodies, no neutral public figure to enforce or settle dis-putes; in *this* vacuum, there is violence, and a kind of violence that consumes the most vulnerable—children, the "harmless" drunk, and generations of people who have no idea where the violence came from or when it will ever end. The least well-off are most commonly the victims.

"My conscience got to stirring me up hotter than ever . . ."

That very insight, that human beings can be so awful, cruel, and predatory, never penetrates Huck's heart in such a way that he sees Jim and other black people as its most serious victims. Throughout the story, Huck sees slaves as servants, as property, as "niggers," but he never questions the morality or legality of slavery itself. Although the American constitution envisioned and protected slave property in numerous ways, including through the fugi-tive slave provisions in Article 4, Huck's experience with slavery is a more normalized condition, as is his understanding about what he or anyone else should do when discovering runaway slaves. That is, the American Consti-tution and subsequent legislation governing fugitive slaves are not the source of this knowledge, nor do they form the core of Huck's dilemma about Jim.

But this is not surprising: by the mid 1800s, various forms of fugitive slave rules were already about 150 years old, dating to long before the American Revolution and the American Constitution, as the colonies had passed rules about fugitive slaves as early as 1650.[11] Fugitive slaves were common, and Huck would certainly not have been the first white boy to ponder what to do when confronted with one.

And like all white people, Huck just knows that he is not to help and that he must report fugitive slaves as all "good" people should. Even this boy, so removed from the civilized world, worries that "It would get all around, that Huck Finn helped a nigger to get his freedom; and if I was to ever see anybody from that town again, I'd be ready to get down and lick his boots for shame." He associates this duty with the "right" thing to do, a religious and customary duty whose breach will cause harm to the Widow, a (white) person who he considers as having been nothing but kind to him. When faced with the dilemma about what to do about Jim, Huck cannot figure out how to square his sympathies for Jim, his sympathies for Jim's owner, "poor Miss Watson," and his crude yet fixed understanding of what morality requires him to do. He must report Jim as a fugitive rather than help him become free. He is stupefied by the choice, and instead of choosing, he puts off the decision, then gives up morality altogether and decides to do whatever is most convenient. Indeed, for most of the novel, Huck is rendered "stupid," if we understand the word to mean "stunned" or "benumbed," and thus deals with the problem mostly by avoiding it. This is further evidence of his immaturity, and how awful we feel for Jim that he must share his raft and be so dependent upon this boy.[12]

Yet Jim behaves as though he is fully aware of his vulnerability, and he comes to rely on Huck. Shortly after he finds Jim on Jackson's Island, Huck has a number of opportunities to report Jim as a fugitive slave. In the first instance, Huck is disguised as a girl when he comes upon Judith Loftus' house in St. Petersburg: she quickly discovers that he is a boy, that he doesn't quite know where he is, nor does he know that the townspeople are looking for the "runaway nigger" accused of killing Huck Finn. She tells Huck that her husband and "another man" will head to Jackson's Island in the hopes of collecting the $300 reward for Jim. In this instance, Huck reveals nothing to Mrs. Loftus, but rather rushes back to Jim, and both escape. His words to Jim are telling: "'Git up and hump yourself, Jim! There ain't a minute to lose. They're after us!'" Clearly, both Huck and Jim have reasons to remain hidden: Huck wants the townspeople to believe he is dead; and Jim is a fugitive slave who will face severe consequences for running away. "They're after us!" reveals a common interest in evading the white men who are looking for both Huck's killer and the reward for finding the fugitive slave. On a deeper level, the phrase binds the two together, representing for some scholars the moment that Huck commits himself to Jim.[13]

But Huck and Jim are not the same: there is no reward per se for finding Huck's killer, but there is one for finding the "runaway nigger." It's doubtful that Mr. Loftus and his friend would risk the trip unless Jim was worth so much. And it's not clear that Huck wants to save Jim from these men so much as save himself from being returned to a custody dispute that could lead back to his Pap. Still, the fact that Huck would warn Jim about the approaching men indicates to Jim that the boy is more an asset than a liability.

In another instance, when Jim and Huck come upon a shipwreck, they find two men contemplating the murder of a third, all of them drifting on a sinking ship. The two men decide not to kill the third man directly, but they agree to leave him to drown. The men are terrifying, and Huck and Jim are more terrified when their own raft is no longer tied to the wreck—they have no choice but to steal the boat that belongs to these bad men to make their own escape. As they float away, leaving all three to the sinking ship, Huck "[began] to worry about the men." "I begun to think how dreadful it was, even for murderers, to be in such a fix. I says to myself, there ain't no telling but I might come to be a murderer myself, yet, and then how would *I* like it?"

Huck tells Jim to hide himself and the boat, and he eventually reports the wreck to a watchman, telling him a tale suggesting a reward for anyone who rescues the sinking ship. Huck waits until the ferry boat leaves on its mission. Huck is even pleased with his own sense of empathy: "[Take] it all around, I was feeling ruther comfortable on accounts of taking all this trouble for that gang, for not many would a done it. I wished the widow knowed about it. I judged she would be proud of me for helping these rapscallions, because rapscallions and dead beats is the kind the widow and good people takes the most interest in." He says nothing of Jim to the watchman.[14]

To the thirteen men aboard the "monstrous long raft" that they encounter next, Huck also avoids mention of Jim entirely, and makes up more tales to avoid getting in trouble with these men. It was Jim's idea for Huck to board the raft, as he might listen as the "[men] would talk about Cairo." Cairo is the town where the Mississippi and Ohio Rivers meet, the place where Jim intends to turn their raft up the Ohio and toward his freedom. Even Huck recognizes his planning: "Jim had a wonderful level head, for a nigger; he could most always start a good plan when you wanted one." The men aboard the raft frighten Huck with their singing and ghost stories— when he is discovered, Huck panics and escapes, and he doesn't learn where they are after all. Yet Huck does not reveal who he really is, nor does he tell the men about Jim.[15]

Though he is disappointed not to know where he is, Jim *senses* that he is tantalizingly close to freedom. This makes Huck feel horrible. As Jim gets closer to freedom, Huck is plagued by his guilty conscience, feeling as though he has harmed Miss Watson, maybe also laying the foundations for Jim to buy, even "steal," his own children in the future, "children that belonged to a man I didn't even know; a man that hadn't ever done me no harm." Huck evaluates Jim's desire for his freedom and his family in negative ways, and he comes to hate himself for having aided this fugitive slave. He wants to turn Jim in: "My conscience got to stirring me up hotter than ever, until at last I says to it, 'Let up on me—it ain't too late yet—I'll paddle ashore at the first light and tell.' I felt easy and happy and light as a feather right off." This boy can empathize with (white) murderers, but he seems incapable of seeing Jim as a good person who deserves to be free.[16]

"You can make some money by it . . ."

The subtlety and genius of Twain's prose, though, suggests that Jim himself knows that the boy might be turning. Aware that Huck might betray him, Jim is excessively appreciative: "Pooty soon I'll be a-shout'n' for joy, en I'll say, it's all on accounts o' Huck; I's a free man, en I couldn't ever ben free ef it hadn' ben for Huck; Huck done it. Jim won't ever forgit you, Huck; you's de bes' fren' Jims ever had; en you's de ONLY fren' ole Jim's got now." Jim manipulates Huck's emotions, and at this critical point, where Huck intends to report the fugitive, but then tells him that he is only trying to locate where they are on the river, the tension becomes unbearable: "I was paddling off, all in a sweat to tell on him; but when he says this, it seemed to kind of take the tuck all out of me." Huck *wants* to report Jim, and Jim knows: "When I was fifty yards off, Jim says: 'Dah you goes, de ole true Huck; de on'y white genl-man dat ever kep' his promise to ole Jim.' Well, I just felt sick."[17]

The two men that Huck encounters are, in fact, looking for "five niggers run-off, tonight." They see Huck paddling from the raft, and they ask Huck who else is aboard. "Is your man white, or black?" More than at any other time, this is the precise moment where Huck can easily betray Jim—both of these men are armed and Huck has had a guilty conscience. And yet he does not tell. He hesitates but then, by leading these men to believe that his entire family has small pox, he gets them to go away. Afraid of this dreaded disease, the two men do not help his "sick family," though they float $20 each to him to assuage *their* guilty consciences. They advise him to look for "runaway niggers," as "you can make some money by it." Huck's reply is revealing and funny: "'Good-bye, sir,' says I; 'I won't let no runaway niggers get by me if I can help it.'" He has again helped Jim, but he is plagued all over by his bad conscience.[18]

Huck finds Jim in the water, holding onto the raft for fear of the two men passing, and Jim thanks Huck for getting the men to leave. Jim has heard everything. Did he also sense Huck's hesitation, the moment where things could have gone either way? If he had, could he have confronted Huck for almost betraying him? Rather than delving deeply into Huck's motives, Jim is simply grateful, again manipulating the boy's feelings for his own ends: "Dat *wuz* de smartes' dodge! I tell you, chile, I 'spec it save' ole Jim— ole Jim ain't going to forgit you for dat, honey."

For the remainder of their time on the raft, Huck reveals nothing of his guilty conscience, and he stays with Jim as they move closer and closer to freedom. But their raft is destroyed in a night fog gray and thick, by an upstream boat "like a black cloud with rows of glow-worms around it . . . all of a sudden she bulged out, big and scary, with a long row of wide-open furnace doors shining like red-hot teeth, and her monstrous bows and guards hanging right over us." For many scholars, this boat is a metaphor for the impossibility of Jim's freedom, perhaps even Twain's own inability to move his narrative into a place where Jim can be free. This disaster propels the story in a different direction entirely: it separates Jim and Huck, Huck meets the Grangerfords and Shepherdsons, and after that ordeal, the two are reunited again only to be subjects of the lawless King and Duke, the two men who will later betray Jim to make some money by it. For a while, Huck's conscience and Jim's freedom are not the central focus of the novel.[19]

"I knowed he was white inside . . ."

For some critics, the arrival of Tom Sawyer at the end of the novel diminishes Twain's work, as the story takes a turn toward the ridiculous and implausible. Jim remains the center of attention, but he does not speak in any articulate way. He is a prisoner at the mercy of these two boys, though clearly Tom is the dominant of the two. When Tom arrives on the Phelps farm where Jim is being held and chained as a runaway, Tom knows that Jim is legally free, yet he withholds this from Jim and Huck and instead insists that they participate with him in an elaborate plan to "free" Jim, a plan that includes unnecessary hardship, constant deception, snakes and spiders, other pointless diversions, and even possibly maiming Jim for realistic effect. Many, many critics have pointed to these chapters as evidence that *Huckleberry Finn* fails as a novel; others claim that, whether Twain intended to or not, these chapters can be read as a commentary about the sad, absurd condition of "free" African Americans after Reconstruction; and still others claim that these chapters are consistent with the rest of the novel, which is fundamentally a work about "bad faith," that horrible willingness to deceive oneself and others to benefit from their exploitation. Again, in the last interpretation, Jim has no choice but to remain silent—as a captured runaway slave, his very life is in danger, and he knows that he cannot speak or evade without risking his life as he had earlier in the story.[20]

This third interpretation appears as the most persuasive, though I will argue here that there is more, as Tom appears twice in the novel, at the beginning and at the end, when Jim is a captive, held by the Widow and then by the Phelps family. His appearances have interesting, thematic parallels. At both beginning and end, Tom tricks Jim and to an extent, Jim uses Tom.

At the beginning of the story, when Tom tricks Jim into thinking that he had been visited by witches, Jim turns the story into an ever more elaborate account of flying and haunting that impresses all who hear it. Huck reports that "[niggers] would come from all around there and give Jim anything they had" to see Jim's bedeviled coin and to hear his story. Here, Tom had tricked Jim and Huck went along, but it was Jim who ultimately benefited from the trick and turned it to his own ends. When Huck observes that "he was most ruined for a servant, because he got stuck up on account of having seen the devil and been rode by witches," Huck misses the point, as he cannot see how this slave (or any slave) can turn a trick into profit through his own devices.[21]

On the Phelps farm, when Tom appears as Cousin Sid, the two boys are ostensibly involved in a much more elaborate trick, again involving Jim, but one where much more is at stake for the captive than at the beginning of the story. Jim knows he will be consigned to a horrible fate. The Phelpses do not pay much attention to him, if at all—he is a runaway who will be sold into a condition about which they couldn't care less. When Huck first appears and becomes aware of Jim's presence, and then when Tom appears as Sid and also reveals himself to Jim, Jim's response is immediate and unequivocal— he goes along. He himself does not tell the Phelpses that Huck is Huck, Tom is Tom, Huck is not Tom, or Tom is not Sid.

Jim *participates* in this deception, not because he is the gullible, unthinking slave that these white people believe he is, but because using the boys and playing along now appears as his only plausible path to freedom. Throughout the novel, Jim has relied on Huck to get free, however thoughtless and imperfect that boy may be; here, faced with a more dire set of circumstances,

Jim must go along. That this grown man must be subject to the pointless play of a boy like Tom Sawyer speaks volumes both about his precarious condition as well as his willingness to use these white boys for his own ends. As painful as this path may be, Jim *does* become free, though he willingly gives up his freedom when the boys make a mess of the escape, when Tom is wounded and facing death, and it is Jim who insists on getting him a doctor.

When the doctor arrives and needs help to save Tom's life, Jim reveals himself and assists, even though he loses (again) his hard-fought freedom. If, after the escape, Jim had simply left Tom to die, could any of us have blamed him? Later in his life, Twain himself revealed contempt for Tom Sawyer, and suggested that Teddy Roosevelt, with all of his imperialist tendencies, was as prone to the foolish, unrealistic heroics as this stupid, literal boy; no grown man should act like Tom Sawyer. It must have been hard for Twain as a novelist to save Tom and sacrifice Jim, though through this sacrifice, the doctor, Huck, the Phelpses, and even the mob come to admire Jim for his selflessness. Huck was at his most admirable when he chose to give up his immortal soul for his friend Jim, and Jim is most ennobled when he sacrifices his precious freedom to save the life of a thoughtless, careless boy. As readers, we see the greatness of Jim as a person, though Huck, typically, misses the deeper point. When Jim speaks in favor of fetching a doctor for the injured Tom, against Tom's own wishes, Huck says of Jim: "I knowed he was white inside, and I reckoned he'd say what he did say—so it was all right now, and I told Tom I was a-going for a doctor." The boys were supposed to free Jim through their play, but it is Jim who rescues one of the most unattractive characters in the entire novel.[22]

Twain ends the story with an interesting twist. Jim has been keeping secrets, too, about Huck's father: "Doan' you 'member de house dat was float'n down de river, en dey wuz a man in dah, kivered up, en I went in en unkivered him and didn' let you come in? Well, den, you kin git yo' money when you wants it, kase dat wuz him." Jim had withheld this until now, and so we learn that almost all of Huck's time floating with Jim was unnecessary, for Huck at least, for there was no need for Huck to flee his father. Jim knew that Pap had died. This sudden conclusion is striking, and perhaps the most obvious indication that the slave had been using the boy to gain his freedom all along. Huck expresses no reaction to the fact that his father is dead, or that Jim had kept this secret for so long, through a plot that endangered and put both of their lives at risk. The novel ends with Aunt Sally ready to "sivilize" Huck once again, and Huck making plans to light out for the West. Huck does not mention Jim, though in many ways, the entire experience has been much more transformative for the slave than it had been for the boy.[23]

Race and Status, Then and Now

Huckleberry Finn is a most wonderful novel for framing the remainder of this present work—its central themes are so powerful, so persistent, and they remain deeply illuminating of our current dilemmas around law, status, and illegality. In Huck's awareness of Jim's condition as a fugitive slave, law is always already there, though the boy himself seems oblivious of the American Constitution, the Fugitive Slave Act, or other complex rules governing slavery. Law is also absent in many of the places where Huck and Jim travel, and this absence allows for conditions where the strong prey upon the weak and where no one seems to know the origins of the violence that permeates all of their lives. Evil, selfish men cheat one another and sell human beings for profit; the central protagonist, the second most likeable person in the novel after Jim, is the boy who helps his friend *avoid* the law for nearly the entire story. The most admirable person in the novel, the one person who values human life the most—the man who misses his wife and daughter and longs for their reunion, the man who weeps at the thought of losing Huck, the man who saves an idiotic boy at the expense of his very freedom—he is the one who is lawfully not a full person. The law does not capture who he is, nor is he ever "heroic" in the eyes of the white people he encounters, despite the overwhelming evidence of his virtue. Even Huck cannot see Jim in all of his humanity, although he experiences Jim's kindness and his best qualities firsthand.

Perhaps the saddest phrase in *Adventures of Huckleberry Finn* occurs when Jim saves Tom and then Huck thinks Jim was "white inside," a phrase that reveals how the boy can *never* see past Jim's race and status. If there is a perverse power in the law and in the ideology of white supremacy, it is this ability to blind people to one another through the categories that they come to embrace without thinking or reflection—to see their other's legal status first and their common humanity later, if at all. This problem of seeing, this dilemma about what we must do when we find "unlawful people" among us, is very much a *Huckleberry Finn* problem, and it has become again one of the most obvious problems in our places of work, in the federal courts, in city ordinances, in the practice of police departments, at our schools and universities, and in virtually every social and political institution in the United States over the past four decades. Although the phenomenon of illegal immigration is not new, the size and shape of yet another "unlawful population" is growing—ironically, it has grown precisely because of more rigid federal laws designed to diminish this very population. Despite overwhelming evidence that immigration restrictions and immigration rules have not worked as they were intended, many Americans have insisted on more of the same—taller fences, more enforcement, and harsher rules.

Toward the end of this book, I shall argue also that there seems an entrenched, slavish devotion to a set of laws that make no sense and might create more disobedience and injustice than respect for the law, a predicament that appears without end. The "illegal immigrant" is as much a creation of the law as the "fugitive slave," primarily because their "offense" arises when they come within a jurisdiction where their presence itself is rendered unlawful. In response to such people, many Americans reflexively consider and support their removal, while other Americans have hidden them, aided them, and otherwise refused to report them. Indeed, as we examine the various institutional and individual responses to undocumented persons, we are struck by the wide range of reactions, from ambivalence and uncertainty, to petty and mean enforcement of the law, and also to hyperexploitation and to circumstances that might be best defined as a kind of lawlessness. In response, in order to protect unlawful people, there have been deliberate efforts to ignore the law, to create new laws that undermine existing rules, and to engage in utter and outright disobedience of settled federal rules. All of these reactions have analogues in the story of Jim and Huckleberry Finn and in the circumstances that surrounded them, and so we return to this masterpiece and its themes again and again.

II

The Company of Others

Slavery and Wage Slavery

Company

The word *company* is made by combining the Latin prefix *co-* with the Latin root *pan*. *Co-* means "together" or "with," *pan* means "bread." A *company* refers, in its most fundamental sense, to a group of people who make or share nourishment together, and this central idea carries through in nearly all definitions of the word: inviting company over to one's house involves good food and drink; a company of soldiers is a common unit to provision in the field, consisting of a certain number of men who will eat, sleep, fight, and die together; and to this day, men and women have made money together and thus have earned their "bread" in many, many different companies. Bread, labor, and money have been interchangeable concepts in our language. When he criticized the Confederates for their obstinate defense of slavery, for example, Abraham Lincoln observed: "It may seem strange that any men should dare to ask a just God's assistance in wringing their bread from the sweat of other men's faces, but let us judge not, that we be not judged."[1]

That men and women have earned their bread together, but that there have been both good and bad kinds of companies—some sharing the fruits of their labor more fairly while others abused and exploited—these circumstances are as old as the ancient Latin. Within companies, some members have been more powerful than others, some are better rewarded, and many still struggle to bring out the advantages of mutual cooperation while suppressing those darker tendencies toward exploitation. Even to this day, some still think nothing of "wringing their bread from the sweat of other men's faces." On a basic level, between Huck and Jim, there is company in the purest form: two people together, sharing food and companionship, their deepest thoughts and concerns, and caring for one another as equals. For many readers, it's very pleasant, just the idea of these two people unencumbered and floating down the river together, and it's no wonder that this is the image that has adorned the covers of so many editions of *Huckleberry Finn*. Nothing gold can stay: the Duke and the King are the first to force themselves into Jim and Huck's company, and in this new arrangement, the scoundrels use Jim and Huck, then sell Jim for money. They betray Jim. It is the most wicked act in the novel.

Slavery and Freedom

Slavery—the lawful sale and exploitation of human beings—has been the ultimate example of people and societies at their worst, the worst possible way to benefit from the labor of another. Few can doubt that the owning, breeding, trading, and working of slaves for profit was one of the most repulsive aspects of American economic history, even though prominent scholars had once argued, not too many decades ago, that the institution of slavery was neither profitable nor central to the main currents of American law and society. At least four generations of scholarly work have shown that American slavery *was* profitable, that it *was* central, that it shaped the very conceptions of freedom and liberty that all white Americans cherished, if only because they conceived "freedom" and "liberty" in direct opposition to the condition of slaves. The British themselves pointed out the irony of American slaveholders complaining about how British policies were reducing them to slavery, and it wasn't difficult to see that the Bill of Rights looked like the inverse of colonial slave codes. Slaves did not get to assemble freely, for example; nor did they have the right to bear arms, nor the right to jury trials, nor the right to be free from cruel and unusual punishment. They did not receive, nor would they ever receive, "just compensation" for their labor. When white Americans conceived their freedom, they did so with their slaves in mind.[2]

The crime of slavery dominated Twain's novel and the nation's history, and it warped all possibilities for collaborative, mutually beneficial forms of work between blacks and whites in the early United States. And rather than being antithetical to the Market Revolution or the Industrial Revolution, slavery had been an important part of it, not just in the South, but throughout the country. The United States was a "slave-holding republic" to the extent that all sections benefited economically from the labor of slaves.

Companies based in the North insured slave property, financed slave sales, and processed the raw materials so commonly associated with slavery, including cotton and sugar. Entire careers and family fortunes in areas far removed from "lawful" slavery were tied to the labor of slaves. There were other, more disturbing aspects about slavery that influenced whites irrespective of class: no matter how poor they may have been, whites could look upon slaves and be assured that they themselves could not be beaten, chained, sold, bred, or hunted.[3] Miss Watson may have liked Jim as her slave, but for "a big stack o' money," she could sell him away from everything and everyone he loved.

These arrangements of white over black, of free over slave, were sometimes muddy, though, if only because slaves often worked alongside free whites and free blacks, especially in early manufacturing and transportation industries. Strict rules separated free and slave labor, of course, but it wasn't always the case that free labor was more "protected" than slave labor, as some recent historians have argued: "In comparison with slave-owners and livestock owners, free workers of the nineteenth century enjoyed less protection from what modern observers might consider unsafe working conditions."[4] Because slaves "hired out" were owned by powerful, wealthy men, and because slaves had an economic value that courts could discern through local slave markets, slave owners often recovered losses when employers did not take sufficient care to protect slave property. If, however, a free man were injured on the job, the common law often favored the employers: "assumption of risk," "the fellow-servant rule," and other legal doctrines shielded employers from liability in many instances. In an odd way, then, employers who'd hired slaves had economic incentives to protect those workers while using free laborers for more risky work. The practices that they used collectively to protect *slaves* appeared often in court cases throughout the South and, in turn, these court cases provided unusual legal precedents for *free* laborers who sued to improve their working conditions or to recover when they themselves were injured on the job, long after the abolition of slavery.[5]

In the early Republic, free men knew that slave-holders could recover even when they couldn't, and these anxieties marked labor relations for much of American history, as Eric Foner and other eminent scholars have pointed out. First, the terms *free* and *slave* had to be defined and redefined constantly throughout the antebellum period. That white men should not be "wage slaves," that they should have a more privileged position than either slaves or free blacks or other people of color—this was an ideological position heavily contested in the United States both before and after the Civil War. The stakes grew higher for a greater fraction of the white population:

between 1830 and 1860, more than five million new immigrants arrived from Europe, most as illiterate, poor, and unskilled workers. These white men and women had to discover, even to invent, novel forms of white privilege, as most knew that they could not be yeoman farmers nor small producers, especially not in the developed cities of the East.[6] These European immigrants would have to work for capitalists, and because there were many more of them compared to the few wealthy men capable of providing employment, the latter had the upper hand.

To poorer white men, the Republican platform championing "free labor" was especially attractive: this ideology said, in essence, that free white men should have decent wages, at least enough to acquire property through their labor and to support a household beyond just the bare necessities of life. They should also have some level of certainty in the length, terms, and conditions of their employment, as well as minimal standards for their safety in the workplace. Outside of work, social and political arrangements should allow laborers to envision a brighter future for their children, so that Americans might break free from the stifling class and caste arrangements of the Old World—common men should have enough for leisure and recreation, and their children should have an education to experience better opportunities. Free labor should produce free men.[7]

Above all, labor leaders warned that without political and social reforms, predatory industrialists would push working men down to the "level of slaves," and as a consequence, most "free" men would not be able to afford families. The "sacred" retreat into domesticity would itself become the exclusive province of a wealthy class. Public and private anxieties like these inspired Americans to create new political parties, which would in turn refashion the role of the state and thus have an impact far beyond labor relations. As this movement grew ever more radical by the middle of the nineteenth century, prominent Republicans would call for the complete abolition of slavery itself, so as to free labor everywhere in the United States as part of a larger project to re-envision American society.[8] Fear of slavery—fear of being reduced to the condition of expendable human resources—formed the core of what it meant to be a free person.

"The immense superiority of Chinese labor . . ."

At the same time that the white working classes struggled to defend the dignity of labor, other Americans were looking for novel sources of cheap labor, worried both about the abolition of slavery and the rising cost of free white workers. Westward expansion throughout the nineteenth century brought new opportunities, but without resolving older, fundamental tensions: what would be the status or position of Native Americans, especially where they were organized into formidable tribes and confederations in the Great Plains or in the Far West? What of Spanish and Mexican landholders in the wake of the American victory in the Mexican American War? Would slavery follow the American flag, and where exactly would it do that? These were vexing, persistent questions, but not everyone was paralyzed thinking too hard about them.

Few American presidents were as aggressive as James Polk, as he sent federal troops to take Mexico City, wrested control of the Southwest from Mexico to the United States, and supported the entry of vast new territories like California and Texas into the American sphere, one as a free state, the other as a slave state.[9] Though the American Civil War would turn the country into a "republic of suffering" that spared few white American families, federal troops would be strong enough to destroy even the most organized Native American tribes in the two decades after that conflict.[10] By the latter half of the nineteenth century, persons of Mexican and Spanish ancestry in the Southwest struggled with issues of whiteness and citizenship within the new racial and political order imposed by the Americans.[11] The entire region was fraught with uncertainty amid a changing legal landscape: would the conquered Native Americans be reduced to chattel slavery, or could land-owning Mexican Americans become capitalists, defined as they were as "white" under the Treaty of Guadalupe Hidalgo?

Again, even before these questions could be settled, new immigrants complicated matters further. In the British West Indies, English planters had been experimenting with Chinese laborers, or "coolie labor," as some called it, in the wake of their own abolition movement. Some said this was slavery in another form; others insisted that Chinese laborers were "free," although they also insisted that the Chinese could be induced easily to work hard for little pay, to tolerate corporal punishment, and to agree to indefinite labor contracts. According to a pamphlet published in 1854 by a Th Bailly-Blanchard, an entrepreneur in New Orleans, the Chinese were the perfect labor force for sugar plantations, and for the black-white society of Louisiana: "It is a well established fact that there is no objection whatever, on the part of the Chinese and Coolies to intercourse with the negro slaves. They are docile and intelligent, and evince no jealousy on account of the whites being able to obtain higher wages than themselves, because they respect and acknowledge the superiority of the white race, and on the other hand, they are neither quarrelsome nor disputatious in their intercourse with slaves." The most obvious, compelling reason for Chinese labor was that it would be cheaper in every way: "If . . . we take into consideration the very low rate at which we have calculated the estimate of [Chinese] deaths, and the fact THAT THE DEATH OF EACH NEGRO IS A TOTAL LOSS OF SO MUCH OF THE PLANTER'S CAP-ITAL, the immense superiority of Chinese labor cannot fail to be recognized." Bailly-Blanchard even appended a helpful model labor contract, a "Form of Engagement Usually Signed by the Chinese," through which planters might bind their pliable Chinese workers for as long as they wished.[12]

Was this just another form of slavery? Moon-Ho Jung, in his history of race and labor in the nineteenth century, noted that Abraham Lincoln thought so: he signed into law "An Act to Prohibit the 'Coolie Trade,'" in 1862, and Jung noted that this was "the last of America's slave trade laws, unambiguously framed as such by Republican legislators."[13] But neither this law, nor the Civil War, dampened the enthusiasm of some Southern planters for acquiring "coolies." Famous and notable Southerners, includ-ing Nathan Bedford Forrest, the former cavalry officer in the Confederacy and the first Grand Wizard of the Ku Klux Klan, hoped for a new source of cheap labor now that African slaves were otherwise unavailable after the Civil War. Yet the few Chinese laborers brought to the sugar plantations of the South did not work out as planned, for they ran away and they re-fused to work when their "employers" resorted to methods like beating. "The Chinese . . . continued to deviate from the racial images preceding them."[14] Many Southerners gave up on Chinese labor, as they concluded that the Chi-nese were not inexpensive, nor pliable, nor expendable, nor easily exploited or abused. They were not at all what Bailly-Blanchard and other labor mer-chants had promised.

Yet in the West, after some companies had exploited Chinese laborers successfully, the "Chinese question" came to shape the politics of California and then the entire nation. This process occurred slowly: like many other immigrants, the Chinese arrived to strike it rich just like other prospectors during the Gold Rush. They were small operators, but unlike white miners, they were soon subject to a Foreign Miners' Tax, both to raise revenue for the new state and to discourage them from mining at all.[15] Some felt that they had to find other work, and leading industrialists saw in them a unique opportunity. Reluctant at first, the managers of the Central Pacific Railroad hired small teams of Chinese when their Irish workers went on strike for bet-ter wages. The experiment turned out well—the Central Pacific hired and hired, and it seemed to the managers that the Chinese worked just as well as white men.

Not surprisingly, the early industrialists who'd relied on Chinese labor often developed confusing, ambiguous attitudes toward Chinese immigrants. In 1861, for example, Leland Stanford had been elected the first Republican Governor of California, and in his inaugural address to the state legislature in 1862, he affirmed clear, anti-Chinese sentiments: "To my mind it is clear, that the settlement among us of an inferior race is to be discouraged, by every legitimate means. Asia, with her numberless millions, sends to our shores the dregs of her population. Large numbers of this class are already here; and, unless we do something early to check their immigration, the question, which of the two tides of immigration, meeting upon the shores of the Pacific, shall be turned back, will be forced upon our consideration, when far more difficult than now of disposal." The Chinese, he continued, were "a degraded and distinct people," whites were "the superior race," and so he supported "the repression of the immigration of the Asiatic races."[16] Based on these remarks, California voters could be assured that Governor Stanford would support federal rules to exclude Chinese laborers, just as President Lincoln would do later in 1862. About three years after he gave these remarks, though, Stanford's men "experimented" with Chinese laborers, and Stanford discovered then that using Chinese labor could pay.

In a letter to President Andrew Johnson in October 1865, Stanford praised his Chinese workers: "As a class they are quiet, peaceable, patient, industrious and economical—ready and apt to learn all the different kinds of work required in railroad building, they soon become as efficient as white laborers. More prudent and economical, they are contented with less wages."[17] The Chinese worked so well that Stanford's recruiters went to China searching for laborers willing to work in railroad construction. Stanford sympathized with leading industrialists, many of whom complained that there was a shortage of labor in the state; together, they saw in the Chinese a plentiful, cheap labor supply that was vital to the economic development of California. Stanford led by example: more than twelve thousand Chinese workers laid track for the Central Pacific in the mid-1860s. "By the time the two sections of the railroad met at Promontory in Utah in 1869, fifteen thousand of the seventeen thousand workers who had worked on the railroad from the West Coast were Chinese."[18]

Like their compatriots in the South, however, the Chinese on the railroads protested the unjust treatment that they endured under their corporate managers. They knew that they were given dangerous assignments that no white man would tolerate; they knew that they were receiving less pay for longer days and fewer benefits, including housing; and they were whipped by their overseers, even as they were tied to labor contracts that seemed to bind them to these cruel masters no matter what the conditions. Five thousand Chinese men refused to work for the Central Pacific in June 1867. Charles

Crocker, one of the founders of that infamous company and a close associate of Governor Stanford, approved of drastic measures: "To break the strike, the railway company attempted to transport ten thousand African Americans to replace the Chinese. When the attempt failed, Crocker stopped the provisions to the strikers and, stuck in their camps in the Sierras like virtual prisoners, without food, they were forced to give in within a week."[19] Crocker himself later boasted of how he brought the Chinese to heel, and his white employees took to calling his Chinese workers "Crocker's pets," or "Chollie's Boys." Chinese laborers did receive a small increase in pay, but this meant that they were earning slightly more than two-thirds of what white workers in similar positions received.[20]

Overlooking incidents like these, or perhaps because of this outcome, corporations in the United States would consider the Central Pacific's use of Chinese labor as a great success, and leading politicians would for a time promise to give them as much of this labor as they had wanted. This attitude, though, struck fear into poorer white men on the West Coast. What would this mean for the United States, for unskilled white laborers, if the "Asiatics" could come in an "unlimited" supply from across the Pacific? White Californians formed labor unions to discourage the immigration of Chinese altogether, and the Chinese thus served throughout the nineteenth century as the political foil wrapping together European immigrants from Ireland and Italy, from Boston to Baltimore: "The Chinese Must Go," the new Workingmen's Party said, and their incessant lobbying brought dramatic results.

The very titles of the public laws in California reflected a gradual, more organized hostility: the Foreign Miners' License Tax in 1850 was raised to higher levels in 1852; another Act to Provide for the Protection of Foreigners, and to Define Their Liabilities and Privileges was approved in 1853; then came the Act to Discourage the Immigration to This State of Persons Who Cannot Become Citizens Thereof in 1855; followed by an Act to Prevent the Further Immigration of Chinese or Mongolians to This State in 1858; and then, in the same year that Lincoln would prohibit the "Coolie Trade," California passed its own rule to Protect Free White Labor against Competition with Chinese Coolie Labor, and to Discourage the Immigration of the Chinese into the State of California. Members of the Workingmen's Party and other politicians sympathetic to their motto became the government of California, holding city offices and seats in the state legislature. No credible political candidate could be in favor of Chinese immigration and hope to win office in California by 1860.[21]

The ones that were elected sponsored rules that moved from vaguely nativist to openly white supremacist and then straightforward anti-Chinese.

By 1879, when anti-Chinese legislators were at the height of their political power, they made sure that Article XIX of the state's new constitution would say "Chinese." Its provisions punished corporations for hiring Chinese laborers and forbade all public agencies from hiring them as well, arguing that "Asiatic coolieism is a form of human slavery, and is forever prohibited in this State, and all contracts for coolie labor shall be void." California's legislature approved of subsequent legislation in 1880 that fined and even imprisoned the officers of any corporation hiring "Chinese or Mongolians." Stanford himself must have been worried about the new rules. Perhaps to his relief, a federal court overturned these rules that same year, arguing that this was beyond the police powers of the state. But these efforts nevertheless represented striking attempts to control what American *companies* could do to pursue profit. Politically, the message was quite clear: American corporations should be punished for hiring foreigners ineligible for citizenship.[22]

Poorer whites had framed themselves as the victims of coolie labor, and by 1882, their sponsors in Congress agreed to protect them by passing the Chinese Exclusion Act, whose title and purpose were unambiguous. Although many scholars have also debated the cultural and social dimensions of Chinese Exclusion, no one could miss the central focus of the Act on Chinese labor—merchants, tourists, and students from China were not excluded under the new rule, but laborers clearly were. The Act was designed to protect (white) American workers from Chinese labor; put another way, the Act deprived American corporations from employing a "degraded" work force, and in doing so, from driving down wages for white workers. It did so on a national scale, and so this was, then, one of the most important federal rules to limit a certain kind of laborer in the United States, at least since the constitutional provision about the importation of slaves.[23] This was a national rule designed to shape the American labor market.

"My race prejudice . . . inclines me to my own people . . ."

Prominent early supporters of Chinese labor responded in interesting ways during this period of Chinese Exclusion. Leland Stanford changed his mind about the Chinese yet again. Though he and his associates had hired many Chinese laborers, Stanford was not embarrassed or defensive about these decisions when he was not active in politics. He served one two-year term as Governor. In fact, when it was time for the ceremonial golden spike at Promontory Point in 1869, Stanford and Crocker acknowledged publicly that Chinese laborers had been indispensable, and that they were free laborers, not slaves. Stanford said that "without [the Chinese], it would be impossible to complete the western portion of this great national highway within the time required by the acts of Congress." By contrast, other prominent politicians had ignored the Chinese contribution altogether, saying that it was "the commingled blood of the four great nationalities of modern days," including "the impetuous daring and dash of the French, the philosophical and sturdy spirit of the German, the unflinching solidity of the English, and the light-hearted impetuosity of the Irish."[24] Popular photographs of the event in May 1869 circulated throughout the United States, but they showed no Chinese workers, though some said that this was because Stanford's foreman, James Strobridge, had invited his Chinese men to a banquet held in their honor.[25] Stanford seemed to embrace the Chinese working for his company, and by extension, he defended the right of all employers to hire them. This did not last.

His position changed in response to the growing resentment against Chinese workers forming in his state over the next decade. Stanford won a seat to the United States Senate in 1885, too late to vote for the Chinese Exclusion Act, but not too late to suffer politically for having employed so many Chinese workers, not just through the Central Pacific Railroad, but in his private vineyards in Tehama County and on his farm in Palo Alto. In Red Bluff, a small town in northern California, the Anti-Coolie League sent an angry letter to the senator in 1886, demanding that he fire all of his Chinese workers at the nearby vineyards in Vina. Stanford dismissed the request at first: "The Chinaman is entitled to the same just treatment, while in our country, as any other foreigner, or as any other citizen." The agitation against the Chinese did not stop, nor did the demands for Stanford to "foreswear" Chinese labor.[26]

Over the next few months, though, Leland Stanford relented: "I have the right to dispose of my own property and my own means as suits me best, so long as I obey the laws. If my humanitarianism impels me or my interest incline me to employ Chinese labor, I hold that I have a perfect political right to do so, it being a matter of my own conscience and its dictates." Though he started from that Republican position, Stanford sought a final peace with his white neighbors: "My race prejudice, however, inclines me to my own people, and I am desirous of giving them all suitable occasions the preference. I have, therefore, in harmony with my own inclinations, strengthened by your request, given instructions to my agent to direct that preference for white labor be very carefully exerted." In a separate letter, conceding the new political reality with respect to the Chinese, he said: "I believe the sentiment of the people of California is very largely hostile to more Chinese coming to our country, also that most of our people sincerely wish the Chinese now in the country were out of it; and, in obedience to that will, and in harmony with my own judgment, I shall do, here, in my public duty, whatever I can justly to restrict Chinese immigration."[27] He sounded again like the politician he had once been in 1862.

Stanford's two turns—from a politician hostile to the Chinese, to a supporter of Chinese labor, and then to a man of "race prejudice"—represented on a more intimate level the ultimate victory of white working class interests over the preferences of powerful, landed men. Stanford, the great railroad builder, industrialist, and farmer, a man who'd held two of the highest offices in the state, was bound by white labor unions and had to sympathize publicly with their race prejudices. And yet there was a caveat to all this: as much as Stanford had promised to direct his agents not to hire Chinese laborers, this instruction did not seem to extend to his wife Jane. In Palo Alto, at the newly established Stanford University, she employed Chinese immigrant gardeners to tend to the grounds, as well as other Chinese laborers to clean the dormitories and to cook for the new students, including Herbert Hoover. Jane Stanford was most proud of her flower beds, the work of Jim Mock and Ah King, two Chinese immigrants who had labored to make sure that all of the visitors to Mrs. Stanford's private residence would see gardens that were as impressive as they were immaculate. Jane Stanford never once considered firing these men simply for being Chinese, and as far as we can tell, no one bothered to complain about their employment.[28]

"An impenetrable maze of discrimination . . ."

American politicians and labor leaders agreed that Chinese Exclusion was a *fait accompli*—it was the result of a bitter debate that few wished to revisit. President Grover Cleveland conceded as much in his Inaugural Address in 1885: "The laws should be rigidly enforced which prohibit the immigration of a servile class to compete with American labor, with no intention of acquiring citizenship, and bringing with them and retaining habits and customs repugnant to our civilization."[29] He didn't say "Chinese" anywhere in his speech, but everyone knew that this was what he had meant, just as much as the constitution never said "slave" or "slavery" even though everyone knew what that had been about, too. Four years after the Chinese Exclusion Act, when several national unions formed the American Federation of Labor, one of the key organizers for this singular achievement, Samuel Gompers, tied the rising fortunes of white labor to the necessary exclusion of Chinese labor. Gompers was not as diplomatic as Cleveland. He supported the indefinite extension of Chinese Exclusion in his famous essay, "Meat v. Rice," submitted to the United States Senate in 1902, the year that Congress did make Chinese Exclusion permanent. Gompers summarized the tensions between "American Manhood against Asiatic Coolieism."

As the first President of the American Federation of Labor and one of the greatest champions of working men and women in the late nineteenth and early twentieth centuries—a white man who'd insisted on including African American laborers in this movement from its inception—the racist tone of his "Chinese" essay remains totally depressing. Gompers repeated there every horrible racist invective against Asian immigrants. More importantly, he framed Asian labor as being a more serious threat than African slavery: "Slave labor degraded free labor. It took out respectability, and put an odious cast upon it. It throttled the prosperity of a fine and fair portion of the United States in the South; and this Chinese, which is worse than slave labor, will throttle and impair the prosperity of a still finer and fairer section of the Union on the Pacific Coast."[30]

Sentiments like these explained why, for many, many politicians in the late nineteenth and early twentieth centuries, a friend of labor was an exclusionist, and a racist, too. A decade later, when a labor dispute in Lawrence, Massachusetts, galvanized workers across the country, "unskilled immigrant workers of extraordinary diverse backgrounds were at the center of the drama." Looking at this period, scholars like Janice Fine and Daniel Tichenor have noted that the Industrial Workers of the World, under the leadership of Eugene Debs, became a multiethnic labor organization unlike any other in American history: "[the] level of cooperation among workers across ethnic lines stunned contemporary observers. Their ranks included Italians, Germans, Poles, French-Canadians, Franco-Belgians, Lithuanians, Syrians, Greeks, Latvians, and Turks." The Chinese had wanted to join this powerful labor movement, but they had been rebuffed numerous times, not just in California, but in New York and in Pennsylvania as well.[31]

White supremacy in the labor movement extended to other groups, too. At the turn of the century, when Filipinos or multiracial Japanese-Mexican agricultural workers formed their own unions on the West Coast, major national organizations refused to acknowledge them.[32] The Japanese were especially vexing for American politicians and for many of the nation's major labor unions on the East Coast and in the Midwest—Japanese immigrants and their descendants were quite militant and successful in places like Hawaii, developing alliances with workers of other Asian ancestries and even with Europeans. But labor leaders did not yet think of Hawaii as part of the United States, perhaps even less so because so many Japanese lived there among other Asians, their polyglot labor unions beyond what many considered possible or desirable in North America. Laborers in Hawaii worked to bridge racial divides, but this was not always the case in other parts of the country. "By the early twentieth century, the American Federation of Labor embraced eugenicist conclusions about southern and eastern Europeans, Asians, and Africans, becoming an unwavering and important advocate first for a literacy test and later for national origins quotas."[33] Labor unions *extended* exclusionist principles in the immigration law during this period—to protect the dignity of labor, they chose to close the door to prospective immigrants on explicit racial grounds.

Moreover, within the United States, the racial logic popular in the labor movement had a profound impact on African Americans, when many of them moved away from the South in the wake of emancipation. During the Great Migration, millions of African Americans remade the United States over four decades of internal migration—from the South to the Midwest, to the great cities of the East, and to the West Coast. Nearly everywhere they went, though, they faced exclusion based on race, and white labor unions were often the worst culprits. Within the South, in cities like Memphis, rapid industrialization did not lead to racial equality. According to many labor historians, "Jim Crow created an impenetrable maze of discrimination; regardless of ability, blacks were banned from most skilled and white collar employment." White workers harassed their African American colleagues, spoke to them in disparaging, racist ways, and vandalized their property. More than a few corporations hired private thugs to murder African American who sued for back wages or complained of harsh working conditions; they did these things with impunity in a number of high-profile cases, and these tactics let all African Americans know just how vulnerable they were in the new urban South.[34]

On an insidious, routine level, African Americans also knew that the workplace was segmented. The best positions went to white people, and the ones that paid poorly or were dangerous, the ones that led nowhere—these were offered to African Americans at wages that unionized white workers would never accept. "This color-coded labor market existed in every region of the United States and could not be avoided." African Americans who proposed interracial labor unions were threatened with violence, as whites overwhelmingly rejected "nigger unionism." African American women faced some of the most intense barriers: "mired for generations in jobs as domestic workers, servants, cleaning and washer women, waitresses and maids, [they] knew better than anyone the American axiom of last hired, first fired, and worst paid."[35] Three generations after slavery, African Americans had to take the toughest jobs, the lowest pay, and under the most dangerous circumstances, and pervasive segregation within the schools and universities made their entry into the professions almost impossible. And yet African Americans who worked in these conditions were still not the worst off: unemployed African Americans were expelled or imprisoned under vagrancy statutes, and they were often incarcerated under an expanding criminal justice system that some scholars characterized as "worse than slavery." State and local police officers trolled cities and towns, they collected men for crimes like "loitering," and then subjected them to various forms of penal labor and involuntary servitude.[36]

Circumstances were hardly better in areas beyond the South, as many African American migrants discovered. The Great Black Migration occurred at a moment when American labor relations were especially tense, when unions went on strike even though the companies dependent on their labor refused to acknowledge them. When some companies hired African American migrants from the South as strikebreakers under these circumstances, white labor unions retaliated against the African American "newcomers." Scholars have described such riots like the one in East St. Louis, Illinois, in 1917 as "pogroms" against African Americans, a deliberate spasm of "racial cleansing" conducted by the members of unions and by public officials to mark clearly the geographic and economic boundaries between blacks and whites. In the historical accounts of this and other race riots in the early twentieth century, labor relations and race relations were intertwined—just as Stanford's employment of Chinese workers incensed white labor unions, the very thought of industrial plants using "cheap," desperate African Americans migrants could send white laborers into a fury. State police officers and many local newspapers in Illinois sided with the angry white workers rather than protecting the victims: in Eldorado in 1902, in Brooklyn in 1903, in Springfield in 1908, and in Belleville in 1909, African Americans were lynched, burned, and beaten, often at the hands of the police. The ones who survived were arrested and then driven from their homes if they weren't imprisoned. In a state like Illinois, African Americans could not trust the unions to protect the dignity of their labor, nor public officials to protect their lives or property.[37]

"They will come in conflict with white labor . . ."

Local white resistance to African American migrants became widespread throughout the United States over the first half of the twentieth century, and labor unions that had been struggling for political support and legitimacy found in the arrival of black migrants new sources of support, economically and politically, among poorer whites anxious to protect themselves from any competition. When the economy turned bad, segregation in the labor markets grew even worse: during the Great Depression in Chicago, "white unions were refusing colored workers membership, keeping colored wages low, restricting the work that migrants could do, and leaving them unprotected during cutbacks."[38] Beyond Chicago, the unions said that they were responding to the desires of their rank and file members: "In the North, companies and unions said that, however much they might want to hire colored people, their white workers just wouldn't stand for it. And, for the sake of morale, the companies and unions weren't going to force the issue."[39]

By the middle of the twentieth century, black exclusion from mainstream white labor unions was so complete that it was taken for granted. Scholars of the American labor movement have argued that with few exceptions the labor movement has been understood to be both working class *and* white in the United States. Labor unions excluded people of color so successfully from their ranks that "their privileges, and sometimes the very fact that they have a racial identity, go un(re)marked." "[American] labor . . . in iconography, public discourse, and historical writing, has often been assumed to be white and male."[40] Among the white men who dominated and shaped the American labor movement in the late nineteenth and early twentieth centuries, the overwhelming consensus seemed to include a complete rejection of the idea that white and African American workers should be making their bread or money together in positions of equality.

Yet in this period, African Americans also feared for their positions and lobbied for other kinds of restrictions as well. For African Americans, the Pullman Porters and their Brotherhood of Sleeping Car Porters was one of the most significant organizations in American labor history, the first black-led labor union recognized by the American Federation of Labor in 1935. Before the Civil War, railroad companies in the South owned slaves, leased others, and used them all for various kinds of work, much of it dangerous. Many of the first porters to work for George Pullman's new company after the Civil War were former slaves; accordingly, they were paid very low wages, relied on tips for a good portion of their income, and spent hours in unpaid, preparatory labor on the railroad cars upon which they worked. To prospective customers, Pullman promised a "hotel on wheels," but this level of service required hundreds of reliable workers at a low wage.

The typical Pullman porter was a well-dressed, cheerful African American man paid horribly for the amount of time he was required to spend at work. At least for railroad work in the late nineteenth century, a black porter was as expendable and as exploitable before or after emancipation within the network of railways that was, in essence, a monopoly. Pullman's company built a model town for its employees in 1880 about fourteen miles south of Chicago, a place with brick homes, parks, and a shopping area with a theater and a bank for its white skilled workers, and a much more modest version for Pullman's porters and maids. The town of Pullman didn't have a bar, though, and none of the workers owned their homes or exercised anything that could resemble self-government. Pullman thought the arrangement sufficient to dampen any discontent: as a sign of the times, shoddier North Pullman was nearly all African American, while South Pullman was better built and maintained, and nearly all white.[41]

To the white patrons who used their services, the black porters were just "George," the standard name for any black man wearing the porter uniform. For African American men, however, a job as a porter meant a lot more. Carrying luggage and freight for white passengers would appear demeaning, as it certainly was, but in light of the other options available to black men at the time, this one was not completely unattractive. "To the black community in the early decades of [the twentieth] century, the porters appeared to have jobs with 'status,' jobs that provided the opportunity for a better income through liberal tips and a chance to travel throughout the country."[42] After *Plessy v. Ferguson* in 1896, railway cars and practically everything else was segregated by race, and so the only time on their journeys that white men and women saw black men was as porters. And many distinguished black men had once been porters, including Claude McKay, Langston Hughes, and Thurgood Marshall. These men were never as passive or as subservient as George Pullman and his associates would have liked: in time, these black men formed "organizations," including the Brotherhood of Sleeping Car Porters in 1925, after more than three decades of rejection from more established unions like the American Railway Union.[43]

The Pullman Company did not respond well. Even before the Brotherhood became official, the Company sought to hire Filipinos in an effort to threaten its African American employees. These Filipino men had come to Chicago as "nationals," from a territory that the Americans had controlled since 1902; they were not "aliens" subject to American immigration law. After the United States took the Philippines from Spain, and after the Americans suppressed a nationalist independence movement within the Philippines, the American federal government sponsored the arrival of many Filipino migrants, often as students who might learn how to remake the Philippines under an American model. These men took working class jobs to support themselves, and when the Pullman Company offered places within the Commissary Division, 300 Filipino men took the jobs over the next two decades.[44]

Now, the Pullman Company employed about 12,000 African Americans in various positions by 1920, so the handful of Filipino men employed in 1925 were not a grave, immediate threat to the Brotherhood, but still, what if the Company could have more of them? The Company featured their exotic new employees in advertisements: they were put aboard deluxe trains like the "Cuban Special" and the "Broadway Limited," where white passengers could pay extra for well-dressed, cheerful Filipino men to attend to them. Only the most senior, experienced African American porters had been given these kinds of assignments before, and A. Philip Randolph, the first President of the Brotherhood, pointed that out to his brothers: "The Company has attempted to break your spirit by putting some Filipinos on a few club cars in utter and flagrant violation of the seniority principle."[45]

Despite Randolph's protests, Filipino workers remained with the Company through World War II, but in 1934, after the Brotherhood and other local organizations formed the International Association for Railway Employees, labor leaders continued to worry about strikebreakers and scabs from Asia. By this time, leading labor organizations, including the American Federation of Labor, had voted to include African American labor unions within their national efforts, and so in spite of lingering and persistent hostilities against African Americans, the labor movement was integrating. African American labor leaders were meeting with their white counterparts, the more progressive white leaders wanted their full incorporation into the labor movement, and all parties were searching for common ground. As the Brotherhood and the International Association struggled to speak with one voice, they found that they could agree upon some obvious things: in a list of complaints drafted in 1934, they alleged a number of abuses at the hands of their employers, including the Pullman Company. Labor organizers had been fired; more militant workers had been relieved of their most important responsibilities, their pay cut accordingly; and labor contracts were often breached without a care. The Association claimed that in a number of instances, key organizers and workers had been attacked by Company thugs, even assassinated for forming labor unions. One new concern, however, stood out among the statement of grievances: the Association called for "congressional protest against the use of Filipinos to displace Negro Pullman and dining car employees."[46]

This position put the Association in political agreement with men like Senator Millard Tydings, the Democrat from Maryland, who worried more for white working class men than anyone else: "It is absolutely illogical . . . to have an immigration policy to exclude Japanese and Chinese and permit Filipinos en masse to come into the country. . . . If they continue to settle in certain areas they will come in conflict with white labor . . . and increase the opportunity for more racial prejudice and bad feelings of all kinds." Tydings had co-sponsored the Tydings-McDuffie Act of 1934, a rule that on the one hand, promised complete Filipino independence from the United States by July 4, 1946, and on the other, reclassified all Filipinos in the United States as "aliens." The Tydings-McDuffie Act then set an immigration cap of fifty persons per year from the Commonwealth of the Philippine Islands.[47] Again, fearful that foreigners would take opportunities away from lawful American citizens, Americans—even African Americans—moved to restrict immigration and ban another racial group considered undesirable. That an African American labor union had spoken in favor of restrictions against Asian immigrants was a new development during the course of this particular labor dispute, but it wouldn't be the last time that lawful people of color—claiming citizenship—would identify other people of color as a threat to their livelihood. Like race itself, immigration status emerged in the late nineteenth century as another powerful form of discrimination in the labor market, one that would preoccupy a substantial fraction of American labor relations throughout the twentieth.

Race, Status, Labor

In the United States after the abolition of slavery, American citizens and foreigners alike still experienced circumstances where some jobs and occupations were understood to be available only to members of a certain race or class. Before the Civil War and in the two decades after, entire categories of people—namely Asians—were to be excluded altogether, in the hope that they would never share bread or company in the United States. Although the Chinese may have built key portions of the transcontinental railroad and developed other major industries in California and on the West Coast, "good Americans," full citizens, seemed to have no trouble rejecting these same people who made the bread and did the work. By then, it was a recurring problem, in politics and in rhetoric: the Constitution could not say "slave," nor could Grover Cleveland bring himself to say "Chinese," as if to utter such things would spoil the sacred document or a simple inaugural speech. Under all the loathing, beneath all of the racism and contempt, the good Americans shared that fear of falling (or is it being pulled down?) into the status of the people who did the work, the people who labored and were abused throughout, the people without whom all that bread and money would not be possible. The fears of slavery and of wage slavery have been pervasive aspects of American labor relations.

That, too, has been a recurring pattern. White working class people saw that slaves were, oddly, better protected than they were, and so they moved to protect the dignity of their labor. They imagined a more privileged place in the labor market for themselves, and as we shall see in another chapter, entire spaces free of all black people. White working class people also turned their attentions against Chinese immigrants, disciplining capitalists in the process, and supporting national legislation to regulate what the country could now envision as a national labor market. The Chinese Exclusion Act said that there should be no Chinese here. White supremacists and white labor unions—they were often the same—also responded to African Americans from the South by enforcing a violent, virulent segregation throughout the country. Protecting the dignity of labor has often meant pushing others to suffer indignities. Just as Huckleberry Finn never really *sees* Jim as a human being and as a full person, as fully human as any white man and far more virtuous than most, the desire to push away the Other and to formalize that discrimination has been a near permanent feature of American public life.

In that light, there has been something especially sad about people of color turning against each other in similar ways, just as they themselves acquired the citizenship that they so coveted. One has to imagine only for a moment the first time that an African American porter encountered a "Filipino boy," dressed in crisp whites, in segregated railroad cars, trying to get his mind around the new man. Was the Filipino porter there to take his job and his bread? What should he make of his own union's demand, joined as it was to a new black-white brotherhood, to "protest against the use of Filipinos to displace Negro Pullman and dining car employees"? Should he also, perhaps, support the Repatriation Act of 1935, the rule that would send Filipinos back to the Philippines at government expense?[48] As we shall see in the next chapter, the labor movement in the first half of the twentieth century produced a powerful set of new federal laws, and it gave his union not just collective bargaining rights, but a political voice as well. But in the postwar period, after the Civil Rights Movement, after immigration law became race-neutral, after more people of color joined the mainstream labor force and mainstream labor unions, it would seem for a moment that a rising tide would lift every boat, that bread and money could be earned together from positions of equality, not status. Yet in a way that few could have anticipated, immigration status would emerge as another major axis of inequality in the labor market, dividing those with full citizenship and legal residency from those who didn't have it.

Illegal Workers

"Liberty of contract . . ."

Even as Congress approved Tydings-McDuffie in 1934, and thus excluded Filipino laborers to the United States, the most intense political debate that year surrounded the two bills sponsored by Robert Wagner, the Democratic Senator from New York. The first bill, the Social Security Act, sought to protect Americans from the vagaries of modern life, including unemployment leading to poverty, poverty in old age, and poverty resulting from the injury or loss of a breadwinner in the family. The second bill, the National Labor Relations Act, hoped to empower working class Americans by protecting them from "unfair labor practices." This new federal rule would ensure the right of all employees to join labor unions and bargain collectively with their employers, and then to strike and to demand relief when companies attempted to undermine these novel statutory rights. The National Labor Relations Act was what organizations like the Brotherhood and its Association had wanted for many, many years: companies like Pullman could no longer interfere, restrain, or coerce employees from forming or joining labor unions, nor discriminate or terminate any employee for doing the same, nor could the company refuse to bargain with a union once it had been certified as a legitimate bargaining unit by the new National Labor Relations Board created under the Act. President Franklin Roosevelt signed this stunning new law in August 1935 after years of debate, and it still remains one of the most important pieces of legislation passed during the New Deal.

Organized labor unions provided the critical political support necessary for the passage of this law. For several decades, labor unions had played an important role in state politics, as they had supported political candidates who approved of minimum wage rules, rules against child labor, workplace regulations, rules regulating how long a person could work per day, and similar measures designed to protect workers from the very companies that had employed them. By the early twentieth century, even Congress had approved of rules that set minimum wages and forbade child labor. On a number of occasions, however, the United States Supreme Court had overturned many of these rules in cases such as *Lochner v. New York* (1905), *Hammer v. Dagenhart* (1918), and *Adkins v. Children's Hospital* (1923). In these instances, the Court held that legislatures had gone too far: minimum wage rules like the one Congress had approved in *Adkins* interfered with employers and the women who might wish to work for less, the Court said. In the Keating-Owen Child Labor Act of 1916, Congress forbade the sale across interstate lines of anything made by children under the age of fourteen; the Court said in *Hammer* that Congress lacked authority to pass such a statute.[1]

The earliest of these cases, *Lochner*, was by far the most famous; subsequent decisions along similar lines came to be associated with the *Lochner* era, a period during which the United States Supreme Court regarded "liberty of contract" as so important as to endanger any state or federal rule that might interfere with the "sacred right" of employers and employees to strike their own bargains free from government interference. In the case itself, the State of New York had approved of rules limiting the number of hours that a baker could work; the Court said that this was an impermissible labor regulation, an "unreasonable, unnecessary and arbitrary interference with the right and liberty of the individual to contract." In dissent, Justices Oliver Wendell Holmes and John Marshall Harlan both suggested that the New York legislature reflected the will of a majority of New Yorkers, that their new rule wasn't completely unreasonable, and so they should have what they wanted. Both men knew that labor unions exerted great influence over elections in New York and that the state legislature was giving the unions through legislation what they could not have through collective bargaining. Holmes was no great friend of workingmen or of labor unions, but he objected to using constitutional provisions to protect employers from the will of state majorities: "a constitution is not intended to embody a particular economic theory." In their view, the United States Supreme Court should not take sides in political disputes between labor and capital.[2]

This, however, was not the majority opinion, and in cases like *Coppage v. Kansas* (1915), the Supreme Court did seem to take sides. In *Coppage*, the

Court said that the states could not outlaw "yellow-dog contracts"—contracts that required employees to foreswear joining labor unions as a condition of their employment. In other words, employers could demand that their employees never join a labor union as a condition of employment. New York, again, had been a pioneer in banning such yellow-dog contracts, as it had in 1887, and more than a dozen other states had done the same before the Court undid all these rules in 1915. Such state rules were struck down by a Court that interpreted property rights in strict terms, in favor of people who had lots more property over people who had very little or none at all, people who had only their labor and the right to vote. When they could not join labor unions without fear of losing their jobs, and when their state legislatures passed rules that their employers' lawyers overthrew in the federal courts, labor organizations again shifted tactics, toward national politics and toward much more aggressive national legislation.[3]

All of these developments occurred against a backdrop that few Americans could have imagined in the two decades after the Revolution. American presidents in the early nineteenth century had sent explorers across the continent just to figure out what was west of Ohio; presidents in the late nineteenth and early twentieth centuries had acquired vast territories that they had no intention of incorporating into states, and they had a military reach that Washington or Adams would not have believed. The Spanish American War gained the Americans the Philippines and brought Filipinos to places like Chicago—but territories like Cuba and the Philippines were radically different, full of restless, angry laborers and workers combining to demand better working conditions and land distribution, even if that meant killing a great many landlords. The *Lochner* era took place in a world where revolutions embroiled whole countries, where kings, tsars, emperors, and members of the landed classes were deposed and shot. When Franklin Delano Roosevelt was elected President of the United States in 1932, communists had been in power in Russia for over a decade, ultranationalist fascists had control over Germany and Italy, and the leading industrial power in Asia, Japan, seemed to be an army and navy attached to a nation.

To make his job even more difficult, Roosevelt had to deal with a global economy that had collapsed, a catastrophe that inspired draconian state responses throughout the world. Leaders in Europe and Asia had varying answers for the economic troubles in their countries—Stalin pursued collectivization programs despite early, repeated reports of mass starvation; Hitler proposed an eastward expansion for Germany, where non-Germans would be reduced to slavery while their new German masters took their lands by force; and Japan proposed a Greater East-Asia Co-Prosperity Sphere, under which Asian peoples would be at once "liberated" from Western imperialists and tied to a massive, maritime Japanese Empire.[4] Conservatives in the United States insisted that Franklin Roosevelt was a socialist, a radical, a communist—a "traitor to his class" who was dangerous to private property and free markets, and a panderer to the uneducated masses locked in a class struggle with leading capitalists, financiers, and industrialists. Roosevelt insisted that he was none of these things: he claimed that government should play a greater role in protecting "forgotten men" and working class people, too many of whom could be driven to poverty and desperation when capitalists, financiers, and industrialists were so unregulated and unfettered that they could drive the entire country into ruin.[5]

"Unfair labor practices . . ."

Roosevelt's proposed legislative solution to the country's "class struggle" was at once radical and pragmatic. The two major pieces of legislation addressing labor issues—the Norris-LaGuardia Act of 1932 and the National Labor Relations Act (NLRA) of 1935—framed the state as a neutral referee between labor and capital, with one important change: under these federal rules, laborers could combine and bargain collectively. Under Norris-LaGuardia, companies could not forbid their workers from joining labor unions as a condition of their employment, nor could the federal courts issue injunctions against labor unions for strikes and work stoppages, as they had since the Pullman Strike of 1894. "Yellow-dog contracts" were forbidden now as a matter of national policy. Furthermore, under the NLRA, employers who discouraged employees from joining labor unions or bargaining collectively could face serious penalties if found to have engaged in such "unfair labor practices." The newly created National Labor Relations Board could also order companies to reinstate employees who had been wrongfully terminated, as well as to pay wages that were lost as a result of the employer's interference with the workers' collective bargaining rights. On the one hand, this was quite radical, as this legislation undid several major Supreme Court decisions governing labor relations; on the other hand, the new rules balanced the power of corporations against the emergent power of labor unions.[6]

In this new arrangement, "liberty of contract" would be preserved by allowing workers to bargain in a corporate form, thus recognizing that gigantic corporations had for some time had an upper hand against *individual* workers in any single bargaining transaction. Given a choice between a horrible wage and starvation, and given no chance to discuss with others who were similarly situated about whether such a choice was even fair or humane, an industrial worker had no choice at all. Treating workers as atomistic individuals reduced all of them to wage slavery, much to the benefit of corporations and, in Roosevelt's view, to the detriment of the country as a whole. Indeed, in a nation with vast and powerful productive capacities, the reality of huge numbers of poorly paid, destitute workers made no sense at all. Their poverty and vulnerability were, in the end, the result of industrialists and capitalists having too much leverage over wages and working conditions. But rather than having government legislate, endlessly, wages and safety rules and retirement benefits, the federal government could protect workers who wished to bargain for such things through labor unions. The federal government did set some minimal standards during this period, through rules like the Fair Labor Standards Act in 1938, but such rules set minimums that by then, nearly everyone could agree were a low floor—restrictions against child labor, a federal minimum wage, and definitions for what should count as a "work week" or "overtime."[7]

To many labor leaders, this wasn't direct government intervention so much as a fundamental reframing of the role of government. Instead of taking over private industries, as a true communist would, labor unions—not government—could bargain with powerful corporations, and then perhaps make a new kind of capitalism that would be more fair, even more rational, in a world where free markets were threatened as much by laissez-faire ideologies as by revolutionary communists and fascists. In 1937, key leaders like John Lewis of the United Mine Workers framed a distinctive, American compromise to class struggle: "American labor . . . stands between the rapacity of the robber barons of industry of America and the lustful rage of the communists, who would lay waste to our traditions and our institutions with fire and sword." Lewis and other labor leaders had persuaded Roosevelt that low wages had eviscerated the purchasing power of American workers, and that this had made many commodities unaffordable to the very workers who had made them.

A robust capitalism required workers who could afford to become consumers, people who could purchase more than just the necessities of life: "Not a living wage! We ask more than that. We demand for the unskilled workers a wage that will enable them to maintain themselves and their families in health and modern comfort, to purchase their own homes, to enable their children to obtain at least a high school education and to provide against sickness, disability and death."[8] Through this middle way, Lewis proposed *saving* capitalism from the capitalists, through public laws that would legitimate robust collective bargaining. Finally, free from court injunctions and yellow-dog contracts, labor unions could represent labor interests in powerful, corporate forms—they could demand better wages, safer workplaces, and benefits like health insurance and retirement plans.[9]

Fire and sword did consume the world in the 1930s and 1940s, as World War II destroyed every industrialized country except for the United States. Although the United States was attacked at Pearl Harbor and in the Philippines in 1941, its industrial infrastructure grew well before it formally entered the war. Through policies like Lend-Lease, Roosevelt had approved the sale of wartime materials to nearly any country opposed to Imperial Japan and fascist Germany and Italy. After the war destroyed industrial and agricultural production in the Soviet Union, France, Great Britain, and China, the United States provided direct aid to its allies, again stimulating industrial production in the United States to levels that were unprecedented in American history.

After 1945, American policymakers still continued to finance the reconstruction of both their wartime allies and their enemies; rather than imposing indemnities and other financial penalties for starting the war, as the victors had done after World War I, American policymakers sought to fold their former allies *and* adversaries into a broader circle of democratic, free-market systems, primarily to defend against the spread of global communism. World War II and the new Cold War strengthened American industries: American steel and concrete were used to rebuild Japan, the Philippines, and Western Europe, and then South Korea, too. The American economy enjoyed a postwar growth that saw enormous increases in household income for working class families, where many more Americans could own their homes, get a college education, and plan for an even brighter future for their children. Some of the most astonishing victories in the labor movement occurred within a decade after the end of World War II, and they would make sure that Americans were the most highly paid industrial workers in the world.[10]

"A massive foreign labor force for agriculture . . ."

The tremendous mobilizations of governments and of people during World War II itself created conditions for labor shortages, or at least the perception of labor shortages, and this was a remarkable turn in a nation where unemployment had been a crippling reality just a few years ago. For people of color, the war provided many economic opportunities: African Americans entered mainstream industries, often in wartime production, and after the war, many more joined labor unions in numbers unthinkable a generation before; Asian Americans, Mexican Americans, and even Native Americans saw their fortunes rise also, both by participating in wartime production and in the economic boom that followed.[11] The war generated massive migrations, and some of the most significant ones were internal movements, sometimes in opposite directions: African Americans further dispersed to major industrial centers across the country, for example, to the urban Midwest, the East and West, and to emergent cities in the South itself, like Mobile and Savannah; on the other hand, Japanese Americans were concentrated—nearly 120,000 of them were moved by war, by their own government, as they were subject to curfews, then evacuated, and then interned, as if to cleanse the West Coast of enemy aliens, even though most of the internees were American citizens.[12]

The war produced striking international migrations as well, setting up another recurring set of concerns about immigrants and citizenship, as well as wage slavery and exploitation, that have shaped labor relations ever since. The federal government played a central role in this new immigration: pleading labor shortages, and having convinced government officials of dire threats to agricultural production, growers in the Southwest demanded labor, and they would have it from across the southern border. Although for all practical purposes the Bracero Program had been in existence for several months before its formal approval, Congress enacted rules to govern the Program in April 1943, and at the insistence of agricultural companies, portions of the Program continued well into the 1960s. For a policy that would, over time, brings hundreds of thousands of Mexican migrants to the United States during the war itself and would thereby solidify migratory relationships between the two countries, the Bracero Program was not at first the subject of great concern.[13]

Yet it was unique and unprecedented on both sides of the border: here was Congress approving the direct involvement of federal agencies to bring foreign workers to private employers. Such a thing, on such a scale, would have been unimaginable during the period of American slavery or Chinese Exclusion. Leading scholars of immigration have noted the novelty of the Program: "[The Bracero Program] was born virtually overnight and with remarkably little fanfare. . . . This program, that delivered millions of Mexican farm workers to employers in the United States, is unique in U.S. immigration history. For over two decades, the U.S. government recruited, distributed, and controlled a massive foreign labor force for agriculture."[14] The Program reversed the formal *emigration* policies of the Mexican government: since the Mexican Revolution of 1910, and under the Mexican Constitution of 1917, Mexican laborers wanting to leave the country had to acquire the formal permission of their municipal government as well as the Mexican consulate; leaving without such permission amounted to unlawful emigration, a policy designed to discourage the departure of low-wage, unskilled workers. Leaders of the Mexican Revolution had promised all workers a great improvement in their quality of life; millions of them leaving would represent an embarrassing failure to deliver on that promise, not to mention a huge loss of cheap labor available to Mexico's own nascent industries.[15]

Because the Bracero Program, at least initially, preserved strict emigration controls even as it "invited" an ever growing number of underemployed and unemployed Mexican workers to the United States, Mexican workers who did not participate in the Program migrated anyway. Under the Program, about two million Mexican agricultural workers arrived in the United States between 1942 and 1964; outside of the Program, migrating without permission, an untold number of other Mexican workers found employment in the United States during that same period. At least initially, the Bracero Program was to represent mutual cooperation between two countries at a time when both were opposed to fascism. Here was a more modern, advanced state with improved agricultural methods helping its neighbor acquire new knowledge—perhaps even modernity itself—through the hosting of agricultural workers, and here was a neighboring state with surplus labor and a desire to contribute to the cause of freedom, sending its men willingly to "soldier" in American fields. The *braceros* were to remain in the United States for short periods of time, to learn whatever they could about agriculture and business, and then to return home as model citizens and leaders to a country that could benefit from their experiences abroad.[16]

At the beginning of the Bracero Program, neither Mexico nor the United States thought that the temporary workers from Mexico would become a permanent part of the American labor market. They were not Americans, and so they were not to be involved in American labor disputes, nor in collective bargaining agreements, and the entire Program that brought them was considered necessary only for wartime agricultural production. Production was of paramount concern: during World War II, Franklin Roosevelt had asked Congress to approve the National War Labor Board, a federal agency that would mediate labor disputes so as to prevent work stoppages that might cripple any industry. Between business and labor, the government supported a "No Strike" policy for the duration of the war, even though this meant that wages were kept low. In addition, new federal policies, including the work of the Fair Employment Practice Committees, enlarged economic opportunities for people of color, but as they too entered the mainstream workforce, they were, by the end of the war, ready for collective bargaining and higher pay across the entire labor market.

When the war did end, when labor activists saw how agricultural producers had come to depend upon the federal government to "deliver" *braceros* to the fields, American labor leaders turned against the Program and against the *braceros* themselves.[17] In agriculture, the common understanding now was that foreign labor depressed wages, and in the absence of war, there was no justification for the use of foreign labor. In their opposition to the Bracero Program, labor leaders like Cesar Chavez behaved in ways that would make immigration status an obvious and legitimate form of discrimination in the American labor market.

"Institutional support for an unlawful practice . . ."

Within this context, the Immigration and Nationality Act of 1952, often referred to as the McCarran-Walter Act, deserves special attention, as it highlighted the ways that federal law criminalized illegal immigrants while shielding the industries that hired them. The Act of 1952 was the most important, comprehensive piece of immigration legislation in the postwar period: it set categories for "immigrants" (people who intend to reside permanently in the United States) and "non-immigrants" (persons who intend to visit, as students, tourists, or on business) that remain good law today; it retained the National Origins System in the Immigration Acts of 1917 and 1924, thus preserving the bar against immigration from Asia and Eastern and Southern Europe; and it did all this over the veto of President Harry Truman, who considered the law embarrassing, a kind of insult to important Asian and European allies during the Cold War. As American troops arrived in places like South Korea and Greece in near-permanent arrangements, South Koreans and Greeks could wonder why the Americans still saw them as so racially unfit that they should never be allowed to migrate to the United States.

For Senator Pat McCarran, the Democrat from Nevada, the portions of the law most offensive to Truman were its best parts: in the *Congressional Record*, the Senator said that federal immigration rules should protect American society from being "over-run, perverted, contaminated, or destroyed." McCarran supported the existing bars against Asians and Eastern and Southern Europeans, making clear the origins of such threats. McCarran considered himself the staunchest warrior of the Cold War, hateful toward all communists and subversives, and the sponsor of other rules like the McCarran Internal Security Act of 1950, also known as the Subversive Activities Control Act, yet another law that he'd passed over Truman's veto. Like many anti-communists during that period, McCarran was much more comfortable with free market capitalists and just as suspicious of "leftists," including nearly all leaders of organized labor. When Harry Bridges rose to prominence as the head of the International Longshore and Warehouse Union in San Francisco, for instance, McCarran insisted that he was a dangerous communist who should be deported back to Australia. People like Bridges were not "admissible" under either the Act of 1950 or the Act of 1952, as "communists" were forbidden under these new rules. Still, as a successful politician from the West, McCarran was also careful not to offend agricultural interests in his region and in his state even as he insisted that immigration rules ought to be enforced strictly, as though the nation's security depended upon it. In his new immigration law in 1952, he framed labor problems in a novel language that combined vagueness and paranoia.[18]

The Act of 1952 did not eliminate the Bracero Program, but it codified a provision about "bringing in and harboring certain aliens," using language that also appeared in the Act of 1950: an American citizen who "[knows or recklessly disregards] the fact that an alien has come to, entered, or remains in the United States in violation of the law, conceals, harbors, or shields from detection, or attempts to conceal, harbor, or shield from detection, any alien in any place, including any building or any means of transportation." The plain meaning of this provision would be that American citizens and anyone else lawfully present in the United States could be fined and imprisoned for aiding someone they knew to be here unlawfully. In 1952, in light of how so many growers were hiring and using both *braceros* and people who were out of status—even as they knew that they were out of status—the law should have applied to agricultural producers in the Southwest. Instead, Congressional supporters insisted that the provision would be most applicable to people aiding "wetbacks" along the southern border; nowhere in the Act of 1952 did Congress provide for sanctions against employers who knowingly hired undocumented workers. This was not an oversight: in the Act of 1952, in order gain support from legislators in the Southwest, Congressional leaders added a "Texas Proviso," a clause that limited the definition of "harboring," so that "for the purposes of this section, employment (including the usual and normal practices incident to employment) shall not be deemed harboring."[19]

Throughout the 1950s, through Operation Wetback in 1954, employers were thus shielded from any liability or responsibility, while "wetbacks" were framed as a serious threat to the American republic. An article published in the *Stanford Law Review* in 1954 was typical of how Americans talked about "Wetbacks"—indeed, that was the title of the piece—as it described this migration in terms similar to the ones used against Chinese migrants not too long ago, as an "invasion in its current proportions," "a vast alien labor force," "a critical threat to the health, safety and general welfare of the people of the border states." The author listed the problems caused by the presence of illegal immigrants in states like Texas and California, and then suggested measures that the states could take to address these problems. The federal government had not acted because of "political pressures" and "interest groups," and the article said at the very end that growers should be held accountable through state rules for hiring people who were undocumented. Still, the primary thrust of the piece was to center "wetbacks" as sources of disease and crime. Even as this article circulated in the law schools, the federal government did act under President Eisenhower to deport hundreds of thousands of persons through new federal enforcement actions over the next few years, while doing little to punish the growers who'd hired and supported their migration.[20]

In much of the legal and political discourse about illegal Mexican immigration during this period, the most notable trend was that the people who had economic and political power successfully avoided law and regulation, while the people who were often exploited at their hands were defined as *the* problem. Agricultural "interests" were so powerful that they got exemptions from federal laws that governed nearly every other industry, trade, and market. The NLRA did not apply, and neither did the Immigration Act of 1952: here was a rule that criminalized the "harboring" of persons, "knowing or in reckless disregard of the fact that an alien has come to, entered, or remains in the United States in violation of law," and yet the principle behind the rule did not apply to the very people who seemed to be doing most of the harboring. Agricultural growers did, after all, house their workers, provide food and other necessities, and otherwise assist persons that they knew to be out of status. They did these things to take advantage of their labor, to make money.

Yet the federal policies approved after 1952 did not touch such interests at all, at least not directly. Instead, federal rules criminalized "illegal aliens," as other Americans first spoke of them in disparaging terms—as "wetbacks" or as "stray dogs"—and then the federal government itself used militarized methods to secure the southern border and to remove the "invaders" into the interior of Mexico. Still, throughout the 1960s, even as the Bracero Program ended in 1964 and after the Immigration Act of 1965, the flow of unauthorized migrants from Mexico to the United States continued—it had become by then an entrenched pattern, the result of years of "institutional support for an unlawful practice." Ellwyn Stoddard, an anthropologist at the University of Texas in El Paso, predicted in 1976 that because of tacit federal support and indifference, as was evident in the comprehensive Act of 1952, the persistent clout of growers, and the worsening economic and political climate in Mexico, unauthorized migration in his region and throughout the West would continue.[21] He was absolutely right.

"There was instant reaction . . ."

As many immigrants from Mexico seemed to travel within the Bracero Program as without it. By 1954, agricultural producers in Mexico, conservative politicians in the United States, established Mexican Americans, and even the *braceros* themselves complained about "illegals," accusing them of lowering wages and working conditions for American citizens and foreign workers alike. Responding to reports of workers abandoning entire regions in Mexico, the Mexican government requested greater collaboration with the American government "to prevent the illegal entry" of Mexican workers; similarly, responding to reports of illegal immigrants "taking" work that belonged to American citizens or Mexican *braceros*, the United States hired more Border Patrol agents and deployed them to known illegal crossing points.[22]

Federal enforcement grew more severe after the war, when the Bracero Program continued to provide a seasonal flow of labor from Mexico to the United States. Undocumented immigration continued as well. To prevent this unauthorized flow, the federal government announced in 1954 that it would implement new measures to deport all unlawful foreign workers from the United States. In the Attorney General's statement, no one could miss the location or complexion of the problem that the government had had in mind: again, using even more Border Patrol agents along the border with Mexico, the enforcement action would be called Operation Wetback, and it "would be an intensive and innovative law enforcement campaign designed to confront the rapidly increasing number of illegal border crossings by Mexican nationals." Over the next several years, under Operation Wetback, workplace raids, road blocks, and mass deportations were implemented, some of which did not bother to distinguish between Mexican nationals and American citizens who "looked like" illegal immigrants. A staggering two million persons were forcibly deported under Operation Wetback, many to the interior of Mexico to diminish the chances that they would ever cross back into the United States.[23] In subsequent decades, however, it became clear to everyone that the southern border had become like a revolving door, with new immigrants coming unlawfully even while others were deported.

In the late 1950s and early 1960s, prominent Mexican Americans themselves favored tougher enforcement measures against undocumented aliens despite hearing credible reports of abuse. To defend against a "wetback invasion," they argued that unscrupulous growers had grown dependent on cheaper, more exploitable illegal immigrants for agricultural work; that this undermined efforts for Mexican Americans and lawful immigrants to improve their wages and working conditions, especially through collective bargaining; and that the illegal immigrants themselves damaged Mexican American aspirations for full citizenship in the United States in the postwar period.

In Texas, important figures like Hector Garcia emerged as critics not just of illegal immigration, but of the Bracero Program itself for these very reasons. Garcia was a physician who had travelled to agricultural labor camps throughout the state, and he saw first-hand how *braceros* and illegal immigrants were both subject to deplorable living and working conditions. As a leader of the American G.I. Forum in Texas, Garcia sent telegrams and letters to rising politicians, notably Lyndon Johnson, asking them for tougher legislation to stop poorer, desperate Mexican nationals from entering Texas. Garcia contrasted the plight of poorer migrants against the aspirations of Mexican Americans, framing the former as threats to the latter: "It is no secret that Texas has for the past 100 years and to a certain extent still [is] segregating our children, hoping to retard them and to discourage them from seeking higher education so that they would furnish cheap labor. . . . It has been stated that the children like to pick cotton. It isn't so; if they pick cotton it is because they have to."[24] To disassociate all persons of Mexican ancestry from the status of "cheap labor," Garcia spent fifteen years lobbying against the Bracero Program, recommending, among other things, detention camps for illegal migrants, more border patrols, and "the airlifting of wetbacks to the interior of Mexico." In another letter to Johnson, Garcia softened, but not by much: "I believe that our government should give protection and opportunity and good pay to its workers before importing outside workers."[25]

California growers were no less dependent on a steady supply of agricultural workers, as many scholars have shown, and *braceros* were no less controversial there. The Bracero Program generated similar forms of antagonism in that state: Cesar Chavez, the celebrated founder and leader of the United Farm Workers, took a position in California nearly identical to Hector Garcia's stance in Texas. Chavez came to this conclusion after hearing an unexpected set of complaints from his compatriot farm workers in Oxnard in 1958 and 1959: "[They said,] 'The *braceros* have all our jobs. What are you going to do about that?'" Like Garcia in Texas, Chavez concluded that the federal government had been providing local growers with *braceros* and thus replacing American citizens with foreign workers: "The jobs belonged to local workers. The *braceros* were brought only for exploitation. They were just instruments for the growers. *Braceros* didn't make any money, and they were exploited viciously, forced to work under conditions the local people wouldn't tolerate. If the *braceros* spoke up, if they made the minimal complaint, they'd be shipped back to Mexico."[26] Wanting to rally a burgeoning movement of agricultural workers in California, Chavez seized upon this issue to unite them: "We always felt that ending the program would be the best thing we could do for them and for everybody. So I changed the attack at house meetings to the issue of fighting to get those jobs from the *braceros*. There was instant reaction."[27]

Hector Garcia had appealed to politicians to stop the Bracero Program, but Cesar Chavez took a much more grassroots approach: "I studied the issue and learned that, according to the law, *braceros* could not be used if there was local labor available. But they were being used, and the people could not get jobs."[28] To remedy this situation, Chavez proposed that American citizens seize back these opportunities: "People would come and tell us that they needed work as irrigators or tractor drivers or in the sheds. I said, 'You want to drive a tractor? Okay. You go find me a bracer on a tractor, and you've got a job.' That worked like magic. People were going all over the valley." Sharing with American citizens knowledge of how the immigration law worked, Chavez helped lawful workers by encouraging them to report illegal immigrants: "When they found a *bracero*, we'd call the federal people and say, we want this job right on the spot."[29]

That Cesar Chavez supported efforts to criminalize the hiring of Mexican nationals—even though he was, without a doubt, one of the greatest champions of farm workers and a pioneer in the movement to organize low-wage farm workers—has been the source of a great deal of scholarly debate about his legacy. Chavez condemned the federal government and local growers for exploiting and using *braceros* as cheap labor, and yet in his initial political positions regarding *braceros* themselves, he did not embrace their incorporation into *La Causa*. Instead, he placed them outside the movement to defend the dignity of farm labor, and he encouraged "legal" workers to report the presence of their "illegal" peers.[30] Still, throughout this period, Chavez's position and the position of his new labor union was fraught with contradiction: over the next two decades, Chavez would support federal efforts to detain and remove illegal immigrants from the agricultural labor markets throughout the Southwest even though "the [United Farm Workers] had undocumented immigrants within its ranks for years."[31]

"The unorganizable . . ."

In light of these conflicting tendencies, it wasn't surprising that the United Farm Workers supported federal legislation that also seemed to be at cross-purposes. In 1965, when Lyndon Johnson signed into law a new set of Immigration Amendments, federal immigration law became more race-neutral than ever before. Commonly known as the Immigration Act of 1965, the new rules abolished the national origins system that had been in place since before World War I, a system that had been openly nativist and racist. Johnson's Act would bring immigration law into the Civil Rights Movement: the Immigration Act of 1965 was the first race-neutral immigration law governing admissions in American history, allowing for all countries to send permanent residents to the United States. Yet the Act of 1965 "regularized" immigration from Mexico, in essence abolishing the Bracero Program, and so Cesar Chavez supported the law and envisioned its immigration consequences as positive for "native" American workers in the agricultural sector. By cutting off the supply of cheap foreign labor and by affirming that illegal immigration was a national problem, the Act of 1965 represented "the window of opportunity for domestic farm workers to demand better pay and working conditions."[32] Though his detractors had criticized him and his union for being more Mexican than American, Cesar Chavez and other Chicano activists supported a rule that they knew would reduce lawful migration from Mexico. Still, in the next two decades after the Act of 1965, undocumented immigration would prove to remain an intractable problem.

Two decades later, the United Farm Workers supported again another immigration law that targeted illegal immigration from Mexico. Under the Immigration Reform and Control Act of 1986, Congress expanded border enforcement and punished employers who had hired illegal immigrants. The Act of 1986 had an interesting political history, and portions of it had been inspired by federal court decisions that suggested an ongoing problem: undocumented aliens had been barred from coming to the United States under federal law, but federal law did not explicitly prohibit American employers from hiring undocumented aliens. Other portions of the Act of 1986 suggested an evolving position among the leaders of the United Farm Workers and other important constituencies—they supported "legalizing" hundreds of thousands of people, especially in the agricultural economy, shifting them from "undocumented aliens" to lawful permanent residents. Cesar Chavez supported the Act of 1986 because he believed that undocumented workers were too vulnerable and too afraid to join the UFW; by folding them into American society, he hoped to grow the union, and thus to organize the "unorganizable."[33] But like the Bracero Program itself, the Act of 1986 did not have the consequences that anyone, including Cesar Chavez, had hoped.

Looking back at the entire system through which the federal government procured Mexican workers for American growers, the Bracero Program had many unintended consequences on both sides of the Southern border. For example, in response to widespread reports of *braceros* being abused and exploited by their American employers, the Mexican government had protested and demanded that the United States monitor the behavior of its companies. Otherwise, the Mexican government had warned, it would end the Program. But as experience with this transnational migration continued, as *braceros* continued to work and to send money back home to their loved ones, the Mexican government had to reconsider whether it could afford to end this or any migration that sent so much money back into Mexico. The government of Mexico had once feared losing too many of its workers to the United States, but it realized that their departure brought about other gains: "By the 1950s, [*braceros*'] remittances comprised the country's third-largest source of hard currency and a fundament for Mexico's economy and the state's modernization projects, just as international financing of development projects was decreasing dramatically."[34] What was once conceived as a net economic loss turned out not to be so. After the war, for this and other reasons, subsequent Mexican governments would maintain an ambivalent attitude toward emigration, both lawful and unlawful, and they would attempt no serious measures to deter unlawful crossings into the United States. In a society that had been torn apart by peasant revolts and by massive social unrest, emigration could bring both economic gain to Mexico and perhaps even prevent political turmoil, by sending away, on a regular basis, classes of people who might otherwise feel trapped and then turn revolutionary.[35]

In the United States itself, Mexican "temporary" workers were becoming a permanent fixture of the agricultural economy, cycling in and out of the fields through regular schedules kept by the federal government. Federal agencies provided *braceros* to domestic growers, some of whom were quite awful: from the beginning of the program, labor abuses were common, but whenever *braceros* complained of mistreatment, unscrupulous growers threatened to have them sent back to Mexico. *Braceros* could appeal to Mexican officials, but stuck in remote portions of a country they didn't know, and working under conditions they didn't control, *braceros* were vulnerable to obvious and egregious abuses, not to mention casual racism, biological notions about their "fitness" for back-breaking stoop labor, inadequate housing and food, and lukewarm support from their own government.[36] Formal complaints were filed, but long after the abuses had occurred. It did not help that Mexican *braceros* entered an industry that had been lawless in general: growers exercised a great deal of political power in the Southwest, and they devoted a substantial portion of that power to keeping government regulations from telling them what to do. The politicians they'd supported made sure that farm workers would be exempt from the protections of the NLRA; well into the first half of the twentieth century, agribusiness in the West and South could almost be described as semi-feudal, with growers insisting that they did not need any government intervention in their industry. Federal recognition for collective bargaining did not exist in the agricultural sector even under the New Deal.[37]

Yet labor unions, strikes, and other forms of collective action against agricultural producers were common before World War II, and they resumed in the postwar period. In 1947, during a strike against the Di Giorgio Company in the San Joaquin Valley in California, domestic farm workers found that their own government was supplying the company with *braceros* in ways contrary to the original designs of the Bracero Program. The strike dragged on for over two years, and although labor leaders attempted to unionize some of the *braceros*, and even to reach out to undocumented workers, the company used "agreements" with the federal government to procure more foreign laborers to break the strike. Leaders of the American G.I. Forum, including Hector Garcia, pointed to these kinds of instances in their opposition to the Bracero Program—domestic farm workers, he had insisted, would never be able to elevate their economic status if companies were to engage in such unfair labor practices. If the federal government provided foreign scabs at every strike, federal protection for collective bargaining would be meaningless.

Over the next few years, labor leaders in California and elsewhere argued among themselves over the best strategy to deal with the presence of foreign workers. Some favored outright exclusion through new immigration laws, while others advocated for the incorporation of all farm workers into the labor unions, and then full protection for collective bargaining under the NLRA. The federal government seemed set against any of these goals, and according to some commentators and scholars, it continued to furnish foreign workers whenever agricultural producers wanted them and without any care for organized labor. The very flexibility of the system, its loose interpretation of law, proved attractive to American capitalists, especially growers in the West and Southwest, as Kitty Calavita and other scholars have written: "Paroling illegal immigrants to their employers, periodically opening the border to aspiring *braceros* who were documented on the spot, and collaborating with the Department of Labor on unilateral recruitment, the Immigration Service used its discretion to paste together an uninterrupted system of imported farm labor for over two decades."[38] Such habits would be hard to break.

"No employer shall knowingly employ an alien who is not entitled to lawful residence . . ."

For the next two decades, without question, unauthorized immigration not only continued, but grew: in 1965, the Immigration and Naturalization Service (INS) reported approximately 120,000 persons apprehended for undocumented entry into the United States, but in 1986, it detained over 1.5 million persons.

The INS itself estimated that for every one person caught, another three persons weren't.[39] Given that some persons were apprehended more than once while others left within a year or two, no one knew how many people were in the United States unlawfully at any given time, nor how much of an overall impact this population was having on the American labor market. In the 1970s, Presidents Nixon and Ford both supported employer sanctions for companies that had knowingly hired undocumented workers, but neither was successful in forging a compromise between organized labor and agricultural interests on this issue. In the early 1970s, states, including Connecticut and New York, debated similar policies without any clear resolution.

In 1971, however, Governor Ronald Reagan of California signed a new labor law that moved in that direction. It said that "no employer shall knowingly employ an alien who is not entitled to lawful residence in the United States if such employment would have an adverse effect on lawful resident workers."[40] The new rule was the subject of a major lawsuit when domestic farm workers sued a subcontracting firm that employed large numbers of illegal aliens; the plaintiffs sought "a permanent injunction against respondents' willful employment of illegal aliens." In response, a California Appellate Court struck down the law, partly on the grounds that this was in essence an immigration rule and thus within an area where the federal government should have supremacy. The Court pointed to the Act of 1952, to the Texas Proviso, concluding that Congress did not intend to penalize employers for hiring unauthorized workers.[41]

The state appealed, and in 1976, in *De Canas v. Bica*, the United States Supreme Court reversed that decision through an opinion issued by Justice William Brennan. He agreed with the plaintiff De Canas and other farm workers that Bica and similar contracting firms were violating a valid state rule. Brennan said that although the law in question did refer to immigrants and immigration, it was as a whole similar to child labor laws, state-sanctioned minimum wage laws, occupational health and safety laws, or other rules regulating the state's economy, all of which the Court itself had held constitutional in many other instances. Whether the state rule did in fact conflict with existing federal rules governing immigration was unclear, as several other federal statutes indicated that foreign workers, even in agriculture, should be registered and authorized to work. Moreover, Brennan said that the state had shown compelling reasons, "within the mainstream of such police power regulation," when it legislated against the hiring of unlawful immigrants, because the very presence of such persons harmed American citizens and lawfully admitted workers in that state.

Traditionally, state police powers encompassed regulations that addressed the morals, health, safety, and general welfare of the state's citizens. Implicit in the Court's opinion was an agreement with the state's claim that the presence of unlawful workers in California did threaten the morals, health, safety, and general welfare of the state citizens.[42] Other states may not have passed similar rules, the Court said, but this might be because they weren't so close to Mexico, nor did they have such a large group of growers and farmers that depended on the labor of undocumented workers. That Congress had not acted did not mean that California had to wait forever. The Court was unanimous in its opinion, and it was also striking that Justice Brennan, one of the Court's most liberal members, wrote for the majority, as if he too had accepted the view that illegal aliens posed significant social problems that the states could address. Brennan and Reagan did not often agree, but this proved to be one area of overlap. Over the next decade, a dozen states also approved bipartisan solutions similar to the one upheld in *De Canas*.

At the federal level, pressure was also building for Congress to legislate against employers who'd "knowingly hired" persons who were out of status. Here, too, a set of test cases revealed a trend: in 1979, the Ninth Circuit Court of Appeals issued a decision in *NLRB v. Apollo Tire Co.*, a case involving "undocumented aliens not entitled to work and reside in the United States." Apollo Tire was alleged to have cheated its workers, not giving them proper overtime pay, and laying off some of them because they had complained about this to the Wage and Hour Division of the Department of Labor. In subsequent hearings, the National Labor Relations Board found that the company had committed several serious unfair labor practices, including coercion and intimidation of its workers. Three sentences from this case were amazing: "In March, 1977, Hilda Niz, employee Lobos' mother, complained to company General Manager Bostanian that her son had not received overtime pay due him. She stated that, if Bostanian did not pay it, she would go to the 'Labor Commission.' Shortly thereafter, Bostanian asked employee Figueroa, Niz' husband, if it was true that his wife had complained to the Department of Labor, and stated that if so, he would have her killed."[43]

Apollo's attorneys conceded that the labor dispute had gotten out of hand, but they argued that as a matter of law, the company's undocumented employees should not enjoy the protections of the NLRA of 1935. They said that Congress intended to exclude such persons in subsequent legislation, most notably in the Immigration and Nationality Act of 1952, which drew clear distinctions between lawful and unlawful immigrants. Moreover, Apollo's attorneys cited the same California state law that had appeared in *De Canas*: "no employer shall knowingly employ an alien who is not entitled to lawful residence in the United States if such employment would have an adverse effect on lawful resident workers."

The federal appellate court rejected both arguments: Judge Eugene Wright, a Nixon appointee, said that absent specific instructions from Congress or from a higher federal court, "employees" as defined by the NLRA should include undocumented workers, and absent a specific finding by the California courts about how its labor laws were or were not consistent with the federal Immigration and Nationality Act, undocumented workers should be entitled to the same forms of relief as lawful workers under the NLRA. Circuit Judge Anthony Kennedy filed a two-sentence concurring opinion: "If the NLRA were inapplicable to workers who are illegal aliens, we would leave helpless the very persons who most need protection from exploitative practices such as occurred in this case."[44] In its decision, the federal appeals court in California relied on a similar set of findings made by their colleagues handling yet another case notable for intimidation and abuse. In both instances, an emerging trend was becoming clear: undocumented workers were being subjected to horrible forms of abuse, and federal law offered little or no meaningful protection for them.

"Employees"

Two leather processing companies based in Chicago, Sure-Tan, Inc., and Surak Leather, were being sued by the people who'd worked there in 1976. As their dispute appeared in *Sure-Tan Inc. v. NLRB*, John Surak became incensed when several of his workers signed union cards authorizing the local chapter of the Amalgamated Meat Cutters and Butcher Workmen to represent them. Sure-Tan and Surak Leather only had eleven employees between them, but eight of them were so upset with their working conditions that they sought collective bargaining rights through the union. This incensed Mr. Surak: according to his own workers, he called one of them a "Mexican son of a bitch," another "stupid," yet another "a lazy bitch," and still another group "motherfucking sons of bitches." Surak himself denied that he ever intimidated or abused his workers for their union activities, even though his workers insisted that in time, John's brother, Steve, with whom he co-owned the two companies, joined in the intimidation and abuse. Despite all this, in early 1977, eight of the eleven workers voted in favor of union representation, and when the NLRB certified this result, Mr. Surak then contacted the INS and asked its agents to investigate all of his employees. It did so, five employees were then arrested, and rather than contesting their immigration status in the courts, these workers accepted "voluntary departure" on a bus bound for Mexico.

The National Labor Relations Board ruled that Surak's companies had violated the NLRA by retaliating against these employees for supporting a union, a finding that seemed obvious. The NLRB demanded that Surak reinstate his employees with back-pay, a rather standard remedy for this kind of unfair labor practice. But as with the employers in *Apollo Tire*, Sure-Tan's attorneys argued that because these workers were out of status, they really shouldn't be eligible for back-pay, as they were not legally "employees" entitled to pay in the first place, nor should they be reinstated, for the simple fact that they were in Mexico and thus unable to get their jobs back. On appeal, the federal Circuit Court tried to resolve this confusion by ordering that the company's reinstatement obligation be held for four years, so that the dismissed workers could have at least some time to return to the United States and resume working for Sure-Tan lawfully. Moreover, the appeals court said that the NLRB could require from the company a minimum of six month's back-pay for each of the workers dismissed through Sure-Tan's unlawful labor practices. This would compensate at least some of the workers for lost wages while deterring other employers from engaging in the same unlawful labor practices.[45] Sure-Tan appealed, and in 1984, the United States Supreme Court handled this most peculiar case. The Court, too, proved divided and confused.

Writing for a cobbled majority, Justice Sandra Day O'Connor said that the workers were, in fact, "employees" within the meaning of the NLRA, even though they were unlawfully present in the United States while working at Sure-Tan. It followed, then, that Surak had committed an unlawful labor practice by retaliating against them through the INS—using deportation to thwart lawful union representation. O'Connor saw Surak as a villain:

he knew that his own workers would be deported, "[and] there can be little doubt that Surak foresaw precisely this result when, having known about the employee's illegal status for some months, he notified the INS only after the Union's electoral victory was assured."[46] By one account, Surak brought up his employee's immigration status just two hours after they voted for the union. He was not a nice person, and O'Connor portrayed him as a flagrant violator of the NLRA. O'Connor, however, struggled with the remedies appropriate for his workers, including both back-pay and reinstatement.

Justice O'Connor said that the NLRB imposed remedies that seemed too "speculative": no one could say if or when these workers could ever resume their jobs, and the six-month back-pay remedy seemed somewhat random. Why hold their spots for four years? Why not two or ten? Also, why back-pay for six, or three, or twelve months? O'Connor suggested that if, say, one of the workers was discovered out of status through some other means just a day before the union vote, he would have been deported and Sure-Tan would have owed him nothing. If, on the other hand, Surak's workers were lawful citizens and Surak's actions deprived them of their jobs for a year or more, six months of back-pay would be way too little. After all, the workers had voted for a union in January 1977, the federal appeals court ruled in their favor in February 1982, and the Supreme Court didn't reach its decision until June 1984. This was over seven years, during which Surak's workers had lost their right to work due to Surak's illegal actions.

O'Connor's colleagues also wrestled with what seemed like a truly impossible subject. Justices Brennan, Marshall, Blackmun, and Stevens disagreed with her analysis, saying that they thought the remedies proper, because these workers were employees under the meaning of the NLRA, and because Surak and his company committed several egregious unfair labor practices. One scholar suggested a new term for what companies like Sure-Tan and Apollo Tire had done to their undocumented workers after they voted for collective bargaining: this was "retaliatory reporting," and if any one employer could get away with this kind of thing, more employers would also engage in similar, egregious labor abuses because they would know in advance that their victims would be deported.

On the other side, Justices Powell and Rehnquist agreed with O'Connor that the remedies were improper, but they disagreed with her over the reason why: these illegal immigrant workers, they said, should not be counted as "employees" under the NLRA at all. "It is unlikely that Congress intended the term 'employee' to include—for purposes of being accorded the benefits of that protective statute—persons wanted by the United States for the violation of our criminal laws." Surak may have been a villain in this story, but his workers were not innocent of wrongdoing, Powell and Rehnquist said, and so these illegal immigrants should "not [be] entitled to any remedy." Powell and Rehnquist would have overturned not just the lower federal court, but the original decision of the NLRB as well. In a footnote, Powell explained why: by denying a remedy to these workers, there would be "less incentive for aliens to enter and re-enter the United States illegally."[47] Again, here were two members of the Supreme Court framing the problem around the illegal immigrants themselves: they should not have been here at all, and if they had been victimized by people like Surak, they had no one but themselves to blame. They would not have extended any protection to such persons under the NLRA, nor perhaps under any federal law. Over the next decade, Powell and Rehnquist's dissent would become the prevailing view, and those who wished to protect undocumented persons at work would have to find other ways to do so. For employers—especially unconscionable employers—the idea that the federal law would not protect certain kinds of people might have appeared as a strange form of good news, the kind that only an unconscionable person would appreciate.

The King and the Duke

American history, in art and in real life, offers many examples of capitalism at its worst. In *Adventures of Huckleberry Finn*, the King and the Duke personify American entrepreneurship in its most amoral and immoral forms, and Mark Twain was at his satiric best when he was writing about these two horrible characters. They will do anything for a buck. From the moment we meet them in the story, after Huck and Jim have reunited following the episode with the Grangerfords and Shepherdsons, the King and Duke lie to Huck and Jim, then they lie to entire towns, and they attempt to cheat just about everyone they meet; for them, life is one long grift. That these scoundrels can so successfully cheat and steal their way across vast swatches of this landscape underscores the basic theme of lawlessness in *Huckleberry Finn*, but when the townspeople plot their revenge, using rotten vegetables and dead cats, the King and Duke escape and most of it is very funny. Unlike Huck, who has a conscience though an underdeveloped one, the King and the Duke have no conscience. They have no shred of decency. Huck and Jim know that the two men are scoundrels, and yet they follow along through various towns bearing witness to and even participating in their interesting and entertaining forms of dishonesty. More often than not, the people duped by the King and the Duke are unsympathetic, as they are so easily taken in by conjuring, preaching, and bad Shakespeare.

Though most victims of the King and the Duke are cheated from their money, matters take a more serious turn when the cheats come upon the Wilks sisters, for whom the King and the Duke pretend to be long-lost uncles from England. In this swindle, they play the inverse of what they claim to be: they pretend to be relatives who care for the girls upon the death of their father, only to use the ruse to liquidate the family's assets. Because the late Peter Wilks was a man of property, this includes the family's slaves: the black mother and her children are promised to "nigger traders," the mother destined for New Orleans, and her sons to Memphis. Though some in the town "said it was scandalous to separate the mother and the children that way," "the old fool he bulled right along." Huck is partly moved by the sale of the slaves, as well as every scrap of the Wilks estate, but his concerns lie more with Mary Jane Wilks, whose beauty and goodness eventually arouse him to reveal the King and the Duke as frauds. Huck does the right thing here, though impulsively and without thinking, or at least not about the slaves. When the King suspects that Huck has stolen a bag of money from his bed, Huck does the quintessentially white thing: he blames the slaves.

The two scoundrels are horrible but not very successful, and when they are with Huck and Jim again after fleeing the Wilkses, nothing seems to work. "[Mesmerizing], and doctoring, and telling fortunes" don't earn enough money. And so they victimize Jim. Just as Huck and Jim plot their escape from the King and the Duke, they learn that the scoundrels have struck first: the King sold his "rights" to Jim as a runaway slave for $40 in a bar. Huck is shocked: "After all this long journey, and after all we'd done for them scoundrels, here was it all come to nothing, everything all busted up and ruined, because they could have the heart to serve Jim such a trick as that, and make him a slave again all his life, and amongst strangers, too, for forty dollars." The King and the Duke have sold Jim back into slavery not because this was what they thought was morally required or just, but because they wanted the money. They do not suffer guilty consciences because they *have* no consciences. They sold Jim because he was black, and because black people could be sold just like that. This betrayal precipitates the great moral crisis for Huck that many commentators have regarded as the core of the novel, where Huck condemns himself to hell as he promises to "go to work and steal Jim out of slavery again." Huck undergoes a "counter-conversion," condemning himself as he commits to rescuing his only friend.[48]

For a short time, the King and Duke disappear from the story as Huck, and then Tom Sawyer, work to "free" Jim from the Phelps farm. In time, though, Huck witnesses the demise of these two men, revealed as frauds by Jim no less, though their fate is again another example of frontier justice.

The King and Duke are tarred, feathered, and paraded on rails, exactly the fate that the tender Mary Jane had wanted to see for them. Yet the sight of the "poor pitiful rascals" makes Huck reflective: "It was a dreadful thing to see. Human beings *can* be awful cruel to one another." Huck shows again how he can sympathize with the most awful kinds of white people, even as he does not see how this was Jim's revenge against the two men who sold him for $40.

The story of the King and the Duke is important here because of their close resemblance to people like General Manager Bostanian or John Surak, the antagonists in cases like *Apollo Tire* and *Sure-Tan*, men who cheated and sold out the very people who'd helped them make their bread and money. They cheated, abused, and betrayed as though devoid of any conscience, and their worst betrayals came when it appeared to them cheaper to get rid of their employees than deal with them as people worthy of dignity. In the federal cases involving the separate disputes with their workers, the federal judges acknowledged that men like Bostanian and Surak were unsavory, even vicious, in their willingness to threaten and to inform upon the people with whom they collaborated for months or years. Their threats and their actions—against people who are vulnerable, people they *knew* to be vulnerable—shock the conscience within the dry prose of the federal appellate cases where they were recorded.

The greatest disappointment, however, might be that the federal courts still cannot get beyond status: confronted with undocumented workers, people who've clearly been the victims of threat and betrayal, the courts have been reluctant to apply the federal law designed specifically to protect the most vulnerable employees from predatory, horrible, and exploitative employers. In *Sure-Tan*, Justice Powell hoped that such reluctance would provide "less incentive" to undocumented people to come work in the United States, but his hopes have not fit reality. Undocumented immigration continued well after *Sure-Tan*, many more employers continued to behave like the King and the Duke, and federal labor law continued to be unhelpful to their many victims, trapped, as it always has been, on questions of status. In their own peculiar way, perhaps inspired by utopian aspirations for a nation free of all unwelcome immigrants, the architects of the federal law and the prevailing federal precedents have created the very conditions for American capitalism at its worst.

Immigrant Activism in the Shadow of Law

Immigration Reform

Cases such as *Apollo Tire* and *Sure-Tan* stimulated a great deal of scholarly and policy discussions about the need for "immigration reform," for a comprehensive set of rules that might settle once and for all the problem of illegal immigration, employers' hiring practices and conduct, as well as the future of undocumented aliens already in the United States.[1] Leading economists, policy analysts, and other scholars published studies to examine whether undocumented workers were harmful or helpful to the economy as a whole and to measure the extent of their involvement in the American labor market. This debate took place during a time when many Americans feared that the United States was losing permanently the pre-eminent economic position that it had enjoyed since the end of World War II. East Asian and Western European countries had been rebuilt through huge infusions of American foreign aid, and now their economies were productive in ways that competed directly with American industries and producers. American workers had enjoyed high wages in the postwar years, but in a global marketplace, with much greater levels of foreign competition, that era was ending.[2]

Hostility toward immigrants—especially immigrants perceived to be a drain on the economy—became more intense in the 1980s. Cases like *Sure-Tan* exemplified several important trends: the degree to which poorer undocumented immigrants were now working in a wider range of industries in the American economy, the willingness of employers to exploit them and to favor non-unionized workers in general, and the importance of immigration status as an established form of discrimination in the labor market. Not every court, though, read the federal law so as to leave undocumented workers unprotected. In peculiar circumstances, in some parts of the country, even when undocumented workers were "discovered," the federal courts sometimes authorized them to pursue claims for unfair labor practices.

In reply, Congress enacted rules that reaffirmed the lines between unlawful immigrants on the one hand and legal residents and citizens on the other: American employers were to face new penalties for hiring people who were out of status, under the theory that such persons would be discouraged from coming here knowing that they were unemployable under the law. After 1986, in addition to new regulations at the workplace, Congress also devoted greater sums to border enforcement and border control, even as it attempted to erase, at least for a time, the number of people who were out of status by adjusting them into permanent residency. Cesar Chavez and other labor leaders supported this move to "legalize" undocumented workers, as well as the efforts to ensure that more would never come. If all of these rules seemed to flow at cross purposes, perhaps it was because they did.

"[Their] wage loss is easily and accurately calculated . . ."

Not every federal court abided by the majority decision in *Sure-Tan*. Two years after that case, in *Local 512 v. NLRB*, a federal court allowed undocumented workers to press for collective bargaining rights and better wages and working conditions, and to seek relief from their employer's unfair labor practices. In this California case, the managers at Felbro had dismissed a number of workers involved in a union drive at their company in South Gate. The company manufactured wire and tubular displays, the metal and plastic racks and shelves that one might see at any retailer. In circumstances similar to those at *Sure-Tan*, the workers at Felbro had voted to join Local 512 of the Warehouse and Office Workers' Union. Soon after, the company laid off and fired many of these workers, listed in the federal appellate case by their last names—Machuca, Casteneda, Zacarias, Ramirez, Santizo, and Zayas. After an administrative law judge agreed with the National Labor Relations Board that the company had committed an unfair labor practice, Felbro rehired the same workers, but then refused to abide by the labor contract negotiated between the company and the union. The company's managers also insisted that several of its unionized workers were illegal immigrants ineligible for back-pay for the period between their dismissal up to the time when they were rehired.[3]

But as the Ninth Circuit Court noted, "no Felbro employee has been the subject of any INS deportation proceeding." Because they were available to work, because they were working at the company at the time of the case, "the Felbro discriminatees' wage loss is easily and accurately calculated by multiplying the loss per day per employee by the number of days in the back-pay period." The back-pay calculation wasn't, in that sense, "speculative," in the same way it might have been in *Sure-Tan*. A majority of the Court thus approved the back-pay award in *Local 512* by applying *Sure-Tan* and yet avoiding one of its central holdings at the same time.[4]

Cases like *Local 512* surprised many members of Congress, who were alarmed that federal judges were protecting undocumented immigrants, not just in labor disputes but in other areas as well. Important policy makers did not like the idea that any illegal immigrant could benefit from federal labor law, and they saw as a problem the fact that organizations like the Mexican American Legal Defense and Educational Fund had sided with Local 512 and the undocumented workers that it represented, all working to limit the extent of *Sure-Tan*. All of these tense discussions were included in congressional debates in the mid-1980s, when Ronald Reagan was president and his administration was trying to coordinate a compromise on immigration, just as the new president engaged in a much publicized crusade against "big government" and federal social welfare policy. In his second term, within months of the decision in *Local 512*, Ronald Reagan signed the Immigration Reform and Control Act of 1986, thus approving a set of compromises that Congress had been debating for nearly two decades.

Under this important new law, President Reagan approved a federal version of the rule he'd signed as governor of California: employers in the United States were not to hire undocumented aliens, and those that did were now subject to fines and other penalties. One of the chief architects of the Act of 1986, Wyoming Senator Alan Simpson, believed the economists who told him that a great number of undocumented aliens were coming unlawfully to work in the lower ranges of the American job market, as agricultural laborers, in domestic service, or in other unskilled work. The influx of such workers on that lower end of the labor market hurt poorer American citizens and lawful residents the most; on this point, the United Farm Workers, the AFL-CIO, the National Association for the Advancement of Colored People, and Attorney General Edwin Meese agreed. American companies should be prevented from hurting poorer American workers in this way.

The approach was to discipline American employers: if they refused to offer jobs to undocumented aliens, such persons would have no incentive to migrate for work, and then wages for unskilled American citizens would go up. To protect American citizens and lawful residents from discrimination—lest employers refuse to hire them for their close resemblance to illegal immigrants—and also to protect undocumented workers themselves from further exploitation, the federal government created a special office to deal with workplace violations. It wasn't clear at the outset what this federal agency, the Office of Special Counsel for Immigration-Related Unfair Employment, charged as it was to protect illegal immigrants, would do with the illegal immigrants after their discrimination claims were settled. Would it turn them over for deportation? Maybe, but maybe not.[5]

The Act of 1986 had other ambitious aspects dealing with undocumented aliens that reflected the same kind of ambivalence and confusion. First, federal spending on enforcement along the border would be increased dramatically: the southern border would now be even more militarized, with a larger number of Border Patrol agents, as well as new physical obstacles and fencing. The prevailing image of undocumented aliens suggested that the majority walked or drove across unsupervised areas of the southern border. Thus, according to government officials, more agents and more enforcement activity in general would deter these prospective, poorer illegal immigrants. To achieve this objective, the federal budget for enforcement would exceed $1 billion for the first three years, with subsequent appropriations tied to the level of activity detected along the border.[6]

Still, as if to acknowledge that the federal government could not or would not deport hundreds of thousands of illegal immigrants already in the United States in 1986, Congress agreed with the President to "legalize" persons who'd been out of status. Reagan's administration and members of Congress agreed upon a cut-off date: persons who'd been "residing" in the United States before January 1, 1982, could apply to adjust their unlawful status into a temporary lawful status, which in turn could be adjusted further into permanent residency and then into American citizenship. This was to be a one-time amnesty provision, and no one really knew how many people might benefit from it—some figures estimated fewer than a half million persons, others suggested more than 6 million persons, and still other estimates were even higher.[7] Although the scope of this provision was unclear, proponents of the plan argued that immigrants who'd been in the United States for at least four years would likely have strong family and community connections, and deporting large numbers of such persons was going to be too painful and unpopular. Indeed, governments in the twentieth century that had moved or removed so many people at once were not admirable in any historical perspective, as they included Nazi Germany and the Union of Soviet Socialist Republics under Joseph Stalin. This fact may not have been lost on President Reagan himself, who saw his nemesis, the Soviet Union, as an "evil empire" for having done such things.

"[She was] a member of the Union's organizing committee . . ."

Over two million people adjusted their immigration status under the legalization provisions of the Act of 1986. Again, even though some scholars and government officials suspected that this figure would be high, perhaps higher, many other politicians and commentators were just shocked that so many people had been living in the United States without authorization. This number did not even count people who'd entered unlawfully after January 1, 1982, nor did it include people who'd entered after the Act of 1986 went into effect. It was quite plausible, then, that in a few years, another two or three or ten million people would be out of status, and Congress would have to consider yet another "one-time" amnesty. Disappointment with the Act of 1986 was widespread: enforcement along the southern border did not stop people from still trying to cross, and $1 billion was not nearly enough to police that entire stretch between the United States and Mexico. When one area was policed more heavily, migrants seemed to cross at another. In the next two decades, Presidents Bush, Clinton, and then the other Bush requested additional money for enforcement along the border, such that federal spending there grew to at least $1 billion every year by the beginning of George W. Bush's first term. By 2005, the Border Patrol consisted of more than 10,000 agents, and so it had become the largest single police force in the United States. Yet in spite of all of this policing and enforcement, despite harsh new rules like Proposition 187 in California in 1994, as well as the harsh new federal rules approved two years later, despite the miles and miles of new fencing and obstacles, the number of persons who were out of status grew, and grew, and grew. By the end of George W. Bush's second term, there were probably more than ten million persons out of status in the United States.[8]

Many of the structural problems that drove unlawful immigration—political chaos and revolutionary civil wars in Central America, or ongoing wage differentials between Mexico and the United States—could not be solved in Congress. Moreover, because undocumented people were available to work, and because many employers still hired them, provisions like the employer sanction rule in the Act of 1986 were often disregarded. Based on evidence collected in Southern California and elsewhere, many scholars observed that "employer violations are widespread and that the continued hiring of undocumented workers is a direct consequence of the high benefits that employers derive from this course of cheap labor, coupled with the low risks associated with this 'white-collar' crime."[9] Employer sanctions never did have a promising history: in 1972, when Governor Reagan funded the first state law to impose employer sanctions, he provided for only six staff members to investigate companies who'd been accused of hiring unlawful workers. One guy, the "Lone Ranger," "was responsible for nine counties in the agricultural center of the Central Valley." It wasn't surprising, then, that "the [California] law did not produce a single successful prosecution of any employer for hiring an illegal alien."[10]

The federal version proved only slightly less anemic. Long after the passage of the Act of 1986, employers avoided the penalties attached to hiring illegal aliens by showing that they'd made a "good faith" effort to check for the proper papers. Unless there was some compelling proof that an employer knew or should have known that an employee's documents were forged or faked, employers had little to fear. The federal courts held that even when employers didn't check very carefully, they should not be liable for fines and other penalties rooted in the Act of 1986.[11] Overall, economists, sociologists, and legal scholars have studied the reasons employer sanctions at the federal level failed to diminish illegal immigration; there was some debate as to why they failed, but no one doubted the failure, and it was as if no one expected the law to succeed, especially not newer illegal immigrants. In the agricultural sector, for example, "field interviews [revealed] that new illegal workers continue to enter the United States, saving their pay stubs and receipts in the hope of a second amnesty."[12] Events unrelated to the labor market—like the attacks of 9/11—triggered more interior enforcement among immigration officials, and these could have diminished for a time the number of undocumented persons in the labor force, but even then, few employers suffered penalties for hiring undocumented workers.[13] Rather, the very language of the Act of 1986 had its most devastating impact on illegal immigrants suffering from abuse at the hands of their employers.

A new set of federal cases indicated that trend. For instance, *Montero v. INS* originated as a labor dispute within STC Knitting, a garment factory in Queens, New York, in 1992. Ms. Montero and her colleagues voted to unionize after the company increased the work week without providing overtime pay, among other unilateral actions that its workers had regarded as unfair. STC Knitting blocked their efforts, the laborers in turn filed complaints with the National Labor Relations Board, and after an investigation, the NLRB's regional director in New York filed a complaint against the company for nearly a half dozen unfair labor practices. In the fall of 1992, the workers voted for collective bargaining rights with the help of the NLRB, and they thus joined the Union of Needletrades, Industrial, and Textile Employees. The NLRB certified these results and the union became the collective bargaining unit for workers at STC Knitting.

But Henry Dogin, STC's attorney, was a former District Director for the INS in New York City, and he used his former employer to help his current one. He had made veiled threats to STC's workers during their union drive, and when the drive was successful, he (or someone else) engaged in retaliatory reporting: "Sometime in mid-September, the INS received two anonymous complaints concerning the employment of undocumented aliens at STC. Following the receipt of these complaints, the INS stepped up its investigation of STC and attempted to put STC under surveillance."[14] As before, as with Apollo Tire and Sure-Tan, the INS did the company's bidding: it even told STC the day and time when its agents would come to the company to verify the immigration status of its workers, and STC then provided a set of its own internal documents so that the INS would know who to apprehend. It was all done in a collaborative way: the immigration raid arranged between the INS and STC was "consensual," and STC made sure that only some of its undocumented workers—the ones who'd voted for collective bargaining—would have to deal with the INS. "Conveniently, on the prearranged date of the INS raid, pro-management undocumented workers were told not to report to work."[15]

STC targeted employees like Gloria Esperanza Montero, a native of Ecuador and one of the workers instrumental in the union drive. "[She was] a member of the Union's organizing committee and, later, the Union's negotiating committee."[16] During the raid itself, she was despondent. INS agents questioned her, she did not understand English, they detained her, and they put her into deportation proceedings. Though the federal appeals court observed that the company's actions did appear to be a clear violation of the NLRA, it still upheld the deportations of Ms. Montero and of her undocumented colleagues. The court insisted that it was a captive of the new immigration law: "Montero and the amici argue that permitting deportation based upon evidence obtained in connection with a labor dispute will significantly undermine labor law protections. This concern is misplaced. Under current law, an employer is subject to sanctions under both the NLRA and the INA if it identifies its undocumented employees to the INS in the course of a labor dispute. To the extent that these sanctions are insufficiently severe to deter such conduct, that concern must be addressed to the Congress and not the courts."[17]

Ultimately, the federal appeals court cited the Act of 1986 to settle upon the deportability of Montero and her other illegal co-workers, as if this were a necessary conclusion that must follow Congressional action: "no court ever has interpreted [the Immigration Reform and Control Act] to constrain the Attorney General's ability to deport undocumented aliens once their unlawful presence in the country has been discovered." Indeed, after the Act of 1986, it seemed implausible that Montero could remain in the country even if her employer had behaved unlawfully: "Whether or not an undocumented alien has been the victim of unfair labor practices, such an alien has no entitlement to be in the United States. The rule sought by Montero would permit undocumented aliens to continue to be present in this country, in ongoing violation of the INA, until the INS gathers evidence supporting the alien's deportability independent of any evidence obtained in relation to the labor dispute. In light of Congress' efforts to strengthen the enforcement of our immigration laws by enacting IRCA, it is inconceivable that Congress intended to erect such an impediment to the deportation of illegal aliens."[18]

Another case that same year confirmed the central conclusion that undocumented aliens were moving beyond the protection of federal labor law with respect to collective bargaining rights. The Seventh Circuit Court of Appeals ruled in *Del Rey Tortilleria Inc. v. NLRB* that undocumented workers who had been terminated for union activities were not entitled to back-pay even though, again, their termination was the result of an unfair labor practice. The company produced and sold tortillas from its plant in Chicago, and it had been in business for nearly four decades. The company's managers had hired over one hundred workers by the early 1980s, but a few of the managers began referring to some of their workers as "a bunch of pigs" and as "wetbacks" when they organized in favor of union representation in 1982. Refugio Martinez, the company's vice-president and chief operating officer, warned his workers not to unionize, threatening them that if they did so he would report them to the INS.

About three years later, the company fired Bernardo Bravo and Nicolas Paredez for encouraging their colleagues to vote in favor of collective bargaining rights. Initially, the company admitted to the National Labor Relations Board that it had committed an unfair labor practice, that it would rehire both men, and that it would give them back-pay. But then the company refused to carry out the stipulation agreement: it insisted that under the recent federal rulings, workers like Bravo and Paredez were ineligible for back-pay because they were illegal immigrants. The company did not deny that it had violated federal labor laws; rather, it just insisted that these particular workers were ineligible for this remedy because of their immigration status. The Circuit Court agreed: citing *Sure-Tan* itself, the Court said that because these immigrants were not entitled to be in the United States, they should be regarded as "unavailable for work" and thus ineligible for back-pay.[19] The fact that they might be available to work didn't mean that they should have the right to work, the court reasoned, nor that they should remain in the country at all. This conclusion challenged the Ninth Circuit's earlier decision in *Local 512*, the case from South Gate, California, and so the conflict among the federal courts was thus laid bare: did undocumented workers have collective bargaining rights as employees under the NLRA or under other relevant federal laws?

"Perverse economic incentive . . ."

The United States Supreme Court attempted to settle that question in 2002, in a remarkable case that had begun almost fifteen years earlier. Hoffman Plastic Compounds was a company that supplied other companies with custom-formulated "polyvinylchloride pellets," an ingredient that was then used to make drugs, construction materials, and household products. Working there sounded unpleasant: "Jose Castro [operated] various blending machines that 'mix and cook' the particular formulas per customer order." Castro started at minimum wage, with documents that seemed to verify his lawful status when he began there in May 1988. Toward the end of that year, when the United Rubber, Cork, Linoleum, and Plastic Workers of America began a union drive at the company's plant, Castro took the lead by giving his colleagues union authorization cards and otherwise helping this effort. "In January 1989, Hoffman laid off Castro and other employees engaged in these organizing activities."[20]

The National Labor Relations Board ruled in January 1992 that Hoffman had committed an unfair labor practice through these layoffs and ordered, in part, that these employees be offered reinstatement and back-pay. In a hearing to settle how Hoffman might comply with these findings, "Hoffman's attorney began to question Castro about his citizenship and authorization to work in the United States." "The Board's General Counsel objected" to these questions, "the [administrative law judge] sustained the objection, but not before Castro had stated that he was a Mexican national." Castro then admitted that he was an illegal immigrant, that he had obtained fraudulent documents, including a birth certificate from Texas, a driver's license from California, and a Social Security card. He was not, in fact, lawfully entitled to work in the United States under the Act of 1986.[21]

When Hoffman refused any remedy for Jose Castro, the case went before the federal appellate court in Washington, DC. Judge David Tatel observed that "this case lies at the intersection of two statutory schemes: labor and immigration." On the one hand, even though Hoffman insisted that it was somehow "an innocent employer" in this case, the court noted that Hoffman had not behaved well: the company's managers had interrogated, intimidated, and discharged specific employees who'd favored a union, thus violating established federal labor laws. On the other hand, Jose Castro was by his own admission an illegal immigrant, and thus not entitled to be in the United States and not a "lawful worker" at Hoffman. Hoffman's attorneys may have tricked him into this admission, either by taking advantage of the fact that Castro had to have everything translated from English to Spanish in that fateful hearing, or by grilling him relentlessly about his immigration status. And yet there it was: Castro wasn't in the United States legally, he had to construct a false identity just to work, and so even though Hoffman wasn't being fair to him, it wasn't clear whether he was entitled to the same protections as a "lawful worker."

Was he entitled to back-pay? Ultimately, the DC Circuit Court of Appeals had said yes, citing a number of precedents from the Ninth Circuit Court of Appeals, including *Local 512*, even as it noted the Seventh Circuit's opposite decision in *Del Rey Tortilleria*.[22] All of these cases cited *Sure-Tan*. Judge David Sentelle dissented from Tatel's majority opinion: "It defies logic—indeed it boggles the mind—to suppose that the employer could be compelled by law to pay to the illegal unearned wages which he could not lawfully earn and to which he would have no claim but for his prior successful fraud." The "unearned wages" due to Castro were significant, calculated to be about $67,000.[23]

In 2002, the United States Supreme Court agreed with Sentelle and vacated the back-pay award. Speaking through Chief Justice Rehnquist, the Court reviewed Castro's fraudulent misrepresentations and then characterized them as similar to "serious illegal conduct" and "serious criminal acts" that could disqualify such workers from obtaining relief even when their employers had committed unfair labor practices. The Act of 1986 made federal offenses of Castro's unlawful entry into the United States and his subsequent misrepresentations in order to work. Castro "directly [contravened] explicit congressional policies." Moreover, Rehnquist said, "awarding back-pay in a case like this not only trivializes the immigration laws, it also condones and encourages future violations."[24]

Justice Stephen Breyer dissented. He noted that Hoffman's actions were "crude and obvious violations of labor laws," and that a National Labor Relations Board unable to impose back-pay remedies for undocumented workers might cause employers to hire *more* undocumented workers, knowing that these workers could then be exploited with near impunity. No back-pay for people like Castro would create a "perverse economic incentive": "That denial lowers the cost to the employer of an initial labor law violation (provided, of course, that the only victims are illegal aliens). It thereby increases the employer's incentive to find and to hire illegal-alien employees . . . to hire with a wink and a nod those potentially unlawful aliens whose unlawful employment (given the Court's views) ultimately will lower the costs of labor law violations." Far from making the objectives of the federal labor law consonant with the objectives of the federal immigration law, Breyer said, the Court's decision in *Hoffman* interpreted the latter in a way that would undermine both.[25]

Without a doubt, the majority opinion in *Hoffman* threw an ominous shadow over undocumented aliens working in the United States. No one could doubt that despite harsher immigration rules in 1986, 1990, and 1996, there were more undocumented people in the United States than ever before, and it was equally obvious that they were working across many different areas of the American economy. And yet if they were not entitled to back-pay, even when their employers harmed them, what *else* might they not be entitled to? The response to *Hoffman* was dramatic in academic and legal circles, as various scholars and commentators either condemned or embraced the decision for attempting to settle the complex issues in the case. For critics of the majority, the case represented the further criminalization of undocumented aliens, as the majority stated that illegal entry and unlawful presence itself amounted to a serious crime. For those who favored the majority view, the case represented an important step to discipline the labor market yet again, by disallowing conventional remedies for undocumented aliens who violated federal immigration laws.[26]

The circumstances of the case itself—in particular, the revealing of Castro's illegal status during interviews and discovery proceedings—had inspired serious discussions about attorney-client privilege, the duty to protect or to interrogate someone about immigration status, and the possible impact all of this might have on persons who did, in fact, face exploitative, unfair, or dangerous working conditions. It was as though immigration status might be hereafter the single most important fact about a person complaining in a labor case, or in other cases as well. Some attorneys wondered whether they could advise clients to refuse to answer questions about their immigration status, while others insisted that such an inquiry had to be part of discovery proceedings, for it lay at the heart of the person's identity. In that way, the case has proven quite influential: *Hoffman* has been cited often in other disputes involving undocumented workers, with results that have underscored how these persons have been moved beyond the law's protection, sometimes at that very point where their unlawful status was discovered.[27]

Examples of this trend have been numerous: the Superior Court in Essex County, New Jersey, held in 2004 that Rosa Crespo should not recover anything against her employer, Evergo Corporation, for unlawful termination; a federal District Court in Texas held in 2003 that Enrique Escobar could not recover back-pay related to a sexual harassment complaint against his boss, Mario Fernandez; and a Michigan Court of Appeals said in 2003 that David Sanchez was eligible for wage-loss benefits when he'd been injured at work, but then ineligible after the point at which his illegal status had been discovered.[28] The court in Michigan reasoned that under *Hoffman*, unlawful presence in the United States and misrepresentations about lawful status using false documents—both offenses that Sanchez admitted—were "crimes" that precluded relief under the state's Workers' Compensation Disability Act.

This last case from Michigan is illuminating as an example of how immigration status can reshape an otherwise straightforward case. David Sanchez worked for Eagle Alloy, a company specializing in molded steel and stainless steel castings. He had worked at Eagle Alloy since March 1997, but "in September 1998, Sanchez suffered a right hand injury when one of defendant's machines closed on his hand, crushing and burning it between two heated metal plates."[29] After several surgeries and physical therapy, Sanchez could have returned to work in September 1999, but in the month before, Eagle Alloy received a letter from the Social Security Administration informing the company that Sanchez's documents were invalid. When he applied for workers' compensation benefits, his company claimed that he should be ineligible for such benefits because he was out of status. After lengthy litigation, the Court of Appeals settled on this peculiar compromise: Sanchez would be eligible for benefits from the time he injured his hand to the point at which his unlawful status was discovered, but not after. The Michigan Supreme Court affirmed, but Justice Stephen Markman filed a separate opinion that discussed the irrationality of the compromise itself, the way Michigan labor law now protected workers up to the point that their unlawful status was discovered and then no more. Justice Markman suggested that he would have denied Sanchez any compensation, as his right to work at Eagle Alloy began with wrongdoing—forged documents—and because that should have rendered his labor contract invalid under existing statutes and precedents.

This appeared to Markman as a more logical extension of the principles out-lined in federal labor law, federal immigration law, and the Supreme Court's decision in *Hoffman*.[30]

What was striking, though, was that if all undocumented aliens were guilty of "crimes," just by their unlawful presence, as well as their unlaw-ful misrepresentations—often made in order to work—were they entitled to any protections in the workplace once their illegal status was discovered? The answer being sort of no and his hand injured nevertheless, David San-chez and others like him were in the position of being subject to premodern, pre-industrial legal rules about how workers assumed all of the risks of work, even in dangerous settings, and so should never recover against their employ-ers. For people like him, and for others looking at his condition, American labor law might appear as though it were moving backward, to a time when the doctrines like the "assumption of risk" and the "fellow servant rule" ab-solved employers of any harm that might befall their workers, no matter the circumstances of their work nor the extent to which their employers did or didn't take reasonable protections for their employees. The effective de-nial of collective bargaining rights was even worse: undocumented workers would have few incentives to join labor unions, knowing that they could be deported for even considering that option. Employers could exploit undoc-umented workers, keep only those who didn't complain, and then use immi-gration rules to get rid of those who did, especially the ones who might try to organize their colleagues into bargaining units rather than face exploit-ative employers as single individuals. Considered together, all of these devel-opments threatened to undermine many of the most important progressive victories of the New Deal.[31]

"Serious crimes . . ."

From 2002 to 2010, undocumented workers had few victories in the federal courts, and then only in instances when they veiled their unlawful identi-ties. For instance, in 2004, in *Rivera v. NIBCO*, the Ninth Circuit Court of Appeals in San Francisco upheld a magistrate's protective order in favor of employees who had sued their employer for discrimination based on national origin, in violation of Title VII of the Civil Rights Act of 1964. NIBCO was a manufacturing firm with a plant based in Fresno. The managers there had required all employees to take a basic job skills test that was only given in English; twenty-three of its employees performed poorly on this test, but they alleged that English proficiency wasn't a part of the job description, nor did it impede successful performance of their primary duties. Still, the employees faced a "range of adverse employment consequences," and "eventually, all plaintiffs were terminated in the period between July 30, 1998 and September 24, 1998."

The plaintiffs were all women, immigrant Latinas and Southeast Asians, and during the discovery phase of their lawsuit, NIBCO's lawyers demanded to know their immigration status. "During the deposition of plaintiff Martha Rivera, NIBCO asked where she was married and where she was born. Although Rivera had specified that she was of 'Mexican ancestry' in her answers to interrogatories, Rivera's counsel instructed her not to answer any further questions pertaining to her immigration status." Her lawyers ended the deposition right there, then they sought a protective order from a federal magistrate so as to bar NIBCO from inquiring further into the plaintiffs' immigration status. Rivera's lawyers argued that her immigration status and those of her colleagues had already been verified prior to their employment, that their status was irrelevant to this particular dispute, and that these types of inquiries were likely to have a chilling effect on the plaintiffs' pursuit of their claims, as well as other workers who might pursue similar unlawful discrimination lawsuits.[32] In reply, NIBCO cited *Hoffman*, saying that if the plaintiffs were indeed unlawful immigrants, they had committed "serious crimes" that might bar them from relief.

The Court upheld the protective order, and yet in doing so, nearly admitted that the plaintiffs (or at least some of them) were out of status. The Court observed: "There are reportedly over 5.3 million workers in the 'unauthorized labor' force. Many of these workers are willing to work for substandard wages in our economy's most undesirable jobs. While documented workers face the possibility of retaliatory discharge for an assertion of their labor and civil rights, undocumented workers confront the harsher reality that, in addition to possible discharge, their employer will likely report them to the INS and they will be subjected to deportation proceedings or criminal prosecution." The Court acknowledged here that unlawful immigrant workers were worse off than other workers in the labor market, precisely because their immigration status itself made them "reluctant to report abusive or discriminatory employment practices."[33] The company appealed, hoping that the Court would apply the logic of *Hoffman* to discrimination cases arising under Title VII.

As was obvious by the behavior of NIBCO, one consequence of the *Hoffman* decision has been that employers in labor disputes now have powerful incentives to see about the status of their workers during various kinds of labor disputes. For example, in a case from Michigan in 2005, a group of workers sought a protective order from a court when their employer requested information related to their immigration status; the discovery requests occurred after these workers had alleged that their employer, Brady Farms, had violated provisions of the Fair Labor Standards Act and the Migrant and Seasonal Agricultural Worker Protection Act. Brady Farms, they said, did not pay them for work already performed. But the lawyers for Brady Farms were blunt about what they were attempting to uncover: "There is no question that the disputed discovery requests are designed to uncover Plaintiffs' immigration status. Defendants readily acknowledge such, asserting that Plaintiffs' immigration status is 'relevant for purposes of establishing their entitlement to damages and their standing to sue.' Defendants further assert that Plaintiffs' immigration status is relevant to class certification as well as assessing credibility."[34] The lawyers cited *Hoffman*. As in *Rivera*, the federal magistrate in this case limited the reach of *Hoffman*, and she granted the workers' request to keep certain aspects of their identity hidden during this labor dispute. They were protected from disclosing their tax returns, federal and state W-2 forms, "all identification documents and information regarding worker status," in addition to "any documents or information likely to lead to the discovery of Plaintiff's immigration status."[35] In these ways, even as the Supreme Court majority in *Hoffman* limited the remedies available to undocumented workers, some of the lower federal courts limited the reach of *Hoffman* by condoning the right of these same workers to hide their identities as undocumented people, as if they had a right not to tell.

The confusion persisted throughout the United States. In *Agri Processor Co. v. NLRB*, another case before the DC Circuit Court of Appeals in 2007, Agri Processor did not check the status of many of its employees until after they voted to unionize. The Court described the company "as a wholesaler of kosher meat products based in Brooklyn, New York," the dispute with its employees arising when "[they] voted to join the United Food and Commercial Workers union." The company claimed that many of its employees—many of the people who'd voted for the union—were not entitled to be considered "employees" eligible to participate in such a vote because they were out of status. "In a hearing before an administrative law judge, the company claimed that after the election it put the Social Security numbers given by all the voting employees into the Social Security Administration's online database and discovered that most of the numbers were either nonexistent or belonged to other people. Based on this evidence, the company alleged that most of the workers who had voted in the election were aliens unauthorized to work in the United States."[36]

Though the Circuit Court spent most of its analysis on the National Labor Relations Act, *Sure-Tan* in 1984, the Immigration Reform and Control Act of 1986, and *Hoffman* in 2002, the most interesting phrase might have been "after the election": had the company checked the online database when it first hired these potential employees, it would have discovered their unlawful status. It didn't do so. It didn't do so until after they'd voted to join the union, when such a decision would no doubt raise the labor costs faced by the company, and when the company thus sought to nullify the results. Had the company treated its employees much better, or had the company never hired them at all, this would not have become a federal case, said the Court. The subtext was that Agri Processor had been behaving badly and shouldn't get away with it. The Court held that the original plaintiffs were, in fact, "employees" protected by the NLRA, that the decision in favor of the union was valid, and that the company had to bargain with that unit even though some of its members were undocumented.

Throughout these cases, the federal courts could not decide, sometimes within a single case, whether undocumented workers are too vulnerable to be left unprotected by labor law, or too "guilty" of the "serious offense" of being out of status, or some combination of both. In cases where the federal courts ruled in favor of undocumented workers, the courts emphasized that the undocumented plaintiffs were victims, and their employers were unscrupulous, greedy, or vindictive; in cases where the courts rejected claims for protection, they framed the unlawful immigrants as wrongdoers who did not deserve the protection of the law, without dwelling too much on the behavior of their employers. Clearly, however, win or lose, immigration status had become one of the most important aspects of a person's identity in the workplace, the aspect of a person that can either trigger substantial protections through federal law, or what is now termed, euphemistically, "processing" and "removal." Given that undocumented workers have been participating in such a wide range of industries—from animal processing and agriculture to all manner of light manufacturing—the most interesting and most volatile developments in the law revolve around who a person *is* rather than what they've done at work, or what was done to them in the workplace. Where work and immigration now intersect, questions of identity have an odd and eerie significance, and it is in that place that we face again that same question of whether—if we meet someone out of status and we know it—to tell or not.

"They receive the same wages and benefits as legal workers . . ."

For people who work with and among undocumented aliens, the fact that these persons are often abused precisely because they are out of status has been obvious. Undocumented workers have reported unsafe work conditions and safety violations in the workplace, they have been much more likely to receive substandard wages and to work longer hours without overtime pay, and they have been much less likely to belong to collective bargaining units capable of negotiating improvements to all of these conditions. These circumstances have been prevalent across a range of industries for undocumented workers, whether they have worked in established corporations, in private homes as maids or nannies, or when they have been picked up as irregular day laborers for odd jobs from street corners, near local businesses, at strip malls, or from "hiring halls," the temporary agencies that have arisen in many major cities to help match employer and employee "on an as-needed basis."[37] Most disturbing of all, as many of the cases discussed in this chapter have suggested, employers have pointed to the illegal status of their workers, or began to inquire about this status, only *after* these workers have protested their conditions or after they formed or joined unions. During the labor dispute itself, all of a sudden, the employers turned on their troublesome employees.

Under the Act of 1986, federal law has obliged employers to check the legal status of all the workers they hire, but as we have seen, ample social science evidence has shown that most employers do not take these rules seriously: employers may examine a person's identity, they may even file an I-9, the standard form that verifies employment eligibility for citizens and noncitizens alike, but much of this can be done in a cursory way. So long as an employer has made a "good faith" effort to check, he has not been held liable to pay any fines or face other penalties if, in fact, the people he's hired are not lawful workers. Indeed, under the Act of 1986, only an employer who *knows* he's hiring an unlawful worker—either by "accepting" identification documents that any reasonable person could see were false, or by not checking a worker's identity at all—is liable for penalties under the rule. Only the most careless or the most stupid employers will ever suffer serious consequences for hiring unlawful workers. For everyone else, the Form I-9, "the fundamental document created to enforce the [Act of 1986]," functioned to trigger formal compliance among employers, not to give them an incentive to inquiry genuinely into a person's immigration status: "The I-9 system has been perverted so that the purported enforcement mechanism functions instead as a laundering device."[38]

At best, the state of the federal law is now ambivalent about the range of protections that undocumented workers can have, so much so that it lacks any reasonable predictability. In some jurisdictions, undocumented workers seem to be protected under wage and safety laws, but because Congress and the Supreme Court have agreed that being out of status and then using false documents to work has been a "serious crime," employers have structural incentives to discover and to report the immigration status of their workers in *any* labor dispute; they will continue to do so in the hope that the federal government might "remove" their labor troubles long before another agency of that same government forces the employers to pay higher wages, stop abuses, or improve the workplace.

That threat of deportation looms over everything, so much so that complaining about workplace conditions or even thinking about joining a labor union has been so fraught with anxiety as to deter people from saying anything at all. Again, these circumstances have been reminiscent of the ones discussed in *Coppage v. Kansas*, that case from 1915, where the United States Supreme Court undid state rules banning yellow-dog contracts, those bargains through which employers had coerced employees to forgo unions and collective bargaining as a basic condition of their employment. The Norris-LaGuardia Act of 1932 overruled *Coppage*, banned yellow-dog contracts, and protected the right of laborers to seek union representation. The new immigration law now undoes that protection for workers who are undocumented, by raising the stakes for any such person wishing to join or organize a union; thus the threat of deportation now achieves the same effect for these persons as a yellow-dog contract. Again, in a disturbing way, American law seemed to be moving backward.

Those less troubled by this result have insisted that unauthorized persons have committed federal crimes so serious that they ought to be ineligible for relief when they've been harmed by the companies who've employed them, then exploited and intimidated them as well. The classic idea in criminal law has been that when the law confronts two wrongdoers, neither should be entitled to recover; it would seem, then, that the federal courts, including the United States Supreme Court, have simply applied this principle in cases where a company has done unlawful things to unauthorized workers. By insisting that one cannot be an unauthorized worker *and* benefit from key protections in federal labor law, important members of the federal judiciary have hoped that this would be enough to deter unauthorized workers from coming to the United States to work at all. That was the crux of Justice Brennan's opinion in *De Canas*, Justice Powell's opinion in *Sure-Tan*, and Justice Rehnquist's opinion in *Hoffman*; yet by that logic, the unauthorized worker already in the United States—"unremoved" and still working—may never be entitled to a federal minimum wage, to unpaid wages, to a safe workplace, or to any other protections provided by law. It wouldn't be surprising at all that predatory employers, people who might resemble the King or the Duke from *Huckleberry Finn*, may well prefer to use and to exploit such persons over the ones protected by federal law.

Justice Breyer's dissent in *Hoffman* centered on that concern: by creating, through its own decisions, a class of persons unprotected by federal labor law, the United States Supreme Court may be making their exploitation more possible and more attractive to a wide range of employers. In a case like *Agri-Processor*, the lower courts have struggled to apply *Hoffman*'s majority opinion strictly, and in that intermediary position, the odd conclusion seems to be that undocumented aliens may only benefit from settled protections when they hide or "cover" their true identities during a labor dispute— while they are un-deported, they have rights and should be considered the same as lawful workers. The majority opinion in *Agri-Processor* suggested a deep aversion to drawing too bright a line between legal and illegal persons: "Undocumented workers and legal workers in a bargaining unit are identical. While undocumented aliens may face penalties for violating immigration laws, they receive the same wages and benefits as legal workers, face the same working conditions, answer to the same supervisors, and possess the same skills and duties."[39] They are, in other words, indistinguishable from everyone else, and they may be best off when they "cover" that unlawful aspect of themselves.[40]

Nearly all of the judges involved in that appellate case admitted, however, that emphasizing the rights of undocumented workers was a "somewhat peculiar" conclusion, even though the point of the decision was to reduce the incentives for companies like Agri-Processor to take advantage of its most vulnerable workers. And exploit them it did: a year after the Circuit Court's decision, as part of President George Bush's policy in 2007 to authorize more workplace raids against companies suspected of hiring unlawful workers, federal immigration agents swept through Agri-Processor's parent company in Postville, Iowa. Much of what they found revealed a lawless company. Federal prosecutors alleged that for many years, several of the company's senior officers had committed egregious violations of labor law, including numerous unlawful accounting practices and outright fraud. Progressive journalists and union leaders had long accused the company of this type of wrongdoing, and so the federal indictments were not surprising. Yet the consequences of the federal raids for the workers were devastating, too. In May 2008, federal authorities arrested nearly 400 employees at the Iowa site, and "over the course of the next few days, 297 of them pled guilty to aggravated identify theft based on their use of false documents to obtain employment."[41] Within a week, these people were in removal proceedings, and their children and loved ones were scattered in all directions. In such instances, federal efforts to punish lawless employers have produced consequences that have been more awful for the very workers employed and abused by these companies.

"That collective action caused chaos . . ."

In light of such developments, that phrase—"the undocumented alien may face penalties for violating immigration laws"—has an ominous resonance. Given the mixed developments in federal law and new policies that target the workplace for sudden raids and removal, it's not surprising that for advocates of undocumented workers, one common approach has been to avoid the law entirely, or rather to apply it in ways that have been strategic and mindful of immigration consequences. Labor organizers across the country have developed a wide range of tactics that combine older strategies from the labor movement with new ones that account for the vulnerability of unauthorized workers. Many workers themselves have avoided the law, for they know in advance that being in the country unlawfully has become a most dangerous condition. Yet they have still resisted in ways that have been surprising, even funny, and the organizations that have helped them range in size and mission: some are very small, others are bigger, a few work with government agencies, and others collaborate with sympathetic government officials and avoid the ones that aren't. For obvious reasons, these organizations have not always attracted attention to themselves or to their clients.

Across academic disciplines, various immigration stories about undocumented workers have illustrated many of strategies through which such workers and their allies have coped with a harsher immigration law. For example, in her recent study of the emerging class divisions among Chinese Americans and Chinese immigrants in the United States, Xiaojian Zhao related a story of how a group of underpaid and abused workers at a Chinese restaurant got back at their officious owner. "On the opening day of the East China Buffet Restaurant on Long Island, owner Zheng Tianming invited a number of guests and local dignitaries to see what the best Chinese restaurant could offer, only to find that the entire kitchen staff did not show up to work because he had refused to meet their demands for higher pay. That collective action caused chaos on the otherwise celebratory day for Zheng and he was quite bitter about it." We can imagine the restaurateur, Zheng, dressed in his finest, his best Peking duck just sitting in the kitchen with no one to cook or serve it. Zhao tells us that the workers also took their revenge by attacking the reputations of their abusive employer, both by "bad-mouthing" him and others like him in public, and by writing about the atrocious behavior in the ethnic newspapers. This form of public shaming did not extend into the English-language press, and nothing further may have come of it for Mr. Zheng, but Zhao suggests that this kind of action serves to warn other Chinese immigrant employers that there will be consequences for exploiting their workers.[42]

Beyond the irregular work stoppages, unauthorized workers have also benefited from more organized forms of resistance. In their separate studies, Ruth Milkman, Jennifer Gordon, and Janice Fine have all identified novel organizing strategies among workers in a broad range of settings—from urban, corporate high rises and the janitors who clean them, to nursing homes in the suburbs and the low-wage orderlies who care for the elderly and for the sick. For Fine, for example, the formation of "worker centers" has been one of the most interesting developments in American labor history. Such organizations are not conventional labor unions, nor job-placement agencies, nor social service agencies, but odd combinations of all of these things at once: at these centers, low-wage workers who are out of status can share information about their basic rights as workers, about "good" and "bad" employers, and about places where they can learn English or find other services. Fine has observed that immigration rules like the ones discussed in this chapter have amounted to "a national immigration policy that has created a permanent underclass of workers," and in the absence of other organizations to help them, the worker centers have filled a void, albeit imperfectly.[43]

In Jennifer Gordon's account, the worker center that she helped to establish—the Workplace Project, the very object of her study—has been like a labor union in its mission, as it helps workers "to demand better wages, safer work and respect from their employers." But it has essential differences from more established unions: the Workplace Project was established in Long Island, not New York City; its primary clients have been first-generation immigrants, many of whom are out of status; and the Project must help people who take jobs from one workplace to another, often between long spells of unemployment. Above all, organizers of the Workplace Project have educated newcomers about their "rights," however tenuous those might be; they remind all workers, for example, that federal rules like the Fair Labor Standards Act of 1938 still apply to them, and that they are entitled to a minimum wage and to standards governing maximum hours of work and of overtime pay. In a fundamental way, the staff at the Project have reiterated to their immigrant clients an important message—within a broader environment where these men and women face xenophobia and hostility, every worker deserves to be treated with dignity and respect irrespective of their status. This message appears more powerful if taken in the inverse: the Workplace Project helps people who have been out of status, and its members have not revealed the "illegality" of their clients to people or public officials whose job is to remove them. The organization takes special measures to protect unauthorized workers from being detected at all, and like other worker centers, its staff have emphasized public laws that provide basic, minimum rights to all workers irrespective of status.[44]

Such has been the practice for a wide range of organizations in similar settings. Monisha Das Gupta and Angie Chung have described, in their separate works, groups of taxi cab drivers or of domestic workers, and groups that "campaign" against horrible workplace practices within broad industries in ethnic-specific communities. Das Gupta's study of "unruly immigrants" was set in New York, where unskilled South Asian immigrants have eked out a living in taxis or in domestic service. For those working in private homes, federal law hasn't applied—the National Labor Relations Act exempted household workers when it was approved in 1935, and in addition, any union would have difficulty organizing these workers across hundreds of private homes. Also, most South Asian employers in the New York region depended on South Asian domestic workers, but "the state and individual employers mutually benefit from the arrangement by constructing these women as a particularly rightless group of people on the grounds that they are immigrant and often undocumented." Middle class and professional South Asians depend upon the household labor of co-ethnics, so much so that they sometimes seize the immigration documents of their domestic workers and threaten to report the ones who complain of intolerable conditions.[45]

Das Gupta's study showed how organizations in New York attempted to educate the most vulnerable men and women trapped in these circumstances. These advocacy groups have not been labor unions or social service agencies or civil rights organizations; rather they have helped such workers, either individually or in small meetings, by teaching them about their rights and by offering them practical strategies to deal with a wide range of labor problems. The staff members at these organizations have also underscored federal laws that provide basic minimums related to work—the federal minimum wage, for example, or state and federal health and safety standards. In addition, Das Gupta and other scholars have discussed at length the Domestic Workers Committee, an organization that has provided helpful, pertinent advice about how to *avoid* certain federal statutes: "domestic worker advocates remind women who are hired locally that they have a right not to answer questions about their immigration status and need only to provide a copy of one of many documents (passport, Social Security card, temporary resident or permanent resident or employment authorization card, birth certificate, or refugee travel document) if asked for work authorization."[46]

Where federal law has been unhelpful, members of the Domestic Workers Committee have talked about other sources of "law" and rights, including the U.N. Migrant Rights Convention that came into effect in 2002. That Convention outlined a set of international norms that embraced concepts like the right to travel freely, the right to family reunification, and the right to economic security. Members of the Committee believed that just knowing about these things can be empowering to people treated as though they were without any rights at all. Moreover, to prevent further abuses, domestic workers' advocacy organizations have educated employers as well: "Organizers distribute fliers that describe employers' legal responsibilities toward their employees and contact information for their organizations." If employers had questions about the minimum wage, overtime pay, workers' compensation, or health and safety rules, the organizers helped them stay within federal guidelines, thus using legal authority in ways that were highly selective, and with an understanding that unlawful status could disqualify an employee from enjoying basic rights available to lawful residents and citizens.[47]

"A reimagining of Koreatown . . ."

In another part of the country, in cities like Los Angeles, similar organizations have come to similar approaches, albeit through very different kinds of struggles. The Korean Immigrant Workers' Advocate is one example of an organization that has taken odd twists and turns in response to the changing nature of work and life for low-income people in that city. In a way, its experiences reflect the turmoil within federal law where immigration and labor intersected, especially after the Act of 1986. Formed in 1992, the original founders were labor organizers and campus activists who sought to help working class Koreans in Koreatown, the burgeoning immigrant enclave to the west of downtown Los Angeles. In less than a decade, having had extensive experience with the diverse group of working class people living in Koreatown, the organization had changed its name to the Koreatown Immigrant Workers Alliance (KIWA), that change reflective of broader changes in strategy: the organization that was once bilingual (Korean and English) became polyglot (Korean, English, Spanish, Chinese, and Vietnamese). Its key staff of community organizers was now a mixture of people informed by the labor rights struggles in South Korea, as well as survivors of the civil wars of Central America and rural workers from Mexico. At a time when most residents of Koreatown spoke Spanish, many of KIWA's clients were neither Korean nor "legal" in terms of their immigration status, and many of the employers there were Korean nationals or transnational corporations based in Korea.

In Angie Chung's account, KIWA itself had been born in a raw moment, after the Los Angeles riots in 1992 had leveled Koreatown and Korean American politics began to fracture. Earlier community groups, including the Korean Federation of Los Angeles, had focused on economic development and political recognition for the region that became "Koreatown" under Mayor Tom Bradley's administration in the late 1970s, but after the riots exposed painful economic and racial divisions there, a range of people proffered urgent, dramatic answers for the problems facing Koreatown. The first Korean American politician to win a seat in Congress ran a campaign that underscored how many of the people arrested for rioting were illegal immigrants: in the ethnic Korean press and at numerous fundraisers in Koreatown, Jay Kim promised to get control of immigration, to force the federal government to identify illegal persons and then "to throw them out." In campaign rallies, he also talked of cutting off any public assistance to persons who could not prove lawful status and to poorer legal immigrants generally, not dwelling on the fact that many of the Koreans in his audience *were* poorer legal immigrants. On the opposite end of the political spectrum, the founding organizers for KIWA—including Danny Kim and Roy Hong—pointed to chronic unemployment and underemployment in the wake of deindustrialization in places like Los Angeles, in addition to other structural conditions that lead to poverty for too many people, all of this prone toward a hopelessness that had spiraled into chaos.[48]

Korean American entrepreneurs were much better established in Koreatown, and they gave Jay Kim a lot of money to run successfully for Congress in 1992, 1994, and 1996. Although he resigned in the face of campaign finance violations to which he'd pled guilty in 1998, Kim did indeed support significant changes to immigration law and policy approved by Congress in the fall of 1996, rules that severely limited social welfare for lawful immigrants and facilitated the "removal" of aliens convicted of crimes. Meanwhile, the organizers of KIWA re-imagined it as a new kind of community-based organization. In fact, KIWA became quite estranged from the mainstream Korean American business community in the early 1990s, as this set of entrepreneurs expanded by then to include venture capitalists from South Korea, the owners of gigantic supermarkets and chain stores, and many smaller entrepreneurs who operated a full range of restaurants and businesses all over Southern California. Koreatown was rebuilt after the riots, and its new business community became much more influential and transnational than ever before, but poorer, unskilled laborers struggled to make a living there. In the midst of these new divisions of class and race, KIWA supported or organized several of the most public labor disputes in Los Angeles since the riots in 1992. The actors varied by race, class, and immigration status: wealthy Korean entrepreneurs, financed by partners overseas, ran businesses that relied on poorer Latino and Korean immigrants, some of whom had formal immigration status, although many did not.[49]

They fought complicated disputes that appeared to represent a near constant estrangement between capital and labor in Southern California over the past two decades: in 1992, for example, when a South Korean transnational firm bought the Hyatt Wilshire, KIWA took the side of the seventy-five unionized Latino workers who'd been abruptly fired. Shortly after, when Hanjin International fired nearly six hundred unionized workers from a much larger hotel in the heart of downtown, KIWA joined with mainstream labor unions to protest these practices as well. KIWA's leaders were in a unique position to point out that these South Korean corporations investing in Los Angeles had an atrocious record against their workforces in South Korea; they had depressed wages and suppressed unions in ways that would have been clearly illegal under United States labor law. The South Korean investors—accustomed to being courted by American politicians and businessmen—were taken aback at the brazen criticism, coming as it did from other Koreans. KIWA had by then grown to develop alliances with similar organizations and to collaborate with progressive associations in Los Angeles, including Latino community groups, simply because a great number of more affluent Koreans grew hostile to its activities.[50]

Over the past two decades, KIWA and its allies have targeted the owners of supermarkets, restaurants, and skyscrapers, in conjunction with the men and women who work as butchers, stockers, bus boys, cooks, and janitors. In these efforts, KIWA built alliances with both established labor unions and emergent workers' centers in Los Angeles, including the Service Employees International Union, the National Day Laborer Organizing Network, and Enlace, a transnational network of worker centers in the United States and Mexico. Staff at KIWA also reached out to churches, legal advocacy organizations, and students and academics at local colleges and universities. With many of these allies, KIWA's staff articulated projects that won competitive funding from major philanthropic foundations. Yet it was during this period that the federal law governing immigration developed in ways that tended to undermine strategies like the pursuit of collective bargaining rights or other traditional approaches to substandard wages and working conditions.

Having been influenced by the Korean labor movement, which had to operate without any state support for many decades, KIWA's organizers and allies tended not to focus on law and policy in their early years. Rather, they often *performed* in public to illustrate injustices: one can only imagine the money lost at the Chosun Galbi Restaurant, a target of KIWA's protests in 1998, as its patrons avoided the spectacle of eating inside while outside others were starving themselves in protest for days on end. In the late 1990s, the organizers at KIWA could not do this for every restaurant as part of its campaign to draw attention to the restaurant industry in Koreatown, but Chosun Galbi was special: "the owner [had] threatened to report the workers to the immigration authorities" when they had organized to improve their working conditions. At least five dozen other restaurants in Koreatown had workers who had become clients of KIWA, having asked the organization to help with workplace issues of one kind or another, and most of these disputes were settled without a hunger strike. But when the managers of this particular restaurant threatened deportation rather than engaging in negotiation, KIWA became militant: the bad publicity itself drew the attention of government agencies, including the Department of Labor, which subsequently cited Chosun Galbi for irregular payroll practices. (The managers often paid their workers in cash, so as to avoid the necessary paperwork and the payroll taxes associated with it.) This quality of acting swiftly, publicly—pricking the conscience of the owners and the patrons—became part of KIWA's reputation, and more than any other strategy, it struck fear into at least some of the businesses in Koreatown, as more than a few had "paid under the table" for ordinary and necessary business expenses. Should they attract similar attention and have their books examined, they knew that they too would not come out well.[51]

Creative Tactics

In other instances, KIWA collaborated with mainstream labor organizations to help low-wage workers in Los Angeles, but those efforts proved less effective, precisely because immigration rules were shifting in the opposite direction. In the Assi Supermarket case, for instance, when workers approached KIWA staff about their working conditions, leaders within the organization were persuaded that they needed to conduct a union drive. Pointing to the NLRA, union leaders for the United Food and Commercial Workers International (UFCW) thought they could reach out to workers at multiple sites in the ethnic grocery industry, starting at Assi and with help from KIWA. They considered this as the first step in a massive labor drive that could encompass other ethnic supermarkets in Los Angeles and throughout Southern California. The staff at KIWA, the UFCW, and everyone else in Los Angeles County knew that the ethnic supermarket industry was vast—it wasn't just Koreans, but the Vietnamese, Chinese, Mexicans, Central Americans, Armenians, and Thai, among others—and all of them had entrepreneurs who were running ethnic-specific grocery stores that were bigger and seemed more profitable than ever before. It didn't take a whole lot of research to figure out, though, that many of these places paid their workers poorly and required them to work under conditions similar to the ones that had inspired state and federal labor laws during the Great Depression. If workers at Assi could be persuaded to unionize, if they then saw real gains in wages and better working conditions through collective bargaining, then other workers in other grocery stores could be persuaded to do the same. Because the industry was so large, because it was so public, touching the lives of workers and numerous consumers in the region, this union drive at Assi was a highly risky, highly visible affair.

It didn't end as expected, as the leaders of the traditional unions underestimated the extent to which immigration policy now undermined established labor strategies. When the campaign began in late 1999 and into 2000, KIWA organized a community-based labor union centered in Koreatown—the Immigrant Workers' Union (IWU)—a bilingual organization that reflected the mixed Latino and Korean workforce at the Assi Supermarket on 8th and Western Avenue, about two blocks from KIWA's main office. In a profound way, for staff members at KIWA, this was more a neighborhood fight than a fight against an entire industry: the managers at the local supermarket down the street had rebuffed informal entreaties, they disparaged their Latino workers, and they were not much nicer to the Korean staff. Assi was not a small mom-and-pop operation, either, and it also had had ambitious plans: in the wake of the riots, Assi was just one example of the transnational Korean and American firms that had reshaped Koreatown.[52]

Assi was tied to an international conglomerate, one that had deep pockets and long-term plans for growth in California and other states. This was a company that wasn't going to roll over in the face of a union drive. Assi hired lawyers, expensive ones, and they forced delays for the vote that would decide whether all of the workers at that site would get collective bargaining rights. The UFCW had lawyers, too, but its representatives were surprised that an "ethnic market" would or could devote so many resources to prevent union representation. Managers and one of the owners of the market, Daniel Rhee, also appealed to ethnic solidarity: they met privately with Korean workers at Assi, promised them better conditions if they would vote against collective bargaining, and claimed that organizations like KIWA and the UFCW were pro-Latino and anti-Korean. Ultimately, in March 2001, the formal union vote was split at sixty seven votes apiece—with no majority in favor of the union among the workers, Assi had won. KIWA, the IWU, and the UFCW had faced a major, humiliating defeat.[53] This was the year that *Hoffman Plastics* was making its way through the federal appeals courts and when lawyers across the nation were debating whether undocumented workers even had collective bargaining rights.

As if to settle that issue even before it was settled formally before the United States Supreme Court, about three months after the failed union vote, managers at Assi presented about seventy "no-match" letters to their employees, informing them that the information they'd submitted on their I-9 forms did not match up with federal Social Security records or with any other employment databases. In essence, having been advised by its own counsel, the company was telling these workers—many of whom had supported the union drive—that they would be terminated because they had no lawful right to work in the first place. A disproportionate fraction of workers receiving these letters were Latino, some were the most active members of the IWU and KIWA. Now, many of the workers thus targeted did not have to be familiar with *Hoffman*, *Del Rey Tortilleria*, or *Agri-Processor*; they did not wait for the federal courts or for anyone else to decide whether this was an unfair labor practice, nor did they have to be told where any of this was headed. Many left their jobs, some left Los Angeles. Assi's move infuriated KIWA's members and allies.[54]

Discarding traditional labor organizing, and stung by the willingness of Assi's managers to use immigration law to remove their own workers, KIWA once again employed "creative tactics" to press the company: in 2002, KIWA's staff and volunteers showed up at the tony neighborhood of one of Assi's owners and managers in Rancho Palos Verdes, banging Korean folk gongs and drums, and holding placards that would be embarrassing for any neighbor. Mr. Rhee was also said to be a devout Christian, and so KIWA organized an outing to his church on a Sunday. They passed out helpful flyers informing Mr. Rhee's fellow congregants of his actions. Would a good Christian call the immigration service to deport his own people, to retaliate against them just for asking for better wages and working conditions? Really, what would Jesus have done? Several workers offered vivid testimony of how a devout Christian had cursed them with racial slurs or had told the

Korean workers to think of their Latino colleagues as dogs, while pressing all of them to work like animals.

In addition to these cathartic performances, KIWA and its allies organized regular picket lines in front of the Assi supermarket itself, and they helped file lawsuits against the company for health, safety, and labor law violations. The picket lines were not ordinary: in a conventional union standoff, a strike would increase the costs for business owners by forcing them to replace staff, by creating bad publicity, and by generally disrupting normal operations. Workers, too, would lose wages, but these losses would be offset by various wage-replacement schemes organized by the union itself in preparation for things like a strike. Members of a union could thus draw funds to sustain themselves as they marched along the picket lines. KIWA's "action" against Assi, however, was not conventional in that sense: many of the people picketing the supermarket had never worked there; the whole point of the "strike" was to bring a steady stream of bad publicity against Assi and to "educate" shoppers before they went into the store; and most interestingly, KIWA's staff and its allies had to raise money to support striking workers in the absence of any formal union support. Private philanthropies supported KIWA, KIWA in turn supported the IWU, and the IWU tried as much as possible to make sure that the workers from Assi had some means of financial support.

On and off, KIWA's staff and allies picketed Assi Supermarkets for over four years, while sympathetic federal officials within the Los Angeles office of the United States Department of Labor investigated claims against Assi. The evidence that they uncovered proved crucial to the lawsuit against the company. It was, however, by any measure, a grueling and agonizing neighborhood struggle, one that many of the original workers who'd first complained about Assi's employment practices could no longer afford to see to the end. The end came in 2007, when Assi agreed to a class action settlement for $1.475 million to be distributed to former and current employees. KIWA held a press conference in front of the neighborhood supermarket, and although there was a sense of triumph and vindication, the organizers who'd started the campaign in 2001 knew that many of the workers who'd inspired them were gone. The settlement sounded large, but spread over so many years and so many workers, it was indeed a settlement, not a resounding victory.[55]

Yet it was a transformative experience. During the course of this campaign, the Korean Immigrant Workers Advocates became the Koreatown Immigrant Workers' Alliance. KIWA was still KIWA, but the change in name "signaled not only internal organizational changes but also a reimagining of

'Koreatown' as community and social space, and a repositioning of KIWA within that space."[56] KIWA became a polyglot organization willing to stand up to powerful corporations whenever there was evidence that they exploited their workers—*any* workers, irrespective of ethnicity, race, or immigration status. Among the members of KIWA was a fierce commitment to the idea that all persons—whatever their color or wherever they were from—deserved a living wage and a certain level of dignity, that the businesses within that space called "Koreatown" should behave decently, and that the ones that didn't should be made to feel ashamed of themselves. During and after the struggle with Assi Supermarkets, leaders within KIWA changed the tenor of their efforts; like the Domestic Workers Committee and other worker centers on the East Coast, KIWA focused on initiatives to push for a living wage for all workers, and to educate both workers and employers about minimum wage and safety rules that applied in general to all workplaces. They insisted that these economic and social minimums should apply to people even if they were out of status.[57] These commitments arose from bitter experiences, ones where employers continued to exploit undocumented workers and felt that they could get away with it.

In response, KIWA and other worker centers have chosen to help people irrespective of immigration status, knowing full well that a great many people they'd helped were indeed out of status. This willingness to educate, to defend, and to assist illegal immigrants isn't something that ethnographic sociologists, urban anthropologists, or legal scholars have highlighted explicitly, and yet this recurring fact is what connects these workers' rights movements to much older, moral problems in those places where status, migration, and personhood have collided in federal law and daily life. The problems arise from the lived experiences of having dealt with such persons: if confronted with a worker trying to get by in Los Angeles, should a community-based organization be required to check that worker's immigration status prior to rendering help? If that same worker has been abused, underpaid, or cheated, is the worker's immigration status more compelling than the fact that he was abused, underpaid, or cheated?

Collectively, the response of worker centers and community-based labor rights organizations suggests that their participants have *avoided* federal immigration rules in servicing their clients. Rather than telling immigration authorities, they have interpreted some federal rules to retain the dignity of all workers, but they have done so by ignoring the ones governing immigration. In other words, if an unauthorized worker in Long Island visits the Workplace Project for help with an employer who has paid him four dollars per hour for several months, the staff there is much more likely to educate that person about minimum wage laws and back-pay rather than inquire about immigration status. Even if such a client could not produce the proper papers, the staff members would be much less likely to tell him to leave the country at once, or to inform federal authorities to accomplish the same. Across the country, strategies have evolved in the same direction, such that the staff at KIWA will behave as though the immigration status of an abused worker is irrelevant to her pursuit of a fair remedy.

Often for selfish and self-serving reasons, many abusive employers have cared about immigration status only after one or more of their workers have complained about an unfair or exploitative labor practice. Once a labor dispute arises, immigration status seems to be the only thing that the employer comes to care about, largely because they know that the federal law will be more helpful to the employer than the employee. In turn, the advocacy groups sympathetic to such workers have tended to avoid the law in favor of other strategies and methods. In some instances, federal officials from the Department of Labor or from the Equal Employment Opportunity Commission have helped enforce standards that have benefited and protected undocumented workers, but in nearly all of these cases, it was the advocacy groups that were instrumental in facilitating such outcomes, often after persuading these officials that their primary mission did not include immigration enforcement. The curious result might be that from a certain perspective, one set of federal officials enforces laws that will deport and remove the labor problems of employers who often behave in horrible ways, while another set of officials has been persuaded to maintain labor standards irrespective of the legal status of the people who have been doing the work or suffering from abuse.[58]

"Vulnerable workers . . ."

As long as employers can use immigration law and immigration enforcement to discipline and exploit their employees, worker centers and other civil society institutions will have to rely on creative strategies to help people irrespective of their formal status. The federal immigration law itself has been unhelpful: by further criminalizing persons who are out of status, federal rules and precedents ensure that retaliatory reporting will remain an effective tool against collective bargaining, as well as a credible threat against any worker contemplating a workplace grievance. The decisions in the several cases that have delineated these rules—including *Apollo Tire, Sure-Tan, Montero, Del Ray Tortilleria, Hoffman,* and *Agri-Processor*—reveal a federal law that gives employers incentives to betray their own workers. In recent years, despite substantial resistance among rank-and-file members, some of the most powerful labor unions in the United States have made public commitments to organize and to assist undocumented persons in order to prevent and to address such abuse—both to revitalize the labor movement and to acknowledge the significant presence of foreign workers in the American economy. And yet so long as federal law defines unlawful status itself as a serious crime, traditional labor organizing will not be very effective, and thus worker centers will remain more relevant for such persons.[59]

Of course, many people have favored the federal law prohibiting undocumented workers, and they have pressed even further for additional measures that will diminish or eliminate them from the labor market. Some influential scholars of immigration and labor studies have proposed more workplace enforcement and stricter immigration controls in general to support American workers, especially poorer Americans who compete most directly with unskilled newcomers. These arguments have evoked a patriotic nationalism with economic dimensions: "Interior enforcement . . . must be raised to the same level of concern as border management, or the entire effort to reduce illegal immigration by the federal government must be regarded as a cruel hoax for American workers." These arguments are familiar, as many white Americans once complained about Chinese workers in similar ways in the late nineteenth century. And yet such scholars have insisted that all forms of lawful immigration admission, including asylum claims, have been abused by desperate, poorer migrants looking for work, and so they've proposed getting tougher on all such persons: "With numerous military bases across the country being decommissioned for budgetary reasons, why not convert some of them to humane detention centers where asylum applicants— those whose cases are not obvious—could be held until final decisions can be rendered?"[60]

Immigration detention has, in fact, expanded since 2000 to include a wider range of persons with no other offense than unlawful entry, but because so many people in the United States have regarded unlawful entry as a serious problem, public law and public policy has continued to move in that direction. Critics of this trend have pointed out, often in vain, that illegal immigrants have been "framed as job stealing mobs rather than desperate workers."[61] But because an undocumented worker can face indefinite detention *and* deportation even if she has a legitimate claim for abuse at work, the agencies and people who might help her with that complaint have had less and less incentive to discuss her immigration status at all. For people who empathize with such persons, one common euphemism to emerge has been "vulnerable," as in "vulnerable workers," or "more vulnerable workers."

The terms "illegal immigrant" has receded in favor of other terms that describe the condition as a peculiar kind of "vulnerability," a heightened condition of exposure, even helplessness, that is the result of law, but that doesn't or shouldn't subtract from the essential humanity of the person described in that way. For scholars and activists who take this view, protagonists like Jose Castro, Gloria Montero, or the dozens of Latino and Korean workers who took on Assi Supermarket all appear as admirable people—these were workers who took great risks to pursue collective bargaining rights for themselves and their fellow co-workers. The fact that they were subject to deportation for their sincere attempts to improve the workplace revealed just how unhelpful American immigration law has become in the workplace.[62]

Indeed, for advocates of the "undocumented" and "vulnerable," the federal law governing immigration has been one of the key impediments to the pursuit of justice and fairness for the many thousands of workers in the American economy. It is no wonder, then, that so many advocates who've been pursuing justice and fairness together with "vulnerable" workers have all avoided the federal law in rather obvious, self-conscious ways. For them, the federal law punishes all of the wrong people, as surely as it once would have returned a man like Jim into slavery even after he had saved Tom Sawyer's life. For how long this can go on, no one can say, but like so many Huckleberry Finns, some people who have legal status now seem to have sworn *not* to tell when they encounter people who don't have it, even if other Americans might wish them to hell for it. A few federal courts have recognized and sometimes supported such strategies of evasion, as if to acknowledge that horrible employers shouldn't get away with their misbehavior just by digging into the backgrounds of the people they've abused. Covering, telling, and not telling—all these indicate how immigrant activism to protect the dignity of struggling workers will thus continue in the shadows of American law.

III

Getting an Education

The Bread of Knowledge

"An unpardonable offense . . ."

The education of some Americans was once illegal, and so it, too, had to occur outside of the law. Work and labor were structured along racial lines for most of American history, and education also was available in that way for some and not others. A few found ways around this, though. In his autobiography published in 1845, Frederick Douglass explained how he had learned to read: "The plan which I adopted, and the one by which I was most successful, was that of making friends of all the little white boys whom I met in the street." He noticed that many of the white boys were poor, and so they had less access to food than he did. "This bread I used to bestow upon the hungry little urchins, who, in return, would give me that more valuable bread of knowledge." Even decades later, Douglass remembered with great affection these white boys who had taught him how to read, though he did not repeat their names in his autobiography because "it might embarrass them." Aside from embarrassment, law and custom also made the education of people like Douglass a crime: "It is almost an unpardonable offense to teach slaves to read in this Christian country."[1]

For Douglass, though, literacy was contagious: when he was hired out to a Mr. Freeland, Douglass taught the slaves there, John Harris and Henry Harris, how to read. In time, other slaves learned about this new teacher, and they came for lessons on Sundays "at the house of a free colored man" who lived nearby. The slaves knew that they had to keep quiet: "It was understood, among all who came, that there must be as little display about it as possible. It was necessary to keep our religious masters at St. Michael's unacquainted with the fact, that, instead of spending the Sabbath in wrestling, boxing, and drinking whisky, we were trying to learn how to read the will of God." Reading, even reading the will of God, was a threatening activity in the eyes of nearly all whites. Many slave owners had insisted that Africans had no interest in learning, and even if they did have such an interest, that they had no natural aptitude for it; slaves were only fit for labor, they said, and without discipline, they reverted to unruly, childish pursuits. Other owners knew that slaves could be taught to read, but they feared what literacy could do—literate black slaves, like the rebels Denmark Vesey of South Carolina and Nat Turner of Virginia, seemed the most dangerous, and so it was absolutely necessary to keep all slaves as illiterate as possible so as to prevent the likelihood of destructive combinations among them. Educating slaves was almost the same as "damaging them": in 1755, for example, the colony of Georgia prohibited all persons from teaching slaves to read and write, "an act that elicited a penalty of fifteen pounds sterling." The late historian Leon Higginbotham has observed that under these rules, "the financial penalty for teaching a slave was fifty percent greater than that for willfully castrating or cutting of the limb of a slave."[2]

A small minority of white slave-owners taught their slaves to read in spite of these prohibitions: it brought them a deeper appreciation for scripture, they said, and so this made them better Christians. Provided that the slaves were taught to obey their masters rather than thinking of themselves as like the Hebrews in Egypt or the Christians in Rome, literacy with supervision could serve the cause of slavery. As Douglass noted in his *Autobiography*, however, and as many scholars have pointed out, public law in the Southern states reflected a public consensus against education for slaves. It truly was an "unpardonable offense" for anyone to teach black slaves how to read.

Douglass took pleasure in breaking this rule, just as my own students now take pleasure in hearing about him do it. Douglass felt the most intense satisfaction as the teacher of more than "forty scholars." But the school itself would not last, as whites closed it down, and in 1806, in response to a Virginia statute requiring manumitted slaves to leave the state, Maryland also approved its own rule forbidding the settlement of freed blacks in Maryland. Legislators focused on how the very presence of free blacks—people who might be able to read and would be tempted to encourage others of their color to do the same—would be inherently disruptive. By 1860, Maryland had passed new rules against any "public assemblage" of blacks for "educational purposes." Educating blacks in any kind of institutional setting was thus declared unlawful in Douglass' home state on the eve of the Civil War, this development no doubt a response to the popular writings of its most literate black man. For the most part, these rules proved effective, as an estimated 95 percent of the black population in the southern United States was illiterate in 1865.[3] But in a contemporary classroom, when we discuss the story of Frederick Douglass and his students, their desire to read and to teach one another, and the resistance of white people who organized against both, up to the point of passing public laws forbidding these activities, there is no question about whom we should regard as the villains and whom we should celebrate as the heroes.

"Negro worshipper . . ."

As we all know, the Civil War did not resolve the mixed feelings of whites about the education of former slaves. To be sure, many Radical Republicans wanted the federal government to attend to the welfare of freed slaves, especially in those states where teaching any black person had been unlawful, but resistance to such plans came from many places, as numerous white communities beyond the South did not support the education of black people. For instance, when Prudence Crandall proposed admitting "Young Ladies and Little Misses of Color" to her boarding school in Canterbury, Connecticut, in 1833, the locals held a meeting where "disapprobation of the school was unanimously voted and the town was pledged to oppose it at all hazards."[4] Crandall had opened the school in 1831, at the request of several wealthy families in that town, and at first, she wanted to admit just one black "scholar," Sarah Harris, a household servant who had shown a desire for learning.

The townspeople were concerned, though: the good people of Canterbury wondered whether a mixed school would then lead to mixed pews at church, which then might lead, of course, to that great white worry, miscegenation. Like many Northerners, white citizens in Canterbury generally favored sending all black people back to Africa, and local members of the Friends of Colonization in Africa insisted that Crandall's plan of educating African girls in their town moved the country further away from that more preferable goal of a complete, oceanic separation between blacks and whites. Resistance to Crandall's plan became intense. Though as devout a Quaker as his daughter, Pardon Crandall urged her to give up. Prudence was called a "Negro worshipper," her parents accused of failing to teach their daughter appropriate feminine manners. All of the Crandalls, including Prudence's sister, were threatened with violence. Although William Lloyd Garrison and other prominent abolitionists supported her, people like them were not the majority in Connecticut in 1833.[5]

Majorities in Canterbury rather favored imposing an older colonial rule, the Pauper and Vagrancy Law, through which they might whip any colored girl for attempting to come within the boundaries of the town to attend Crandall's school. More moderate citizens appealed to the state legislature, and the legislature in turn approved a "Black Law" in 1833, the new rule providing that "no colored people from outside the State should be allowed instruction in any but the free public schools of Connecticut, unless the town gave special permission."[6] By then, though, Crandall had already admitted nearly two dozen young black women, and she proposed doubling their enrollment despite her awareness of the new rule. Crandall was arrested two months after the law's passage, held overnight in a county jail, and put on trial in August of that year.

Crandall lost the trial, then won on appeal, but while these proceedings were winding their way through the courts of Connecticut, her neighbors took matters into their own hands. They poured manure into her well in Canterbury, made the shopkeepers refuse to sell anything to her or to her school, set white boys and girls to pelt the teachers with eggs, broke the school's windows, and set one of the buildings on fire when people were still in it. When anyone at the school was hurt or sick, "physicians would not attend them" for fear of losing other business. Common carriers and stage drivers would not take them for the same reason.[7] About a year after her first trial, some of her neighbors surrounded her boarding school one night and broke the windows again, all at once. "All of the occupants were terror stricken." "Realizing that she and her pupils would ever be the object of injury and insult, she decided, upon the advice of Mr. May and other friends, to give up the school and send her girls back to their homes." Samuel May, a Unitarian minister in nearby Brooklyn, Connecticut, witnessed the whole ordeal, and at the end, he said: "I am ashamed of my state, ashamed of my country, ashamed of my color." May was a white man.[8]

"This prejudice, if it exists, is not created by law, and probably cannot be changed by law . . ."

North of Canterbury, Boston was one of the most progressive cities in the United States and had one of the largest populations of free blacks in North America. Still, although the city was one of the first to structure a large, public, and "free" urban school system, the system had segregated black children since the late eighteenth century. At first, the city had made no specific provisions for segregated schools, but free blacks were appalled that white administrators, teachers, and students ridiculed and abused black children in the public schools. This abuse seemed to grow worse in the wake of the Revolution, so much so that African Americans demanded separate schools. In 1798 and in 1815, with help from white philanthropists, the city supported schools for African American children. Over time, though, when these schools fell into disrepair, and when even the best African American students were ignored and marginalized within the city, prominent African Americans pressed for racial integration. They wanted the same educational opportunities that white students were receiving through the Boston public school system, which by then was financed largely through local taxes and fees.[9]

In 1846, several African American parents submitted a petition asking the Boston Public School Committee to integrate the city's public schools. Segregation created "an inferior class" of students, they said, and the lower overall quality of education in the separate schools for African American children was obvious. The Committee divided. A majority insisted that the separation of races was somehow natural, ordained by God, such that having white children and black children together would amount to a "promiscuous intermingling . . . disadvantageous" to both blacks and whites. The majority also noted that African Americans themselves were the ones that had asked for segregated schools. To this, a minority of the Committee said that the schools should now be open to all irrespective of race; whatever its origin, segregation was a mistake, as it elevated the status of whites just as artificially as it degraded the status of blacks.[10]

After the Committee voted to maintain segregation, Benjamin Roberts sued in 1848. Mr. Roberts had tried four times to enroll his daughter in white schools, but each time, he was told no, and so his five-year-old daughter Sarah had to walk past five white schools on her way to the black school to which she'd been assigned. Prominent people were drawn to the Roberts lawsuit: the family was represented by a biracial legal team, including Robert Morris, one of the first African American lawyers in Massachusetts, and Charles Sumner, who in time would become a United States Senator as a Radical Republican. Despite their efforts, they lost.

In a decision issued in 1849, Chief Justice Lemuel Shaw upheld segregation in the Boston public schools, reiterating many of the arguments proposed by the majority of the Boston Public School Committee when it settled the issue in 1845. Coming from the Supreme Court of Massachusetts, though, the reasons stated for the policy had an unusual force: "It is urged, that this maintenance of separate schools tends to deepen and perpetuate the odious distinction of caste, founded in a deep-rooted prejudice in public opinion. This prejudice, if it exists, is not created by law, and probably cannot be changed by law."[11]

The decision in *Roberts* had repercussions far beyond the Boston public school system. The Court's opinion relied on underlying, democratic assumptions that would be repeated later: that white majorities, having taxed themselves and levied monies to support public institutions, should have what they had expected from those institutions, including race-based segregation; that a racial minority thus segregated shouldn't be able to compel that majority to "mix" against its will; and that there were limits to what positive law could do to overcome prejudices and "differences" between people that may be organic, perhaps even ordained by God. Leon Litwack had observed this overarching set of attitudes in his classic work, *North of Slavery*: "To most northerners, segregation constituted not a departure from democratic principles, as certain foreign critics alleged, but simply the working out of natural laws, the inevitable consequence of the racial inferiority of the Negro. God and Nature had condemned the blacks to perpetual subordination."[12] It did not make sense, then, to use tax money to educate people who were racially inferior, even though they were not legally slaves in a state like Massachusetts.

Such ideas would be re-articulated, of course, in that most infamous case, *Plessy v. Ferguson* in 1896, where a majority of the United States Supreme Court cited *Roberts* at length and then went a step further by suggesting that if African Americans were offended by segregation, it was because they chose "to put that construction on it." A state legislature, according to the Court, was "at liberty to act with reference to the established usages, customs, and traditions of the people, and with a view to the promotion of their comfort, and the preservation of the public peace and good order."[13] After *Plessy*, if white majorities wanted segregation, they could have it, irrespective of that clause in the Fourteenth Amendment about equal protection, and even when the facilities and services for blacks were not at all the same as those for whites. This was especially true in educational institutions, as everyone knew of the substandard conditions of black schools: from 1845 to 1954, not a single white family sued to place a child into a school designated for black children. The idea that whites could segregate public education lasted through *Brown v. Board of Education* in 1954, and by then, "colored" children subjected to this segregation included Asians, Mexicans, and other racial and ethnic groups defined by law as "non-white." Segregation in education was popular in the United States, perhaps one of only a handful of policies that public systems shared throughout the country: at least 12,000 separate school systems had mandated some form of racial segregation in the public schools by 1954.[14]

"A higher law . . ."

In spite of the popularity and pervasiveness of racial segregation, not all Americans behaved in such ways. Once in a while, those who favored segregation and those who opposed it attended the same school. At the Lane Theological Seminary in Cincinnati, for example, students and scholars could get into trouble for talking about abolition or maybe even helping fugitive slaves escape from their masters. The most radical students were prone to thinking that their Christian beliefs required them to help slaves fleeing bondage, but the seminary's administrators moved to dismiss students with such views. The radicals gave up—on the Seminary—and with financial backing from abolitionists in New York and elsewhere, several students and faculty members from Lane formed their own college just north of Cincinnati.

In 1835, a year after they had established the college itself, the board of trustees for the Oberlin Collegiate Institute in northeastern Ohio approved of a resolution saying "that the education of the people of color is a matter of great interest and should be encouraged and sustained in this institution." Other colleges—Bowdoin in Maine, Middlebury in Vermont—had enrolled black students before, but not as a matter of policy and not so publicly. The resolution at Oberlin generated substantial debate, as James Horton and other historians have written, and this debate grew so heated and testy that college leaders moved some of the meetings off campus. Many Americans far away from Oberlin were not amused: "The institution was severely criticized and viewed by many as a danger to the morals and the values of American society."[15] Still, with that progressive direction, and with plans to educate young people irrespective of color, gender, or class status, Oberlin College would enroll about a thousand African Americans over the next fifty years. Only sixty would take a degree during that same period, but even this was much higher than at Yale or Harvard, neither of which graduated a single African American until after the Civil War. Oberlin's relationship with its African American students and alumni was quite often strained and painful, and yet the "radical" idea that African Americans should be educated had been a powerful principle for its progressive constituents throughout the institution's history.[16]

As radical as they were, the early founders of Oberlin were careful to remain within the bounds of federal law. The assumption, often implied rather than spoken, was that African American students at Oberlin were free blacks, not fugitive slaves. Among the black women who had attended the College, most were described as "light-skinned" and from families with "sufficient income and status to afford and desire a college education."[17] Black students were sometimes the sons and daughters of fugitive slaves, like Rosetta Douglass, whose father was the most famous fugitive and abolitionist in the United States. Yet other known fugitives would pose special problems for the school, especially after the Fugitive Slave Act of 1850. Still, the town of Oberlin was itself familiar with fugitive slaves—they were attracted to Oberlin because of its very progressive ideals, and some white citizens took pride that both the town and the college were racially integrated. According to historian Steven Lubet, "Oberliners themselves bragged that their town was 'one of the most notorious refuges of fugitive slaves in the North.'" In 1855, Oberlin had admitted Anthony Burns as a student, a runaway slave who'd been recaptured in Boston, sent back into slavery, and then purchased by abolitionist Bostonians in 1854; Burns' education at Oberlin was financed partly by those same abolitionists, some of whom insisted upon it, under the theory that former black slaves could and should be "elevated" to the level of whites.[18]

White citizens in the town knew that free blacks harbored runaway slaves, and this was because several whites provided for the runaways themselves, either with stipends or shelter while they adjusted to freedom in their new town or headed further north. This was what had happened when John Price came to Oberlin in the spring of 1856. Lubet notes that Price's case was just one of many sensational trials following the Fugitive Slave Act of 1850, but the most striking aspect of this one was how it further radicalized the anti-slavery faction at places like Oberlin. Price had been "kidnapped" by a slave-catcher and taken to a neighboring town just south of Oberlin, but when whites and blacks in both towns heard about this, they were incensed. They subsequently rescued Price, took him back to Oberlin, hid him in the house of a senior professor, and eventually helped him get away to Canada, but not before having a bonfire to celebrate his rescue. Because the fugitive himself had escaped, attention turned to the white people who'd helped him get away, the people who'd violated that clear provision in the Fugitive Slave Act of 1850 requiring "all good citizens . . . to aid and assist in the prompt and efficient execution of this law." Slave owners had rights to recover their property: anyone who "knowingly and willingly obstruct[ed], hinder[ed], or prevent[ed] such claimant, his agent or attorney," or anyone who "shall aid, abet, or assist such persons so owing service or labor," could be subject to severe civil and criminal liabilities under the Act of 1850.[19]

In the Price case, thirty-seven people were indicted in 1859 for violating the provisions of the Act, their prosecutions supported by President James Buchanan and his Attorney General Jeremiah Black, both of Pennsylvania. Only two cases came to trial, both held in Cleveland, but they each became spectacles: the white Oberlin bookseller, Simeon Bushnell, the man who drove the getaway wagon, was convicted by local juries, as was Charles Henry Langston, the son of Ralph Quarles and Quarles' slave, Lucy Langston, of Virginia. For obvious reasons, Langston was the more symbolic figure: he was biracial; his father had been a captain during the Revolutionary War; Ralph Quarles had emancipated Lucy and all three of their children; and he then financed their education, helped to settle them in Ohio, and provided for them in his will.

By the time of his trial, Charles Langston had already become a well-known and well-respected abolitionist in Ohio. Although he had tried only to negotiate the release of Price just before the mob took him, prosecutors fixed upon his involvement and insisted on punishing this criminal behavior. Being such a prominent figure in the Oberlin community, Langston must have seemed a suitable proxy for all of the radicals living in and around Oberlin, these people pushing for abolition rather than accepting political settlements like the Missouri Compromise or the Fugitive Slave Act. Bushnell and Langston were both convicted of violating the Act, but the judge seemed moved by Langston's own eloquent defense of his actions.

In fact, Langston expressed no remorse for what he'd done, and he said he'd do it again: "If ever a man is seized near me, and is about to be carried Southward as a slave, then we are thrown back upon those last defenses of our rights, which cannot be taken from us, and which God gave us that we need not be slaves." He continued: "I shall never be taken into slavery . . . [and] I stand here to say that I will do all I can, for any man thus seized and held." Here in the courtroom, Langston conceded his willingness to break the law, to keep breaking it as often as possible to help fugitive slaves. In the end, Judge Hiram Willson sentenced Langston to just twenty days in prison and a $100 fine. President Buchanan and Attorney General Black were furious that a judge that they had considered sympathetic to Southern rights had been so persuaded by Langston's appeals to a "higher law": "It was the first time that a United States court had even partially recognized the legitimacy of civil disobedience in resistance to the Fugitive Slave Act, and it was certainly the first time that a black man's act of defiance was considered a 'mitigating circumstance' by a pro-slavery judge." The consequences reverberated beyond the trials themselves, as some members of the Oberlin community became openly militant against the entire institution of slavery: on the eve of

the Civil War, two African American students from Oberlin would participate in John Brown's fateful raid at Harper's Ferry.[20]

"Whites only . . ."

The raid failed, but the Civil War proved to be a catastrophe whose dimensions no one had expected, an unending, miserable conflict that reduced the
nation to a "republic of suffering" where hardly any family was spared the
loss of a loved one, and quite often the head of the household. Because so
many men had died in the war, because so many of them had left behind
surviving wives and children, and because so many people had fought and
risked their lives for the Union, many Americans expected government and
civic institutions to provide sources of support that were not available in the
antebellum period. For instance, veterans who had been promised pensions
demanded that the federal government keep these commitments, and widows also organized to make sure that they received their late husbands' pensions as well. By 1890, about forty percent of the federal budget was devoted
to pension payments for the veterans of the Union and their survivors; by
1910, about one in five Americans over the age of sixty-five received some
form of government support. In addition, churches, wealthy donors, philanthropies, and federal, state, and local governments spent thousands of dollars
on new schools, colleges, and universities in the decades after 1870. Large-
scale public education and social welfare policies began in the wake of the
Civil War, and so it wasn't surprising that questions of membership, citizenship, and belonging became more compelling, as Americans debated who
did and didn't deserve publicly financed support.[21]

Those debates had racial dimensions. Newly freed black slaves—the
people whose condition sparked the War in the first place—were, after Reconstruction, nearly cut off from all forms of public support or even public
protection against racial discrimination. In landmark decisions like the *Civil
Rights Cases* (1883) and *Plessy v. Ferguson* (1896), the United States Supreme
Court said that the federal government could not prohibit private actors from
discriminating on the basis of race, nor could it require public institutions to
be racially integrated. The *Civil Rights Cases* were sparked by private acts of
racial discrimination—signs that read "whites only," or employers who refused to hire or to serve African Americans, all of which ought to have been
prohibited under the Fourteenth Amendment and the Civil Rights Act of
1875, according to the African American plaintiffs suing in those cases.[22] The
Court replied that the Fourteenth Amendment prohibited *state* actors from
denying persons the equal protection of the laws, not private actors, and as

such, Congress had legislated beyond its powers in the Act of 1875. Implicit in the Court's argument was the idea that individual liberty—private citizens acting for their own benefit and with their own resources—included the right to racial discrimination. If white Americans did not wish to share property, space, or private accommodations and services with racial others, the Court indicated that the Civil War did not change those fundamental rights.

Extending that logic into the public sphere in cases like *Plessy*, where Louisiana state rules had required racial segregation in railway cars, the Court replied that this too was constitutional insofar as the state provided for "separate but equal" facilities for whites as well as non-whites. This separate-but-equal doctrine also allowed private and semi-private businesses to discriminate and to segregate as they wished, even though everyone plainly knew that the facilities and services provided to African Americans were inferior. Again, if whites did not want to share services, accommodations, or facilities with people they (still) considered racial pariahs, the United States Supreme Court wasn't going to make them do it, and if African Americans had a problem with that, it was *their* problem.[23] If white majorities, acting through their legislatures, wanted private carriers to provide separate railway cars, they should have them.

Yet the most profound impact of this doctrine may have been in public institutions, especially public education, where states and local jurisdictions mandated racial segregation and either didn't provide any schooling for African American children or provided for schools that looked and felt nothing like the ones for white children. The relative disadvantage for African American children and for other children of color was made worse by the explosive growth of public schooling in the post–Civil War period: in the late nineteenth century, most Americans did not finish high school, and a much smaller fraction went to college; by 1940, universal public education was becoming a distinct possibility in major American cities, as funds for public schools doubled in about forty years. Larger public systems grew on a massive scale, in part to provide opportunities for American citizens, and also in part to discipline and normalize the thousands of European immigrants settling in places like New York and Chicago. This was a period of radical transformation: a child born of a deceased Civil War soldier had dim prospects—he was very likely to work in a mine or a factory rather than attend school—but a child of similar circumstances born in 1940 would have had a much better chance of finishing high school, maybe even college. Public schools, private scholarships, and other structured forms of opportunity helped that child, and they also made the entire nation as a whole much better educated than any other nation in the world.[24]

Children of color were either left back or left out. Having the right to learn how to read was one thing, but having the resources to make that possible was quite another. In the words of one scholar, newly freed African Americans had to be "self-taught," they had to rely on one another to provide their children with an education that wasn't going to come from state officials or even from funds raised by their own taxes.[25] Although a number of African Americans became highly educated, many more African American children never got a chance in areas where racial segregation was most severe: in 1933, more than 200 counties in the former Confederate states still did not have a single high school for African American children. Even when African Americans could finish high school or college or receive an advanced degree, they never had access to the same job opportunities to match their educational achievements. The most famous educated African American man in the early twentieth century, W.E.B. Du Bois, was never offered a faculty position at a major research university in the United States. It would be impossible to count the number of utterly mediocre and forgettable white academics who didn't have the same problem during this era.[26]

For other people of color, federally financed education could be horrifying in the opposite direction: for instance, collaborating with religious institutions, the United States government had established a network of boarding schools for Native American children after the Civil War, a set of comprehensive institutions through which these young people might be made into good American citizens—this was to be "assimilation through total immersion." The children enrolled at a Native American boarding school were often given English names, forbidden to speak their native languages, converted to Christianity, and otherwise stripped of the cultural markers of their Native American heritage. For some white progressives, this seemed the only way to incorporate the remnants of the defeated civilizations of North America, to "kill the Indian, and save the man." For many Native Americans, however, this was an insidious and obvious form of cultural genocide accomplished with widespread public support and with steady streams of federal money. This was one area where federal law and policy shaped American education in radical and transformative ways, to expand vastly not just educational institutions, but the very meaning of education for a republic desperate to stitch itself together in the aftermath of the Civil War. At the beginning of the nineteenth century, Thomas Jefferson had once surmised that Native Americans could be folded into the American republic as yeoman farmers and citizens—the Native American boarding schools were a set of institutions based on that premise, carried through by federal officials in the late nineteenth century who seemed again more mindful of national questions about belonging, citizenship, and race. Their preoccupations and theories had enormous consequences for everyone.[27]

"Children of Chinese and Mongolian descent . . ."

If Native American children were subjected to hyperassimilation on the one hand and African American children were neglected by state and local governments on the other, Asian American and Asian immigrant children were caught in various in-between categories with respect to public education. When Congress approved the Chinese Exclusion Act in 1882, the popular consensus was that Chinese people were "unassimilable," and so they should be discouraged from coming to the United States at all, let alone from educating their children here. There, again, was the hope for a complete, oceanic separation between Asians and whites. When the United States Supreme Court upheld the principle behind the Act, as well as the harsher, subsequent pieces of legislation that supported it, the Court itself confirmed that the Chinese were to be placed beyond the pale of American citizenship: Chinese migrants were members of a "vast horde," and it was their fault for arousing hostility against them, as "it seemed impossible for them to assimilate with our people or to make any change in their habits or modes of living." That many Chinese immigrants did, in fact, want to pass into American citizenship was immaterial.[28]

Such immigrants did exist in places like California, the heart of the anti-Chinese movement. The title of historian Mae Ngai's remarkable book, *The Lucky Ones* (2010), suggests an unconventional story, and indeed, the Tapes were an unusual Chinese American family in San Francisco. First of all, they were a family during a time when "Chinese" and "family" were not synonymous—most Chinese migrants were male, and whether married or single, there were very few Chinese women among them. Many Chinese women who did migrate in the 1860s and 1870s were like the Chinese girl who lived on Franklin Street, the one called Mary McGladery; she had been a *mui tsai*, an "indentured servant," or "slave girl," the term that the early white Americans used for these unaccompanied girls and women from China. Mary arrived in San Francisco before her teens, and the landing of persons like her had inspired Representative Horace Page to sponsor a new federal rule barring the arrival of "lewd and debauched women" into the United States. Mary's passage and circumstances in San Francisco were horrifying.

Mary herself had escaped her captors and then sought the help of Reverend Augustus Loomis of the Presbyterian Chinese mission. Loomis faced a delicate situation, "for no one could have safely harbored a runaway slave girl without fear of reprisal and abduction." Loomis looked outside of Chinatown for someone to take in this girl, and that was how she came to the Ladies' Protection and Relief Society on Franklin Street. The Chinese girl was named after a white woman, Mary McGladery, the assistant matron at the Society. "Her Chinese name was never recorded in America, and she herself never acknowledged it."[29] When the Chinese Mary McGladery met Jeu Dip in 1875, the same year that Congress had approved the Page Act, she was eighteen and her suitor was twenty-three. Ngai says that they had courted in English, as Jeu Dip himself had arrived in San Francisco without parents, and had since lived and worked mostly among white people. Within six months, the Reverend Loomis married the two immigrants, Jeu Dip and Mary McGladery, who then in turn became Joseph and Mary Tape. If their first child had been a boy, Loomis might have suggested Jesus, but they had a girl instead, and so they named her Mamie, after her mother.

Mamie grew up in a neighborhood known as Cow Hollow, an area south of the Marina District and away from Chinatown. Joseph and Mary were bohemian, even for San Francisco: he took up hunting and she was an amateur painter, specializing in landscapes. All of their neighbors were white, and some of them were convinced that the Tapes were white enough to attend the local public schools. The city did have a school for Chinese children, but it was financed by missionaries and Chinese merchants, and although the city had had an important case about non-white children in the public schools in 1874, it wasn't clear how this case might apply to Chinese children.

Harriet Ward had attempted to enroll her daughter Mary in the Broadway Grammar School; they were African Americans. They demanded that Noah Flood, the principal of the School, admit Mary as a student, but the California Supreme Court replied that Flood had a right to exclude Mary Ward because of her race. The Court held that the California School Law of 1870 was not unconstitutional nor in violation of the Civil Rights Act of 1866, even though it said specifically that "the education of children of African descent, and Indian children, shall be provided for in separate schools." There was a school for colored children in the city, the Court said—Mary Ward had to go there. The Ward family received the exact same reasons for this policy as the one that the Roberts family got from the Supreme Court of Massachusetts, chiefly because Chief Justice William Wallace of California's Supreme Court quoted that earlier decision at length.

The constitution of Massachusetts had prohibited "particular and exclusive privileges" dividing its citizens, just as the Fourteenth Amendment provided for the "equal protection of the laws." The provisions were sufficiently similar, Wallace reasoned, such that if the segregated system in the Boston public schools was legal under Massachusetts law, then the new California rule in 1870 was also constitutional in spite of the Fourteenth Amendment.[30] The California Supreme Court noted, however, that under the state's political code, education for all children was a statutory right, and where separate schools were unavailable or not yet established for colored children, those children should be admitted to the public schools without regard to race.[31]

For a moment, California's Legislature did not know quite what to make of this decision, nor of the repeated petitions of Chinese parents, laborers, and merchants, not to mention their supporters, including prominent religious leaders. On the one hand, in 1878, a federal court had ruled that Chinese immigrants could not become naturalized American citizens—neither "white" nor of "African nativity," the Chinese immigrants would be perpetually foreign.[32] Yet they and others clearly noted their contributions to American society: that same year, Chinese immigrants had sent a petition to the California Senate and Assembly, one that had highlighted the taxes that they paid collectively to the same state that now deprived their American-born children of an education. Indeed, the great irony was they had been subject to discriminatory taxes ever since their arrival during the Gold Rush, and so the Chinese complained of taxation without public education. Anyone mindful of the American Revolution would have appreciated such an argument: "We respectfully represent that for many years we have been taxed for the support of Common Schools, and that for the year 1876–1877 we paid for this purpose, in San Francisco alone, in taxes on real and personal property, and in poll taxes, a sum exceeding $42,000."

The Chinese petitioners said that the city was denying to at least 3,000 Chinese students access to public schools that the Chinese helped finance. They demanded "the establishment of separate schools for Chinese children, and for universal education." Whether this argument had any impact on the white legislators of California, no white legislator would admit, but in 1880, they approved of a new school law that said all children were entitled to public education without reference to race.[33] The new code, though, did say this: "Trustees shall have the power to exclude children of filthy or vicious habits, or children suffering from contagious or infectious diseases."[34]

When Mary Tape tried to enroll Mamie in the Spring Valley Primary School in 1884, the principal there, Jennie Hurley, refused to do it. The Tapes were incensed: they hired William Gibson, a prominent attorney in the city, a graduate of Harvard Law School and the son of Otis Gibson, himself a tireless Methodist missionary who'd worked on behalf of Chinese immigrants through the darkest days of Chinese exclusion and anti-Chinese violence. The younger Gibson noted that Mamie was born in San Francisco, that the family had no intention of leaving the United States, that Joseph was employed and paid taxes, and that the family was in other respects highly assimilated—they spoke English, Joseph didn't wear his hair in a braided ponytail like other Chinese men, and so he showed no allegiance to the Chinese emperor, Mamie and Mary also dressed "in the American costume," they were all Christians, and Mamie certainly didn't have filthy or vicious habits, nor any contagious or infectious diseases. They portrayed themselves as a model minority family, just as many other middle-class people of color would do in the late nineteenth and early twentieth centuries, when racial segregation became common.[35]

Rather quickly, in January 1885, the Superior Court handed the Tapes a major victory, and in a more surprising turn, in less than two months, the California Supreme Court upheld the decision. Unlike other cases from the period involving Chinese plaintiffs, this one relied on straightforward statutory interpretation, and it was thus free of dicta about how the Chinese were mendacious, vicious, unassimilable, or otherwise terrible.[36] But to give Jennie Hurley what she'd wanted, to allow the city to segregate Chinese children in the public schools in spite of the Tape case, the California legislature approved of a new rule authorizing separate schools for "children of Chinese and Mongolian descent." The School Superintendent for the city, Andrew Jackson Moulder, supported Jennie Hurley when she denied, for a second time, Mamie a place in the Spring Valley Primary School. Moulder and Hurley had pushed for the new rule, then used it against Mamie.[37]

Mamie's mother was furious. In an open letter to the *Daily Alta*, she also revealed more than anything the hurt inflicted upon her family by the entire experience: "Is it a disgrace to be Born a Chinese? Didn't God make us all!!! . . . Do you call that a Christian act to compel my little children to go so far to a school that is made in purpose for them[?]"[38] In the space of a year, the Tapes had been insulted, then they had won a major set of court victories, only to be insulted again, and not just by Jennie Hurley or Andrew Jackson Moulder, but by the legislature and governor of California. Many other Chinese plaintiffs in other states would feel a similar hurt for the rest of the nineteenth and most of the early twentieth centuries in the United States.[39]

Colored Children

Getting a formal education was in this way an uphill battle for Asian Americans. About forty years after *Tape v. Hurley*, in a case from Mississippi, the United States Supreme Court observed that there was a consensus among the federal and state courts that Asians were not white and thus could be segregated as non-whites in public education and in other areas. In many respects, the central protagonist of that case, Martha Lum, was similar to Mamie Tape: Martha was the daughter of middle-class Chinese immigrant parents; they were members of a Chinese Delta community in Mississippi that had taken pains to distance itself from African Americans and to embrace local whites; and they had done this because they knew that Mississippi was a racist place, that being "non-white" meant being cut off from good public schools, from social services, and from other opportunities. In the town of Rosedale, where a handful of Chinese immigrants and their families had been allowed to attend the public schools, news of the relative openness of its public system stimulated other Chinese immigrants to move into town, or to send their children to live with residents there just so that they could attend the public schools designated for white children. When school officials blocked Chinese students from attending those schools, Gong Lum, Martha's father, sued and won. Judge Alcorn of the Mississippi State Circuit Court agreed with Mr. Lum that the Chinese were "Mongolian," not "Negro," and thus that the discrimination against them had no statutory basis, and was also "unreasonable, unjust, and arbitrary." The Chinese paid taxes, he said, they were "members of a race wholly different from [Negroes] in racial characteristics," and so they should be allowed to attend the public schools in Rosedale.[40]

The Mississippi Supreme Court reversed Alcorn, and the United States Supreme Court then affirmed in 1927 that the people of Rosedale and their school officials should have the right to exclude Chinese students on the basis of their race, in accordance with the Mississippi Constitution of 1890. The Court, speaking through Chief Justice William Howard Taft, said that the state's Constitution mandated segregation in this language: "Separate schools shall be maintained for children of the white and colored races." "Colored," according to Taft, meant "non-white," and because the Chinese were "yellow," and because yellow was indeed a color, public schools could exclude these "colored" children just as it had excluded other colored children in the state of Mississippi, and as a practice that dated back to Sarah Roberts' case. It did not matter, Taft replied, that Gong Lum was a taxpayer or that Martha was fit for an education. Local majorities had had the right to segregate public schools for several generations, and the people of Bolivar County should have that same right against these "non-white" children.[41]

Taft's opinion continued a pattern of lawful Asian exclusion, and it came as one of many judicial opinions during that era where Asians were defined increasingly as "nonwhite," either in strict "biological" terms, or within "common sense" definitions of whiteness.[42] Though the federal and state courts had divided over who was or wasn't white for purposes of lawful segregation, through naturalization cases like *Ozawa v. United States* (1922) and *United States v. Thind* (1923), the United States Supreme Court held that white majorities had the right to determine for themselves that Asians were not white, that they should be thus ineligible for the same public services assigned to whites, and that they could also be restricted from owning property and from access to other resources reserved for American citizens and those capable of citizenship. Being nonwhite, and thus being "aliens ineligible for citizenship," Asians could be barred lawfully from owning or leasing agricultural land, as they'd been in California and in at least a dozen other states, even if such rules may have harmed white farm-owners and sellers. Asians would thus be subject to segregation, kept away whenever whites were determined to keep their schools and neighborhoods for whites only.[43]

"The whites who taught at the Cleveland School suffered substantial criticism . . ."

Without any doubt, these formal decisions were harmful economically and politically to the majority of Asian Americans struggling to survive in the United States. They also limited the aspirations of middle-class and wealthy merchants and entrepreneurs, Asian immigrants and Asian Americans alike, who often felt that they should have been exempt from the racist treatment that their poorer peers had to endure every day. After all, they claimed, they themselves were educated, and they and their children had assimilated into mainstream American society: in his naturalization case, Takao Ozawa claimed to be a devout Christian; in his own case, Bhagat Thind noted his honorable service in the United States military; and in the alien land cases, many Japanese farmers argued that they had improved agricultural lands far beyond what their white counterparts had done in places like Fresno or Livingston, California. Japanese immigrants and Japanese Americans, for example, insisted that they were like the "Yankees of the East."

Once in a while, these appeals worked, as when President Theodore Roosevelt persuaded an angry San Francisco School Board not to segregate Japanese children in the public schools there, lest this arouse the Japanese military to disrupt American interests in the Pacific. Short of international pressure, however, Asians would face segregation, and Roosevelt himself let everyone know that deep inside, he favored segregation against the Japanese, too: "[Roosevelt felt that] while both civilizations were 'equally high,' they represented thousands of years of separate lines of development, and the mixing together of peoples from the 'culminating points of two such lines of divergent cultural development would be fraught with peril.'" Roosevelt criticized white American planters for importing so much Asian labor into Hawaii, and he negotiated immigration restrictions with the Japanese Empire to make sure that there would never be too many Japanese children in the public schools with white children in places like California. "Under the terms of the 1908 Gentleman's Agreement, Roosevelt extracted an understanding that Japan would not permit the emigration of laborers to the United States."[44] Still, on average, because of the imperial aspirations of Japan, Japanese immigrant and Japanese American children were better educated than their American peers, even though they continued to face employment barriers after their formal schooling.[45]

The most surprising aspect of this history wasn't that Japanese immigrants and Japanese Americans got to attend public schools, but that other Asian immigrants often received a formal education, too. Segregation was uneven, even in the regions that had pioneered segregation against Asians. Again, the Tapes were an instructive example: stung and hurt as they were, Mary and Joseph plodded on to make sure that their children flourished. Mamie and Frank went to the Chinese Primary School in San Francisco, segregated as it was, but by the time their younger siblings were ready for school in 1892, the family had moved to Berkeley, and Gertrude and Emily started at the Le Conte School, which wasn't segregated. Joseph did well in business, too, so well that he bought a ranch in Hayward. Moreover, both of the younger girls married educated men: Emily married a Robert Leon Park, the first Chinese boy to graduate from Lowell High School in San Francisco, and also one of the first to graduate from the University of California; and Gertrude attended Berkeley Commercial High School, and she married a Herbert Chan, who himself attended the California College of Pharmacy in San Francisco, an institution that was affiliated at the time with the University of California as well. Herbert did not become a pharmacist, but this had nothing to do with his Chinese ancestry. Like many students before and since, he just couldn't pass organic chemistry. The experiences of these Chinese Americans—Emily, Gertrude, Robert, and Herbert—showed that not all educators in the late nineteenth and early twentieth centuries behaved like Jennie Hurley or Andrew Jackson Moulder.[46]

In Mississippi, too, after *Gong Lum* in 1927, some Chinese students continued to attend schools with whites, and some whites continued to help Chinese children get an education. According to one account, written by a Chinese American student, "'If a Chinese family lived in one of the smaller Delta town[s], and was good friends with the *Bok Guey* [whites], they'd let you go to their school. . . . They just didn't know any better. But with the

Gong Lum decision, we weren't allowed to go to the *Bok Guey* schools by law and because there weren't many of us back then, some went anyway. We only had problems when someone in the town objected.'"[47] White teachers, parents, and administrators allowed Chinese students to enroll in the public schools when they did not know or when they did not care about the *Gong Lum* decision. When white people didn't care or complain, an education was still possible.

More significantly, as in San Francisco, religious institutions in Mississippi that had wanted to convert the Chinese to Christianity supported schools for adults and children alike. In 1934, Reverend L.A. Streete opened a mission school for Chinese children in Rosedale, and in that same year, in Greenville, Mississippi, the First Baptist Church sponsored a separate mission school for the Chinese community there. In 1937, in Cleveland, Mississippi, the Cleveland Chinese Mission School was established "with funds solicited from local businessmen and Chinese merchants as far away as Chicago, New York, and San Francisco." "At its apex," according to Sieglinde Lim de Sanchez, "the school hosted fifty-four students, with some coming from as far away as Tennessee and Arkansas." Having heard of this school through contacts in the Chinese Delta community, Chinese parents sent their children to board at the school, which had been under the supervision of both white and Chinese teachers. Here of all places, in a small pocket of Mississippi, Chinese families learned that sympathetic whites were willing to help them acquire land for these schools, to pay for teachers, and to provide a modest education to Chinese immigrant and Chinese American children.[48]

This education was, admittedly, only a partial solution. It wasn't the same as the education that white children received, nor was it exactly nonracist, at least not by our contemporary norms: by converting to Christianity, and by having these semi-public spaces to display their willingness to assimilate into mainstream American life, many Delta Chinese families remained optimistic about being accepted into white society, and so they continued to maintain distances between themselves and African Americans through these same spaces. Chinese leaders in the Mississippi Delta pointed out that the Chinese were a "pure race," that they rejected miscegenation with African Americans, and that they kept their children away from Chinese people who'd had sexual or social relations with African Americans. Along those lines, these schools were places where Chinese families could host Christmas parties and other civic events to show white people that Chinese people could behave like white people.[49]

Still, many whites frowned upon those who would do anything for these "colored people": "The whites who taught at the Cleveland School suffered substantial criticism from other whites." Several teachers learned that they'd been naive to think that whites would respect them or treat them the same as teachers in white schools. Indeed, the white neighbors around the Cleveland School were prone to saying and doing uncharitable, un-Christian things— as a matter of policy, Chinese Baptists could use the First Baptist Church of Cleveland, for example, but only in separate services. In the heart of the seg-regated South, however, through the Great Depression and in spite of the hostility, Chinese and white educators helped Chinese American children get something of an education, and through their own contacts across the country, they sent the brightest young people to finish high school and col-lege in California and in Texas, in public school systems that could have seg-regated Asians and other "nonwhites," but for one reason or another didn't.[50]

Indeed, during this period, Asian Americans and Asian immigrants who had avoided the prevailing practices of segregation and race-based discrimi-nation were the ones most likely to get an education. From the beginning of World War I until the end of World War II, some of the most notable Asian Americans fell into this category: the two most well-known protagonists in the federal naturalization cases of the early 1920s, Bhagat Thind and Takao Ozawa, had both attended the University of California at Berkeley; Emsen Charr, a Korean immigrant who'd also been rejected for American citizen-ship because of his race, had attended Park College in Missouri; the author and artist, Jade Snow Wong, had finished at Mills College; Min Yasui had a bachelor's degree and a law degree from the University of Oregon; and Gor-don Hirabayashi was a student at the University of Washington. Yasui and Hirabayashi were notable because they had challenged the evacuation and curfew orders imposed on all persons of Japanese ancestry during those early months of World War II. After the war, Yasui practiced as a lawyer in Den-ver, and Hirabayashi returned to the University of Washington, where he finished his Ph.D. in sociology.[51]

"Our scholarship resources would be as available to them as to any other student . . ."

Gordon Hirabayashi's formal education was most notable and interesting, if only because he received so much support from his university at a time when the entire world for Japanese Americans seemed to be falling apart. As an undergraduate, Hirabayashi knew that many of his friends and even a few faculty members had voiced their opposition to the mass internment of per-sons of Japanese ancestry; he also knew that this was becoming a minority view. In 1942, Congressman John Tolan, a Democrat from California, had been commissioned to study whether persons of Japanese ancestry posed a threat to the United States. When the Tolan Commission came to gather testimony about Japanese Americans and Japanese immigrants in Seattle, where Hirabayashi was attending college, many organizations and groups spoke in favor of removing all persons of Japanese ancestry from the West Coast. Yet he must have been heartened by this: "Two University of Washington undergraduates testified to the loyalty of their Nisei classmates and urged that Japanese university students be allowed to continue their studies in Seattle."[52]

They were not alone: Jesse Steiner, the chair of the sociology department at the University of Washington; Robert O'Brien, then a graduate student and a staff member in the Dean's office; and Lee Paul Sieg, the President of the University, also testified or wrote on behalf of these students, arguing that internment would be unfair to them, disruptive of their education, and just racist. Not everyone cared, of course: business leaders and politicians and even the Seattle Parent Teacher Association had spoken in favor of mass internment, as had nine of the fifteen state governors west of the Mississippi, the Los Angeles Board of Supervisors, the Mutual Broadcasting Company, *The Los Angeles Times, The San Diego Union*, the journalist Walter Lippmann, several prominent generals, the Western Growers Protective Association, the Native Sons and Daughters of the Golden West, President Franklin Roosevelt, and all manner of thugs, bullies, and vandals who'd attacked and harassed Japanese Americans and destroyed their businesses in the months following Pearl Harbor. None of these people or groups seemed to think through how the exclusion and removal orders would impact the education of persons of Japanese ancestry, these young people and children who had done nothing to start the war or to deserve incarceration.

As we know, these hostile voices eventually prevailed, but even then, supporters of students like Hirabayashi did not give up. "Sieg even allowed Nisei members of the class of 1942 to graduate, despite missing their final quarter of classes. He traveled to the camps himself to deliver diplomas to the graduates."[53] For younger Japanese American undergraduates, President Sieg and other sympathetic university administrators, including Robert Sproul of the University of California and Remsen Bird of Occidental College, had asked a number of institutions outside of the West Coast to admit these students so that they might continue their education and avoid internment. Just a handful bothered to reply.

One administrator, though, President Ernest Wilkins, replied right away. Wilkins wrote back to his friend, Lee Paul Sieg: "We have here in our Sophomore class a young man from Seattle, Harry Yamaguchi, who is making an excellent record scholastically and personally." Based on Yamaguchi's recommendation, Wilkins promised Sieg to take at least four students from the University of Washington to start at his college in the summer session of 1942. "We could not undertake to provide any financial help for them in their first term of attendance: but if in that term they should do well scholastically and otherwise and should then continue in Oberlin, our scholarship resources would be as available to them as to any other student." The first group of students did fine, and by the end of 1943, twenty students of Japanese ancestry were enrolled and finishing their degrees at Oberlin College, which was, once again, serving as a haven of sorts.[54]

Race, Immigration, and the Promise of Equality

"The harsh removal of the Japanese . . ."

In 1954, when the United States Supreme Court issued its decision in *Brown v. Board of Education*, the Chief Justice, Earl Warren, appeared to be a man with some regrets. Warren had had a distinguished career: before being appointed to the highest court by President Dwight Eisenhower, Warren had been elected the Attorney General in California in 1938, then Governor in 1942, and it was between those years that the nation had been attacked and plunged into war. Warren defeated Culbert Olson, the incumbent Democrat, partly by accusing his opponent of having been soft on the question of Japanese civilians on the West Coast. Warren had favored heightened surveillance of all persons of Japanese ancestry, and he pointed out that Governor Olson had once been the honorary chairman of the Fair Play Committee. This Committee was formed in response to the possibility of mass internment, and it had the support of leading faculty and administrators at the University of California at Berkeley, including UC President Robert Sproul and former UC President David Barrows.[1]

As its honorary chairman, Governor Olson agreed that second generation Japanese Americans should at least be treated as American citizens entitled to full constitutional protections. He abandoned that position within two months of taking it, but Earl Warren didn't let the voters forget. Indeed, Warren had taken the opposite view as he plotted his campaign for the governorship: there had been no attack on the West Coast, Warren said, but this was "most ominous." "We are just being lulled into a false sense of security and . . . the only reason we haven't had a disaster in California is because it is timed for a different date." Warren insisted that second generation Japanese Americans were even more dangerous than their parents: law enforcement officials he'd consulted agreed that "there is more potential danger among the group of Japanese who are born in this country than from the alien Japanese who were born in Japan."[2]

With testimony like this, in his capacity as Attorney General, and then as the Governor of California, Warren advocated and helped to organize the mass incarceration of Japanese Americans. He worked with federal authorities to evacuate and to remove these people, just as he had promised. Even after the United States Supreme Court insisted in 1944 that the government should release Japanese Americans that it itself conceded were loyal, Warren was a critic: "he argued that every evacuee was a potential saboteur."[3] One of his biographers, G. Edward White, served as his law clerk after Chief Justice Warren was appointed to the United States Supreme Court, but his remarks about Warren during that moment of his career appear unflattering to this day: "Warren was a vital moving force in the formulation of the Japanese relocation program," and "[he] was the most visible and effective California public official advocating internment and evacuation of the American Japanese."[4]

All of this must have been especially disappointing to the eleven "Japanese" residents of Alameda County who'd once supported Earl Warren when he was running for California Attorney General in 1938. They had written a glowing letter, and Warren's campaign had reprinted their endorsement in Japanese-language newspapers throughout the state. It had read, in part, that "[Warren] is too big a man to stir up race prejudice against Japanese . . . and [not] the kind of man to go out of his way to try to create trouble for the Japanese people of this state."[5] They must have been disappointed as they were being sent to the camps, but they would have been surprised, perhaps, that in the fullness of time, Warren regretted it himself, too. In 1970, when the Japanese American Citizens League advocated for the repeal of Title II of the Internal Security Act of 1952, a rule providing for summary detentions in times of national emergency, the retired Chief Justice Warren sent them a letter of support: "Title II is not in the American tradition. . . . I express these views as the experience of one who as a state officer became involved in the harsh removal of the Japanese from the Pacific Coast in World War II, almost 30 years ago."[6] This was as close as he came to an apology in his lifetime. To his law clerks and to his closest friends and family, Warren acknowledged regret, but he refused to apologize for his role during the war.

The day after Earl Warren died in 1974, however, the Japanese American Citizens League publicly forgave him anyway. In 1977, as if from the grave, Earl Warren said in his memoirs, "I have since deeply regretted the removal order and my testimony advocating it." Most interesting of all, in these private writings, the author of *Brown* expressed remorse about this period primarily in terms of children and school: "Whenever I thought of the innocent little children who were torn from home, school friends, and congenial surroundings, I was conscience stricken."[7] Warren hadn't thought about or hadn't thought through how his actions had criminalized entire communities and families, but then the reality of incarcerating "little children" in remote, desolate camps unmanned him.

"California could legally enact a law . . . [but] has not done so . . ."

In 1947, the State of California repealed formal, race-based segregation in the state's public schools. Many factors influenced that turn, including two major sets of cases: in the first, involving Japanese American internment, the United States Supreme Court had ruled that racial classifications would be regarded as "inherently suspect." *Korematsu v. United States* (1944) was a radical change in American public law: prior to that case, racial classifications had become ubiquitous in American life, and the law of segregation had often been framed by reference to "local customs and usage," as it had been since *Plessy.* The Supreme Court itself had supported white supremacy, or at least white aversion to egalitarian relationships with African Americans; time after time, the Court had refused to strike down segregation because it had agreed that white majorities should be entitled to frame race-based relationships as they saw fit, even if this meant disabling African Americans legally and otherwise. As was said in *Plessy,* if white people wanted rules that made black people feel inferior, black people had to deal with it as *their* problem. After *Korematsu,* however, if race-based rules and prejudices were no longer acceptable constitutionally—if public necessities like war or invasion or some other "compelling justification" were now the only grounds for lawful race-based classifications in the public law—that entire structure of formal white supremacy would be in danger. Fred Korematsu lost his case in 1944, and yet the new constitutional rule that emerged from it would form a cornerstone *against* race-based segregation long after the war had ended. Citing *Korematsu,* the United States Supreme Court would overturn many race-conscious laws over the next two decades, including state and local rules governing restrictive covenants in housing, alien land laws, and miscegenation rules.[8]

Other courts were reaching similar conclusions, and they would have a more proximate influence over California public school districts. In a set of cases in 1946 and 1947, two federal courts had agreed that the segregation of Mexican children in the public schools in Orange County was unlawful. Five Mexican American fathers sued to challenge racial segregation against their children, and in the first manifestation of *Mendez v. Westminster* in 1946, federal District Judge Paul McCormick said that this practice had no statutory basis, though it "[fostered] antagonisms in the children and suggests inferiority among them where none exists." Whatever deficits did exist among white and Mexican American children in California, including their language skills, had been *caused* by segregation, the judge said, and even then, more than a few Mexican American seventh graders outperformed their white peers on standardized tests, thus disproving claims of innate, racial inferiority among persons of "Mexican blood."[9]

In 1947, the Ninth Circuit Court of Appeals affirmed on more narrow grounds: the Court noted that existing state rules allowing for segregation in the public schools did not list "Mexican" as a distinct racial group. State rules dating back to Jennie Hurley and Andrew Jackson Moulder had allowed for the segregation of Native American ("Indians"), Chinese, Japanese, and Mongolian students, but the Court said that because these rules said nothing specifically about children of Mexican immigrants, the Orange County schools were segregating without proper authority. "Conceding for the argument that California could legally enact a law authorizing the segregation [of Mexican children] as practiced the fact stands out unchallengeable that California has not done so." Unlike in 1885, when the legislature quickly amended rules to allow for the segregation of Chinese children after a similar court decision, California moved in the opposite direction just as quickly in 1947: bills to repeal those portions of the California Education Code permitting segregation in the public schools passed in the Assembly and in the Senate by wide margins. Governor Earl Warren signed them into law in June 1947, exactly two months after the Ninth Circuit's opinion. Warren himself was moving in a less racist direction, and for opponents of segregation, this was a major legislative victory, as the political institutions of the state now responded in ways likely to benefit people of color, and along lines that few could have predicted just a decade ago. More importantly, in decisions like *Mendez* and then *Brown*, there was that underlying principle that all children should have access to an education within the state, without respect to race, color, ethnicity, or some other characteristic over which they could have no control.[10]

"The most important function of state and local governments . . ."

But the unanimous opinion in *Brown v. Board of Education* in 1954 was not well received in many parts of the United States. Indeed, *Brown* has been controversial ever since the day Chief Justice Earl Warren read the decision in open court and to an international audience of journalists and other observers eager to see what the Court would say about race and American public law after World War II. Overt racial discrimination was an embarrassment in foreign affairs, where diplomats and others had a hard time explaining how the United States could be at once a beacon of freedom against communism and yet still maintain a harsh racial apartheid. Many federal officials welcomed *Brown* and Warren's public rejection of racial segregation in the public schools. And yet immediately, other public officials insisted that they would oppose any effort to integrate the public schools in particular or American society more generally, as governors, senators, and citizens condemned Warren and his Court for this decision. That schools should be racially integrated was inconceivable for those who'd known segregation and seemed to have imagined nothing else—because so many Americans had made segregation so lawful in numerous state rules, local school board policies, and through a wide array of informal practices throughout the country, the hostility toward *Brown* was bright and enduring.[11]

Less controversial in *Brown*, however, was the Court's characterization of public education itself, of how public schooling had changed in the time between *Plessy* and *Brown*: "We must consider public education in the light of its full development and its present place in American life throughout the Nation. . . . Today, education is perhaps the most important function of state and local governments." Indeed, public spending on schools had reached historic proportions by 1954, across all levels of government. Warren observed that by contrast, formal education for African American children had been almost nonexistent when *Plessy* had been decided in 1896. Since then, universal public schooling for white children had replaced extensive use of child labor, both on farms and in factories, and some cities in the United States had by 1920 more high schools and universities than many European countries. States like California had increased enrollment at public universities by astounding margins—enrollment at the University of California campuses and extension programs had increased by over 400 percent from 1900 to 1920.

As governor, Earl Warren participated in the expansion of public education programs on an immense scale: because of federal grants for infrastructure projects, and because of new policies like the G.I. Bill in the postwar years, higher education enrollments in California tripled just between 1940 and 1950.[12] Even in the Southern states, where public expenditures on education were historically the lowest, spending on public schools, especially urban high schools and state universities, grew to impressive levels. Again, because so much of this expansion was financed with multiple revenue streams, many local school districts and public universities relied on federal money for new construction, to pay teachers, or for student financial aid. All branches of government contributed to the expansion of educational institutions and opportunities, and working class and middle class Americans came to associate formal schooling with upward social and economic mobility.[13]

Exclusion from these growing and influential public education systems, or being consigned to inferior schools and colleges for race-based reasons, was irrevocably harmful, according to the social scientists cited by the Court in 1954: "In these days, it is doubtful that any child may reasonably be expected to succeed in life if he is denied the opportunity of an education." That public education had become central to American life was not controversial, but to insist that it be provided without racial discrimination was: "Such an opportunity, where the state has undertaken to provide it, is a right which must be made available to all on equal terms." Those accustomed to racial segregation complained that there was "no legal basis for such action," and that the members of the Court "undertook to exercise their naked judicial power and substituted their personal political and social ideas for the established law of the land." The critics noted that racial segregation in public education was at least as old as *Roberts v. City of Boston* in 1850, and that "the very Congress that proposed the [14th] Amendment subsequently provided for segregated schools in the District of Columbia." Many whites objected to their tax dollars being spent to educate children of color through systems that they and their ancestors had intended for whites only.[14]

As part of a mass social movement, the political push for racial integration seemed unrelenting in the years after *Brown*, but then so too was the resistance against *Brown*. Major legislative changes were in part inspired by *Brown*: in addition to other major federal court precedents, several provisions in the Civil Rights Act of 1964 authorized the federal government to use sweeping new powers that changed the legal landscape in favor of desegregation in nearly every aspect of public life in the United States. Under one section, for example, the Department of Justice could sue any entity providing "public accommodations," including public school systems and private businesses, in order to implement desegregation; and in another, the federal government could withhold federal money to any program or institution, public or private, that persisted in unlawful racial discrimination. Still, some practices like bussing—this involved transporting one set of kids from one side of a racially divided city to another and vice versa, all to achieve racial integration—incensed many white parents in the decades after *Brown*, and throughout the 1960s and 1970s, urban public school systems became the sites for protracted legal battles, seemingly endless litigation and legislation, and more than a few race riots.

To complicate matters further, another major piece of legislation in 1965 reshaped immigration to the United States: the Immigration Act of 1965 allowed large numbers of nonwhite newcomers to arrive in major American cities. The law itself was very much a part of the civil rights revolution in American public law, the first federal immigration rule authorizing the selection of immigrants in a race-neutral way. Yet its proponents, including Senator Edward Kennedy of Massachusetts and President Lyndon Johnson of Texas, had suggested that a race-neutral immigration rule would not by itself upset the racial or class composition of the United States—the Act of 1965 provided preferences for people seeking to reunite with family members in the United States, as well as employment-based preferences for persons with skills and education. In 1965, most Americans were of European ancestry, and the vast majority of educational institutions were in Europe, too. Thus, its proponents claimed, this race-neutral immigration rule would likely achieve two important effects: first, the communist adversaries of the United States could no longer claim that American immigration rules were racist (as they surely had been), and second, the migration streams coming to the United States would remain relatively unchanged. The proponents were right about the first objective, but completely wrong about the second. Over the next two decades, for a wide range of complex reasons, new immigrants from Mexico, Latin America, and Asia—all allowed under the Act of 1965—would reshape major American cities and institutions, including public education.[15]

Many whites were migrating out of the cities in droves during this same period, as if running from the federal decisions and legislative changes that would so alter the complexion of their lives. Although there were some public school systems that complied with *Brown* without much protest, the decision inspired novel forms of resistance, as many white families put their children into private schools, including parochial schools, while others "homeschooled," or simply abandoned newly integrated urban public schools. A few public systems shut themselves down rather than comply with *Brown*, and some state legislatures helped with that process. "White flight" defined a widespread phenomenon—white families would rather leave an urban district in favor of suburban neighborhoods, and sometimes for no other reason than to enroll their children in public school systems that were far from racially integrated. They were voting with their feet, and one powerful way to understand this trend was to consider it in terms of how public finance and racial politics intersected in places like Virginia and California: many white taxpayers seemed unwilling to support public institutions that they felt no longer met their needs or the needs of their children. So accustomed to segregation and to local control of their schools, they moved into districts and regions where they could be assured that *their* local property taxes would be used to support *their* public institutions, including public schools, beyond the reach of the federal courts and of public laws mandating racial integration.[16]

In many urban systems, the departure of so many middle class and affluent white families within just two decades caused some regional housing markets to collapse, which in turn created new fiscal crises in many American cities. Coupled with deindustrialization in those same cities in the late 1960s and early 1970s, this resulted in public finance in many urban areas coming to be characterized in desperate terms—"urban decay," "post-industrial," or perhaps more euphemistically, "economic restructuring." All of these trends led to new inequalities, as well as widening social and political distances between white suburbs and central cities dominated by people of color, including new immigrants. In the immediate years after *Brown*, in cases like *Cooper v. Aaron* in 1958, from Little Rock, Arkansas, the Supreme Court had repeated that all public school systems should integrate racially "with all deliberate speed," and in other similar cases over the next decade, the Supreme Court had given the lower federal courts the power to assume control over large urban school systems that resisted racial integration. By the mid-1970s, however, the United States Supreme Court was testing the constitutionality of *inter-district* remedies—efforts to integrate black and white children over distances best travelled by interstate freeways. The novelty of such schemes indicated just how far Americans were moving apart in terms of race and place in spite of the stirring commitments to equality phrased in *Brown*.[17]

"A service performed by the State . . ."

A pair of federal cases in 1974 revealed broader patterns for how urban public systems were responding to these rapid changes. In *San Antonio Independent School District v. Rodriguez*, a group of Mexican American parents had first sued in 1968 to challenge how public schools were financed in the state of Texas. Although the case had complicated formulas and charts, the crux of the dispute was quite simple: in greater San Antonio, children who lived in public school districts where property values were low attended schools that were less robust than their peers who lived in districts where property values were much higher. The kids in more affluent areas had better libraries, better athletic programs, teachers who were better paid and qualified, and more teachers per student. Even when families in the poorer areas taxed themselves at a higher rate, they simply could not generate an income close to the annual revenues raised through local property taxes in neighboring, affluent districts. The Texas legislature had provided all public districts with some minimal level of funding, but local property taxes financed the rest, and that was where spending patterns skewed in all directions. Educational outcomes between poorer and affluent districts were obvious, too: the students in poorer areas were much more prone to dropping out of school and much less likely to attend college. A majority of children in the affluent districts attended college, with much brighter life prospects.[18]

In the *San Antonio* case, to illustrate what the educational and financial disparities looked like, the plaintiffs pointed to two districts whose racial compositions evoked racial segregation: Alamo Heights was in northern San Antonio and was nearly all white; Edgewood Independent was east of the city center, it was nearly all Mexican American, and a large fraction of the residents were new immigrants from Mexico. No one needed a history lesson to show how the state of Texas had discriminated against Mexican American children and families throughout a wide range of private and public institutions prior to 1974, nor did anyone need a college education to see that these two places—within the same city—remained very different environments to raise a family or get an education. All it took was a twenty minute drive on the freeway from Edgewood to Alamo Heights. A tour through the high schools in both districts might reveal that perhaps a meritocracy didn't exist in the United States—examined together, the public schools could have been designed so as to propel affluent children into the same class position as their parents, while consigning poorer students to much more limited opportunities, either on purpose or through neglect. But in *San Antonio*, there was no obvious public law that mandated racial or economic discrimination between or across these two school districts.[19]

The United States Supreme Court divided vehemently in this case, although all of the justices acknowledged significant disparities between Edgewood and Alamo Heights. Speaking for the majority, Justice Lewis Powell said, among other things, that the kids in places like Edgewood were not being deprived of an education in any absolute sense, that they did not constitute a "suspect class" entitled to special protection under the Fourteenth Amendment, and that discrimination by wealth and place was not, by itself, unconstitutional. That one area happened to be primarily Mexican American while the other was white was somewhat relevant to the case, but it was not by itself evidence of racial discrimination or racial animus. And, "where wealth is involved, the Equal Protection Clause does not require absolute equality or precisely equal advantages." Moreover, Powell continued, public education was not a fundamental constitutional right, but rather "a service performed by the State," and "it is not the province of this Court to create substantive constitutional rights in the name of guaranteeing equal protection of the laws." State and local rules for the financing of public education were closer to "social and economic legislation," and so its levels and terms were not constitutional matters, but rather political disputes best settled outside the federal courts. Justice Thurgood Marshall and his more liberal colleagues dissented from this analysis, proposing instead that the states should be prohibited under the Fourteenth Amendment from funding their public schools in such an inequitable manner. Marshall said that this inequality in public finance was an obvious legacy of racial discrimination that had been ruled impermissible in *Brown*.[20]

In response to the *San Antonio* case, many state legislatures and state courts addressed economic and funding disparities between public school systems, and yet the distances between affluent suburban and poorer urban school systems has persisted over the past four decades. So long as poorer children had some minimal access to public education, though, state legislatures, the federal courts, and the state courts have been reluctant to override the Supreme Court's willingness in *San Antonio* to give more control to local schools and districts. Unless there were some clear mandates to insure an equitable distribution of resources outlined in state rules or constitutions, state courts also did not regard economic disparities between adjacent public school systems as a federal constitutional issue similar to the ones raised in *Brown*.[21] Also, during this period, school districts were allowed to enforce their local boundaries, either by refusing enrollment to children beyond their district lines or by ensuring that the revenues generated in their districts remained there. Private fundraising within public schools was becoming more common, too, enhancing disparities across districts even further. All of this was enough to give poorer families strong incentives to cheat their children into a more affluent school district, often by lying about where they lived. A poor kid from Edgewood might be better off using an Alamo Heights address so as to have access to the schools there, but this would have made him an illegal migrant of another sort.[22]

"A mockery of public education . . ."

In the same year as *San Antonio*, in another case in which the plaintiffs alleged a near complete deprivation of educational opportunities within a single district, the Supreme Court proved more receptive and unanimous. By 1970, communities like Chinatown in San Francisco were growing as a result of the changes in immigration law, but many of the new immigrants were political refugees or working class migrants from mainland China and Taiwan, now all crammed together in one of the densest neighborhoods in California. San Francisco had been the heart of the anti-Chinese movement since the mid-nineteenth century, and even a hundred years later, the city had, at best, an ambivalent relationship with Chinese immigrants and Chinese Americans. In 1970, Chinatown was still an urban ghetto, racial segregation in the city had been obvious and legal through World War II, and new Chinese immigrants were not just crowded into Chinatown, but chronically underserved there as well. It did not seem to matter to some school administrators, for example, that the San Francisco public school system was offering instruction to Chinese immigrant students in English only. About three thousand students unfamiliar with English had no idea what their teachers or books were saying. After frustrated, repeated attempts to get the district to address this issue, thirteen Chinese American families joined in a class action lawsuit in 1970 against the San Francisco Board of Education, claiming that by failing to provide Chinese immigrant children with the means to acquire an intelligible public education, they were "[doomed] to become dropouts and join the rolls of the unemployed." That case became *Lau v. Nichols*, and it too had far-reaching implications.[23]

In the original district court case, and then in the Ninth Circuit Court of Appeals, the federal courts ruled that this was a local problem and not a constitutional issue. Children arrived in the public schools under a variety of conditions and circumstances, they said, and the public schools needn't be forced under court order to accommodate all of their different needs, especially when public funds were tight. The plaintiffs appealed, and the United States Supreme Court gave them what became a somewhat unexpected landmark victory. Without even reaching the constitutional issue, the Court said, through Justice William Douglas: "We know that those who do not understand English are certain to find their classroom experiences wholly incomprehensible and in no way meaningful." Douglas agreed that just providing the same facilities, teachers, and textbooks was insufficient; to furnish all of these in a language that the children didn't understand was to waste state resources and "to make a mockery of public education." The Court ruled that this form of neglect amounted to unlawful discrimination under the Civil Rights Act of 1964, a portion of which said that "school systems are responsible for assuring that students of a particular race, color, or national origin are not denied the opportunity to obtain the education generally obtained by other students in the system."[24] The Court handed the case back to the lower federal courts and to the school district, with instructions to provide relief to the Chinese American plaintiffs.

In its original manifestation, *Lau v. Nichols* did not mandate bilingual education, nor did it resolve exactly how districts like the ones in San Francisco or Los Angeles or New York would accommodate English-learners, or rather children who spoke Chinese, Korean, Spanish, Vietnamese, Khmer, Armenian, or Russian, just to name a few of the languages spoken in some urban public school systems by 1980. Sustained immigration after 1965 persisted over the next two and then three and four decades, such that the number of students who'd find public education unintelligible in English only grew to levels that could have overwhelmed even the most progressive public school districts. Indeed, *Lau* raised many more questions than it resolved: some saw the case as a move toward retaining and protecting cultural and language diversity in the United States, and they felt that this was a wonderful development; others saw the case in much the same way, as a move toward acknowledging and protecting racial and linguistic diversity, and yet they despaired at the possibility of the United States unmoored from its Anglo roots under a cacophonous tide of immigrants.[25]

Lau inspired subsequent lawsuits, as well as legislation across many states and in the federal government. The Bilingual Education Act, for example, approved by Congress in 1968, was amended five more times after 1974, most often to provide federal money to support what was then understood by 1980 to be a federal, court-ordered mandate implicit in *Lau* to provide bilingual education to immigrant students. Some states and local districts bristled at this new federal requirement, and some legislators and political candidates tied their support for "English-only" rules with their opposition to all forms of bilingual education. Indeed, state English-only rules proliferated in the years after *Lau*, as nearly two dozen states approved or re-approved English as their state's official language after 1975. When American public law was openly white supremacist, few legislators had any reason at all to insist upon English, but after *Lau*, politicians referenced Benjamin Franklin's hostility toward Germans or Teddy Roosevelt's aversion to Eastern Europeans to support their own discomfort with Spanish or Korean. In its own way, however, the *Lau* case was revolutionary: under federal law, public school systems had to accommodate all of their students so as to provide a meaningful, intelligible level of education, even if—or especially if—these students were from a foreign country. Under this decision, the Court preserved the principle of assuring some minimal access to public schooling for all children, irrespective of the conditions under which they arrived in the public schools.[26]

"Fundamental conceptions of justice . . ."

Two concurring opinions were filed in *Lau v. Nichols*, but one was full of worry. Justice Harry Blackmun was vexed that there were just a lot of kids in San Francisco who didn't get English. Without saying it directly, he blamed their parents: "We may only guess as to why [these children] have had no exposure to English in their preschool years." Blackmun then became blunt: "Earlier generations of American ethnic groups have overcome the language barrier by earnest parental endeavor or by the hard fact of being pushed out of the family or community nest and into the realities of broader experience." These remarks were curious: was Blackmun saying that Chinese immigrant parents weren't encouraging their kids to assimilate into American life quickly enough or early enough? Was he saying that these Asian immigrants were less assimilable, that they were too clutchy or clannish, so unlike other "American ethnic groups"? Indeed, when Blackmun referred to "earlier generations of American ethnic groups," did he really mean to say "white people," and did he think that white people were better at fitting into American life than these hopeless, forever English-limited Chinese people? We may only guess. Blackmun did side with the Chinese plaintiffs in *Lau*, but he insisted in his own concurring opinion that it was mostly because there were a *lot* of kids there in San Francisco who didn't understand English. Having been appointed to the Court by President Nixon, perhaps Blackmun was moved most by the argument that these Chinese kids might be otherwise "[doomed] to become dropouts and join the rolls of the unemployed."[27]

The connections between (potentially) illiterate immigrants, irresponsible immigrant parents, their innocent little children, and higher, long-term social welfare costs came to the fore one year after *San Antonio* and *Lau*, when the state of Texas in 1975 passed a rule withholding from local schools any state money for the education of children not "legally admitted" into the United States. The logic of the rule proved persuasive for a clear majority of legislators in Texas, though no one seemed to have given the rule much consideration in any legislative hearing: the rule allowed school districts to charge tuition to any student who couldn't prove legal residency. Once the rule came under scrutiny, its supporters insisted that the law targeted irresponsible, criminal immigrants, people who'd broken other laws to get into the United States, and so what was the sense in using state money to finance the education of their children? It was like rewarding law-breakers, perhaps even giving them an incentive to violate immigration rules knowing that they'd have access to free public schools. Opponents of the rule, including leading civil rights organizations like the Mexican American Legal Defense and Educational Fund (MALDEF), saw the state law as part of a broader pattern of racial discrimination against Mexican Americans and Mexican immigrants in the state of Texas, where state legislators had approved of rules since *Brown* that were facially race-neutral, and yet bore obvious, race-based disadvantages to people of color. In the Texas public schools, MALDEF had fought practices that included inadequate or nonexistent bilingual education programs, "academic" tracking policies that resegregated public schools internally, and the mapping of boundaries in ways that created one-race districts and schools.[28]

The first lawsuit to challenge the new state rule against undocumented students failed quickly, and the plaintiffs also realized that they might be subject to deportation, as the lawyer in Houston who'd filed their case had used their real names. Given that they were undocumented persons, this was a real problem. MALDEF's lawyers then moved carefully to design a test case. In his legal history of *Plyler v. Doe*, Professor Michael Olivas tells us what happened next: "The MALDEF lawyers found their Linda Brown in Tyler, Texas, where the brothers and sisters in the same family held different immigration status. Some had been born in Mexico, while those born in Texas held U.S. citizenship." Just by looking at these kids, one couldn't tell the Mexicans from the Americans, but under the state rule, the Mexican kids had to pay $1,000 every year to attend the public schools in Tyler, Texas. Supporters of the rule didn't think a trial necessary: they asked federal agencies to deport the plaintiffs, designated as "Doe," "Roe," "Boe," and "Loe," in the original complaint. In reply, the lawyers for MALDEF said that this was trial-tampering. Federal officials based in Texas tended to agree, and so they did not sweep or deport. The trial proceeded. James Plyler, the Superintendent of the Tyler Independent School District, was named as the defendant, and in 1978, Mr. Plyler lost. Other lawsuits popped up throughout Texas to challenge the same rule as it was being applied in local districts, such that within a year, about a dozen lawsuits were arrayed against it. All of these actions were consolidated under *Plyler v. Doe* when the case headed to the United States Supreme Court in 1981.[29]

As in *San Antonio*, the Court divided in a 5–4 decision, but in this instance, the immigrant plaintiffs won. Speaking through Justice William

Brennan, the Court majority settled upon a number of contested interpretations: it uncoupled "residency" within a school district from "illegal entry" or illegal status, for example, by suggesting that a person could still be regarded as a legitimate "resident" of a school district even if one didn't have lawful immigration status in the United States. (This struck the dissenters as a very curious argument.) At any rate, Brennan insisted, the children in the case were quite obviously "persons," and the Fourteenth Amendment said "[no] State shall . . . deprive any *person* of life, liberty, or property, without due process of law; nor deny any *person* within its jurisdiction the equal protection of the law." Most important of all, according to the Court, the undocumented children in Texas were not responsible in a thick moral way for their illegal status: "Their 'parents have the ability to conform their conduct to societal norms,' and presumably the ability to remove themselves from the State's jurisdiction; but the children who are plaintiffs in these cases 'can affect neither their parents' conduct nor their own status.'" Punishing the kids to discourage the parents was just Texas being mean: "Even if the State found it expedient to control the conduct of adults by acting against their children, legislation directing the onus of a parent's misconduct against his children does not comport with fundamental conceptions of justice."[30]

Moreover, there was no evidence—at least in this case—that undocumented children eroded the public schools, as the State itself had conceded in the original trial. Legal immigrants from Mexico were far more numerous than illegal Mexican nationals, nor was there any evidence that the removal of undocumented children would improve the schools. Brennan pointed out that even illegal immigrants probably paid more in taxes than they consumed in public services. And even if the rule were implemented as it was intended, it didn't seem rational in the long run: "It is difficult to understand precisely what the State hopes to achieve by promoting the creation and perpetuation of a subclass of illiterates within our boundaries, surely adding to the problems and costs of unemployment, welfare, and crime."[31] The State of Texas said that undocumented children were less likely to settle in Texas, and so were not worth the public investment represented in public education funding; the Court suggested a dimmer view of the federal government's power to deter or to remove anyone who was out of status, and thus concluded that this form of state-encouraged truancy would lead in time to "a subclass of illiterates." This was not a pleasant way of referring to the plaintiffs, and so Justice Brennan emphasized their present condition in another way, by referring to them as "innocent children" in his closing paragraph, emphasizing again that the kids weren't responsible for their unlawful status.[32]

In many ways, the Court's dissenters granted that the Texas rule was a stupid public law: "Were it our business to set the Nation's social policy, I would agree without hesitation that it is senseless for an enlightened society to deprive any children—including illegal aliens—of an elementary education." Speaking for the dissenters, Justice Warren Burger said, however, that it was Texas' right to pass stupid public laws without judicial interference, without the Court itself taking a "policymaking role." Burger reminded his colleagues that in *San Antonio*, a majority had concluded that education was not a "fundamental right," that states should have wide latitude to determine the circumstances under which this "benefit" or "service" could be provided, and that while depriving undocumented children of a free public education might be unintelligent in the long run, it wasn't completely irrational either. "By definition, illegal aliens have no right whatever to be here, and the state may reasonably, and constitutionally, elect not to provide them with governmental services at the expense of those who are lawfully in the state." Burger pointed out that in 1974, Brennan himself, in *DeCanas v. Bica*, had approved of the California rule punishing employers for hiring unauthorized immigrants. Burger suggested that if jobs were finite resources that the states could reserve for lawful residents only in 1974, then why not other state resources like public education in 1982? Indeed, in the late 1970s and early 1980s, everything seemed more finite: *Plyler* arose during a time when state and federal governments were struggling to maintain services in the face of an international recession, when the dominance of the United States economically and politically seemed to be ending, maybe even declining. If the states and local governments wanted to divert "finite" resources away from persons who didn't have a right to be in the United States, Burger said, they should be allowed to do so.[33]

"It unlawfully harbors illegal aliens in its classrooms and dormitories . . ."

Like *Brown*, *Plyler* has proven to be a very controversial decision, and on its twenty-fifth anniversary, James Plyler, the former superintendant of the Tyler Independent School District, gave an interview about his role in the case. He was eighty-two years old in 2007, but he remembered well the case that bore his name: Jim Plyler recalled that the undocumented students impacted by the Texas rule in 1975 were overwhelmingly poor, that they would not have been able to afford the $1,000 that his district was about to charge per child per year, and that many families were worried about what might happen to them if they'd lost their case. It would have amounted to a complete deprivation of any formal schooling for their children. Very few litigants ever confess to being pleased about losing, but Plyler was different: "I'm glad we lost [the case], so that those kids could get educated." Emphasizing his role as an administrator, Plyler said that he didn't have much of a choice about implementing the tuition requirements, but that he was then relieved that the Supreme Court forced him not to do it. During his interview, he revealed also that since the decision in 1982, one of his sons had married a Mexican American woman, and that they'd given him Mexican American grandchildren, their photographs displayed throughout his home in Tyler, Texas.

As for the "winners," the "Does," "Roes," "Boes," and "Loes" were now adults, of course, and they had grown up and some still lived in Tyler, too. Justice Brennan's prediction proved true—they had not been deported, nor did they "self-deport," but instead they settled and valued the education they received in town. Many adjusted to lawful permanent residency or to American citizenship, and so now they could be public about their true names, as Alfredo Lopez, Faviola Tizcareno, and Laura Alvarez Reyna. Ms. Tizcareno credited the public schools with teaching her English and giving her valuable job skills, the very tangible outcomes of her and her parents' victory. Ms. Reyna noted, though, that her own parents had been reluctant to talk about the lawsuit, even though they'd been the victors in one of the most unusual and distinctive cases in American constitutional history. A great deal of scholarly literature and legal commentary had been inspired by *Plyler v. Doe*, but it's a strange case indeed when the loser was pleased with the result and the winners didn't want much to talk about it.[34]

It *was* a peculiar case, a lot had happened in the public schools in the twenty-five years since *Plyler*, and not everyone had been as magnanimous as Jim Plyler. Indeed, discomfort against some of the ideas in the majority opinion in *Plyler* preceded that case, and so the reaction against it was immediate: two weeks after, for example, in *Toll v. Moreno*, Justice William Rehnquist dissented again when the Court's majority struck down a Maryland rule that charged "non-immigrant students" much higher, out-of-state tuition in its public universities. This case was significant because its basic facts showed a growing range of people coming to the United States under various, unusual circumstances—the litigants in *Toll* were people on G-4 visas and their dependents, people who'd been admitted to the United States temporarily to work in an international organization such as the United Nations. They were "non-immigrants," in that they hadn't been given permission to reside permanently in the United States, and yet the G-4 was odd, as it allowed these visa-holders to establish a "domicile" in the United States and gave them other special privileges, too, the most obvious being that they were exempt from paying state or federal taxes on their income. If the litigants in *Plyler* were poor and underprivileged, the ones in *Toll* were quite the opposite. Their dependents were the sons and daughters of diplomats and other high officials, they could live in the United States tax-free for as long as their parents could keep their jobs, and they were being admitted into some of the best universities in the country. The University of Maryland charged them higher tuition because it classified such students as "out-of-state residents," and in 1975, their parents sued the University to test this policy.[35]

The plaintiffs in *Toll* had argued that they all had been lawfully admitted to the United States, that they otherwise satisfied the other criteria used to determine "residency" in Maryland, and if they didn't pay state taxes to support the University, it wasn't their fault, as such exemptions were written into the federal law that had created their visas. The Supreme Court, again speaking through Justice Brennan, agreed with their petition, the result being that all lawfully admitted persons, including these "non-immigrants" who'd paid no income taxes to the state, should be eligible for in-state tuition benefits within public university systems.[36] Brennan reminded the states that a long line of cases now pointed to the troublesome nature of alienage as a discriminatory classification—states could not deny aliens state welfare benefits based solely on their immigration status, for instance, nor could they discriminate against aliens for access to public employment nor restrict them from receiving state licenses nor bar them from certain professions. With respect to higher education, in 1977, the Supreme Court had said in *Nyquist v. Mauclet* that the State of New York could not deny financial aid, including state-funded scholarships, to legal resident aliens even though they demonstrated no intention of becoming naturalized American citizens. And then of course there was *Plyler*. All of this, Brennan suggested, was enough to say that these plaintiffs—no matter how privileged—should have the benefit of in-state tuition rates at the University of Maryland.[37]

In dissent, Justice Rehnquist expressed exasperation, and he suggested that at least some of these developments were all wrong. "The University is substantially supported by general state revenues appropriated by the legislature, and of this sum nearly half is generated by the state income tax." "Just as it may seem unfair for a State to deny to a resident alien the right to participate in public benefits to which he has contributed through taxes, it may seem equally unfair to allow [the plaintiffs] to participate, on a par with tax-paying resident citizens and permanent resident aliens, in public benefits to which they have *not* contributed." Instead, the Supreme Court was acting, in *Toll*, "at the behest of a group of individuals who have been accorded a status by the Federal Government *superior* to that of the average citizen." Rehnquist pointed out that the plaintiffs in *Toll* paid no taxes, that some of their parents worked at the World Bank, and that although they were foreigners, people of such class position were not exactly an oppressed racial minority.

Finally, Rehnquist suggested that decisions like this one eroded the fundamental value of American citizenship. He indicated a legal posture in opposition to the majority opinions in both *Toll* and *Plyler*: "alienage, or the other side of the coin, citizenship, is for certain important state purposes a constitutionally relevant characteristic and therefore cannot always be considered invidious in the same manner as race or national origin."[38] Rehnquist's insight would prove highly consequential in subsequent Supreme Court decisions: immigration status was not like race or racial discrimination, he said, it should not be subject to the same level of judicial scrutiny, and immigrants could be treated differently from citizens in ways that should be regarded as constitutional.

But because Rehnquist had been a dissenter, and because *Toll* and *Plyler* were now valid constitutional interpretations by the end of 1982, state institutions responded to these new precedents in dramatic ways. For instance, states like California had required all noncitizen applicants to provide proof that they were lawful permanent residents; after *Toll*, the state universities in California dropped that requirement in favor of "residency" requirements that did not refer to immigration status at all. There were odd, lingering questions, though; if one combined *Toll* and *Plyler*, for instance, did they mean together that undocumented aliens, persons who'd not been lawfully admitted, could also benefit from in-state tuition at the public universities? The possibility did not sit well with everyone: W. Ann Reynolds, the Chancellor of the California State University, had heard that there could be many such students enrolled in the CSU system, which was by then one of the largest public university systems in the world, and so she asked the California Attorney General for his formal opinion on that question. In 1984, John Van de Kamp said that undocumented aliens should not be considered "residents" for tuition purposes under any circumstances.[39]

A year later, five students at the University of California at Berkeley challenged this opinion in Superior Court in Alameda County; all five, including the lead plaintiff, "Leticia A.," had graduated from high schools in California prior to their matriculation at the University, and on average, they had been "physically present" in the state for about seven years, well beyond the one-year requirement for students to qualify for in-state tuition. With help from lawyers who'd also worked on *Plyler*, the plaintiffs argued that they were "residents" of California in a manner similar to the plaintiffs in *Toll*. In addition, like the plaintiffs in *Plyler*, they said that they were not morally responsible for their unlawful immigration status, as they'd been brought as minors into the state by their parents. The Court agreed with Leticia A. and her fellow plaintiffs, and thus overturned California's Attorney General.[40]

The UC campuses implemented that decision quickly, and so in 1985, undocumented students became eligible for in-state tuition at all of the public colleges and universities in California. The controversy resurfaced, however, when David Paul Bradford, a staff member at UCLA, insisted that undocumented students should not be eligible for in-state tuition benefits. His job entailed making determinations like this, but his supervisors "invited him to resign after he evinced unwillingness to comply with the ruling of the Alameda court." Bradford left, but when he was denied unemployment benefits, he sued to get his job back, and his lawsuit also petitioned the Superior Court in Los Angeles to prevent the public universities from enrolling illegal immigrants, as this was a "waste and misuse of public funds." This time, Bradford won, and a California Appellate Court upheld the decision, thus affirming the original opinion of Attorney General Van de Kamp.

In the *Bradford* case, Judge Joan Klein noted that undocumented aliens faced several *lawful* disabilities under state and federal codes, that much of American public law "discriminates against undocumented aliens in the most basic way," and so "surely the state is not constitutionally required to subsidize the university education of other aliens who have never legalized their status." Klein suggested that if the state of California did offer in-state tuition to undocumented students, it would be open to "accusations that it unlawfully harbors illegal aliens in its classrooms and dormitories." In response to the University's argument that it was following the decision in *Plyler*, Klein noted only that "there is, of course, a significant difference between an elementary education and a university education." She didn't explain, though, why an elementary school shouldn't be guilty of "harboring" when it educated a youngster, but her remarks suggested that although a primary education might be essential or fundamental or at least important enough to overlook unlawful immigration status, a college education just wasn't. By the end of 1990, as a result of Judge Klein's decision, undocumented students were not to be considered "residents" again for tuition purposes at California state colleges and universities.[41]

Taken together, the formal responses in *Plyler*, *Toll*, *Leticia A.*, and *Bradford* indicated stark divisions about what to do with immigration status, public education, and ever more complex questions about the meaning of equality in American public law. In the four decades after *Brown*, no one in the United States had publicly favored a return to segregated schools, at least not by race, nor did anyone say that racial classifications should be used once again in ways to disable or deprive children of color from educational opportunities. Yet in Judge Klein's opinion and in cases like *San Antonio* and *Lau*, Americans revealed a willingness to condone policies that left some children behind, either through disparate financing of public schools, or through practices that ignored meaningful differences between children of diverse backgrounds. These children were coming from all over the world, and for some, it may have seemed that they were crowding in on every kind of American institution. They challenged what were fragile, new promises of equality, and such commitments had never been deeply rooted in American history.

Furthermore, *Plyler* and *Leticia A.* involved minors who'd come to the United States without any formal permission, and again, American legal institutions reflected broader anxieties about whether such persons should be eligible for a public education at all. It was an incredible thing that in the post-civil rights era, states and local governments were contemplating the formal exclusion of children from the public schools based on their immigration status, an aspect of their identities that they themselves did not control. For many Americans who had been uncomfortable with *Brown* or with the different shades of immigrants now surrounding them, though, it wasn't obvious that the principles of equality announced in that landmark case should extend to immigrants, especially not illegal immigrants.

Again, we should remember that *Brown* itself was never overwhelmingly popular: for Americans accustomed to racism and segregation, *Brown* may have made some sense in a world where the United States was compelled to offer itself as a beacon of freedom, and when many other countries were being courted by its communist adversaries. But the communist threat was diminished after 1990. By then, too, many politicians had ample evidence that middle class and affluent white Americans were preoccupied with the education and the fate of their own children rather than with abstract principles of equality and fairness, whether applied to the public schools or to any other set of institutions. And again, there were these immigrants, almost all nonwhite, many coming as they were without inspection, seeking an education for their children within a society where many of its citizens saw their very presence as a threat to the rule of law and as clear evidence of how the law wasn't being obeyed or enforced. Looking back upon these circumstances, we should not have been surprised that in many places, the public law governing education and immigration would become harsh, even though, as a consequence, it circumscribed the lives of thousands of young people struggling to get an education.

Undocumented and Unafraid

"Illegal aliens are not eligible . . ."

As school and university administrators struggled to fashion coherent policies in the wake of divergent federal and state court decisions, activists who'd considered illegal immigration a growing threat were proposing their own solutions. Some wanted to revisit and to overturn *Plyler*, including Governor Pete Wilson of California, as he saw a prime political target in this one issue. As a Senator from California, Wilson had once initiated several legislative efforts to provide agricultural growers in his state with "temporary workers," and he had also supported Ronald Reagan's immigration reforms in the Immigration Reform and Control Act of 1986, including the amnesty provisions. Wilson once considered migrant workers as an important source of labor for the agricultural industry in California, as did many of his political donors. As Governor, however, Wilson blamed many of the state's economic problems on federal mandates related to immigration, and he sued for federal reimbursements for state services consumed by illegal aliens. In an open letter to President Bill Clinton in 1993, Wilson insisted that illegal immigration was one of the gravest problems in the United States, and that Clinton had not done enough to deter illegal immigration or help the states finance the burden of educating and serving so many people who were out of status. Many legislators in his own state did not agree with Wilson, and as they resisted his efforts, he became more emboldened. In 1994, Wilson supported Proposition 187, a ballot initiative that changed everything.[1]

The rule was unequivocal in denying undocumented aliens any access to public schools or to higher education or, for that matter, to any social services. Its first section listed a set of injuries suffered by the people of California because of the presence of so many undocumented aliens, injuries that included "criminal conduct" and "economic hardship." The rule insisted that state and local agencies cooperate with the federal government "to establish a system of required notification by and between such agencies to prevent illegal aliens in the United States from receiving benefits or public services in the State of California."[2] Various reporting requirements under the rule were broad in scope: "Every law enforcement agency in California shall fully cooperate with the United States Immigration and Naturalization Service regarding any person who is arrested if he or she is suspected of being present in the United States in violation of federal immigration laws." Hospitals, social service agencies, and other state agencies could check for immigration status before providing services, and "each school district shall verify the legal status of each child enrolling in the school district for the first time in order to ensure the enrollment or attendance only of citizens, aliens lawfully admitted as permanent residents, or persons who are otherwise authorized to be present in the United States."

The section on higher education indicated the same intentions: "No public institution of post-secondary education shall admit, enroll, or permit the attendance of any person who is not a citizen of the United States, an alien lawfully admitted as a permanent resident in the United States, or a person who is otherwise authorized under federal law to be present in the United States." In preventing undocumented students from even enrolling in the public schools and universities of the state, Proposition 187 went further than any rule or federal court decision up to that point. Scholars and others also noted the resemblance between the reporting requirements of Proposition 187 and fugitive slave rules—just as federal law had once commanded "all good citizens" to report fugitive slaves, the rule in California now required good Californians to check and report for immigration status.[3] Despite months of protest and public demonstrations, a two-thirds majority approved of the rule in the November elections in California in 1994.

A coalition of legal advocacy groups sued in the federal courts for an injunction against Proposition 187, and in time, the Ninth Circuit Court of Appeals upheld a decision that blocked the enforcement of most of its provisions. In one of the initial decisions about the rule, Judge Mariana Pfaelzer held that the state proposition amounted to a "regulatory scheme" that went too far—specific portions of the rule, for example, including the one about barring undocumented children from public education, were unenforceable under the Supreme Court's decision in *Plyler*, and other parts of the rule also contradicted federal laws about eligibility for federally funded welfare benefits and other social services. Pfaelzer herself was not going to say that Proposition 187 was constitutional. Pfaelzer observed that in 1994, many federal rules still provided benefits without reference to immigration status; Proposition 187 clipped them off at the state level to undocumented aliens, denying through state legislation what may have been allowable under federal law. Given these conflicts, she blocked enforcement until these issues could be settled, even as she conceded the new political realities that the thing represented: "The California voters' overwhelming approval of Proposition 187 reflects their justifiable frustration with the federal government's inability to enforce the immigration law effectively."[4]

The frustration flowed beyond California, as its representatives in Congress sponsored several massive changes to the immigration law to produce federal versions of Proposition 187 by 1996. Californians voted for Proposition 187 during the same elections in which Congress shifted from Democratic to Republican control, the year that Bill Clinton lost the congressional midterms in 1994 and thus had to contemplate becoming a one-term president, the year that Newt Gingrich was ascendant and held aloft his Contract with America as a blueprint not just for political campaigns but as a Reaganesque road map for how to run the country. In 1996, when Congress approved and Bill Clinton signed the Illegal Immigration Reform and Immigrant Responsibility Act (IIRIRA), the title of the rule encapsulated the intentions of its sponsors: there was too much illegal immigration, and immigrants in general were not acting "responsibly" once they'd been admitted to the United States.[5]

Along with the Personal Responsibility and Work Opportunity Reconciliation Act (PRWORA) approved that same year, Congress moved to limit public assistance and other forms of social welfare spending to noncitizens. The hostility to poorer, undocumented immigrants was palpable, as members of Congress proposed to cut off illegal immigrants from any and all social services, even during natural catastrophes and other disasters, and to rewrite welfare eligibility rules to deny public assistance to *lawful* immigrants as well as to the ones who'd come without inspection. If Judge Pfaelzer's objections to 187 were rooted in conflicts between federal and state rules governing eligibility for federal support, the federal rules in 1996 moved to eliminate that confusion by drawing brighter lines between citizens on one side and noncitizens on the other.[6]

Portions of these new laws referring to education were meant to be blunt, inspired as they were by Proposition 187, but they engendered more confusion. Illegal immigrants had already been barred from federally funded public assistance programs in other statutes, but Section 505 of the IIRIRA said: "An alien who is not lawfully present in the United States shall not be eligible on the basis of residence within a State . . . for any postsecondary benefit unless a citizen or national of the United States is eligible for such a benefit (in no less an amount, duration, and scope) without regard to whether the citizen or national is such a resident." The language of Section 505 was confusing: some states interpreted the provision to preempt in-state tuition for undocumented students who could otherwise prove "residency" in their respective states; other states thought the rule forbade scholarships and financial aid to unlawful immigrant students entirely; and still others proposed rules to provide in-state tuition to undocumented students, *believing* that Section 505 threatened this possibility. At least one co-sponsor of the rule, Representative Christopher Cox of California, said of the effect of his proposal, "Illegal aliens are not eligible for in-state tuition at public colleges, universities, technical and vocational schools." Others, though, were not convinced that this was purely a federal issue, and so they moved to limit the scope of this provision through new state rules outlining what constituted "residency."[7]

PRWORA had similar language, and if anything, it also made the issue more difficult to understand: one paragraph said that undocumented aliens should not be eligible for "any state or local public benefit," a provision that included "public or assisted housing, postsecondary education, food assistance," and other similar "payment or assistance" "provided to an individual, household or family eligibility unit by an agency of a State or local government." And yet, in another paragraph, it allowed the states to approve rules that provided for these same benefits.[8] Academics and others were befuddled, and so they pushed competing interpretations: some felt that these federal rules forbade any state from providing access to public universities and colleges to undocumented aliens; others began drafting legislation to provide specific state authorization allowing undocumented students to matriculate at the same institutions, including provisions to permit them to pay in-state tuition.[9]

That tuition difference was becoming anything but academic—the difference between California residents and nonresidents was already substantial by the 1990s, when California residents paid about $1,600 per year for "registration and educational fees" for full-time enrollment at a University of California campus, while out-of-state students paid about $7,000 per year for "tuition and fees." In 1922, by comparison, the difference between residents and nonresidents had been about $150 per year. Those days were over: by 2010, residents of California were paying about $12,000 in fees and tuition to attend a campus like the University of California at Santa Barbara, while nonresidents there paid about $35,000. If UC Santa Barbara admitted a few dozen students who didn't have legal immigration status, however, it wasn't clear how they could afford $1,600 or $12,000 per year (before living costs), let alone $35,000, with no access whatsoever to state or federal financial aid.[10]

"Through no volition of their own . . ."

Since 1996, many states have been unwilling, unable, or confused about what to do with students who are out of status and yet otherwise qualified to attend colleges and universities. From 2001 to 2010, following California and Texas, ten other states approved in-state tuition for undocumented students, though twice as many states debated such measures, with a few rejecting the policy outright. In nearly all of these statutes, eligibility for in-state tuition benefits was phrased in terms of "residency": anyone who'd attended a high school in California for three years and had graduated, for example, would be considered a "resident," without further reference to immigration status. In California and in Texas, "resident" students were to sign an affidavit promising to file an application for lawful permanent residency "at the earliest opportunity the individual is eligible to do so"; of course, lawful residents and American citizens didn't have to worry about that provision, and this rule covered both lawful nonimmigrant students (persons granted formal permission to study temporarily in the United States) as well as undocumented students. Marco Firebaugh, the Assemblyman from South Gate, California, had written AB 540 in response to federal rules like IIRIRA and PRWORA, and he had framed the law in such a way that undocumented students were not the *only* beneficiaries of the new residency rules, even though he and every legislator and supporter conceded that such persons would likely be the primary beneficiaries.[11]

Critics complained that by outflanking IIRIRA and PRWORA, state legislators were engaging in "immigration nullification," thus "rewarding those who violate the law with a valuable subsidy while penalizing those aliens and out-of-state U.S. citizens who play by the rules." Professor Kris Kobach of the University of Missouri School of Law insisted that the courts should overrule state residency rules designed to benefit students who didn't have lawful immigration status, and that Congress should also approve new penalties against the states for providing such benefits. To facilitate the first strategy, Professor Kobach helped to challenge a Kansas in-state tuition rule in the federal courts while also participating in a lawsuit against the California in-state tuition rule in the California state courts. He lost the federal case in *Day v. Bond* in 2007, and then lost again before the California Supreme Court in *Martinez v. Regents* in 2010; the United States Supreme Court then refused to review either of these cases. Elton Gallegly, a California congressman, obliged the second of Kobach's strategies by proposing a rule in Congress in 2011 that would have cut off federal funds to any higher education institution that provided in-state tuition benefits to "illegal aliens." That measure failed, too.[12] Still, by 2011, only a minority of states had approved changes to state residency rules to admit students who were out of status.

Most of the states were deeply divided: in Utah, Virginia, and Arizona, legislators had introduced competing bills, some to provide in-state tuition, but others to ban admissions for anyone who was "illegal." Oklahoma passed a rule in 2003 allowing undocumented students to pay in-state tuition, then it rescinded the same policy in 2007, under a "Taxpayer and Citizen Protection Act." Utah passed a rule providing in-state tuition in 2002, but then its House approved a bill to repeal this policy in early 2011. During the debate in Utah, the Republican sponsor of the repeal, Carl Wimmer, framed undocumented students as lawbreakers, much as did his peers in Oklahoma: "One of the key questions you're going to have to ask yourselves is if you're OK with $5.5 million of your constituents' money going to subsidize illegal aliens going to college." During this period, Arizona, Colorado, Georgia, and Indiana passed rules that denied in-state tuition rates to any student who could not prove lawful immigration status, and South Carolina and Alabama required university administrators to check for lawful immigration status for all students matriculating into their public colleges and universities, just as California had once attempted to do under Proposition 187. By 2011, many more states had either refused to amend residency rules to help undocumented students or they had barred undocumented students entirely, and for reasons that men like Kobach and Gallegly would have approved.[13] Again, helping students who were out of status with in-state tuition benefits was not an overwhelmingly popular public policy after 1996, despite the media attention often accompanying these debates when one or two states had moved in the opposite direction.

At the federal level, the divisions around this issue have also led to a legislative deadlock more often than not. In 2001, aware that the states were also dealing with issues involving undocumented students, the Republican Senator Orrin Hatch of Utah first proposed the Development, Relief, and Education for Alien Minors Act, commonly known as the DREAM Act, a rule that had multiple sponsors from both major parties. Like Rick Perry, the Republican Governor who'd supported in-state tuition benefits in Texas, Senator Hatch emphasized how the primary beneficiaries of the DREAM Act were "children who have been brought to the United States through no volition of their own."[14] In its original manifestation, the Act proposed "adjusting" undocumented students who'd finished at least high school in the United States, so long as they satisfied other age and residency requirements.[15] Supporters included Senator Barack Obama, who continued to support the DREAM Act after he became President; the opponents of the bill said that it was another "back-door amnesty" for illegal immigrants and that it might stimulate even more illegal immigration. Although the Act was approved in Senate committees, it was blocked in 2002 and again in 2003; the Act was also folded into comprehensive immigration bills in 2006 and 2007, but again these bills failed; and in 2007, when Senator Richard Durbin of Illinois proposed the rule as part of a defense appropriation bill for the following year, it failed again, even though Durbin's versions included adjustment of status for undocumented aliens who'd served honorably in the United States military for at least two years.[16]

In 2010, after the midterm elections produced a new Republican majority in the House, key political leaders once again expressed their hostility toward any rule that might be interpreted as another "amnesty" for persons who were out of status. As if reading from the same script, Representative Lamar Smith of Texas and Senator Lindsay Graham of South Carolina both referred to the DREAM Act as a "nightmare," a rule through which undocumented students could displace American citizens and lawful permanent residents at American colleges and universities. In many respects, in order to garner more political support, advocates of the Act had limited the scope of the rule to reflect a much higher threshold for anyone seeking its benefits—to be adjusted for permanent residency under the 2010 version of the DREAM Act, for instance, a person now had to finish a college degree or complete military service. A high school diploma was not enough.

In reply, as the new chairman of the House Judiciary Committee, Representative Smith proposed that anyone found out of status—including those already enrolled at colleges and universities—should be deported. When his Democratic colleagues voted in favor of the DREAM Act in the House, Senator Lindsey Graham refused to support a similar vote in the Senate, even though he had suggested previously that this could be one part of comprehensive immigration reform, one that had to include border security. Other key supporters of the bill, including Senators John McCain and Orrin Hatch, said that they would abandon it, as adjustment of undocumented students alone would not be possible. Thus the bill failed in Congress in December 2010, and an undocumented student captured the disappointment of her allies with a rather American phrase on that day: "we were all like super bummed out." Again, at the federal level, as in the states, helping students who were out of status has not been a popular or winning position.[17]

Once the federal DREAM Act failed again, state legislators moved to authorize state versions. In 2010, lawmakers in Illinois moved toward what they'd considered a compromise position: undocumented students who'd established "residency" could already pay in-state tuition, but they were ineligible for state or federal financial aid; Representative Edward Acevedo of Chicago proposed establishing a state-wide commission to raise private scholarship money for any Illinois resident otherwise ineligible for state or federal financial aid. The Democratic Governor of Illinois, Pat Quinn, signed the bill into law in August 2011. In California, the Democratic Governor, Gray Davis, had supported AB 540, and ten years later, when another Democratic Governor, Jerry Brown, came into office, he was willing to make these same students eligible for certain forms of state financial aid to attend public colleges and universities. Brown's immediate predecessor, the Republican Governor Arnold Schwarzenegger, had vetoed similar bills since 2006.[18]

With Brown's election, Assemblyman Gil Cedillo of Los Angeles sponsored and amended a California version of the DREAM Act in 2010, and it was passed in two pieces in June and October 2011. Under the rule, known collectively as the California Dream Act, AB 540 students would be eligible for private scholarships and state aid, including two of the largest sources of aid for low-income students, Cal Grants A and B. As urgent as the need for such aid may have been, though, the California Student Aid Commission said that AB 540 students would not have it for at least another year; the existing rules for Cal Grants A and B, for example, had required all applicants to provide a Social Security number, an alien registration number, or a permanent residency card. Undocumented persons could not get any of these legally. To work out alternatives, the Commission needed time, even as opponents of the California Dream Act vowed to fight it in the courts or to seek its repeal in the legislature. Assemblyman Tom Donnelly of San Bernardino reiterated familiar arguments against this rule: "It's morally wrong. We have just created a new entitlement that is going to cause tens of thousands of people to come illegally from all over the world." Within a month, Donnelly attempted to collect enough signatures to repeal the rule through a statewide initiative process, but by January 2012, that effort had fallen short.[19] If court challenges and other efforts to block the rule also fail, California will become the first state to offer formal financial assistance for undocumented students attending its public colleges and universities, and all this within two decades of having approved Proposition 187.

"Undocumented and unafraid . . ."

But given the pattern of federal and state responses to students who've been out of status, a majority of states will likely not follow California's example, and a federal version of the California rule, authorizing financial aid for undocumented students, will meet the same level of resistance that the DREAM Act has received for over a decade. And yet what has been most surprising about these debates, about the fate of the so-called "Dreamers," these students lobbying to have access and support for a college education and even for graduate study, has been the change in their own attitudes about their status, their own public claims about their place in American society, although they've never been formal members of the United States. Some social scientists have found preliminary evidence that in-state tuition rules, like the ones approved in Texas and California, may have already increased the likelihood that poorer, out-of-status students will attend college; others have suggested that once admitted, these students finish college at rates similar to their peers with lawful status.[20] But more surprising than either of these findings has been the rather public character of their appeals—on-line, in the streets, and on college campuses, undocumented students have pressed their claims with a visibility that belies their vulnerable legal status.

A number of social scientists have discussed how undocumented students have changed simply by participating in struggles for state or federal immigration reform, including political debates about the various manifestations of the DREAM Act or other pieces of legislation. In recent years, these students have participated in marches, rallies, petition drives, and other public events, where they've often been quite open about their unlawful immigration status. They were not always this way: in Professor Leisy Abrego's ethnographic studies, for example, she followed undocumented students and some of their families for more than ten years, and when she first met her informants, they spoke of fear and anxiety, the result of living in a condition in which they could be removed from the United States for a traffic violation or because of a raid at their workplace or on account of some other random and unexpected meeting with immigration authorities or any authorities. When undocumented people were amongst themselves, "individuals shared stories of common crime and violence that went untold in their neighborhoods because people were worried about the police questioning their legal status."

Parents who were out of status often didn't take their own children to school, even though their children were born American citizens. The fear and anxiety could be overwhelming, and saddest of all, some undocumented people, including minors, revealed through their thoughts and actions how they themselves often felt less than fully human, as though they were undeserving of rights, dignity, or protection. Like the children in *Brown*, American immigration rules appeared to have lowered the self-esteem of people who were out of status: feeling "worthless," such persons rarely made public claims for relief or justice, and they often felt estranged from their own parents, even when they understood that their parents had brought them to this country for their own sake. The stigma of being out of status could feel crushing.[21]

The success of rules like AB 540, the law that permitted undocumented students to attend California public colleges and universities at in-state tuition rates, may have changed these attitudes among the law's intended beneficiaries. Feelings of shame among undocumented students have transformed to a sense of harboring a "stigma"—the stigma of being out of status—that was not the result of anything one did or didn't do. One student described the status as a kind of "scar," something that marked her, made her ashamed, and caused her to hide that aspect of herself from peers, teachers, and other authority figures. Yet after the passage of rules like AB 540, that same student expressed a new legal consciousness, one that made her feel as though the problem was not so much her and her family, but public laws that punished them for a status that others took for granted, a status disconnected from merit or moral dessert. Now that she could go to college legally, "I'm motivated to speak up for change whenever I feel strongly about it." Another student framed his predicament in language suggestive of how American citizens enjoyed privileges and rights that were undeserved, to a degree that prevented them from seeing the injustice inherent in his own status: "Students who are born in the U.S. are completely different from me. . . . None of them have experienced rejection from a program even when they have completed all the requirements needed to participate just because of their legal status. None of them know what it means to work hard and to have all the doors close in their face."[22] In comments like these, undocumented students themselves revealed a more critical view of American immigration rules, as well as a willingness to assert their own position in the United States despite their unlawful status.

On college campuses, organizations that support undocumented students have become increasingly common. Ten years after approval of AB 540, all of the University of California undergraduate campuses had organizations that were led or supported by students who did not have lawful immigration status. While many were cautious about revealing their identities, others claimed a more public profile: in 2003, a group of students at UCLA formed IDEAS, an acronym for Improving Dreams, Equality, Access, and Success, and the organization developed several branches and affiliated organizations over the next five years. Originally formed as a support group for students who were out of status, IDEAS has since grown into one of the most visible and influential student organizations within the UC system. With support from faculty and staff at UCLA, the organization has hosted numerous public events, its members have made films and books about undocumented students and their families, and they have raised money for students struggling through college. All of these activities were interrelated: the films and books, for instance, were produced at UCLA, with its institutional support, and proceeds from screenings and sales were directed to students otherwise ineligible for state or federal financial aid. Although IDEAS started as a support group, the organization itself drew a great deal of support, both on and off campus, and many of its members were quite open and public about being out of status.[23]

Indeed, members of the organization have lobbied state legislators and representatives in Congress, and they have also participated directly in litigation about public laws that could shape their lives. In 2007, for example, one of its founders, Tam Tran, testified before the House Judiciary Committee's Subcommittee on Immigration in favor of the DREAM Act. Three days later, immigration agents detained and then released members of her family in Orange County, even though these authorities claimed that their actions had nothing to do with her testimony before Congress. As implausible as that sounded to some, Tran's visibility had the odd effect of protecting her and her family: leading immigrants' rights organizations, congressional members of the subcommittee to which she'd testified, and private attorneys working pro bono assisted Tran and her family on both coasts. Zoe Lofgren, the Democratic congresswoman from San Jose, suggested that immigration authorities were intimidating a witness before Congress, and she demanded that Tran's family members be released pending the outcome of their appeals, including a bid to re-open their asylum petitions. These interventions worked: in time, Tam Tran started a doctoral degree at Brown University in, of all things, American Civilization.[24]

In litigation, students who've had no lawful immigration status have nevertheless participated in prominent cases where their rights have been at stake; in so doing, they've changed popular conceptions of undocumented students. For instance, when the California Supreme Court heard challenges to AB 540 prior to its decision in *Martinez v. Regents* in 2010, important civil rights organizations filed briefs on behalf of undocumented students, many providing ample testimony about what it felt like to go to school and to college without legal status. In its own amicus brief, the Asian Pacific American Legal Center based in Los Angeles made two interesting points: Asian Pacific Americans were about 40 percent of all students in the University of California receiving tuition relief under AB 540, and thus they were the second largest group in the state to receive such relief, and AB 540 students who were Asian Pacific Americans also reported that the UC system would have been out of reach without AB 540. Citing a report published by the University itself about AB 540 students, the lawyers for the Center noted that although a small fraction of affluent families benefited from AB 540—families who looked more like the privileged plaintiffs in *Toll* rather than the underprivileged litigants in *Plyler*—the overwhelming majority of AB 540 students were struggling and fighting, financially and otherwise, for a college education. Even among members of this purportedly "model minority," being out of status was not an uncommon condition. The experiences of many of these Asian Pacific American students were channeled through these important avenues, and they thus portrayed themselves in ways that would elicit great empathy for their position, to the point that leading Asian American civil rights organizations devoted substantial resources to supporting them.[25]

Similarly, since 2007, many more students at various colleges and universities across the country have "come out" to their peers and in their communities in related ways, as "undocumented and unafraid," as more willing to participate in debates about their future. At several college campuses, student organizations have hosted public events where they've shared "counternarratives" about their experiences, stories that again challenge prevailing notions about how "illegal aliens" are horrible people out to destroy American society. At UC Santa Cruz, for example, Students Informing Now (S.I.N.) worried that members of their audience might report them to the immigration authorities after their public event, but they went ahead anyway with performances that they felt could "humanize" people who were out of status. Across the country, at the City University of New York, at Brooklyn College, and at Baruch College, students and faculty have organized immigration clinics, hosted teach-ins, and offered "safe spaces" for undocumented students to share resources openly with one another and with their peers. They designed these efforts not just to create support networks for people who don't have lawful immigration status, but also to build solidarity between people who do have lawful status and those who don't. For many faculty, students, and staff on college campuses, meeting a young person facing these circumstances has been a sobering experience, a rather visceral moment to see how public law makes unlawful people.[26]

Student activists have attempted to share such moments with a wider audience. When Congress again debated the DREAM Act in 2010, several undocumented students "outed themselves," some expressing a sense of "elation" that they were talking publicly about their status in the nation's capitol. One student said, "I think losing the shame overshadows the fear. . . . I'd much rather clarify to the public that being undocumented is just a circumstance I find myself in. I'd much rather have that out in the public than just living in fear."[27] Rhetorically, the idea of "outing" oneself has always had a powerful resonance in American political and cultural thought—to take a status or condition, seen widely as a source of stigma or shame, and to turn that into a positive identity, perhaps into a source of pride, has long been an effective political strategy. Nowadays, as much as their gay, lesbian, and transgender peers might "out" themselves in college in similar ways, these public expressions of identity undermine the idea that all people who are "illegal" ought to be ashamed of that status. By revealing themselves in the open, their precarious status presented before everyone, these students suggest that the network of federal laws that defined people like them as law breakers and as social problems may itself be the problem.

Checking and Not Checking

Nevertheless, as of January 2012, the DREAM Act had yet to be approved, minors and college students who were out of status still faced removal along with their parents, and any rule—comprehensive or otherwise—that could adjust the status of millions of people without lawful immigration status faced certain, stiff opposition in Congress. The states and local jurisdictions seemed to move in opposite directions, but quite often in favor of rules that checked for immigration status prior to the delivery of any social service or benefit, and the public schools were no exception. Throughout the country, school officials have checked for immigration status in spite of *Plyler*, in efforts that some critics have said were designed to deter undocumented families from settling in those districts at all. In many local schools, all parents must establish residency prior to enrolling their children, but in Arlington, Virginia, in 1988, school administrators told a family that they could not enroll their children without proof of immigration status. In 1995, in Long Island, New York, proof of residency included lease agreements, mortgage statements, and other documents that people out of status would have difficulty procuring; and in Randolph, Massachusetts, school officials demanded birth certificates and other evidence of lawful permanent residency prior to formal enrollment as well. In Arizona and in New Mexico, school officials have sent scouts in recent years to watch for children crossing the southern border to attend the local schools, or they've demanded proof of residency every year that a student attempts to enroll in the public schools.[28]

According to a study released by the New York Civil Liberties Union in 2010, about one in five school districts in that state required proof of lawful immigration status as a prerequisite for enrollment, a practice that has also appeared in states like Maryland, Nebraska, and New Jersey. In 2011, the Office for Civil Rights within the United States Department of Education issued a letter to the states and to local school districts advising against the implementation of any residency requirements that might have a "chilling effect on a student's enrollment in school." And yet later that year, the state of Alabama approved a new rule *requiring* the public schools to check the immigration status of students at the time of their enrollment, just as Proposition 187 had once proposed in 1994. Proponents insisted that the rule in Alabama was designed only to keep track of the number of illegal immigrant children educated with state funds, so as to help the state make a more solid case in lawsuits and other actions for federal reimbursements, but many critics didn't see any other point of the law than to deter such persons from enrolling in the public schools at all.[29]

At the federal level, issues of residency and status have reappeared largely in response to state policies that have allowed for the enrollment of undocumented students at colleges and universities. Since 1974, the Family Education Rights and Privacy Act (FERPA) had required all educational institutions that received money from the United States Department of Education to protect the private educational records of students. Under the Act, institutions may not divulge these records without express written permission from students or their parents (if the students are minors), nor could they divulge such records to other government units without similar consent. But for a variety of reasons—in the wake of the 9/11 attacks and also in light of spectacular acts of violence on college and school campuses—law makers and others have questioned whether FERPA's privacy protections should remain in place under some circumstances.

FERPA had been interpreted to provide privacy protections to all students, including immigrants and other noncitizens, but that principle has been amended in recent years given these developments. For example, provisions of the USA Patriot Act of 2001 gave federal authorities the right to petition a court for student records related to a terrorism investigation, and in other, less controversial areas where immigration and education have intersected, new rules have already authorized the release of what was once considered private information protected under FERPA. In 2002, under a new set of policies to keep track of nonimmigrant foreign students in the United States, Congress gave the Attorney General the authority "to collect from approved institutions of higher education . . ." "information [about] non-immigrants," including "international students and exchange visitors."

These policies have been implemented through Immigration and Customs Enforcement, such that federal authorities have established a national database that attempts to keep track of all international students and scholars in the United States. Within a few minutes, educational institutions and others can check on-line whether a candidate has lawful immigration status. Programs like this one have been extensions of other similar programs, most notably E-Verify, first established in 1997 as a pilot project among a small number of states and then expanded to include biometric data within a massive new searchable, national database by 2007. Through E-Verify, employers can check on-line to see about the immigration status of prospective employees, and since 2009, Congress has required all federal contractors and subcontractors to use this system. Some policy makers have imagined similar systems to test the eligibility of anyone seeking admission into a college or university or applying for any social service, or to see about someone's status during routine police stops. Checking for immigration status continues to be a preoccupation for a wide range of American institutions, including now educational institutions, and this will no doubt create anxiety for even the bravest student, no matter how "unafraid" she might be of her immigration status.[30] In an era when the federal government has removed more people more efficiently and more often than ever before, that anxiety will likely remain the one singular reality that cannot be ignored for anyone who is out of status, no matter whether they are or were enrolled in our schools, colleges, or universities. On the other end, for those who teach and run these institutions, the decisions to check or not check for immigration status will provide many occasions to consider whether to trigger or to ignore the formidable force of American law.

Under these circumstances of surveillance and policing, what has been so striking has been the plea—coming so often from undocumented students and others facing similar conditions—for those of us who have lawful status to recognize first the common humanity of those who don't, as well as their desires for a place in this country and for an education here without stigma, shame, or fear. They have asked many people to *ignore* laws that have frustrated these ends, and their pleas have grown ever more urgent and more powerful. For example, following policies approved in North Carolina and South Carolina, the Georgia Board of Regents voted in 2010 to ban illegal immigrants from the state's five largest public universities, a policy that went into effect in fall 2011. In response, students at the University of Georgia and at Georgia State University asked their respective administrators not to comply with the policy; undocumented students persuaded the Student Government Association at the University of Georgia to resist its implementation, and at Georgia State, their peers held rallies in the spring of 2011 to ask the University's President, Mark Becker, to do the same. Some complained that these students were asking public officials, including university officials, to break the law and to harbor people who had no right to be in the United States; the protesters themselves insisted that their requests were in the best traditions of American political protest, where the victims of race-conscious, unjust rules had often issued pleas for help and protection.[31]

Several undocumented students took great risks in these protests. They signed and delivered an open letter to President Becker urging him not to comply with a policy that would exclude each of them from the Georgia State University. They used their real names—Dulce Guerrero, Jose Rico Benavides, Georgina Perez, and many, many others, both in the letter and when they were addressing the media that came to cover these events. They noted in the letter and in the protests that followed that the ban against undocumented students at the most competitive state universities in Georgia amounted to the creation of a two-tier system of education, an "institutionalized discrimination" that reflected and echoed some of the darker aspects of American history and culture. Such policies, they said, should not be followed. This policy was unjust and unfair, and the fact that it was lawful did not absolve administrators and others from making their own decisions about what to do with such rules, at least in the ways that they were manifest in the state of Georgia. Several students were arrested in the demonstrations of April of 2011, but none seemed ashamed or afraid of that. Instead, they were hopeful: that they were so public, so open, was on purpose and it had a political point, if only to let others like them know that they were not alone and that they too could have a voice. What was an act of empowerment for them horrified others—some legislators in the state of Georgia saw lawlessness in these protests, and they promised new rules to ban all undocumented students from all public universities in Georgia.[32]

Despite the appeals, in their separate replies, President Becker of the Georgia State University and President Michael Adams of the University of Georgia both stated their intentions to comply with the Regents' policies, and they gave as a reason the fact that they were simply required to do so by law. The petitioners were of course disappointed, but not surprised. What was surprising, however, was that in subsequent months, several faculty members at universities in Georgia and across the country pledged to educate and to advocate for these students and others like them at a new kind of institution based somewhere in Athens, Georgia. Exactly where this institution was located, they would not say. Started by five professors from the University of Georgia, the newly established Freedom University attracted to its board of advisors senior scholars from Yale University, the University of Texas, the University of California, the University of Wisconsin, Harvard University, and New York University. Hundreds of other faculty members and students gave money and offered their time. Soon, Freedom University had a Web page and an Amazon wish list, a site where supporters could donate gas cards and textbooks. Its founders conceded that this University would never replace the University of Georgia or Georgia State University, and that its mission was primarily political from the beginning, a public expression of support for undocumented students and a rebuke against state rules denying them access to an education for which they were otherwise well qualified.

The founding faculty at Freedom University planned a curriculum of sorts for the fall of 2011, the first seminar being, of all things, a class on American civilization. It may be fitting if they were to review, in their first lesson, the circumstances under which Frederick Douglass learned how to read or how he then established a "school" to teach other slaves to do the same. That lesson might allow the undocumented students at Freedom University to place themselves in an American historical narrative of which they were also now a part. The more profound and damning lesson might have been the one for the rest of us, people who had legal status, the American citizens who had voted for politicians who then in turn supported policies that made institutions like Freedom University necessary. From a certain perspective, it would appear that such people were repeating collectively some of the most unfortunate episodes of their own history.[33]

History, Memory, and Regret

All students of American civilization ought to read *Adventures of Huckleberry Finn*, as they would see in that story how, in American history and American fiction, many people did not favor the education of others whom they considered pariahs, for reasons that could only be described as racist and irrational. The very fact that even one racial pariah had gotten an education offended such people, as Pap Finn himself indicated in his tirade in chapter 6 of Twain's novel. Shortly after kidnapping his son into a remote cabin, Pap complained about "govment," that entity that kept him from possessing his own son, or at least his son's money. Pap then described the educated black man he'd seen in town, the ultimate example of that same "govment's" failure in other respects. Pap couldn't stand the sight of "a free nigger there from Ohio—a mulatter, most as white as a white man." This man was a professor, fluent in many languages, and "knowed everything." Pap heard that this man could vote in Ohio. (Pap must have misheard, though—prior to the Civil War, Ohio restricted the franchise to white men only. Being drunk most of the time, Pap was one of the most unreliable of unreliable narrators.) And yet just the very thought of this *educated, enfranchised* black man was enough to send Pap into a violent fit: Pap said he had shoved the man, demanded that he be sold at auction, and was amazed again when he learned that the professor must be in Missouri for at least six months before he could be sold lawfully as a slave, this "prowling, thieving, infernal, white-shirted free nigger."

Not everyone in Missouri was like this, of course. Against Pap's disapproval, a few Christian missionaries had set up schools for black children, including slave children, more than two decades before the Civil War. However, a majority of white citizens tended to agree with the town drunk of St. Petersburg: in 1847, Missouri passed a rule forbidding the education of "any Negroes," and anyone found in violation could be fined up to $500 and sent to prison for up to six months. Sober people in Missouri voted in ways that Pap would have approved.[34] Even now, such political behavior among American voters might represent that dim tendency to push down and disable other people, believing that this might raise their own precarious status somehow or make them safer, as though they might be better off simply by making others more miserable. When we encounter an undocumented student who has finished college, despite substantial obstacles that their peers can only imagine, some of us see a great triumph, and we see in such a student the possibility of a society that can support the education of all people who come among us. The education of anyone appears as an intrinsically good outcome. And yet others still react like Pap, and they express disappointment at their current "govment," pointing as they've done to such young people as if to indicate that their presence and success represents a failure. Such thinking is hard to understand, then or now. When Barack Obama (a former professor, no less) announced in June 2012 that the federal agencies in his administration would no longer deport some undocumented students, a few of the immediate responses in Congress could best be described as Pap-like. The President and his opponents saw the same people in such profoundly different ways.[35]

These fractures in vision are as old as the Republic. As he attested in his autobiographical writings, Mark Twain grew up like Huckleberry Finn and like Pap, just knowing and *seeing* as a child that black people were to be treated as inferior human beings, as slaves, "niggers," and people without rights for whom an education was inappropriate. He nevertheless wrote one of the most compelling antiracist novels ever, and we can see, in his art and in his life, how his inspirations were all around him. For instance, to escape the fires and violence of her neighbors in Connecticut, Prudence Crandall married and relocated with her husband to Illinois in 1834, and then to Kansas. After months of conflict, she decided, finally, that her white neighbors in Canterbury were simply too racist and too violent to tolerate a school for the education of colored girls, and rather than further risking their lives and hers, she left. But in 1886, when Crandall was eighty-three years old, Mark Twain supported a Connecticut state rule that apologized to Ms. Crandall for what had happened to her and to her students. Twain had published *Huckleberry Finn* a year earlier, and so his support for Crandall suggested something deep about the direction of his sympathies, both in life and in his fiction. Perhaps Twain was thinking about Jim, or maybe Jim's daughter, when he wrote in support of Prudence Crandall. Or maybe Twain was thinking of Pap Finn. Twain knew better than most the kind of people who'd tormented Ms. Crandall and her students, and so it may not have been surprising at all that he wished to support a person like her and to restore her memory to the people of Connecticut.

The legislature in Connecticut obliged, Crandall was given a pension for $400 per year, and she collected it until her death in 1890. About fifty years later, the Prudence Crandall School for Negro Girls was listed as an historic building, and it was repaired and restored at the state's expense; in 1970, the federal government added the site to the National Register of Historic Places. It now houses the Prudence Crandall Museum. In 1995, more than 160 years after she'd been driven from Canterbury, the Connecticut legislature declared that Prudence Crandall should be the state's official heroine, her life to serve as an ongoing lesson to children in the state's public schools.[36] Like Frederick Douglass' life, Crandall's determination and dedication to the education of all children are celebrated there as part of Black History Month.

This desire to celebrate people once considered pariahs has continued into our own time, and its occasions have arisen from the most unexpected places. In 2004, for instance, at the University of California at San Francisco, an elderly Japanese American woman inquired as to how she might finish her nursing degree, as her studies had been interrupted by World War II. It was an unusual request: in 1941, Aiko "Grace" Obata had been a nursing student at UCSF, having finished preparatory coursework at Berkeley, but because of the internment and her subsequent relocation, Obata had to complete her studies in Minnesota. She did become a nurse, she married, and as Grace Amemiya of Ames, Iowa, she and her husband had made a life together far from California with their two children after the war. As it was for many internees, though, the experience had been haunting, so much so that even after she retired, Ms. Amemiya wondered whether she might have some recognition for the academic work she'd completed at the University of California.[37]

Grace Amemiya's request drew the attention of Zina Mirsky, an Associate Dean at UCSF. Mirsky was very sympathetic, but she saw that Amemiya had not finished all of the requirements for an academic degree and that the university would have to make a rare exception to offer anything for her. In time, though, other administrators and faculty throughout the system were receptive to the idea that Ms. Amemiya, along with approximately seven hundred other students whose studies had been interrupted by the war and by internment, might be awarded an honorary degree. These administrators included Joseph Castro, a Vice Provost at UCSF, Judy Sakaki, the Vice President for Student Affairs at the UC President's Office, William Kidder, a lawyer and a member of Sakaki's staff, and Daniel Simmons, a law professor at UC Davis. Working with other faculty and staff across the four UC campuses that had been established by 1942—Berkeley, Los Angeles, Davis, and San Francisco—they formed a committee to study the possibility of awarding honorary degrees to former internees, even though the University of California had not awarded any such degrees since 1986.

Ms. Amemiya was eighty-eight years old in July 2009 when she came to San Francisco and testified to the Regents of the University about what had happened to her almost seven decades before. She bore no hard feelings, she said, but she still thought about Cal and UCSF, she visited the campuses from time to time, and she said that she was now hopeful that "the university is recognizing that what the government did was wrong, and now my classmates and I can finally take our place as full-fledged UC alumni." Many were in tears after hearing her testimony, and this was how the Regents approved special honorary diplomas for former students like Amemiya. Later that year and into the next, the four UC campuses hosted special ceremonies to award these degrees to former internees or to their surviving relatives, and Ms. Amemiya received her diploma in San Francisco on December 4, 2009. In the photographs, she was beaming.[38] Governor and Chief Justice Earl Warren had taken two degrees from Cal, he'd been an officer of the Alumni Association at Berkeley, and so one naturally wonders how he might have felt about these events, or what he might have said to Ms. Amemiya on that special day.

In 2009, though, the same year that the University of California was awarding diplomas to students who'd been interned during World War II, the place of undocumented students in American education and in American higher education was still uncertain, and it would likely remain uncertain for the foreseeable future. For those who struggled for equal access in the shadow of American law, people like Frederick Douglas, Prudence Crandall, or Grace Amemiya could be inspirational, but the more proximate inspirations came from fellow students, albeit the circumstances surrounding them could be profoundly sad. Tam Tran, that graduate student of American Civilization at Brown University, and her friend, Cinthya Felix Perez, had been tireless advocates for the DREAM Act for most of their time together at UCLA. Tam was the undocumented student from Vietnam and Orange County; Cinthya's family was undocumented also, from Mexico and East Los Angeles. After UCLA, Tam had gone to Brown, Cinthya to Columbia University for a master's degree in public health. They were travelling together in Maine in the spring of 2010 when they were both killed in a car accident. Tam would have been twenty-eight years old in October 2010, and Cinthya had just turned twenty-six that January.

Death and grief for people so young and promising are unimaginable. They are private affairs. And yet these women were mourned in public, first by the University of California, whose President, Mark Yudof, embraced the student organization where both young women had been so active. In his remarks, Yudof said that "the on-going work of IDEAS, we believe, stands as a lifelong tribute to the dreams of these young women," this language suggesting his own longtime support for the DREAM Act. President Yudof's actions indicated a moral and political position regarding undocumented students that was quite different from the ones taken by his peers, including President Mark Becker of Georgia State and President Michael Adams of the University of Georgia. On the other side of the country, students and faculty at Brown University mourned Tran's death in private and in public events, and faculty members in her department awarded her a graduate degree in American Civilization posthumously. Most surprising of all, in a joint resolution authored by State Senator Rhoda Perry of Providence, the legislature of Rhode Island sent formal condolences to Tran's family five days after the accident, expressing its deepest sympathies and calling their daughter "an inspiration to us all."[39]

It may seem strange for such American institutions to mourn the passing of these young women who had no lawful status in the United States, one from a family that the federal government had attempted to deport almost exactly three years before her death. Yet throughout American history,

Americans have celebrated and mourned those people who were outside the boundaries of American law, as they appeared so obviously American when their lives were considered from a distance, even though they were denied membership or citizenship in any formal way during their lives. It would seem now that through these formal celebrations, many Americans still believed that this was a nation where citizens have long cherished principles of equality irrespective of status, where citizens could also celebrate people who've devoted their lives to those principles. The incomprehensible death of women like Tran Tam and Cinthya Perez give us pause, however, to reflect upon our own laws and to assess those commitments, in light of a history that other Americans will measure and assess long after we ourselves are gone. When we consider how our own rules and policies have made life dreadful (again) for a great many young people, we can foresee with reasonable accuracy how these laws may well leave our own descendants wondering just how and why we've managed to repeat ourselves in the most unfortunate ways.

IV

Unlawful Migrations in American Law and Society

Utopian Visions and the Unlawful Other

Utopian Visions and People of Color

Mark Twain's *Huckleberry Finn* was set in the world before the Civil War, and although we know in the end that Huckleberry himself intended to head west, Jim's fate as an emancipated slave was less certain. Neither Huck (nor Twain) discussed Jim's future in the conclusion, as Huck (and Twain) complained of "what a trouble it was to make a book." But Jim's story was at least as compelling as Huck's, and that leads us back to that question: Where could he have gone? Would Jim have gone back to St. Petersburg, Missouri, to purchase his family, or would he have pursued that goal in some other state, either in the East, in the Midwest, or in the far Western frontiers? Given the low prevailing wages for free black laborers in the years before the Civil War, however, Jim might have stolen his family instead, as he had once intimated to Huck, running with them together, maybe to Canada. Being a good father, aware that his younger daughter was disabled, and knowing what could happen to vulnerable slave girls when they came of age, Jim would have sought to protect his wife and children. But then again, his whole family would have faced the same migration problem.

This was because in areas where slavery was unlawful after the American Revolution, hostility toward blacks was intense and pervasive. White supremacy was a dominant, powerful ideology throughout the country, not just in the South, and as part of its routine political practice, its proponents supported public laws that discouraged the settlement of free blacks, segregated them from public institutions, discriminated against them in employment and in nearly every other aspect of civil society, and mandated their political disenfranchisement in almost all of the so-called free states. African Americans like Jim knew that manumission did not lead to fundamental equality with whites, and one key aspect of that inequality was that he would have no obvious place where he could be secure in his own property and person, prosper through his own labor, or reunite with his family.

Indeed, one of the most common forms of discrimination against all African Americans, free and slave, was a set of migration restrictions that had emerged shortly after the American Revolution. Citizens of all the states expressed their desire for all-white communities through these public laws. For example, for veterans of the Revolutionary War, the new federal government had set aside lands in the Ohio River Valley—the city of Cincinnati was named after that famous Roman dictator who gave up his weapons to resume farming, and so too veterans of the Revolution were given lands there to start their lives anew as American citizens. This involved, of course, "removing" and subjugating the Native American tribes of the Ohio River Valley, and it did entail displacing ancient civilizations of great sophistication. But having executed those policies as though they were the equivalent of clearing the land of wildlife, many successive American presidents favored white settlements on the frontier, as they saw this as a source of economic and political stability essential to the survival of the fledgling republic. Even as mobility and economic opportunity were now possible for white Americans—many of whom were poor and landless before the Revolution—the vast majority of blacks suffered exclusion. Unless they could "become Christian," take up settled agriculture, and otherwise cover all evidence of their tribal identities, Native Americans fared worse.[1]

Without question, white racial identity was the one essential prerequisite for American citizenship in the early United States. The phrase itself became part of American law—the Naturalization Act of 1790 had stated that only "free white persons" could pass into American citizenship, and this necessarily excluded "Indians not taxed," understood to mean Native Americans who did not exercise private property rights, in addition to white indentured servants, African slaves, and free African Americans. No state wanted free blacks, and many states excluded all black persons within a few months of achieving statehood: in the regions "north of slavery," "Ohio provided a classic example of how anti-immigration legislation could be invoked to harass Negro residents." "That state's restrictive statutes, enacted in 1804 and 1807 as part of the Black Laws, compelled Negroes entering the state to post a $500 bond guaranteeing their good behavior and to produce a court certificate as evidence of their freedom."[2]

Ohio had become a state in 1803, and its citizens knew that a $500 bond would have been impossible for the vast majority of free blacks. But the rule bore a more fundamental political point: Ohio's legislature had made it clear that the state did not want African Americans, and though the law was not strictly enforced in the immediate decade after its passage, white residents used these rules against the entire black community in periods when they felt economically or politically threatened. Under law, any African American who didn't have such a bond could be imprisoned or removed. If rules like the Naturalization Act of 1790 revealed a utopian vision of America where "free white persons" could come from all over Europe to collaborate with one another as equals and as fellow citizens, Ohio's migration rules in 1804 and 1807 indicated that even free people of color stained that vision, and should thus be made to feel unwelcome. Free blacks and fugitive slaves did settle in Ohio and in the old Northwest after the American Revolution, but there, "most of them had to contend with legal discrimination, bigotry, poverty, and the ever-present threat of recapture." As we saw earlier in this book, not even progressive towns like Oberlin were completely safe.[3]

Race, Migration, and Anxiety

Other states took similar approaches, as citizens across the country worried about what might happen with slavery in the South. In the slaveholding states, several prominent masters, including George Washington, had felt remorse for holding slaves while fighting for independence, and so they had manumitted their slaves. Washington's biographers tell us that his remorse about slavery was a private affair, though, because he enjoyed the worldly comforts slavery provided and because he did not want to disparage publicly an institution that had been a part of his life and the life of his fellow white Virginians for many generations. After all, Washington himself had acquired his first slaves through an inheritance when he was eleven; if slave-holding was a sin, it had been passed onto him. But in time, after making other provisions to provide for the material comforts of his surviving children, George Washington freed his slaves just like Miss Watson had done, through a provision executed through his will after both he and his wife had died.[4]

Miss Watson's former slave would have had a hard time settling in the Midwest because an earlier generation of whites had opposed the arrival of former slaves like the ones who'd worked Mount Vernon. By the early nineteenth century, white residents in Indiana and Illinois were anxious that manumitted slaves would flood their respective states, especially in light of Ohio's new restrictions, and so each passed their own anti-immigration rules against free blacks. In 1813, settlers in southern Indiana counties petitioned the territorial government to prohibit the settlement of free blacks, and they passed their own local rules toward that end. They threatened violence along their borders, suggesting images of men with rifles to discourage the migration and settlement of African Americans. By 1829, the governor of Indiana proposed state-wide rules against the growth of a "Negro population": the historian Eugene Berwanger wrote that "because the neighboring states had passed or were considering laws to prevent their immigration, Indiana, in order to protect herself from becoming a dumping ground, must enact the same type of legislation."[5] Governor James Ray was right about what the other states intended to do: Illinois included immigration restrictions against freed blacks in its state constitution in 1848, Indiana itself did the same with its own constitution in 1851, and so did Oregon just four years before the Civil War.[6]

In all of these states, the legal status of African Americans mattered less than the fact that they were African Americans. In other words, states in the Midwest and in the Far West did not care whether they were legislating against African American slaves or free African Americans; they favored the exclusion of *all* African Americans, as if to avoid entirely the political questions of African American citizenship and status that had so vexed the entire nation.[7] Statewide restrictions were the result of popular elections: majority decisions exemplified hostility against African Americans throughout the frontier. It was as if, at the local level and in various states, white voters simply did not want racial pariahs from the north or slaves from the south to tarnish the communities that they were establishing in the newly acquired territories. In doing so, just as previous generations of Americans loathed both free blacks and African slaves, white men in the Far West were repeating a pattern of exclusion that had been common in nearly all of the "free" states of the early Republic.

Moreover, throughout the antebellum period, the political justifications for this hostility were most often rooted in recurring fears about what impoverished African Americans might do within the local communities where they would settle. In New Hampshire, for example, whites feared that "fugitive slaves would line the streets with their huts and burden the town with paupers and vagabonds."[8] Whites worried that, having nothing in their possession and fleeing the approach of slave-catchers, African Americans would pose significant social problems, and so whites legislated against the very possibility of fugitive slaves and free blacks within their towns and cities. These restrictions were only partly successful, however: African Americans *did* settle in East Coast cities, in cities in the Midwest, and throughout the frontier, albeit in uneven numbers. Under law, they were illegal migrants, although for them as well, the rules against their settlement proved easier to enact than to enforce. In time, as both free blacks and fugitive slaves continued to leave the South before the Civil War, despite the multitude of state and local prohibitions against their arrival, their communities would play an important role in the abolition of slavery itself when the War finally came.[9]

This was because African Americans, even the ones who'd been legally freed, were never quite free from the specter of slavery, and so it wasn't surprising that many fought and died to abolish the institution altogether. Whites in the North may have been confused about why they were fighting in the Civil War, but for all African Americans, it was about slavery, about how slavery could reduce them to commodities and how it caused insecurity and anxiety far from the states were it was legal, as the constant threat of being identified as a fugitive and of having to return to slavery was very real. In his history of free people of color, James Horton told the story of George Washington McQuerry, a slave who had escaped from Kentucky into Ohio in 1849, where he eventually married and established a family. "He and his family lived [in Miami County] for four years before his master, who had learned of his whereabouts, had him arrested by the federal marshal. Despite the attempts of Ohio blacks and abolitionists forces to prevent it, McQuerry was finally returned to slavery in Kentucky." McQuerry's story was not uncommon, as many fugitive slaves could live for many years outside the South believing that they were free, at least until their owners claimed otherwise. The letter of the law favored their "return." Many whites did not have to pay much attention to cases like these, but free blacks and fugitives alike saw in these instances stark reminders of how American legal institutions did not protect them, did not distinguish carefully who was or wasn't free, nor care what African Americans might have thought about their own status. So long as slavery survived, any African American could be dragged back into it, a fact that no African American could ignore.[10]

After 1850, when the Fugitive Slave Act gave Southern owners enormous powers to "reclaim" their property against state rules that in some cases worked to protect black citizens from being treated as slaves, it was even more abundantly clear that "no African American was safe from slavery."[11] Kidnappers who captured and sold freed blacks were a notorious threat to all African Americans, prompting many to move to Canada or to support colonization schemes outside the United States.[12] The Fugitive Slave Act gave whites huge structural incentives to abuse black citizens and make money in the process—if they were simply identified as slaves, African Americans were regarded as having no legal right to mount a defense, to testify on their own behalf, or to petition government institutions to protect their freedom. Slave catchers could thus convert free African Americans into chattel. Kidnapping—a problem for free blacks since the legalization of slavery—became an even more serious menace and a source of pervasive anxiety among all African Americans. Given that they had been rendered subject to this odd form of lawful lawlessness, leading black citizens and abolitionists recommended that free blacks arm themselves, that they regard all slave-catchers as "wild beasts," and that they protect one another from this collective threat to their community. In 1851, posters put up within major cities warned African Americans to be ever vigilant of ruthless slave-catchers.[13]

"The Chinese Must Go . . ."

In 1850, after the Mexican American War, even as the frontier became more open for whites, restrictions against free African Americans followed the American flag: Utah, Colorado, Texas, and New Mexico passed rules similar to the ones in the Ohio Valley. Many of these states also curtailed the civil rights of African Americans—they were typically not allowed to vote or testify in court against whites, and were subject to various forms of segregation. In California, where the Gold Rush accelerated the migration of people from all over the world, quickly making this one state the most populous and politically important place in the Far West, restrictionist sentiments took violent turns, and in ways few would have predicted in 1830. Like in other states, early white settlers in California had envisioned a "white man's republic" even before 1848, and demographically, they outnumbered Mexican citizens by a considerable margin long before Mexico and the United States went to war. "'We desire only a white population in California,'" said the editor of an early newspaper in that state, and "although he 'dearly loved' the Union and wanted California to be a part of it, he preferred complete independence from the United States unless Congress approved the prohibition of both slavery and 'free Blacks.'"[14]

California was admitted as a "free state" after the Mexican American War, but its leading citizens stood opposed to African American citizenship: by 1852, its legislature had passed its own version of the Fugitive Slave Act, mandating the capture and return of runaway slaves to their masters.[15] State officials made some African Americans into slaves; in 1857, for instance, the director of California's state prisons sent inmates to New Orleans to be sold into slavery. African Americans were constantly threatened with removal in this way. According to one historical account, "In March of 1858, the California legislature came close to passing a punitive anti-black immigration bill that would have required current black residents to carry registration papers and would have deported blacks who newly entered the state." In light of these debates, African Americans complained that the early white Californians were far worse in their prejudices than slaveholders in the Deep South.[16] Very few came to California: "Blacks . . . remained a very small population throughout the nineteenth century. Black immigrants numbered around 5,000 in 1860 and 1870 and climbed to just over 6,000 in 1880. The black population in the state would increase steadily after that date to over 11,000 at the turn of the century."[17]

For early white Californians, however, African American migrants turned out not to be the most serious threat to their "white man's republic." The Chinese took that position. Indeed, when Chinese migrants began arriving in California in ever greater numbers in the first decade after 1848, California became the place through which federal immigration law would rise to a new level, driven by concerns over a unique type of racial threat to the nation. The very motto of one of the state's most powerful labor unions summarized this sentiment succinctly: "The Chinese Must Go." Many Americans described the trans-Pacific arrival of Chinese immigrants as yet another kind of racial problem, a new and emergent threat to the nation, one that grew in the midst of the crisis of secession and then continued through the following decades. If slavery had led to the Civil War, some argued, what was the sense of allowing yet another racial pariah into the country? And the threat was of an entirely different magnitude: leading exclusionists noted that there were many more Chinese in the world compared to the "lovely white," and so even if a small fraction of the Chinese were to come to America, the trend would prove a national disaster, quickly. By 1855, over 20,000 Chinese migrants had come to California, having made a journey by sea on ever more reliable ships across thousands of miles. The subsequent political response greatly enhanced federal power, created new institutions to manage immigration admissions, and moved the United States toward becoming a "gatekeeping nation."[18]

About forty years ago, Asian immigration occupied, at most, a paragraph or two, perhaps just footnotes, in the great histories of American immigration. In recent decades, however, several outstanding historians have written at length about the origins of the Chinese Exclusion Acts and their impact on American public law and American culture, including Ronald Takaki, Sucheng Chan, Charles McClain, Lucy Salyer, Mae Ngai, Madeline Hsu, and Erika Lee, among several others. In these histories, what has been most interesting has been the discovery that a much greater fraction of Chinese immigrants were "illegal aliens" from the perspective of the new federal immigration laws that they'd inspired. Like the state rules that barred African Americans from migrating and settling in various states and towns, federal laws against the Chinese were only partly successful, as they were difficult to enforce and required constant adaptation.[19]

Federal immigration policies had to adapt because the Chinese used various strategies to get around the spirit of Chinese Exclusion. For example, the Act of 1882 and its subsequent revisions allowed merchants, students, and tourists—people not likely to be a public charge, persons staying temporarily in the United States, or both—to be admitted. When immigration officers excluded members of these exempt classes, the United States Supreme Court chastised them for being "overzealous." And so, many poor Chinese pretended to be merchants, students, and tourists. Among the more enterprising, there were Chinese men who claimed to be Cuban merchants or Mexican businessmen. This involved borrowing money for nicer clothing, practicing a certain demeanor, "passing" as a richer man, perhaps a few Spanish lessons. Immigration officials resorted to long detentions to ascertain why so many "merchants" were now coming from China. In response, members of the Chinese community "coached" prospective migrants, and then some developed other identities. American-born Chinese were American citizens, according to most prevailing interpretations of the Fourteenth Amendment, and the United States Supreme Court upheld this interpretation by a bare majority in *United States v. Wong Kim Ark* (1898). And so, thereafter, many Chinese pretended to be native-born American citizens and thus not subject to exclusion at all. There was no way that all of these claims could be true, however, as this would mean that every lawfully admitted Chinese woman would have had to bear hundreds of children.[20]

Indeed, a great many Chinese immigrants stayed in the United States through misrepresentations. One method became common: a "paper son" is a fictive relative, a man who typically bought the right to an American "father" who claimed him only for immigration purposes. As they were mostly not stupid, immigration officials interrogated Chinese migrants to sort through true kin from paper son; in response, the Chinese already in the United States "coached" prospective immigrants much more thoroughly. Frustrated, the officials then built a prison in San Francisco Bay, where the coaching would be more difficult because the "family members" could be kept apart. The Chinese adapted further: the historian Erika Lee shows us in her book the banana peels and hollowed peanut shells smuggled into "relatives" for long-distance coaching. Immigration detention could last longer than two years, and as the Chinese kept coming, the authorities had to build a cemetery for those who didn't survive on Angel Island. In the restored museum there today, we can see how some inmates had carved poems on the prison walls, most telling how badly it felt to be held there so close to the Gold Mountain. Yet in spite of such obstacles, most Chinese migrants succeeded in their ruses; only one in ten were sent back to China.[21]

And there were other ways to get to America. A great many Chinese entered without inspection. Many crossed the southern border; others came through Canada, through cities like Detroit, Michigan, and through towns in upstate New York, including Buffalo. Along this northern border, unlawful Chinese immigrants made for a kind of mirrored migration to that of fugitive slaves about five decades before: for fugitive slaves, Detroit, Michigan, was called "Midnight," and Windsor, Canada, the town on the other side of the bridge, was code-named "Dawn"; people operating the underground railroad made arrangements to cross at Midnight and meet at Dawn. For many Chinese immigrants, also migrating unlawfully, the sun just rose and set in the opposite direction. We have no idea how many made this crossing—because they came without inspection or were "paper sons," the large community of Chinese immigrants in the wake of Exclusion left few public records of their lives.

Ironically, the most obvious public records about this population were kept by the federal officials charged with excluding them in the first place— endless reams of interrogation records, birth and marriage certificates (often false), and written testimonials now sitting in boxes, catalogued by the National Archives at research libraries across the country. What we know now for certain was that a great many Chinese immigrants lived with untruths: most were not, indeed, related to the American citizens or lawful residents who had petitioned for family reunification; most were not merchants or students who had been exempt from federal exclusion; and by World War II, nearly all Chinese had a close "relative" or associate who had proffered elaborate lies to gain admission to the United States. Many Chinese Americans were born to illegal immigrant parents. These issues were spoken and not spoken among Chinese Americans themselves: in the ethnic Chinese newspapers, American immigration law and policy—including endless speculations about when, if ever, Chinese Exclusion would be repealed, or when, if ever, naturalization into American citizenship would be possible—was a constant, recurring preoccupation throughout the early twentieth century.[22]

In the wake of exclusion, the Chinese American community was supposed to "die off," but although the Chinese American community shrank and became marginalized, it did not die, and its survival did depend largely on the willingness of Chinese migrants to misrepresent who they were and thus to avoid those rules designed to eliminate that entire community. And it's here that we find instructive parallels: the rules designed to govern the Chinese were similar to the ones passed against free African American migrants and even fugitive slaves in the period before the Civil War; members of each community responded and adapted in ways that the other would have recognized; and the entire community was rendered vulnerable and prone to exploitation because of their precarious legal and political position. In the North, most free blacks knew someone who'd been a fugitive slave. Many had been fugitives themselves. Many more African Americans were free because their ancestors had run from slavery and had avoided capture. For many decades, the survival of free black communities depended on widespread evasions of the federal law.

"Driven out . . ."

Nevertheless, like the hostility against African Americans, Chinese Exclusion was a violent collection of local affairs directed against all Chinese people both long before and decades after it became a national issue. Hostility against the Chinese was a visceral thing in the gold fields and small towns of California, and recent accounts of how Chinese workers were "driven out" of early California communities remind us of just how intimate exclusion had been. In her account of the widespread, local hostility against the Chinese, Jean Pfaelzer noted two distinct methods through which whites tried to purge themselves of Chinese residents: through the "Eureka method," whites organized swift pogroms and threatened violence if the Chinese didn't leave; and through the "Truckee method," civic leaders deprived the Chinese of the necessities of life, slowly starving them and forcing their departure. "Everywhere the Chinese defied the violence, but with few exceptions, both the Eureka and Truckee methods worked."

Wherever the Chinese were recalcitrant, things devolved further: "Ultimately both methods turned to night raids and torchlight parades in the Chinese quarters. And when the Chinese refused to leave, the pogroms climaxed in apocalyptic violence and fire." In the early decades of their arrival in the United States, Chinese migrants were spread throughout the Far West, as they participated in mainstream economic activities, especially mining. In turn, they also participated in early farming in California, as well as commercial fishing, light manufacturing, and massive infrastructure projects, the most notable example being their participation in the construction of the transcontinental railway, as employees of Leland Stanford's Central Pacific

Railroad. After many years of persecution, however, Chinese Americans were segregated in urban Chinatowns, a residential pattern that was the result of sustained forms of ethnic cleansing committed against them across many towns and cities throughout the West. Public officials, vigilante groups, and local unions all collaborated to expel the Chinese during this period.[23]

Even after Exclusion, this problem persisted. In some places, it grew worse, as news spread that the Chinese were not wanted, that they would never become American citizens, and that a great many were in the United States illegally. Some of the most notorious massacres of the Chinese occurred after the Chinese Exclusion Act of 1882, and as the Chinese were forced to settle into the cramped quarters of San Francisco Chinatown, the city leaders there saw this trend as an occasion for even harsher public rules to discipline and punish the Chinese. When plague struck the Chinese quarter in 1901, for example, the mayor and supervisors did not blame racial discrimination or residential segregation throughout San Francisco, which caused severe overcrowding in Chinatown, nor the impoverishment of Chinese men due to intense discrimination against them in the state's economy. They blamed the Chinese, just as African Americans had been blamed for an outbreak of yellow fever in Philadelphia in 1793, as well as periodic outbreaks of the same disease in New Orleans through 1905.[24]

All the while, the Chinese in California and across the United States had to worry about immigration authorities, about being "discovered" as an unlawful immigrant and then being removed from the country. In 1896, the United States Supreme Court held that the power to deport an unlawful alien was the natural extension of the federal power to exclude undesirable aliens. The Court also upheld the power of federal officials to detain aliens suspected of being unlawful prior to their deportation.[25] Because of decisions like this one, Chinese immigrants had every incentive to avoid public officials at all times. In a number of instances, lawful Chinese immigrants and some American citizens were detained, and several were threatened with removal. In one infamous case, the Supreme Court supported the deportation of a Chinese man whom a lower federal court had determined to be an American citizen—Justice Oliver Wendell Holmes said that the lower court had taken this case improperly, against Congressional procedures designed to facilitate the removal of unlawful Chinese immigrants. That the man of Chinese ancestry was, in fact, held to be an American citizen by the lower federal court was immaterial, said Holmes, as the federal courts should be regarded as unavailable to such persons in the first place.[26]

In this way, Chinese Americans shared a sense of anxiety that many freed blacks and fugitive slaves would have recognized in the years before the abolition of slavery. American law defined both groups as being suspect, as being in an improper place given who they were, even if they happened to be American citizens. Local, state, and federal officials could detain and remove them, applying laws that gave few rights to members of either group and extensive powers to government officials to return or to deport these persons to their "proper" place—whether that meant back into slavery or back to China. Both African Americans and Asian Americans were not part of the utopian visions that so appealed to majorities of white Americans, even after the Civil War and the abolition of slavery. Unable to vote or to participate in politics directly, members of these racial groups lived with a constant fear of removal, the anxiety of knowing that the public laws so widely supported in state and federal politics did not protect them or their families, nor even recognize their basic rights and humanity.

Both people of color and white majorities participated in a vicious cycle, because when people of color resisted white supremacist rules, white citizens supported even harsher state and federal laws in efforts to overcome that resistance. Many African American slaves did run away, as they were unwilling to exist within the harsh confines of this peculiar institution. The Fugitive Slave Act of 1850 was perhaps the most grotesque federal law that attempted to resolve that problem. In the same way, many Chinese also came unlawfully to the United States. Federal officials had grounds to believe that a great many Chinese were violating the Exclusion laws and thus avoiding the will of the American people. They were, indeed, correct in their suspicions. But in response, Congress and the United States Supreme Court fashioned an immigration jurisprudence that warped American law entirely, moving it further from settled principles of government restraint, of judicial review, and of procedural fairness. And as American law grew harsher to account for the many forms of disobedience, the sense of anxiety also grew more severe among people subject to the law.

We all know now that given the choice of living with such anxiety or obeying the law, many people of color chose the former. We know as well that many people who had both unlawful and lawful status—including many white people—continued to facilitate multiple forms of resistance in spite of the federal and state rules, the summary procedures, the patrol and police officers, and the new prisons and jails all designed to coerce their obedience. We know all this in part because we celebrate at least once or twice every year the people who violated white supremacist rules rather than the others who'd embraced white supremacy. Whether it's during Black History Month or Asian Heritage Week, our elected leaders, our teachers, our professors, and many parents tell their children that American laws were once terrible, and that resistance to those wicked rules could be brave, correct, and just. The people who approved them were racist, we say, not like we are now. We are now a nation devoted to the rule of law, and it would be wonderful to believe this to be true, both during these events and after, too.

Ethnic Studies and the Rule of Law

That we are a nation governed by settled rules, by an independent judiciary, by core public institutions that check one another and that allow for the people governed by the law to shape it through elections and other forms of representation—these have all been essential aspects of a civil society devoted to the rule of law. The most important idea behind that fundamental concept has been that settled rules—rules that provide clear, stable, and prospective direction for human behavior, and rules that do not command the impossible—these should govern society, not individual men who command obedience through force and violence. Horrible governments have ruled *through* law, using rules in instrumental ways to persecute their political opponents, to structure oligarchic economic arrangements, and to otherwise pillage and murder and steal from the people under their control, people who have no say over who shall rule nor for how long nor under what terms.[27] In *Huckleberry Finn*, the Grangerfords and Shepherdsons, as well as the murderous Colonel Sherburn, represented this kind of lawlessness. They structured their own separate worlds closer to a state of predation, whether through custom or sheer will. In their worlds, the strong killed the weak, violence repeated in endless cycles, and men dictated harsh realities with guns and force.

When we consider our immigration rules in light of those collective aspirations to be, or at least to become, a society devoted to the rule of law, and to move away from a tragic history of authoritarian, violent, and unjust rules, the lessons of American ethnic studies are especially instructive. Those lessons are everywhere. When American have looked upon their past and have come to the conclusion that their laws were once unjust, that realization comes with a hope that our laws might now be just and fair to all who appear before our institutions. Americans have regretted the systemic reduction of African Americans into commodities, as well as the brutal abuse they suffered, not just at the hands of cruel white masters and overlords, but under legal institutions and rules that justified such suffering and allowed it to continue for generations and for centuries. While slavery existed, the rule of law was an empty and insane concept, if only because obedience to law reduced human beings to things and because law itself tolerated that "full dominion of the owner over the slave" so antithetical to our considered judgments about what justice requires. By demanding that slaves submit to the institution of slavery, law commanded the irrational and the impossible. Such laws should have been violated and breached at every conceivable opportunity, and that is why we believe that people like Harriet Tubman and Frederick Douglass were great American heroes worthy of celebration and praise.[28]

Immigration restrictions—whether based on racial otherness or a desire to keep out the poor and displaced throughout the world—have always been troublesome because they have reflected the exercises of national sovereignty in their rawest forms. When nation-states pass a law or build a fence or carve some corner of the earth for themselves for the sake of the people already there, we should consider the unnatural quality of such political actions. There is nothing natural about an international boundary, less so when it's been fortified with moats and fences and patrolled by plane and by car and by men and women with guns. In addition, when some people are simply given citizenship because they were born on one side of that boundary rather than another, citizenship itself loses all connection to justice or fairness. Citizenship assigned in such a way is about as fair as being born into slavery or into freedom during another era—a kind of lottery where considerations of justice did not exist nor made sense, and where a slave child (if he was light-skinned enough) and a free child (if he could pass as a light-skinned black child) could easily be switched without anyone noticing.[29]

One look at the international boundary between the United States and Mexico south of San Diego tells us that there is nothing intrinsically just or natural about the miles of walls and obstacles separating these two countries that are not at war—the boundary there is a passive yet powerful expression of force, it was designed to keep out people who don't belong and to say that they are unwelcome, and yet if it expressed the will of a majority of Americans, we can only observe that a majority of Americans did nothing exceptional to acquire their citizenship in the United States, which is the very thing that gives them that power to build such a hulking, monstrous thing. As Americans, we might also say with some confidence that the boundaries constructed there have obvious connections to portions of American history unworthy of any celebration. No one I respect looks fondly upon the Chinese Exclusion Act nor thinks of Japanese American internment as a great triumph nor embraces Pap Finn's attitudes toward black people, but when a sheriff in Arizona routinely asks Latino citizens if they have a right to be here, demanding to see their papers—never considering how or why he has that same right, nor carrying any papers of his own—he presents himself as a contemporary Colonel Sherburn, a thoughtless, violent, and dangerous man who cannot distinguish between force and law.[30]

We cannot expect such a man to acknowledge a truth: that the state of Arizona, like the rest of the United States, was born of violence and dispossession, was seized in fits of violence, and is now patrolled through violence. Yet to recover any possibility for the rule of law anywhere in the United States, Americans must begin with a thick, unwavering commitment to human dignity and equality above all else, a commitment to *see* the fundamental humanity of every person of every color on every side of every border. That so many Americans have done this throughout American history—even if they've faced contempt and violence for it—should give us hope, as they've shown how people on the margins of our society have often forced people in the middle to make moral judgments, to question their deepest convictions, and to do what their conscience demanded of them, even though that was not always what was legal. That is, in fact, the best lesson that Americans have to offer the world, that enduring commitment to see beyond the pariah status created and enforced through positive law. By acknowledging and insisting upon the dignity of the other in spite of and against rules that commanded otherwise, they have been "an inspiration to us all." This gift of sight has been a rare but precious form of empathy found throughout American culture and history, and the recognition of that gift remains the reason why we ought to celebrate people like Prudence Crandall and Mark Twain, Gordon Hirabayashi and Lee Paul Sieg, and Tam Tran and Cinthya Perez.

"Something there is that doesn't love a wall . . ."

The border between the United States and Mexico will not wither away because of moral approbations or a better reading of history, but perhaps in time, it will become a relic of sorts, like the Great Wall of China or Hadrian's Wall or the Berlin Wall, all consigned now to history. These other boundaries were used to keep out unwanted people in other times, but they are pointless now, as they sit as curious monumental structures once designed to define and prevent against threats that only historians can remember or explain. These walls did cause misery to people on both sides of them, and though they may have made some sense to build at one point or another, the builders of one may have suggested to the builders of the other that they really shouldn't have bothered. Of course, no one would have believed them: the people who built the Great Wall of China would have been shocked to learn that the "barbarians" would come in anyway and then assimilate so successfully into Chinese ways as to become almost indistinguishably Chinese, at least to someone who was British, the people who'd come to China by sea many centuries later. If you'd told the Roman builders that Hadrian's

Wall would be pointless in a few hundred years, that the people on the other side would help build an empire of their own far more vast than Rome, the Romans might have considered such a thing impossible. They would have built anyway, never imagining that the descendants of the savages on the other side would sail in ships in the opposite direction, to conquer and settle a continent no one in Europe could have imagined in the second century after Christ.[31]

And in our own time, even as the Berlin Wall fell and ever since it fell, it has been curious to see other walls go up, in Israel, in South Africa, and of course, in the United States. The one in the United States might be the most curious of all, as many scholars of immigration know that a great many people who are out of status originally got here by plane. Fugitive slaves ran on foot, sometimes on horses; the Chinese and other Asians came mostly by ship, first by sail and then by steam; *braceros* took trains and buses; nowadays, flying is cheap and fast, and getting cheaper and faster still as more people fly everywhere. On average, since 2003, the federal government recorded 170 million instances of people coming legally to the United States through various "non-immigrant" visas, including roughly 50 to 60 million tourists every year. Indeed, the revolution in global communication has made the United States one of the most popular tourist and business destinations in the world, just as the newest transportation technologies have put this country (and every other affluent country) within reach of many more people than ever before. The Americans were on the cutting edge of both revolutions—in communication and in transportation—and so it's not without some irony that these forces have remade the United States in ways that would have shocked the original American revolutionaries.

Some things are irreversible, though: a great many foreigners have come and will come here by plane, and although by law all are supposed to go back, if just half of one percent decide not to go back home and make this country their new home, and if the same fraction behave the same way for about ten or twenty years, it's not clear how a fence would make any sense at all. Even if those unlawful immigrants were adjusted to permanent residency through a general amnesty, the pattern repeating again in the next ten or twenty years would replicate the same troublesome population at about the same magnitude, and thus it would engender the need for yet another general amnesty. People incapable of understanding this simple math might get angry at the politicians twenty or forty years from now, but perhaps by then, they might figure out that fences were not an answer. In 2006, though, the senior Alabama Senator, Jeff Sessions, said in support of more fencing along the Southern border, "Good fences make good neighbors." It wasn't clear that he was quoting Robert Frost, but then again, even if he was, it was quite possible that he didn't understand the math or the poem at all.[32]

Avoiding *La Migra*

Over the past two decades, in many areas of the United States, Spanish-language radio has become ever more popular. In addition to programming that can feature Mexican, Central American, Cuban, and South American music, reflecting the great diversity of origins and tastes among Spanish-speaking Americans and immigrants, radio stations have also hosted call-in shows, where a doctor, a lawyer, a politician, or some other experts can field questions from listeners about a wide range of topics. As Dolores Ines Casillas has noted, however, "[I]t is clearly the billing of a guest immigration attorney that consistently attracts a high volume of caller participation." The anonymity of this medium—the attorney being a disembodied voice coming out of a box or a car stereo, the caller also participating by phone or on a cell, first name only—has led to frank and honest discussions about the callers' methods of entry, their length of "residency" in the United States, and what, if anything, can be done to help them become "legal," or at least avoid "*la migra*" and "deportation." An attorney can then explain that the United States doesn't "deport" people anymore, but it still does "remove" them, and that having an American relative or family members to support in the United States doesn't protect against this "removal," at least in nearly all circumstances. As the attorney attempts to explain some of the nuances and weirdness of American immigration law—the difference between "deportation" and "removal," for instance—their listeners have shared that sense of anxiety that comes from living a day-to-day existence outside the law itself.[33]

That anxiety has grown intense in recent years because of changes in federal law and policy. Indeed, many new laws and policies since 1992 revealed ongoing frustrations with the growth of illegal immigrant populations and a willingness to inflict the harshest of measures: there was Proposition 187 in California in 1994; then the whole battery of federal laws in 1996, including new rules encouraging local police to collaborate with immigration officials; which was then followed by 9/11 and the subsequent reorganization of federal immigration enforcement. The Immigration and Naturalization Service ceased to exist, but within the newly created Department of Homeland Security, the lead enforcement agency became Immigration and Customs Enforcement, or ICE, a colder, blunt description for "*la migra*." Federal policy makers approved even more new programs for ICE to collaborate with state and local law enforcement agencies, including rules like the REAL ID

Act of 2005 or the Secure Communities program in 2008. ICE has become a formidable federal agency: immigration detainees now account for the fastest growing population of people under federal incarceration, and "removal" happens more swiftly and more often than ever before. Under President Barack Obama, the federal government has "removed" about 400,000 persons every year since 2009, a rate that was more than twice as high as when President George W. Bush first took office, and about ten times the rate when President Bill Clinton won office. Deportation from the United States has created an entirely new and unconventional diaspora in recent decades.[34]

Many legislators in the United States have believed that all of this was still not enough, while others have felt that this was too much. Indeed, a new round of local and state rules passed since 2000 have required some local and state law enforcement officers to behave like immigration authorities, to hand over anyone "suspected" of being out of status. Other local rules have required all persons to prove legal residency before applying for any job, renting an apartment, or registering a child in a public school. But, as we've discussed in the last chapter, vulnerable immigrants and their advocates were also successful in persuading some states and local jurisdiction to approve rules to expand opportunities for some categories of unlawful people, especially students. In addition, some urban police departments and other local law enforcement agencies have declared that they will not cooperate with federal immigration authorities to remove people suspected only of immigration-related offenses. A clear majority of states and local governments have moved toward greater enforcement of federal immigration laws, but local resistance has been quite significant as well. To explain these trends, scholars of immigration law and policy have proposed concepts like "immigration federalism" to describe the overlapping, confusing, contradictory, "multi-layered jurisdictional patchwork" of local, state, and federal laws governing immigration in general and illegal immigrants in particular. Just between 2006 and 2008, state legislatures approved of over five hundred new pieces of legislation concerning immigration or illegal immigration, the vast majority designed to facilitate federal enforcement activities.[35]

In the midst of all this hostility, Spanish-language radio stations have reported *la migra* sightings at local intersections, companies, and schools, these warning sent to their listeners so that they might avoid immigration officials or any officials lurking around certain areas. This has become but one novel adaptation to a life out of status: "The *migra* alerts function as a subversive 'traffic report' for immigrants to avoid certain roads and highways in their commutes to work. . . . [Radio] shows help callers maneuver through their delicate routes toward citizenship, as *migra* alerts caution the listening public against deportation." The warnings have appeared sometimes in ways that mix humor and alarm: in central Texas, "*limones verdes*—or green limes— are sprouting near the highway, an announcer warns over the radio, using shorthand for the agents' green uniforms." For many years, the radio has told people in urgent bulletins to avoid the immigration checkpoints that pop up on Jimmy Carter Boulevard in Atlanta, the occasional raids at the laundromats and supermarkets in Escondido, California, or the possible sweeps at the popular flea markets in San Jose. Immigration officials never swept through the flea market in San Jose, but so many customers stayed away that one weekend that the businesses suffered anyway.[36]

The technologies through which communities of color in the United States have communicated with one another have changed since before the Civil War, through the turn of the last century, and now into this new one, but some of the most pressing messages have remained similar: watch for the authorities, be careful and take care of yourself, and be alert to public officials and others who might use the law to remove you. African Americans north of slavery got that message through posters and printed bills that they circulated to one another, as they cautioned all black people to "avoid conversing with the watchmen and police officers of Boston," as the Fugitive Slave Act of 1850 had turned them into "kidnappers and slave catchers." In San Francisco in 1904, the Chinese-language newspapers warned all Chinese immigrants to carry residency certificates at all times, because Chinese people in America were treated like dogs, and "the dogs must have with them [these] necklaces." Without residency certificates that could be produced on demand at the whim of any white officer, the Chinese "would be arrested as unregistered, unowned dogs and would be herded into a detention camp."[37] If African Americans in 1850 or Chinese Americans in 1904 had access to radios, their programs might have sounded the same as the ones coming from the Spanish-language media over the past twenty years.

It's sadder still to think in the opposite direction: if Jim could have had a cell phone, if cell reception was decent on a raft in the middle of the Mississippi River at night, and if he could have called an attorney to help him sort through what to do with himself, his family, and the white orphan boy travelling with him, we can only imagine what the well-meaning counselor on the other end might say. Perhaps Jim would not have bothered. Instead, maybe he would have called his wife and daughter, still on Miss Watson's farm. As a husband and father, Jim could have used this technology to convey messages of love and of longing similar to the ones sent every day by the many thousands of people now here in the United States, separated as well from their families through our own immigration rules.

Acknowledgments

L ike many authors who've worked on a project for years, I cannot say when exactly I got the idea for this book. Maybe it was when I re-read *Adventures of Huckleberry Finn* after meeting Shelley Fisher Fishkin in Austin in 2000, when she told me that *Huck Finn* was really about Jim. Or maybe it was when Douglas Daniels, my former Chair, advised me in 2005 to take risks in my academic work, as this was one of the great things about having tenure, and that I should try something different. Or maybe it was about a year after publishing the book with Ed in 2005, when we were talking in Santa Barbara about what to do next, and he said that my idea about *Huckleberry Finn* and illegal immigration was by far the most interesting. Always a font of advice, Ed explained *why* it would be a compelling project, and that was how he encouraged me in a Jedi mind trick kind of way to devote the next six years to this book. I should thank my own children for giving me ideas throughout that time: around 2008, Zoe learned about Harriet Tubman during Black History Month, and Isabel and Sophie were playing with Strawberry Shortcake and her friend, Huckleberry Pie. In their own way and without meaning to, my lovely daughters reminded me that the past was not even past.

I also gave public lectures during those years, and I was inspired by the interesting remarks from the (sometimes) kind audiences in Santa Barbara, Los Angeles, Boston, Amherst, and San Francisco. During the same time, always with my brother, I'd met with members of labor organizations, community groups, and legal advocacy centers who'd worked with undocumented people. In an era when fences, removal, and other boundaries were once again politically popular, I was inspired by so many professionals who'd devoted their entire lives to people living on the margins of American society. Even more inspiring were the men and women who fought for their basic rights together within these organizations, though they had no formal status in the United States.

As a professor, I've had sadder, more compelling forms of inspiration. On occasion, students across campus came to my office hours, the ones who'd heard that I had once worked in an immigration law firm and now taught a class on immigration law and policy. Maybe I could be trusted. These young people told me in solemn tones, as if they were confessing, that they were "illegal." Could I help them? Most of the time, I could not, at least not in the ways they'd hoped. But this book is an attempt to be helpful, maybe hopeful, too, if only by reassuring these young people that their predicament isn't a new one in American law and society, and that they themselves will have an important role in shaping our common history and future.

Over the past five years, many people have helped me think through the basic ideas presented here. I've shared portions with audiences at the annual conferences for the Association for Asian American Studies, the American Studies Association, and the Law and Society Association, as well as with audiences at the Harvard Law School, the UC Irvine School of Law, the American University College of Law, and several events hosted on my own campus. Mary Romero and Marie Provine were enthusiastic when this project was still forming, and Rick Su, Maria Santos, Neil Gotanda, Angela Harris, and Ofelia Cuevas assured me later that this project, as strange as it was, could work. At UCSB, Xiaojian Zhao, Diane Fujino, Melvin Oliver, Mary Nisbet, and Howard Winant were especially encouraging and supportive throughout, and I've been very fortunate to have these senior colleagues as mentors and friends. When the end was in sight, three outstanding research assistants, Rachel Jensen, Ariana Dumpis, and Stephanie Tran, located and discovered wonderful material—I hope they'll enjoy finding their work again in these pages.

My editor at Temple University Press, Janet Francendese, has been most awesome. Not every publisher was thrilled about a work that combined Mark Twain, illegal immigration, and comparative ethnic studies, but Janet embraced this project in all of its funkiness, and I'm grateful to her for getting this book into the world. Two anonymous reviewers for the Press conveyed important messages through Janet, and I hope they'll receive my gratitude as well. Other people read the manuscript in its entirety and offered helpful suggestions, including Ed (of course), Xiaojian, Diane, Howie, erin Ninh,

Steven Allaback, and Robert de Neufville. My two friends Phong Le and Ramie Dare recommended many changes to make the manuscript more accessible, and I'm so grateful for their attention and constant friendship. With great care, Peggy Gordon turned that manuscript into this book.

Finally, for giving me deadlines and then forgiving them, I'm thankful to my wife, Gowan. Books, learning, teaching, the yearning for a timeless wisdom on a page—these are amazing things, the best aspects of a scholarly life. She reminds me, though, that the best parts of life itself are family, home, the nurturing of plants and of trees, and the laughter of children, especially our children. Oh, it all sounds nice, but let's face it, for an obsessive academic, all of these things (including spouses) can be distracting, too, and they sometimes take a lot of work, and it's hard to write when these vexations have been laughing and goofing, often at my expense, while I've been trying to *think*. Yet I know that my life only works because Gowan keeps everything together, especially me, and because she's a good director. She achieves a finer balance—with her countless silken ties of love and thought, my dear wife persuades me of what it means to love and be loved and to pay attention every day to the passing of ephemeral things, those that are more beautiful because they are fleeting.

Notes

CHAPTER 2: RACE, LAW, AND PERSONHOOD IN *HUCKLEBERRY FINN*

1. As one might imagine, literary criticism about *Adventures of Huckleberry Finn* is voluminous. I've benefitted from several influential, book-length monographs: ROBINSON (1992), QUIRK (1995), ARAC (1997), CHADWICK-JOSHUA (1998), WIECK (2004), and MESSENT (2007). Excellent essay collections about the novel and about Twain include: NEW ESSAYS ON 'ADVENTURES OF HUCKLEBERRY FINN' (Louis Budd, ed., 1985); ONE HUNDRED YEARS OF 'HUCKLEBERRY FINN': THE BOY, HIS BOOK, AND AMERICAN CULTURE (Robert Sattelmeyer and J. Donald Crowley, eds., 1985); SATIRE OR EVASION? (1991); MARK TWAIN'S HUMOR (1993); MARK TWAIN: A COLLECTION OF CRITICAL ESSAYS (Eric Sundquist, ed., 1994); MARK TWAIN: TOM SAWYER AND HUCKLEBERRY FINN (Stuart Hutchinson, ed., 1999); and HUCK FINN (1990). My own reading of the novel has been heavily influenced by Professor Shelley Fisher Fishkin's work; see FISHKIN (1994) and FISHKIN (1998). All of these books, though, represent only a small sample of the many scholarly works about Mark Twain and *Adventures of Huckleberry Finn*.

2. Huck's awkward position in his society is a common theme. See, for example, the collection of essays in HUCK FINN (1990), especially the essays by Leslie Fiedler, Roy Pearce, and Harold Beaver.

3. Nearly every literary critic has noted the central place of Jim and Huck's relationship in the novel. See, for example, the discussions in ROBINSON (1992) and MESSENT (2007). A few critics have read the novel as a story primarily about Jim, as a kind of fugitive slave narrative; see, for example, the essays by Charles Nilon, Bernard Bell, and Betty Jones, in SATIRE OR EVASION? (1991), as well as Harold Beaver, *Run, Nigger, Run: 'Adventures of Huckleberry Finn' as a Fugitive Slave Narrative*, 8 J. AMER. STUD. 339 (1974).

4. TWAIN (2001), ch. 5. Throughout, I've relied on this University of California Press edition of Twain's novel, edited by Victor Fischer, Lin Salamo, Harriet Elinor Smith, and Walter Blair. For an interesting discussion of Huck and Pap, see: Harry Segal, *Life Without Father: The Role of the Paternal in the Opening Chapters of 'Huckleberry Finn,'* 27 J. AMER. STUD. 19 (1993). Pap wants Huck's money, and Huck got his money through the events described in Mark Twain's THE ADVENTURES OF TOM SAWYER, published in 1876. His gold was once the unlawful treasure of Injun Joe, the main villain of *Tom Sawyer* and the character who was buried alive near the end of that novel.

5. On this disturbing episode in the novel and its literary origins, see: Joseph Gardner, *Gaffer Hexam and Pap Finn*, 66 MOD. PHILOLOGY 155 (1968).

6. Slaves ran away for many reasons, but a great many escapes were precipitated by violence and were achieved violently; see, generally, FRANKLIN and SCHWENINGER (2000), especially chs. 3 and 4. Franklin and Schweninger's book, along with other scholarly works about slavery in recent years, shows that slavery was never the benevolent institution that Southerners readily claimed it was, but rather a perpetually violent relationship between master and slave, exemplified not by the happy, settled slave content with his master, but rather by the seething runaway who wanted to kill him. The methods of both Jim's escape and Huck's escape were typical of runaway slaves. See also: HERBERT APTHEKAR, AMERICAN NEGRO SLAVE REVOLTS (1937, 1993); STAMPP (1989); and GENOVESE (1976). Jim and Huck differ in the asymmetry of their reasons: Jim runs to avoid being separated from his family, Huck to avoid being "reunited" with his father.

7. Huck and Jim meet on Jackson's Island in chapter 8. Three essays that attempt to explain how Huck might consider his "duty" to report Jim are very helpful: Jonathan Bennett, *The Conscience of Huckleberry Finn*, 49 PHIL. 123 (1974); Laurel Bollinger, *Say It, Jim: The Morality of Connection in 'Adventures of Huckleberry Finn,'* 29 COLL. LIT. 32 (2002); and Nomy Arpaly, *Moral Worth*, 99 J. PHIL. 223 (2002). In each of these pieces, the authors wonder, as we do, whether Huck has the intellectual capacity—as an uneducated boy—to make a fully informed moral choice, whether he is able to grasp Jim's humanity or the morality of slavery, and in a way to give context to his moral decision-making. This uncertainty can't be good for Jim, as he must at once depend on this boy and yet live with the possibility that the boy might turn at any moment. This first exchange between Huck and Jim underscores the anxiety: Huck can't understand why Jim, as a slave, must hide rather than eat.

8. The Grangerfords and Shepherdsons appear in chapters 17 and 18. For a discussion of this section, as well as an interpretation of Twain's attitudes toward codes of honor, duels, and unending violence, see: Arthur Pettit, *Mark Twain, the Blood-Feud, and the South*, 4 SO. LIT. J. 20 (1971); and Dale Billingsley, *'Standard Authors' in 'Huckleberry Finn,'* 9 J. NARRAT. TECH. 126 (1979). Billingsley notes that "Grangerford" suggests a family of farmers, the descendants of Cain, and "Shepherdson" suggests a family of herders, the descendants of Abel. Whether the members of the families realize this or not, Twain's names imply a murderous family feud that has primeval origins, perhaps woven into humanity itself.

9. This theme is a recurring one in legal theory, especially theories that attempt to explain the concept of the rule of law. For helpful discussions about the rule of law, see: TAMANAHA (2004) and BINGHAM (2011). Again, the theme is ancient, as all of

these authors have pointed out. We will return to this same theme toward the conclusion of this work.

10. Sherburn murders Boggs in chapter 21. For a discussion of Arkansas as the wildest portion of the South in Twain's novel, see Elmo Howell, *Mark Twain's Arkansas*, 29 Ak. Hist. Quart. 195 (1970). Sherburn appears as a perverted, Nietzschean superman, an Ubermensch, beyond good and evil. To some scholars, the Grangerfords, the Sheperdsons, Sherburn, and Pap are "isolated grotesques" in the novel, characters that are not quite central to its overall narrative structure. For this, see: Martin Shockley, *The Structure of Huckleberry Finn*, 20 So. Cent. Bull. 3 (1960); and Jonathan Arac, *Nationalism, Hypercanonization, and Huckleberry Finn*, 19 Boundary 2 14 (1992). The phrase "isolated grotesques" appears in Arac, on 32. Other scholars, however, have argued that law, lawlessness, and rule by men instead of law represent, collectively, one of the most important themes in the work, and these episodes are connected by that theme. I agree with this view, and for that alternative perspective, I relied on Robinson (1992), 144–150, and on these two essays: Leo Levy, *Society and Conscience in Huckleberry Finn*, 18 Nineteenth Cent. Fict. 383 (1964); and Walter Blair, *The French Revolution and 'Huckleberry Finn,'* 55 Mod. Philology 21 (1957).

11. Fugitive slave rules receive a great deal of attention in Franklin and Schweninger (2000), but for other instructive discussions of fugitive slave rules before and after the Revolution, see: Allen Johnson, *The Constitutionality of the Fugitive Slave Acts*, 31 Yale L. J. 161 (1921); Lorenzo Greene, *Slave-Holding New England and Its Awakening*, 13 J. Negro Hist. 492 (1928); and Reuel Schiller, *Conflicting Obligations: Slave Law and the Late Ante-Bellum North Carolina Supreme Court*, 78 Va. L. Rev. 1207 (1992).

12. Again, for Jim's precarious dependence on Huck, see: Beaver, supra note 3; and Bennett, supra note 7. Among professional philosophers and ethicists, the character of Huck Finn has become a textbook case of a person who does the right thing for emotional, empathetic reasons, even though he thinks the opposite intellectually. See, for example, Chad Kleist, *Huck Finn and the Inverse Akratic: Empathy and Justice*, 12 Ethical Theo. & Moral Prac. 257 (2009). Few of these philosophers, though, have dwelt very long on the anxieties that Huck's stunted ethical calculations might have had on Jim.

13. Discussions about the significance of this moment in chapter 11 appear in Chadwick-Joshua (1998) and Robinson (1992), as well as more directly in David Burg, *Another View of Huckleberry Finn*, 29 Nineteenth Cent. Fict. 299 (1974).

14. This episode appears in chapter 13. Huck remains oddly sympathetic to white people, no matter how awful they might be—he sees white people as suffering beings, and yet constantly has trouble seeing the same thing about black people or empathizing with black people. For a discussion of this curious tendency, see: Gregg Camfield, *Sentimental Liberalism and the Problem of Race in Huckleberry Finn*, 46 Nineteenth Cent. Fict. 96 (1991). Camfield's essay suggests that Twain's wider audience has since had a similar problem—they tend to sentimentalize Huck, Tom, even Jim, without *seeing* slavery, Jim's suffering, or the plight of fugitive slaves more generally as central themes in Twain's novel. For a full treatment of this theme, see Fishkin (1998).

15. This episode appears in chapter 16.

16. Again, this is a critical moment in chapter 16, and several scholars have pointed to this episode where Twain pays close attention to Jim's humanity, and the

author himself has trouble dealing with it. For a helpful discussion that points to other scholarly work about Jim, his family, and Huck's reaction in this portion of the novel, see: Gene Jarrett, *'This Expression Shall Not Be Changed': Irrelevant Episodes, Jim's Humanity Revisited, and Retracing Mark Twain's Evasion in 'Adventures of Huckleberry Finn,'* 35 AMER. LIT. REALISM 1 (2002). Toni Morrison's Introduction in THE OXFORD MARK TWAIN (Shelley Fisher Fishkin, ed., 1996) is also an interesting take on fatherhood in Twain's novel, and what it meant for Huck, for Jim, and for Twain himself.

17. On Jim's willingness and ability to sway the boy, see: Bernard Bell, *Twain's 'Nigger' Jim: The Tragic Face Behind the Minstrel Mask*, and Betty Jones, *Huck and Jim: A Reconsideration*, both in SATIRE OR EVASION? (1991), as well as Beaver, supra note 3.

18. For a discussion of Huck's repeated "failures" to do the "right" thing by turning Jim in, see Bennett, supra note 7.

19. Again, more than a few scholars have suggested that Twain had problems figuring out what to do about Jim and his freedom. For more, as it pertains to this section of the novel, see: Richard Gollin and Rita Gollin, *Huckleberry Finn and the Time of Evasion*, 9 MOD. LANG. STUD. 5 (1979); Leo Marx, *Mr. Eliot, Mr. Trilling, and Huckleberry Finn*, in A CASE STUDY IN CRITICAL CONTROVERSY (Gerald Graff and James Phelan, eds., 1995); Christine Macleod, *Telling the Truth in a Tight Place: Huckleberry Finn and the Reconstruction Era*, 34 SO. QUART. 5 (1995); and Henry Wonham, *'I Want a Real Coon': Mark Twain and Late Nineteenth Century Ethnic Caricature*, 72 AMER. LIT. 117 (2000).

20. See ROBINSON (1992), part II. The ideas there also appear here: Forrest Robinson, *The Characterization of Jim in Huckleberry Finn*, 43 NINETEENTH CENT. LIT. 361 (1988), and in relation to James Cox, *A Hard Book to Take*, in ONE HUNDRED YEARS, supra note 1. For discussions about how the ending of the novel might represent an artistic or some other kind of "failure," as even Ernest Hemingway had once suggested, see: Robert Ornstein, *The Ending of Huckleberry Finn*, 74 MOD. LANG. NOTES 698 (1959); Chadwick Hansen, *The Character of Jim and the Ending of 'Huckleberry Finn,'* 5 MASS. REV. (1963); and Bollinger, supra note 7. Several critics have said that Twain did not take Jim's plight seriously, that Twain says nothing about what might happen to Jim after he realizes he's been emancipated—will he reunite with his family, for example, or where will he go? That Twain doesn't address these issues, coupled with Jim's general passivity in the final chapters, could suggest that Twain didn't really care about black people, or at least didn't know what to do with his black characters. For this, see Julius Lester's essay in SATIRE OR EVASION? (1991).

21. Many scholars note that Tom is an extremely unlikeable character in *Adventures of Huckleberry Finn*, while mostly a clever and wily one in *The Adventures of Tom Sawyer*. In his private letters, Twain himself reveals a souring toward Tom—the little trickster in that earlier novel ties up Jim, then hatches this horrible plan to free a freed man in *Huckleberry Finn*, endangering himself and Jim in the process. Tom in *Huckleberry Finn* is a super creepy character, immature in the most dangerous and cruel ways, a "creature of delusion." For a sample of this discussion, see: Judith Fetterley, *Disenchantment: Tom Sawyer in Huckleberry Finn*, 87 PMLA 69 (1972). "Creature of delusion" appears there on 70, and a sampling of Twain's letters about Tom appears on 69.

22. Scholars have dwelled at length about what exactly Huck (and Twain) meant when he described Jim as "white inside." Having been with Jim for the entire journey

and having witnessed his humanity at every turn, Huck seems still incapable of seeing Jim as a noble, admirable *black* man. Goodness and virtue are so intertwined in Huck's mind with "whiteness" that he must somehow convert Jim into white in order to *see* him as a good man. That Jim remains, in that sense, an "invisible man," a man that white people cannot see as a fully human and virtuous being, is sad indeed, and it's a point made poignantly in Ralph Ellison's essay discussing the novel; see: ELLISON (1995).

23. That Jim manipulates Huck isn't universally acknowledged among literary critics, but it's a recurring theme in Twain scholarship. For an argument that Jim does control Huck for his own purposes, see: Susan Derwin, *Impossible Commands: Reading Adventures of Huckleberry Finn*, 47 NINETEENTH CENT. LIT. 437 (1993). As for the fate of the two main characters, one worries that Huck will get killed in a Cormac McCarthy novel. As for Jim, we return to a discussion of his migration possibilities at the end of this book.

CHAPTER 3: SLAVERY AND WAGE SLAVERY

1. The statement is from President Lincoln's Second Inaugural Address (Mar. 4, 1865).

2. Consider the remarks of John Millar, Professor of Law at the University of Glasgow, in 1774: It is a "curious spectacle" that those "who talk in so high a strain of political liberty, and . . . the unalienable rights of mankind, should make no scruple of reducing a great proportion of the inhabitants into circumstances by which they are not only deprived of property, but almost of every right whatsoever." Millar is quoted in Peter Dorsey, *To 'Corroborate Our Own Claims': Public Positioning and the Slavery Metaphor in Revolutionary America*, 55 AMER. QUART. 353 (2003), on 363. American leaders, including George Washington, were fond of the slavery metaphor to explain how their English king was reducing them to subservience. For American conceptions of freedom and their relationship to conceptions of slavery during the colonial period, especially in Washington's home state of Virginia, see: MORGAN (2003). For a similar discussion of how early Americans dealt with the same themes in the North in the eighteenth century, see: LEPORE (2006). In her discussion of the fires in Manhattan in 1741, Lepore's history explores how many Northerners wished for the end of slavery not because they saw Africans as morally and politically equal to whites, but because they favored a society free of black people. In the middle of the seventeenth century, about twenty percent of the population of New York was enslaved. For influential scholarly works about the economics of slavery and its role in American economic history, both internally in the South and across the nation, see: FOGEL AND ENGERMAN (1995), WRIGHT (1978), and EINHORN (2008).

3. For lengthy arguments that slavery was a national institution, see: BERLIN (2000), FEHRENBACHER AND MCAFEE (2002), KOLCHIN (2003), DAVIS (2008), and VAN CLEVE (2010).

4. WAHL (1998), on 65. On 58–59, Wahl writes: "when slaveowners and employers did not plan for a contingency, judges generally placed liability on the party who could have most cheaply foreseen or prevented the loss. Employers were not to be imprudent or cruel in their treatment of slaves, nor were they to employ slaves with-

out masters' permission. . . . In contrast, legal rules governing nineteenth century free labor markets were more one-sided. Employees of the 1800s rarely succeeded in proving their employers were negligent. If they did succeed, employers usually avoided paying damages by using one of the three defenses: contributory negligence, assumption of risk, or the fellow-servant rule. . . . Southern courts typically held negligent employers of slaves liable for injuries."

5. Id. Wahl notes: "To the extent legal rules protecting slaves led to better workplace safety, of course, free workers may have benefited indirectly if employers hired both free and slave workers." About slave cases serving as precedents after slavery, see Wahl, on 66: "Adult workers who won lawsuits that charged their employers with negligence sometimes used slave cases to buttress their arguments. Over two decades after the Civil War ended, Missouri courts for the first time held defendants responsible for falling items that injured employees—just as in slave case *Biles v. Holmes*—but only if the employer had known about the problem or failed to cover mining cars as required by statute. In 1907, a North Carolina court relied on slave case *Allison v. R.R.* to require employers to furnish safe appliances and careful workers." *Biles v. Holmes* concerned a slave injured when iron drills fell on him while he was in a gold mine pit; *Allison v. R.R.* concerned an employer who had stored an open powder keg under a slave's bed without telling him.

6. For immigration figures, see: BRIGGS (2001), on 18. For a thorough discussion of the "invention" of white privilege among working class whites, see: ROEDIGER (2006), JACOBSON (1999), and ROEDIGER (2007). The topic is vast, but for accessible, notable histories of European immigration into the United States from the late 18th to the early 20th centuries, see: HIGHAM (1984), HIGHAM (2002), and OSCAR HANDLIN, THE UPROOTED (1973, 2002).

7. See FONER (1995). In the preface, on xviii, by way of summary, Foner writes: "The metaphor of wage slavery (or, in New England, its first cousin, 'factory slavery') drew on immediate grievances, such as low wages, irregular employment, the elaborate and arbitrary work rules of the early factories, and the inadequacy of contract theory to describe the actual workings of the labor market. But at its heart lay a critique of economic dependence. Workers, wrote one labor leader, 'do not complain of wage slavery solely on account of the poverty it occasions. . . . They oppose it because it holds the laboring classes in a state of abject dependence upon capitalists.' In perhaps the most influential statement of the 'wage slavery' argument, Orestes Brownson [the noted New England activist and labor organizer from New York] described wages as 'a cunning device of the devil for the benefit of tender consciences who would retain all the advantages of the slave system without the expense, trouble, and odium of being slaveholders.'" For an account of how wage slavery and slavery shaped life in the upper South, see ROCKMAN (2008).

8. See, for example, Frank Carlton, *The Workingmen's Party of New York City, 1829–1831*, POLI. SCI. QUART. (1907); Arthur Darling, *The Workingmen's Party in Massachusetts, 1833–1834*, AMER. HIST. REV. (1923); and Edward Pessen, *The Workingmen's Movement of the Jacksonian Era*, MI. VALLEY HIST. REV. (1956). For a study of the gendered and religious dimensions of the early labor movement in New England, see: TERESA MURPHY, TEN HOURS' LABOR (1992).

9. James Polk remains a controversial figure, though he is not the most well-known among American presidents and certainly not the most celebrated nineteenth-

century American. Two biographers have explored the way Polk made Westward expansion a key part of his presidency: WALTER BORNEMAN, POLK: THE MAN WHO TRANSFORMED THE PRESIDENCY AND AMERICA (2009); and MERRY (2009).

10. The phrase "republic of suffering," is from FAUST (2009). Faust's history contains an extensive bibliography of scholarly works about the Civil War, but for more general histories, see: FOOTE (1986); JAMES MCPHERSON, BATTLE CRY OF FREEDOM: THE CIVIL WAR ERA (2003); and DAVID GOLDFIELD, AMERICA AFLAME: HOW THE CIVIL WAR CREATED A NATION (2011). I also relied on three books that dealt with the culture of violence associated with the war, its origins, and its aftermath, all by BRUCE CATTON: THE COMING FURY (1961), THE TERRIBLE SWIFT SWORD (1963), and NEVER CALL RETREAT (1965). For accessible, scholarly accounts about the fate of Native Americans in the nineteenth century, see: BROOKS (2001); BROWN (2007); HAMALAINEN (2009); and JEFFREY OSTLER, THE LAKOTAS AND THE BLACK HILLS: THE STRUGGLE FOR SACRED GROUND (2010). For a study of how European Americans at once sympathized with Native Americans, even as they victimized them, see LAURA MIELKE, MOVING ENCOUNTERS: SYMPATHY AND THE INDIAN QUESTION (2008).

11. The history of Mexican Americans in the Southwest is quite varied by state; the territory is vast, and some of the more outstanding contributions to late nineteenth- and early twentieth-century Mexican American history in that region would include: MONTEJANO (1987), GUTIERREZ (1991), ALMAGUER (2008), GUTIERREZ (1995), FOLEY (1999), MEEKS (2007), and GOMEZ (2008).

12. I'm very grateful to Mary Lou Eichhorn for telling me about this pamphlet when I was visiting the Williams Research Center in New Orleans in May 2011. The Bailly-Blanchard pamphlet is part of the permanent archival collection, catalogued as *Remarks on the Chinese and Coolies*, R.Pam.RD4875.U5R4 (1854). The most notable Bailly-Blanchard with those first initials, "Th," in 1854 was a Theodore Bailly-Blanchard, Jr., the father of Arthur Bailly-Blanchard, the Ambassador to Haiti from 1914 to 1921. In the New Orleans City Directory in 1876, Theodore Bailly-Blanchard is listed as the Administrator of Police. Bailly-Blanchard's remarks about the suitability of the Chinese are on page 3, his remarks about the cost of slaves compared to the cost of Chinese workers appears on page 12, and the model labor contract is on pages 14 and 15. The emphasis concerning the "DEATH OF EACH NEGRO" is in the original.

13. JUNG (2008), on 37.

14. Id., on 196.

15. In recent decades, many scholars have written about Chinese immigration to the United States. The most influential studies include: SAXTON (1975), SALYER (1995), and LEE (2007). For general histories of Asian Americans since the mid-nineteenth century, see: CHAN (1991), OKIHIRO (1994), and TAKAKI (1998).

16. Leland Stanford, Governor of California, Inaugural Address (Jan. 10, 1862).

17. Letter from Stanford to President Johnson and Secretary of the Interior James Harlan, quoted in NORMAN TUTOROW, THE GOVERNOR (2004), on 248.

18. KWONG and MISCEVIC (2007), on 54. For general background on the Chinese, see: TAKAKI (1998), chs. 2 and 3. For a discussion of the Central Pacific and its workers, see: Cheryl Cole, *Chinese Exclusion*, 57 CAL. HIST. 14–15 (1978).

19. Id., on 55. Kwong and Miscevic observed: "The railway company had clearly been handling the Chinese in a fashion closer to the treatment of black slaves than to the management of free labor, giving substance to white labor's claim that the Chinese

were unfree coolies." Stanford appointed Edwin Crocker, Charles' brother and former legal counsel to the Central Pacific, to the California Supreme Court in 1863.

20. See TUTOROW, supra note 17, 247. See also CHANG (2003), especially ch. 5.

21. For scholarly accounts of the political movement represented by the Workingmen's Party, see: Ralph Kauer, *The Workingmen's Party of California*, 13 PAC. HIST. REV. 278 (1944); Daniel Cornford, *To Save the Republic: The California Workingmen's Party in Humboldt County*, 66 CAL. HIST. 130 (1987); and Eric Fong and William Markham, *Anti-Chinese Politics in California in the 1870s*, 45 SOC. PERSPECT. 183 (2002). For accounts of their electoral success, see: NEIL SHUMSKY, THE EVOLUTION OF POLITICAL PROTEST AND THE WORKINGMEN'S PARTY OF CALIFORNIA (1991); Judson Grenier, *'Officialdom': California State Government, 1849–1879*, 81 CAL. HIST. 137 (2003); and Shirley Moore, *'We Feel the Want of Protection': The Politics of Law and Race in California, 1848–1878*, 81 CAL. HIST. 96 (2003).

22. For early California state rules against the Chinese, see TAKAKI (1998), ch. 3; CHAN (1991), chs. 2 and 3; BAIN (2000), ch. 16; and PARK (2004), ch. 4. For the Workingmen's Party and other white exclusionists and their impact on the California constitution specifically, see: *The Workingmen's Party of California, 1877–1882*, 55 CAL. HIST. QUART. 58 (1976); Cole, supra note 18; and Grenier, supra note 21. The federal case striking down Article XIX was *In re Tiburcio Parrott*, 1 F. 481 (Cir. Ct., D. Cal., 1880). Parrott had been "imprisoned for an alleged violation of the act of the legislature of this state, approved February 13, 1880." That act provided for fines ranging from $100 to $1,000 for hiring a Chinese worker; subsequent "offenses" could triggers fines of $500 to $5,000, as well as jail terms for 200 days to up to two years.

23. The United States Constitution listed in Article I, Section 9, a specific limit on the power of Congress: "The Migration or Importation of such Persons as any of the States now existing shall think proper to admit, shall not be prohibited by the Congress prior to the Year one thousand eight hundred and eight, but a tax or duty may be imposed on such Importation, not exceeding ten dollars for each Person." During his presidency, in 1807, Thomas Jefferson supported restrictions on the further importation of slaves for reasons that are complicated—despite the fact that he had owned over 200 slaves, Jefferson thought the institution of slavery repulsive. The Act Prohibiting Importation of Slaves went into effect on January 1, 1808. His critics noted that although the Act seemed anti-slavery, Jefferson made no further moves to ban slavery, and the Act had the effect of increasing the price of slaves by limiting their supply, which no doubt benefitted people like Jefferson himself. Every biographer of Jefferson (at least in recent decades) has dealt with his complicated attitudes toward race and slavery. See, for example, ELLIS (1998); R. B. BERNSTEIN, THOMAS JEFFERSON (2005); and HAYES (2008). About the original constitutional provision concerning slave importation, the Act of 1807, and the market for slaves in the late 18th and early 19th centuries, see: HERBERT GUTMAN, THE BLACK FAMILY IN SLAVERY AND FREEDOM, 1750–1925 (1976); BRENDA STEVENSON, LIFE IN BLACK AND WHITE: FAMILY AND COMMUNITY IN THE SLAVE SOUTH (1996); and DEYLE (2006).

24. For Stanford's own comments about the Chinese in 1868–1870, see: Alexander Saxton, *The Army of Canton in the High Sierra*, 35 PAC. HIST. REV. 141 (1966), on 144 and 151. The man talking about "comingled blood" was Judge Nathaniel Bennett, quoted in Saxton, on 152.

25. For more about the ceremony and about the significance of the final spike, see: J. N. Bowman, *Driving the Last Spike: At Promontory, 1869*, 36 CAL. HIST. SOC. QUART. 263 (1957); THE GOLDEN SPIKE (David Miller, ed., 1973); and JOHN WIL-LIAMS, A GREAT AND SHINING ROAD: THE EPIC STORY OF THE TRANSCONTINENTAL RAILROAD (1988). These accounts tell us that Chinese workers probably drove the last spike, and so it's odd that they didn't appear in any of the more popular portraits of the event.

26. The first quote from Stanford is from RICHARD STREET, BEASTS OF THE FIELD: A NARRATIVE HISTORY OF CALIFORNIA FARMWORKERS, 1769–1913 (2004), on 357. Street points to a sensational case involving the murder of a white woman by a Chinese man during this period, in that region; this case inflamed white men against Chinese laborers, and led to many acts of violence and lynching against the Chinese in Tehama County. For a discussion of Chinese laborers on Stanford's farm in Palo Alto, see Cecilia Tsu, *'Independent of the Unskilled Chinaman': Race, Labor, and Family Farming in California's Santa Clara Valley*, 37 WEST. HIST. QUART. 474 (2006). According to Tsu, Stanford was not at all "independent" of Chinese workers—he and his wife relied on them to run his farm.

27. Stanford's change in opinion is recorded in GEORGE CLARK, LELAND STANFORD (1931), on 453–454.

28. For Jane Stanford's employment of Mock and King, see Tsu, supra note 26, 487–490.

29. Grover Cleveland Inaugural Address (Mar. 4, 1885).

30. Samuel Gompers, *Meat v. Rice* (1902), reprinted in DOCUMENTS OF AMERICAN PREJUDICE 438 (S. T. Joshi, ed., 1999).

31. Janice Fine and Daniel Tichenor, *A Movement Wrestling*, 23 STUD. AMER. POL. DEV. 84 (2009). About the Chinese and the Knights of Labor, see 92–93. Fine and Tichenor rely on TERENCE POWDERLY, THIRTY YEARS OF LABOR—1859–1889 (1967), and PHILIP FONER, HISTORY OF THE LABOR MOVEMENT IN THE UNITED STATES, vol. 2 (1955). In their own essay, Fine and Tichenor argue against Briggs' earlier work (supra note 6) that claimed, in essence, that organized labor tended always to be restrictionist. Fine and Tichenor argue for a more nuanced position, saying that labor leaders fiercely debated immigration law and policy, and that the restrictionists didn't always win. They identify four factors that help to explain organized labor's position with respect to immigration law and policy: the fluid structure of the labor market, aggregate immigration trends, racial and nativist sentiments against foreigners, and the state's disposition toward organized labor.

32. See, generally, CHAN (1991), ch. 2.

33. The quote is from Fine and Tichenor, supra note 31, 94. For scholarly accounts of labor movements in Hawaii, see RONALD TAKAKI, PAU HANA: PLANTATION LABOR AND LIFE IN HAWAII, 1835–1920 (1983); OKIHIRO (1992); and JUNG (2010). For more about labor unions and immigration restrictions, see HIGHAM (2002).

34. HONEY (2002). The quote is on 43.

35. Id., 46–47. The phrase, "nigger unionism," and the discussion about proposals for interracial labor unions, appears on 83–84. For discussions of African Americans in the workforce and in the labor movement during the first half of the twentieth century, see: DAVID BERNSTEIN, ONLY ONE PLACE OF REDRESS: AFRICAN

AMERICANS, LABOR REGULATIONS, AND THE COURTS FROM RECONSTRUCTION TO THE NEW DEAL (2000); ARNESEN (2002); and JONES (2009).

36. The phrase, "worse than slavery," is a quote from, and the title for, David Oshinsky's study of the penal system in late nineteenth- and early twentieth-century Mississippi. OSHINSKY (1997). Another work, DOUGLAS BLACKMON, SLAVERY BY ANOTHER NAME: THE RE-ENSLAVEMENT OF BLACK AMERICANS FROM THE CIVIL WAR TO WORLD WAR II (2009), deals with the same topic. For vagrancy laws in general, see: Caleb Foote, *Vagrancy-Type Law and Its Administration*, 104 U. PENN. L. REV. 603 (1956). For vagrancy laws in the South, as part of a broader system of involuntary servitude, see: William Cohen, *Negro Involuntary Servitude in the South, 1865–1940*, 42 J. SOUTH. HIST. 31 (1976); Haywood Burns, *Black People and the Tyranny of American Law*, 407 ANN. AMER. ACAD. POLI. & SOC. SCI. 156 (1973); Terrell Shofner, *The Legacy of Racial Slavery: Free Enterprise and Forced Labor in Florida in the 1940s*, 47 J. SOUTH. HIST. 414 (1981); and LITWACK (1980), especially chs. 6 and 8. The federal government was itself complicit in the move toward involuntary servitude, as LITWACK noted, on 408: "When the postwar southern legislatures adopted measures to compel blacks to contract with an employer or face arrests as vagrants, they had merely written into law what the Union Army and the Freedmen's Bureau had already demanded of freed slaves."

37. CHARLES LUMPKINS, AMERICAN POGROM: THE EAST ST. LOUIS RACE RIOT AND BLACK POLITICS (2008); MALCOLM MCLAUGHLIN, POWER, COMMUNITY, AND RACIAL KILLING IN EAST ST. LOUIS (2005); and ELLIOTT RUDWICK, RACE RIOT AT EAST ST. LOUIS, JULY 2, 1917 (1982). The three scholars differ in their interpretations of the origins and consequences of this riot, as well as the effectiveness of "militant" black organizing before and after the event. For a proximate account of the riot, see: Oscar Leonard, *The East St. Louis Pogrom*, SURVEY (Jul. 14, 1917), and for the relationship between this event and the Civil Rights Movement of the latter half of the twentieth century, see HARPER BARNES, THE 1917 RACE RIOT THAT SPARKED THE CIVIL RIGHTS MOVEMENT (2008).

38. WILKERSON (2011), on 271.

39. Id., on 316.

40. David Roediger, *What If Labor Were Not White and Male? Recentering Working-Class History and Reconstructing the Debate in the Unions and Race*, 51 INT. LABOR & WORKING-CLASS HIST. 72, on 73 (1997).

41. For histories of the Pullman porters and their part in the American labor movement, see: BATES (2000) and ARNESEN (2002). For a brief sketch of the town of Pullman, see Richard Schneirov, *'To the Ragged Edge of Anarchy': The 1894 Pullman Boycott*, 13 OAH MAG. HIST. 26 (1999); and Janice Reiff, *Rethinking Pullman: Urban Space and Working-Class Activism*, 24 SOC. SCI. HIST. 7 (2000). For the origins of the company town, Beth Bates, in her book, on 42, wrote: "[George Pullman] believed that capital and labor must cooperate for their mutual benefit, that the task of the employer was to improve employee morale by alleviating the squalor of city life and introducing workers to the advantages of reading rooms, libraries, and concert halls. Behind his devotion to improving his workers' lives was both concern for maximum profits and minimum labor problems as well as an obsession with order and control, concerns that also contributed to his passionate antiunion position. Perhaps most important was making his employees feel they were members of one large, happy fam-

ily, without strife or conflict." To mollify black workers, and to maintain an image of benevolence toward African Americans in general, the Company also contributed to the YMCA in South Chicago, to local hospitals that served African Americans, and to leading African American churches and pastors.

42. Janice Reiff and Susan Hirsch, *Pullman and Its Public: Image and Aim in Making and Interpreting History*, 11 Pub. Hist. 99, on 102 (1989). Reiff and Hirsch continued: "When racial barriers left so few jobs available for black men, that combination of perquisites gave the jobs and the men occupying them an element of prestige."

43. For a discussion of the background for, and litigation following, this strike, see David Ray Papke, The Pullman Case: The Clash of Labor and Capital in Industrial America (1999).

44. For a discussion of Filipinos in Chicago, see Barbara Posadas, *Teaching About Chicago's Filipino Americans*, 10 OAH Mag. Hist. 38 (1996), and Barbara Posadas and Roland Guyotte, *Unintentional Immigrants: Chicago's Filipino Foreign Students Become Settlers, 1900–1941*, 9 J. Amer. Ethn. Hist. 26 (1990). Posada's discussion of Filipinos with the Pullman Company is in *Teaching*, on 39. For general histories of the United States and the Philippines, see: Stanley Karnow, In Our Image: America's Empire in the Philippines (1990); Kramer (2006); and Go (2008).

45. Randolph's remarks were published in March 1926 in *The Messenger*, a publication he had founded with Chandler Owen to support organizations like the Brotherhood. His remarks are reprinted in Posadas, *Teaching*, supra note 44, 43.

46. The quote is from Arneson (2002), 135. For more on the Brotherhood and its relationship to mainstream, white labor unions, see: Preston Valien, *The Brotherhood of Sleeping Car Porters*, 1 Phylon 224 (1940); Alexa Henderson, *FEPC and the Southern Railway Case: An Investigation into the Discriminatory Practices of Railroads During World War II*, 61 J. Negro Hist. 173 (1976); and Yvette Richards, *African and African American Labor Leaders in the Struggle over International Affiliation*, 31 Int. J. African Hist. Stud. 301 (1998).

47. Tydings is quoted in Takaki (1998), 331–332. Many Asian Americanists have emphasized the racist underpinnings of the Tydings-McDuffie Act, while other historians have emphasized also the desire of Congress to free itself from the financial burden of supporting the Philippines as an American territory during the Great Depression, as well as the desire of Filipinos themselves for independence. See, for example, Karnow, supra note 44, on 254–256.

48. For scholarly discussions of Filipino migrations to the United States during this period, see: E. San Juan, From Exile to Diaspora: Versions of the Filipino Experience in the United States (1998); and Rick Baldoz, The Third Asiatic Invasion: Empire and Migration in Filipino America, 1898–1946 (2011).

CHAPTER 4: ILLEGAL WORKERS

1. This period of local, state, and federal legislation over the market has inspired countless scholarly works across a range of disciplines. Of the many, many titles I've relied upon, these provide more analysis of the legal doctrines and political forces that shaped that era: Forbath (1991); Gillman (1992); Stanley (1998); and Wiecek (2001).

2. For two very different accounts of *Lochner*, see: PAUL KENS, *LOCHNER V. NEW YORK*: ECONOMIC REGULATION ON TRIAL (1998); and DAVID BERNSTEIN, REHABIL-ITATING *LOCHNER*: DEFENDING INDIVIDUAL RIGHTS AGAINST PROGRESSIVE REFORM (2011). The quote from Holmes is from *Lochner v. New York*, 198 U.S. 45, on 75 (1905).

3. FRIEDMAN (2005). On 506, Friedman wrote: "The states were too feeble to stamp out the saloon; they were too feeble to control the airwaves, or the railroads, or to stop the trusts, or to uplift the quality of food products made in one state and sold in all the others. Moreover, because the country was a gigantic free trade area, because there were no border guards, custom officials, and inspections, at state lines; and because a factory could relocate at will from one place to another, the states in a real sense competed with each other." Unless a state statute protected women, "the weaker sex," from excessive hours of work, or similarly limited the hours of work for men in "dangerous" occupations like smelting iron or working within a mine, state regula-tions were in danger of being rendered unconstitutional. *Coppage v. Kansas* appears in 236 U.S. 1 (1915); the most influential scholarly discussion of yellow-dog contracts is SEIDMAN (1932).

4. For influential histories of this period, on Europe, see: MARK MAZOWER, DARK CONTINENT: EUROPE'S TWENTIETH CENTURY (2000); RICHARD EVANS, THE COMING OF THE THIRD REICH (2005); and TIMOTHY SNYDER, BLOODLANDS: EUROPE BETWEEN HITLER AND STALIN (2010). For histories of Asia, especially the period of Japanese imperialism, see: RAMON MYERS AND MARK PEATTIE, THE JAPANESE COLO-NIAL EMPIRE, 1895–1945 (1987); W. G. BEASLEY, JAPANESE IMPERIALISM, 1894–1945 (1991); and JOHN TOLAND, THE RISING SUN: THE DECLINE AND FALL OF THE JAPA-NESE EMPIRE, 1936–1945 (2003).

5. For historical accounts of the New Deal and Franklin Roosevelt, see: COHEN (2008); WILLIAM LEUCHTENBERG, FRANKLIN D. ROOSEVELT AND THE NEW DEAL, 1932–1940 (2009); and BRANDS (2009).

6. For scholarly discussions of how labor unions helped to shape New Deal leg-islation that reworked American labor relations, see: COHEN (2008), LICHTENSTEIN (2003), and FANTASIA AND VOSS (2004).

7. That bargaining collectively, between public employee unions and government agencies, and then between workers in private industries and corporations, could lead to better outcomes than state regulation remained one of the most important insights in New Deal legislation and jurisprudence. On this point, see: MICHAEL YATES, WHY UNIONS MATTER (1998); SLATER (2004); and CUSHMAN (1998). On the Fair Labor Standards Act, see: Suzanne Mettler, *Federalism, Gender, and the Fair Labor Stan-dards Act of 1938*, 26 POLITY 635 (1994); Robert Fleck, *Democratic Opposition to the Fair Labor Standards Act of 1938*, 62 J. ECON. HIST. 25 (2002); and Malcolm Davis-son, *Coverage of the Fair Labor Standards Act*, 41 MICH. L. REV. 1060 (1943). Met-tler discusses the gendered dimensions of the rule—certain forms of "male" labor were counted as work and regulated by federal law, while "women's work" wasn't counted nor protected. For a discussion of state rules that were the predecessors to the Act of 1938, see Louise Stitt, *State Fair Labor Standards Legislation*, 6 L. & CONT. PROB. 454 (1939).

8. These quotes from John Lewis are taken from KENNEDY (1999), on 299, where Kennedy argues that Lewis and Roosevelt both came to view the National Labor Rela-tions Act as a political compromise to help workers increase their "purchasing power"

while disciplining more radical, communist elements of the labor movement during the Great Depression.

9. In addition, massive infusions of public money, into everything from interstate highways to public schools and universities, led to a dramatic increase in the standard of living in the United States, a trend that began even before the end of World War II. See, for instance, COHEN (2003).

10. For histories of postwar American foreign and domestic policies, see: COHEN (2003); JAMES PATTERSON, GRAND EXPECTATIONS: THE UNITED STATES, 1945–1974 (1997); GADDIS (2000); and WESTAD (2007). After 1946, American labor unions moved aggressively to bargain for better wages and working conditions from private corporations and to include health care, retirement programs, and pension plans in labor negotiations. Some labor unions offered pension programs to their own members, vastly increasing the attractiveness of joining these unions. For more about these struggles, see: JAMES ZETKA, MILITANCY, MARKET DYNAMICS, AND WORKPLACE AUTHORITY: THE STRUGGLE OVER LABOR PROCESS OUTCOMES IN THE U.S. AUTOMOBILE INDUSTRY, 1946–1973 (1995); ZIEGER (1986); ROSENBERG (2003); and IRVING RICHTER AND DAVID MONTGOMERY, LABOR'S STRUGGLES, 1945–1950: A PARTICIPANT'S VIEW (2003). For an insightful analysis of labor movements in several countries in the postwar period, see BRUCE WESTERN, BETWEEN CLASS AND MARKET (1999).

11. See, for example, RONALD TAKAKI, DOUBLE VICTORY: A MULTICULTURAL HISTORY OF AMERICA IN WORLD WAR II (2000); and FRYMER (2007).

12. For discussions of African American migrations during the war and federal policies designed to lessen racial discrimination in wartime industries, see: BITTER FRUIT: AFRICAN AMERICAN WOMEN IN WORLD WAR II (Maureen Honey, ed., 1999); KRYDER (2001); and TROTTER AND DAY (2010). On Japanese Americans during the war, see: DANIELS (2004), KASHIMA (2004), and ROBINSON (2009).

13. Leading accounts of the Bracero Program include: GALARZA (1964), CALAVITA (1992), and GAMBOA (2000). For an interesting historical reinterpretation of the Bracero Program, see COHEN (2011).

14. CALAVITA (1992), 18.

15. See, Kelly Lytle Hernandez, *The Crimes and Consequences of Illegal Immigration: A Cross-Border Examination of Operation Wetback*, 37 WEST. HIST. QUART. 421 (2006). On 423–424, Hernandez writes: "The administrative restriction rendered legal labor migration of Mexican workers to the United States virtually impossible, because U.S. law prohibited offering contracts to foreign laborers before they entered the United States. For poorer Mexicans, therefore, labor migration to the United States was often a crime south of the border just as their inability to pay U.S. fees and/or pass literacy exams often forced them to surreptitiously cross the border in violation of U.S. immigration law." For a discussion of why both the revolutionaries and industrialists wanted Mexican workers to remain in their own country, see Hernandez, 424–425.

16. For a discussion of how the Mexican state and the American state originally conceived the program, see COHEN (2011).

17. On federal labor policy before, during, and immediately after World War II, see: William Rice, *The Law of the National War Labor Board*, 9 L. & CONT. PROB. 470 (1942); Richard Cortner, *Liberals, Conservatives, and Labor*, 344 ANN. AMER. ACAD. POL. & SOC. SCI. 44 (1962); Julian Zelizer, *The Forgotten Legacy of the New Deal: Fiscal Conservatism and the Roosevelt Administration*, 1933–1938, 30 PRES. STUD.

QUART. 331 (2000); and William Collins, *Race, Roosevelt, and Wartime Production: Fair Employment in World War II Labor Markets*, 91 AMER. ECON. REV. 272 (2001). For a succinct discussion of the strikes that represented a kind of disintegration of the three-way cooperative relationship between business, government, and labor during the war, see CHUN (2009), ch. 2.

18. On the McCarran-Walter Act of 1952, see: Robert Alexander, *A Defense of the McCarran-Walter Act*, 21 L. & CONT. PROB. 382 (1956); and John Higham, *American Immigration Policy in Historical Perspective*, 21 L. & CONT. PROB. 213 (1956). For an explanation for why the McCarran-Walter Act is so important, especially from an historical context, see: TICHENOR (2002) and NGAI (2005). For interesting biographies of Pat McCarran, including an account of his role in the communist scares of the 1950s and his attacks against prominent labor leaders, see JEROME EDWARDS, PAT MCCARRAN: POLITICAL BOSS OF NEVADA (1982), and MICHAEL YBARRA, WASHINGTON GONE CRAZY: SENATOR PAT MCCARRAN AND THE GREAT AMERICAN COMMUNIST HUNT (2004).

19. On the Congressional debates about the harboring provisions of the Act of 1952, see: Eisha Jain, *Immigration Enforcement and Harboring Doctrine*, 24 GEO. IMMIGR. L. J. 147 (2010). The harboring provisions are most similar, however, to the Internal Security Act of 1950. For a discussion, see H. B. Kirshen, *The Internal Security Act of 1950*, 37 BULL. AMER. ASSO. UNIV. PROF. 260 (1951). Agricultural producers often complained that they could not tell the difference between legitimate *braceros* and illegal aliens. Many scholars have been skeptical about such claims, arguing instead that the growers themselves added to their own confusion. Consider this passage from COHEN (2011), on 29: "Paralleling the bracero program's regulated labor stream was a growth in undocumented workers, many of them former *braceros* who knew how to maneuver in the United States. Employers who viewed bracero paperwork as a burden and wanted to retain the men they identified as good workers often encouraged such former *braceros* to return unofficially. In 1952, the U.S. Congress pressed to tackle rising unauthorized migration, passed the McCarran-Walter Immigration Act, making it a felony to harbor undocumented workers, although the bill did not institute penalties for employing them."

20. See: *Wetbacks: Can the States Act to Curb Illegal Entry?* 6 STAN. L. REV. 287, on 288 (1954). As racist as it may sound now, the article was mild in comparison with other popular accounts of "wetbacks." For a discussion of those accounts, see GARCIA (1980).

21. Ellwyn Stoddard, *Illegal Mexican Labor in the Borderlands: Institutionalized Support for an Unlawful Practice*, 19 PAC. SOC. REV. 175 (1976).

22. For a discussion of enforcement actions leading up to Operation Wetback, see Hernandez, supra note 15, and GARCIA (1980). Hernandez's scholarly work on the history of the border patrol, including this period, is also in HERNANDEZ (2010).

23. Hernandez, supra note 15, 429–432.

24. Hector Garcia's letter to Senator Lyndon Johnson is from October 20, 1950, and the quote is taken from Michelle Hall Kells, *Questions of Race, Caste, and Citizenship: Hector P. Garcia, Lyndon B. Johnson, and the Polemics of the Bracero Immigrant Labor Program*, in WHO BELONGS IN AMERICA? PRESIDENTS, RHETORIC, AND IMMIGRATION (Vanessa Beasley, ed., 2006), on 188. Of Garcia's motives, Kells writes, on 189: "[Garcia] believed that a fixed and impermeable border was possible and neces-

sary. Moreover, Garcia failed to see that the United States' economic pull of Mexican nationals across the border was even stronger than the forces pushing them from their homeland. From his perspective as a physician treating a poverty-ridden migrant population, the influx of desperate immigrants competing for the same scarce resources appeared to be the primary aggravating source of his people's suffering. Taking a pathologist's point of view, Garcia envisioned the *bracero* program and the 'wetback invasion' as a social disease."

25. The quotes are from Kells, supra note 24, on 193 and 195.

26. Cesar Chavez is quoted in LEVY (2007), on 128–129.

27. Id., on 129–130.

28. Id., on 130. Chavez knew very well that the *braceros* were exploited and abused, not just by local growers, but by the entire system that the federal government had supported to bring the *braceros* to the fields: "Not only did they pay *braceros* cheap wages, about seventy-five cents an hour, but they brought in three times as many as they needed and worked them every third day. Since all of the *braceros* had to pay board, whether they were working or not, and pay insurance and cigarettes and other things, whether they were working or not, some people became millionaires just from providing food and insurance or other things for them. But the *braceros* were poor when they came, and they were poor when they went back. It was a vicious racket of the grossest order."

29. Id., 142.

30. Philip Martin, *Mexican Workers and U.S. Agriculture: A Revolving Door*, 36 INT. MIG. REV. 1124 (2002), on 1130: "The major issue that would affect farm worker immigration and integration in the early 1980s was what to do about illegal immigration. The unauthorized share of the farm work force was estimated to be about 25 percent in California (and much lower elsewhere in the U.S.) but farmers opposed the Grand Bargain of employer sanctions to stop illegal immigration, and amnesty for unauthorized foreigners that was recommended by the Select Commission on Immigration and Refugee Policy in 1981. Farmers, fearing a loss of unauthorized farm workers, showed that they could block this Grand Bargain in Congress unless they were assured a replacement supply of legal guest workers."

31. For a discussion of this difficult moment in the history of the United Farm Workers, see SHAW (2008), especially 194–198. The quote is from SHAW, on 195. For more on Chavez's initial approach to illegal immigrants, especially when they were used as strikebreakers in the agricultural labor market, see: RICHARD GRISWOLD DEL CASTILLO AND RICHARD GARCIA, CESAR CHAVEZ: A TRIUMPH OF SPIRIT (1995), on 157–160.

32. The quote is from Todd Holmes, *The Economic Roots of Reaganism: Corporate Conservatives, Political Economy, and the United Farm Workers Movement, 1965–1970*, 41 WEST. HIST. QUART. 55, on 57 (2010).

33. See SHAW (2008), 196–199.

34. COHEN (2011), 24.

35. For scholarly discussions about emigration from Mexico, see: Arthur Corwin, *Mexican Emigration History, 1900–1970: Literature and Research*, 8 LATIN AMER. RES. REV. 3 (1973); Douglas Massey and Emilio Parrado, *Migradollars: The Remittances and Savings of Mexican Migrants to the USA*, 13 POP. RES. & POL. REV. 3 (1994); Dennis Conway and Jeffrey Cohen, *Consequences of Migration and Remittances for Mexican*

Transnational Communities, 74 Econ. Geogr. 26 (1998); Yossi Shain, *The Mexican-American Diaspora's Impact on Mexico*, 114 Pol. Sci. Quart. 661 (1999–2000); Jeffrey Cohen, *Transnational Migration to Rural Oaxaca, Mexico: Dependency, Development, and the Household*, 103 Amer. Anthro. 954 (2001); and Delano (2011).

36. See Cohen (2011), on 142: "On rare occasions when men did submit complaints against growers, a principal, though not the only, remedy available to [Mexican] bureaucrats was sending the offending *braceros* back to Mexico. Instead of pressuring growers to honor the letter and spirit of the agreement, administrators too often applied pressure on workers to either back down or return home."

37. For histories of Western agriculture, especially those that focus on the ideological and racial logic of growers in the region, see: McWilliams (2000); Camille Guerin-Gonzalez, Mexican Workers and the American Dream: Immigration, Repatriation, and California Farm Labor, 1900–1939 (1994); Foley (1999); Richard Walker, The Conquest of Bread: 150 Years of Agribusiness in California (2004); and Katherine Benton-Cohen, Borderline Americans: Racial Division and Labor War in Arizona Borderlands (2011).

38. For a thorough discussion of how organized labor leaders felt about and argued over the Bracero Program, see Calavita (1992), chs. 4 and 5. The quote is on 79. For a more similar discussion, beyond the agricultural sector, see Delgado (1994).

39. Wilbur Finch, *The Immigration Reform and Control Act of 1986: A Preliminary Assessment*, 64 Soc. Sci. Rev. 244 (1990). The figures for immigrants apprehended appear on 248.

40. 424 U.S. 351 (1976). The California rule is quoted on 352. For Ronald Reagan's position on this rule in particular, see: Thomas Maddux, *Ronald Reagan and the Task Force on Immigration, 1981*, 74 Pac. Hist. Rev. 195 (2005). On 204, Maddux quotes Reagan: "By cracking down on those employers who knowingly engage in the hiring of illegal aliens, this legislation can help to improve job opportunities for thousands of legitimate California residents."

41. Austin Fragomen, *Supreme Court Rules that States Can Prohibit Unauthorized Employment by Aliens*, 10 Int. Mig. Rev. 253 (1976).

42. Id., on 356–357. Brennan continued: "Employment of illegal aliens in times of high unemployment deprives citizens and legally admitted aliens of jobs; acceptance by illegal aliens of jobs on substandard terms as to wages and working conditions can seriously depress wage scales and working conditions of citizens and legally admitted aliens; and employment of illegal aliens under such conditions can diminish the effectiveness of labor unions. These local problems are particularly acute in California in light of the significant influx into that State of illegal aliens from neighboring Mexico."

43. *NLRB v. Apollo Tire Co.*, 604 F.2d 1180 (9th Cir. 1979).

44. Id., on 1184.

45. The appellate case, from the Seventh Circuit, appears as *NLRB v. Sure-Tan Inc.*, 672 F.2d 592 (1982).

46. *Sure-Tan Inc. v. NLRB*, 467 U.S. on 895 (1984).

47. Id., Justice Powell dissenting, on 913. The phrase "retaliatory reporting" comes from Richard Marks, *Retaliatory Reporting of Illegal Alien Employees: Remedying the Labor-Immigration Conflict*, 80 Colum. L. Rev. 1296 (1980).

48. The Duke and the King first appear in chapter 19, and they are tarred and feathered at the end of chapter 33. I've borrowed the phrase from Norris Yates, *The 'Counter-Conversion' of Huckleberry Finn*, 32 AMER. LIT. 1 (1960). The amorality of Jim's sale fits within a larger theme in Stephanie Le Menager, *Floating Capital: The Trouble with Whiteness on Twain's Mississippi*, 71 ELH 405 (2004), where she argues that the novel is fundamentally a "profound, post-national critique of white mobility on the Western frontier." Slaves like Jim are at once valuable as commodities, but slavery itself as an institution is difficult to value, almost impossible to account for in the face of something like emancipation. The idea is that whites will do or sell anything to get ahead—this is the most troubling theme that Twain explored in his novel, especially at this point where Huck *experiences* his friend reduced to a commodity.

CHAPTER 5: IMMIGRANT ACTIVISM IN THE SHADOW OF LAW

1. There has been a great deal of legal commentary about *Sure-Tan*, its predecessor cases, and its subsequent impact. Some excellent pieces include: Peter Schuck, *Taking Immigration Federalism Seriously*, 2007 U. CHI. LEGAL F. 57; Keith Cunningham-Parmeter, *Fear of Discovery: Immigrant Workers and the Fifth Amendment*, 41 CORNELL INT'L. L. J. 27 (2008); and Stephen Lee, *Private Immigration Screening in the Workplace*, 61 STAN. L. REV. 1103 (2009).

2. Some of these studies would include: VERNON BRIGGS, MEXICAN MIGRATION AND THE U.S. LABOR MARKET (1975); Charles Keely, *The Problem of Illegal Aliens in the United States*, 5 POP. & DEV. REV. 357 (1979); Barry Chiswick, *Illegal Aliens in the United States Labor Market: Analysis of Occupational Attainment and Earnings*, 18 INT. MIG. REV. 714 (1984); Sidney Weintraub, *Illegal Immigrants in Texas: Impact on Social Services and Related Considerations*, 18 INT. MIG. REV. 733 (1984); Jean Baldwin Grossman, *Illegal Immigrants and Domestic Employment*, 37 IND. & LABOR REL. REV. 2450 (1984); Thomas Bailey, *The Influence of Legal Status on the Labor Market Impact of Immigration*, 19 INT. MIG. REV. 220 (1985); and JEFFREY PASSEL, IMMIGRATION TO THE UNITED STATES (1986). For economic histories of the postwar period, see PATTERSON (1997) and COHEN (2003).

3. *Local 512 v. NLRB*, 795 F.2d 705 (9th Cir. 1986).

4. Id., the quotes are on paragraphs 5 and 44.

5. For additional background on the Immigration Reform and Control Act of 1986, see: Alan Simpson, *The Politics of Immigration Reform*, 18 INT. MIG. REV. 486 (1984); Philip Martin, *Harvest of Confusion: Immigration Reform and California Agriculture*, 24 INT. MIG. REV. 69 (1990); Daniel Tichenor, *The Politics of Immigration Reform in the United States, 1981–1990*, 26 POLITY 333 (1994); GIMPEL AND EDWARDS (1999); and Thomas Maddux, *Ronald Reagan and the Task Force on Immigration, 1981*, 74 PAC. HIST. REV. 195 (2005). Attorney General Edwin Meese's testimony and Althea Simmons' testimony representing the NAACP appear separately in *Immigration Control and Legalization Amendments: Hearings on H.R. 3080 Before the Subcommittee on Immigration, Refugees and International Law of the House Committee on the Judiciary*, 99th Cong., Session 4 (1985). Consider this passage, from Shannon Gleeson, *From Rights to Claims: The Role of Civil Society in Making Rights Real for Vulnerable Workers*, 43 L. & SOC'Y REV. 669 (2009), on 672–673: "Discrimination, in particular based on national origin, was a prominent concern amongst legislators and advocates following

the imposition of employer sanctions under the Immigration Reform and Control Act of 1986. Many feared that employers would make assumptions about workers' immigrant status in efforts to avoid violating the law. Consequently, the federal government dedicated specific resources to monitor such situations by establishing the Office of Special Counsel for Immigration-Related Unfair Employment Practices at the U.S. Department of Justice, which was charged with ensuring that employer sanctions did not unfairly impact immigrant-origin workers and did not accelerate the exploitation of undocumented workers."

6. See Simpson, supra note 5.

7. Arthur Corwin, *The Numbers Game: Estimates of Illegal Aliens in the United States, 1970–1981*, 45 L. & CONT. PROB. 223 (1982).

8. On border enforcement since 1990, see: ANDREAS (2009); NEVINS (2001); MASSEY, DURAND, AND MALONE (2002); and HERNANDEZ (2010). For a review of immigration law between 1986 and 2000, see PARK AND PARK (2005) and NEWTON (2008). For estimates of the population of illegal immigrants after 2000, see: Jeffrey Passel, *Unauthorized Migrants: Numbers and Characteristics* (Pew Hispanic Center, 2005), and Michael Hoffer and Christopher Campbell, *Estimates of the Unauthorized Immigrant Population Residing in the United States* (United States Department of Homeland Security, Office of Immigration Statistics, 2006).

9. Kitty Calavita, *Employer Sanctions Violations: Toward a Dialectical Model of White-Collar Crime*, 24 L. & SOC. REV. 1041, on 1042 (1990).

10. Maddux, supra note 5, 204.

11. See, for example, *Collins Foods International v. INS*, 948 F.2d 549 (9th Cir. 1991). Here, a federal appeals court held that an employer who'd offered employment by phone to an employee who'd had a fake Social Security card—one that could have easily been determined to be fake—still did not have "constructive knowledge" that the employee was out of status; consequently, the employer should not be liable for violating the employer sanction rule.

12. For a review of the debate around why employer sanctions failed to deter illegal immigration, see: UNDOCUMENTED MIGRATION TO THE UNITED STATES (Frank Bean et al., eds., 1990); U.S.-MEXICO RELATIONS: LABOR MARKET INTERDEPENDENCE (Jorge Bustamante et al., eds., 1992); HANS JOHNSON, UNDOCUMENTED IMMIGRATION TO CALIFORNIA, 1980–1993 (1996); Cynthia Bansak and Steven Raphael, *Immigration Reform and the Earnings of Latino Workers: Do Employer Sanctions Cause Discrimination?* 54 IND. & LABOR REL. REV. 275 (2001); and Gordon Hanson, *Illegal Migration from Mexico to the United States*, 44 J. ECON. LIT. 869 (2006). The quote about the field survey is in J. Edward Taylor and Dawn Thilmany, *Worker Turnover, Farm Labor Contractors, and IRCA's Impact on the California Farm Labor Market*, 75 AMER. J. AGRI. ECON. 350 (1993), on 359.

13. On this point, see: Pia Orrenius and Madeline Zavodny, *The Effects of Tougher Enforcement on the Job Prospects of Recent Latin American Immigrants*, 28 J. POL. ANALY. & MANAGE. 239 (2009).

14. *Montero v. INS*, 124 F.3d 381 (2d. Cir. 1997). For more about this particular form of retaliatory reporting, see: Michael Wishnie, *Emerging Issues for Undocumented Workers*, 6 U. PA. J. LAB. & EMP. L. 497 (2004).

15. Lori Nessel, *Undocumented Immigrants in the Workplace*, 36 HARV. C.R.-C.L. L. REV. 345 (2001).

16. *Montero*, 124 F.3d on 382.

17. Id., on 385.

18. Id., at 384 and 385.

19. *Del Rey Tortilleria Inc. v. NLRB*, 976 F.2d 1115 (7th Cir. 1992). For a specific discussion of this case, see John Barmon, *The Seventh Circuit Explains Why There Is No Harm in Exploiting Undocumented Workers: Del Rey Tortilleria, Inc. v. NLRB, 976 F.2d 1115 (7th Cir. 1992)*, 24 U. Miami Inter-Amer. L. Rev. 567 (1993).

20. *Hoffman Plastics v. NLRB*, 535 U.S. 137, on 140 (2002).

21. The description of Jose Castro's job is on 140, as well as from an earlier manifestation of the case in the federal appellate court, *Hoffman Plastic Compounds v. NLRB*, 208 F.3d 229 (2000), on 232. The sentence about Hoffman's attorney and Castro's status is also on 208 F.3d 232.

22. Judge Tatel's opinion cited the following cases: *NLRB v. Kolkka*, 170 F.3d 937 (9th Cir. 1999), holding that under the NLRA, an employer may not refuse to negotiate with a union even when some of the workers voting in favor of the union were undocumented aliens; *Contreras v. Corinthian Vigor Insurance Brokerage*, 25 F. Supp. 2d 1053 (N.D. Cal. 1998), holding that an undocumented worker may seek punitive damages against her employer for violating provisions of the Fair Labor Standards Act of 1938; and *Escobar v. Baker*, 814 F. Supp. 1491 (W.D. Wash. 1993), holding that the Agricultural Workers Protection Act of 1983 protects both documented and undocumented workers.

23. 208 F.3d on 252. To support his position, Sentelle cited a number of law review articles *complaining* that *Sure-Tan* had eliminated the possibility of back-pay relief when an employee was undocumented.

24. *Hoffman Plastic Compounds v. NLRB*, 535 U.S. 137 (2002). Rehnquist's discussion of Castro's conduct is on 143, that Castro "explicitly [contravened] Congress" is on 148, and his remark about "trivializing labor law" is on 150.

25. Id. Breyer's dismay with Hoffman's actions is on 153, and his discussion of the "perverse economic incentives" created by his colleagues' majority opinion is on 155–156. On 157, Breyer argued that Congress wanted to avoid precisely this result: "That presumably is why those in Congress who wrote the immigration statute [the Immigration Reform and Control Act of 1986] stated explicitly and unequivocally that the immigration statute does not take from the Board any of its remedial authority."

26. For some examples of the commentary surrounding *Hoffman*, see: Christopher Cameron, *Borderline Decisions: Hoffman Plastic Compounds, the New Bracero Program, and the Supreme Court's Role in Making Federal Labor Policy*, 51 UCLA L. Rev. 1 (2003); Robert Correales, *Did Hoffman Plastic Compounds, Inc., Produce Disposable Workers?* 14 Berkeley La Raza L. J. 103 (2003); Miriam Wells, *The Grassroots Configuration of U.S. Immigration Policy*, 38 Int. Mig. Rev. 1308 (2004); Ruben Garcia, *Toward Fundamental Change for the Protection of Low-Wage Workers: The 'Workers' Rights are Human Rights' Debate in the Obama Era*, 2009 U. Chi. Legal F. 421; and Kati Griffith, *A Supreme Stretch: The Supremacy Clause in the Wake of IRCA and Hoffman Plastics Compound*, 41 Cornell Int'l L.J. 127 (2008).

27. See, for example: Michael Duff, *Three Problems the NLRB Must Confront to Resist Further Erosion of Labor Rights in the Expanding Immigrant Workplace*, 30 Berkeley J. Emp. & Lab. L. 133 (2009); David Weber, *(Unfair) Advantage: Damocles' Sword and the Coercive Use of Immigration Status in a Civil Society*, 94 Marq. L. Rev.

613 (2010); and Kati Griffith, *Discovering 'Immployment' Law: The Constitutionality of Subfederal Immigration Regulation at Work*, 29 YALE L. & POL'Y REV. 389 (2011).

28. *Crespo v. Evergro Corp.*, 841 A.2d 471 (N.J. Super. Ct. App. Div. 2004); *Escobar v. Spartan Security Service*, 281 F. Supp. 2d 895 (S.D. Tex. 2003); and *Sanchez v. Eagle Alloy Inc.*, 254 Mich. App. 651 (2003). For a discussion of these cases and the evolving labor standards that do or don't apply to unlawful aliens, see Keith Cunningham-Parmeter, *Redefining the Rights of Undocumented Workers*, 58 AM. U.L. REV. 1361 (2009), and Wishnie, supra note 14.

29. See *Sanchez*, 254 Mich. App., on 656.

30. The Michigan Supreme Court case appears as *Sanchez v. Eagle Alloy*, 471 Mich. 851 (2004).

31. For discussions of doctrines like "assumption of risk" and the "fellow servant rule," especially as they appeared in American labor history, see: WIECEK (2001), WITT (2006), and FISHBACK AND KANTOR (2006).

32. *Rivera v. NIBCO*, 364 F.3d 1057 (9th Cir. 2004).

33. Id., at 1064.

34. See *Galaviz-Zamora v. Brady Farms*, 230 F.R.D. 499, on 501 (W.D. Mich. 2005).

35. Id. at 503. Other courts ruled that workers in a labor dispute may keep their immigration status private and beyond the reach of their employers during the discovery phase of a lawsuit; see, for example, *Zeng Liu v. Donna Karan*, 207 F. Supp. 2d 191 (S.D.N.Y., 2002).

36. *Agri Processor Co. v. NLRB*, 514 F.3d 1, 2–3 (D.C. Cir., 2008).

37. For government reports about working conditions faced by undocumented workers, see: U.S. General Accounting Office, *Collective Bargaining Rights* (2002); Bureau of Labor Statistics, *Census of Fatal Occupational Injuries* (2002), and Centers for Disease Control and Prevention, *Protecting the Safety and Health of Immigrant Workers* (2002). For studies and commentary discussing common abuses against undocumented workers in general, see: Christopher Ho and Jennifer Chang, *Drawing the Line After Hoffman Plastic Compounds*, 22 HOFSTRA LAB. & EMP. L. J. 473 (2005); Michael Wishnie, *The Border Crossed Us*, 28 N.Y.U. REV. L. & SOC. CHANGE 389 (2003); GORDON (2007); and Lee, supra note 1. For scholarly work about domestic labor, see: Doreen Mattingly, *The Home and the World*, 91 ANN. ASSOC. AMER. GEOGR. 370 (2001); ROMERO (2002); Pei-Chia Lan, *Negotiating Social Boundaries and Private Zones*, 50 SOC. PROBLEMS 525 (2003); and HONDAGNEU-SOTELO (2007). On day laborers and "irregular" laborers, see: Abel Valenzuela, *Day Labor Work*, 29 ANN. REV. SOC. 307 (2003), and Carolyn Turnovsky, *A la Parada*, 24 SOC. TEXT 55 (2006). The phrase "on an as-needed basis" comes from Valenzuela, on 318.

38. The sentence is from *Developments in the Law: Jobs and Borders*, 118 HARV. L. REV. 2171 (2005), on 2240.

39. 514 F.3d on 9 and 10.

40. The concept of "covering"—of hiding, subsuming, or downplaying an aspect of one's identity that is or may be disabling under prevailing public rules and norms—is a powerful way of understanding some of the circumstances faced by persons who are out of status, people who must often pretend that they are "legal" in order to fit in or to avoid the harsh consequences of federal law. For more about this concept, its rela-

tionship to anti-discrimination principles, and its various forms as they've appeared in American public law, see: Yoshino (2007).

41. For more about Agri-Processor and its many legal troubles, see: Karla McKanders, *The Unspoken Voices of Indigenous Women in Immigration Raids*, 14 J. Gender Race & Just. 1 (2010); Hiroshi Motomura, *The Rights of Others: Legal Claims and Immigration Outside the Law*, 59 Duke L. J. 1723 (2010); and Khari Taustin, *Still in 'The Jungle': Labor, Immigration, and the Search for a New Common Ground in the Wake of Iowa's Meatpacking Raids*, 18 U. Miami Bus. L. Rev. 283 (2010). The quote at the end of the paragraph is from Jennifer Chacon, *Managing Migration Through Crime*, 109 Colum. L. Rev. Sidebar 135, 144 (2009).

42. Zhao (2010), on 88.

43. See Fine (2006). On 11, Fine defines worker centers as "community-based mediating institutions that provide support to and organize among communities of low-wage workers. As work is the primary focus of life for many newly arriving immigrants, it is also the locus of many of the problems they experience." As part of her study, Fine surveyed over eleven dozen worker centers across the United States and she offered nine case studies; nearly all of the centers she surveyed served primarily low-wage immigrant workers. Fine's remark about a "national immigration policy" is on 244. Other scholars have written at length about these new organizations, many drawing from Fine's work. Consider, for example, this description from Daniel Widener, *Another City Is Possible: Interethnic Organizing in Contemporary Los Angeles*, 1 Race/Ethnicity 189 (2008), on 202: "Operating outside, and often to the left of labor unions, are multiple types of social justice organizations. Among the most novel organizational forms to proliferate during the last fifteen years are the varied groupings known collectively as worker centers. Marking a key development in the history of multiracial, class-based organizing locally, these centers serve as a bridge between labor unions and place/community or race/ethnically based social justice organizations. As Janice Fine's recent work on the subject details, Southern California is unique for both the quantity and quality of worker centers present. These centers typically focus on those workers only marginally sought by organized labor, and typically conduct outreach away from the point of production or job site. Generally based on ethnicity, geographic origin, or immigration status, worker centers operate as political spaces that offer legal services, provide arenas for discussion beyond those offered by unions, and conduct campaigns that make "social" demands for workers. In contrast to unions, worker centers focus on internal democracy, leadership development, and, in the case of many L.A.-based groups, they do so with an eye toward tackling many of the ethnic aspects of interracial and intra-class tension."

44. For scholarly commentary about the Workplace Project and similar worker centers, see: Jennifer Gordon, *We Make the Road by Walking: Immigrant Workers, the Workplace Project, and the Struggle for Social Change*, 30 Harv. C.R.-C.L. L. Rev. 407 (1995); Saru Jayaraman, *Making Movement: Communities of Color and New Models of Organizing Labor*, 27 Berkeley J. Emp. & Lab. L. 223 (2006); Sameer Ashar, *Public Interest Lawyers and Resistance Movements*, 95 Calif. L. Rev. 1879 (2007); Michael Tusa and Vanessa Spinazola, *Wage Claims of Undocumented Workers and the Fair Labor Standards Act*, 58 L.A. Bar J. 370 (2011); and Gleeson, supra note 5.

45. Das Gupta (2006), on 219–220. On 213, Das Gupta writes: "A well-kept secret behind the immigrant success story is the grossly underpaid labor of South Asian

domestics. A deeply gendered project that enables South Asian households' dependence on women, who are imported for the express purpose of doing domestic work, undergirds the extremely divisive project of portraying South Asians as successful minorities. This dependence clearly demonstrates the interlocking gendered, classed, and sexualized dimensions of the model minority myth." Other scholars have written about "global care work," that phenomenon through which women in poorer countries often leave their own families to care for families in affluent countries. See, for example: GLOBAL WOMAN: NANNIES, MAIDS, AND SEX WORKERS IN THE NEW ECONOMY (Barbara Ehrenreich and Arlie Hochschild, eds., 2004); GUEVARRA (2009); and INTIMATE LABORS: CULTURES, TECHNOLOGIES, AND THE POLITICS OF CARE (Rhacel Parrenas and Eileen Boris, eds., 2010).

46. Id., 221–223.

47. Id. For more about the Domestic Workers Committee and its allied organizations, see: *Remarks of Nahar Alam, Women in the Global Economy*, 22 BERKELEY J. GENDER L. & JUST. 325 (2007); and *The Role of Legal Services in Workers' Organizing*, 13 N.Y. CITY L. REV. 195 (2009). For similar work based in other cities, including Los Angeles, see, Richard Sullivan and Kimi Lee, *Organizing Immigrant Women in America's Sweatshops: Lessons from the Los Angeles Garment Worker Center*, 33 SIGNS 527 (2008).

48. For a thorough account of KIWA's origins, see CHUNG (2007). For the fractures in Koreatown before and after the riots, see: Edward J.W. Park, *Competing Visions: Political Formation of Korean Americans in Los Angeles*, 24 AMERASIA 41 (1998), and Edward J.W. Park and John S.W. Park, *Immigration and the Crisis of the Urban Liberal Coalition: The Case of Korean Americans in Los Angeles*, in GOVERNING AMERICAN CITIES (Michael Jones-Correa, ed., 2002). On the settlement of Koreans in Los Angeles in the wake of deindustrialization, see: LIGHT AND BONACICH (1991).

49. For Jay Kim's role in the immigration reforms of 1996, see PARK AND PARK (2005), chs. 4 and 5. For helpful discussions of KIWA's efforts and the changing economic situation in Koreatown, written by two law students who'd worked at KIWA, see: Daisy Ha, *An Analysis and Critique of KIWA's Reform Efforts in the Los Angeles Korean American Restaurant Industry*, 8 ASIAN L. J. 111 (2001); and Yungsuhn Park, *The Immigrant Workers Union: Challenges Facing Low-Wage Immigrant Workers in Los Angeles*, 12 ASIAN L. J. 67 (2005).

50. CHUNG (2007), 150–160.

51. Id., 161–162. Consider also the analysis by Jong Bum Kwon, *The Koreatown Immigrant Workers Alliance: Spatializing Justice in an Ethnic 'Enclave,'* in WORKING FOR JUSTICE: THE L.A. MODEL OF ORGANIZING AND ADVOCACY (Ruth Milkman, Joshua Bloom, and Victor Narro, eds., 2010), on 27: "Militant street actions are strategies to not only redefine 'Korean American' community politics but also to challenge representations of Koreatown as a Korean entrepreneurial enclave. KIWA's confrontational and highly public demonstrations are cultural performances that function as *definitional* dramas. In addition to communicating grievances and demands for redress from individual businesses, those protests display for the Koreatown public and for the participants themselves an alternative vision of community, cultural space, and social justice. As definitional dramas, they challenge the symbolic economy of Koreatown— the economy of images, the representation of space 'that yields real returns in terms of

attracting new businesses, corporate investment, tourism, and consumption.'" Kwon borrowed the concept "definitional drama" from VICTOR TURNER, DRAMAS, FIELDS, AND METAPHORS: SYMBOLIC ACTION IN HUMAN SOCIETY (1974), and he quoted from SHARON ZUKIN, THE CULTURE OF CITIES (1995), on 7.

52. For accounts of the Assi Supermarket dispute, see: Austin Bunn, *Market Forces*, L.A. WEEKLY (May 3, 2002); Ellis Boal, *Worker Center Fights for Immigrant Workers Rights*, LABOR NOTES (Oct. 2003); and Narges Zohoury, *UCLA Students Join Workers at Supermarket Pickets*, DAILY BRUIN (June 4, 2004).

53. For a description of the early years of the struggle against Assi Supermarket in Koreatown, I've relied heavily on FINE (2006), especially her descriptions on 139–143; and on Kwon, supra note 51.

54. For another account of the ongoing impact of the Assi campaign, see Janet Kim, *Going Into Labor: The Effects of the On-Going Labor Dispute at Assi Market*, KOREAM J. (Feb. 2004).

55. See, Via Max, *Assi Market Workers Win $1.475 Million Settlement*, INDYMEDIA (Apr. 23, 2007).

56. Kwon, supra note 51, 24.

57. KIWA itself published reports that outlined the change in emphasis: see, for example, KOREAN IMMIGRANT WORKERS ADVOCATES, LIVING WAGES IN KOREATOWN SUPERMARKETS: A KEY STRATEGY IN THE COMMUNITY FIGHT AGAINST POVERTY (2005), and KOREAN IMMIGRANT WORKERS ADVOCATES, KOREATOWN ON THE EDGE: IMMIGRANT DREAMS AND REALITIES IN ONE OF LOS ANGELES' POOREST COMMUNITIES (2005).

58. These odd outcomes and dilemmas have appeared with increasing frequency in the academic literature on immigration and labor. See, for example, THE NEW URBAN IMMIGRANT WORKFORCE: INNOVATIVE MODELS FOR LABOR ORGANIZING (Sarumathi Jayaraman and Immanuel Ness, eds., 2005); MILKMAN (2006); and Gleeson, supra note 5.

59. For accounts of how American labor organizations have shifted in their strategies with respect to immigrants, especially undocumented immigrants, see: Dan Clawson and Mary Ann Clawson, *What Happened to the US Labor Movement? Union Decline and Renewal*, 25 ANN. REV. SOC. 95 (1999); Roger Waldinger, *Will the Followers Be Led? Where Union Members Stand on Immigration*, 17 NEW LAB. FOR. 42 (2008); and Brian Burgoon, Janice Fine, Wade Jacoby, and Daniel Tichenor, *Immigration and the Transformation of American Unionism*, 44 INT. MIG. REV. 933 (2010).

60. The quotes come from BRIGGS (2001), 184–185. Other prominent labor and immigration scholars have made similar arguments. See, for example, BORJAS (1991) and BORJAS (2001). For a review of alternative perspectives, see: JULIAN SIMON, THE ECONOMIC CONSEQUENCES OF IMMIGRATION (1999); and MASSEY, DURAND, AND MALONE (2002).

61. The phrase is from Clyde Woods, *Les Miserables of New Orleans: Trap Economics and the Asset Stripping Blues, Part I*, 61 AMER. QUART. 769 (2009).

62. Shannon Gleeson's essay is one example of this rhetorical move away from "illegal immigrant," "illegal worker," and "illegal status." She does not use these terms, but rather includes "undocumented workers" as situated similarly as non-unionized workers and other "vulnerable workers." See, Gleeson, supra note 5.

CHAPTER 6: THE BREAD OF KNOWLEDGE

1. DOUGLASS, NARRATIVE (1994), ch. 7. For a discussion of slave codes governing literacy, see Janet Cornelius, *'We Slipped and Learned to Read,'* PHYLON (1983). It's pleasing to think that the "little urchins" that Douglass described might have looked like Huckleberry Finn, as Huck was exactly the kind of boy who might have traded bread for lessons.

2. DOUGLASS, NARRATIVE (1994), ch. 10. The discussion of Georgia's rule against teaching slaves is in HIGGINBOTHAM (1980), on 258. For other discussions about African Americans, public law, and education in the antebellum period, see: R. I. Brigham, *Negro Education in Ante-Bellum Missouri*, 30 J. NEGRO HIST. 405 (1945); WOODSON (1972); WHITMAN (1997); and BERLIN (2007).

3. For the rule in 1806, see: David Bogen, *The Maryland Context of* Dred Scott, 34 AMER. J. LEG. HIST. 381 (1990). On 406, Bogen wrote: "In 1806 the Maryland General Assembly passed a statute forbidding the immigration of free negroes into the state, fining the illegal immigrant for each week after the second week he stayed in the state, and fining any employer who hired an illegal immigrant. The vote was overwhelming." For a discussion of the rule in 1860, see: Cornelius, supra note 1, 173. For a discussion of black illiteracy in the South prior to the Civil War, see: REESE (2011), ch. 2.

4. Miriam Small and Edwin Small, *Prudence Crandall: Champion of Negro Education*, 17 NEW ENG. Q. 506 (1944). "Disapprobation of the school . . ." appears on 515. LITWACK (1965), on 118–119.

5. C. C. Tisler, *Prudence Crandall, Abolitionist*, 33 J. ILL. STATE HIST. SOC. 203 (1940).

6. Small and Small, supra note 4, 517.

7. G. Smith Wormley, *Prudence Crandall*, 8 J. NEGRO HIST. 72 (1923). The acts of vandalism appear on 77.

8. Id., on 80. Prudence Crandall's story, with some modifications, was also reiterated at length in LITWACK (1965). There, on 118–119, Professor Litwack discussed a similar local panic in New Hampshire that followed Prudence Crandall's experience: "In March, 1835, twenty-eight whites and fourteen Negroes commenced classes at newly established Noyes Academy [in Canaan, New Hampshire]. The school, which had several abolitionists on its board of trustees, admitted all qualified applicants, regardless of race or color. In announcing this liberal policy, the trustees cited the exclusion of Negroes from educational institutions in the free states and proposed 'to afford colored youth a fair opportunity to show that they are capable, equally with whites, of improving themselves in every scientific attainment, every social virtue, and every Christian ornament.'" Reaction to the school in New Canaan was similar to reaction to the one in Canterbury: "The mixing of Negro and white youths set off a series of rumors through the town. Negroes would overrun Canaan; fugitive slaves would line the streets with their huts and burden the town with paupers and vagabonds; the school would become a public nuisance." This school, too, was closed shortly after its establishment.

9. For discussions of the Boston public schools during this period, see: Douglas Ficker, *From Roberts to Plessy*, 84 J. NEGRO HIST. 301 (1999); and James Horton and Michele Moresi, *Roberts, Plessy, and Brown*, 15 OAH MAG. HIST. 14 (2001).

10. Ficker, supra note 9, 302–303.

11. Shaw, in *Roberts v. City of Boston*, 59 Mass. 198, on 209 (1850). Shaw was criticized for his decision, but he may have understood his fellow citizens better than many progressives. In her study of Massachusetts civil rights legislation from 1855 to 1985, Kazuteru Omori noted the following: "In 1855, the Massachusetts legislature passed an act providing that '[in] determining the qualifications of scholars to be admitted into any public school or any district school in this Commonwealth, no distinction shall be made on account of the race, color or religious opinions, of the applicant or scholar.' After the Civil War, Republican assemblymen in the Bay State took a further step by enacting and reinforcing laws against racial discrimination in public accommodations." Yet, as Omori and other scholars have noted, Boston in the late nineteenth and early twentieth centuries remained highly segregated and racially hostile, perhaps one of the most hostile in the Northeast. By itself, in Boston at least, law did seem incapable of producing racial equality. See, Kazuteru Omori, *Race-Neutral Individualism and Resurgence of the Color Line: Massachusetts Civil Rights Legislation, 1855–1895*, 22 J. Amer. Hist. 32 (2002).

12. Litwack (1965), 98.

13. *Plessy v. Ferguson*, 163 U.S. 537, on 550 and 551 (1896).

14. The literature on this topic is voluminous. For some examples, especially drawing from law and society perspectives, see: Patterson (2002); Kluger (2004); and Klarman (2007).

15. James Horton, *Black Education at Oberlin College*, 54 J. Negro Hist. 477, on 488 (1985). See, also, Horton and Horton (1998).

16. Id., on 477. Horton noted, however, that Oberlin and its students often devolved into segregation after the Civil War, as Jim Crow rules became popular throughout the United States. Professors objected to integrated living arrangements, whites refused to sit next to black students during school functions, and white students directed racial insults at their black classmates. "It was evident that these opinions were not merely those of southerners at Oberlin but were widely held racial views among whites from all areas of the nation." African American students, in turn, organized against these tendencies: "Incensed by the changing attitudes among their white classmates, black students condemned the increasingly open expression of racial prejudice on campus and in the town." Horton, on 489.

17. Ellen Henle and Marlene Merrill, *Antebellum Black Coeds at Oberlin College*, Women's Stud. Newsletter on 11 (1979).

18. On Oberlin College in the antebellum period, see: Roland Baumann, Constructing Black Education at Oberlin College: A Documentary History (2010); and Catherine Rokicky, James Monroe: Oberlin's Christian Statesman and Reformer, 1821–1898 (2002). On the Burns case, see Albert von Frank, The Trials of Anthony Burns: Freedom and Slavery in Emerson's Boston (1999); and Maltz (2010). That blacks should be "elevated" to the status of whites is amusing now in light of *Huckleberry Finn*, as these progressives sound so similar to Huck when he says that he knew that Jim was "white inside." We have no way of knowing for certain, but it would seem that many progressives were trying to prove that at least some blacks were white inside, too, all of this suggesting how good intentions could still be so racist as well.

19. Steven Lubet, *A Victory for Higher Law: The Oberlin Fugitive Slave Rescue*, 13 NORTH & SOUTH 30 (2011). See, also, the FUGITIVE SLAVE LAW OF 1850. Section 5 outlines the duties of "all good citizens," and section 7 details the consequences for not complying: "That any person who shall knowingly and willingly obstruct, hinder, or prevent such claimant, his agent or attorney, or any person or persons lawfully assisting him, her, or them, from arresting such a fugitive from service or labor, either with or without process as aforesaid, or shall rescue, or attempt to rescue, such fugitive from service or labor, from the custody of such claimant, his or her agent or attorney, or other person or persons lawfully assisting as aforesaid, when so arrested, pursuant to the authority herein given and declared; or shall aid, abet, or assist such person so owing service or labor as aforesaid, directly or indirectly, to escape from such claimant, his agent or attorney, or other person or persons legally authorized as aforesaid; or shall harbor or conceal such fugitive, so as to prevent the discovery and arrest of such person, after notice or knowledge of the fact that such person was a fugitive from service or labor as aforesaid, shall, for either of said offences, be subject to a fine not exceeding one thousand dollars, and imprisonment not exceeding six months, by indictment and conviction before the District Court of the United States for the district in which such offence may have been committed, or before the proper court of criminal jurisdiction, if committed within any one of the organized Territories of the United States; and shall moreover forfeit and pay, by way of civil damages to the party injured by such illegal conduct, the sum of one thousand dollars for each fugitive so lost as aforesaid, to be recovered by action of debt, in any of the District or Territorial Courts aforesaid, within whose jurisdiction the said offence may have been committed."

20. Langston is quoted at length in Lubet, supra note 19, 37. For a history of John Brown's raid, see TONY HORWITZ, MIDNIGHT RISING: JOHN BROWN AND THE RAID THAT SPARKED THE CIVIL WAR (2011).

21. For histories of social welfare policies, particularly in the post Civil War era, see: SKOCPOL (1995); KATZ (1996); TRATTNER (1998); and GORDON (1998). For histories of public education that focus on late nineteenth- and early twentieth-century developments, see: TYACK (1974); MCAFEE (1998); URBAN AND WAGONER (2008); COHEN AND KISKER (2010); and THELIN (2011).

22. See *Civil Rights Cases*, 109 U.S. 3 (1883). The Civil Rights Act of 1875 read, in part: "All persons within the jurisdiction of the United States shall be entitled to the full and equal enjoyment of the accommodations, advantages, facilities, and privileges of inns, public conveyances on land or water, theaters, and other places of public amusement; subject only to the conditions and limitations established by law, and applicable alike to citizens of every race and color, regardless of any previous condition of servitude." Refusing to hire persons solely on the basis of race and refusing to serve them on the same grounds were, in the plaintiff's arguments, not just a violation of the Act, but also a clear violation of the 14th Amendment's Equal Protection Clause, in section 1: "No State shall make or enforce any law which shall abridge the privileges or immunities of citizens of the United States; nor shall any State deprive any person of life, liberty, or property, without due process of law; nor deny to any person within its jurisdiction the equal protection of the laws."

23. Note the language in *Plessy*, 163 U.S. on 551: "We consider the underlying fallacy of the plaintiff's argument to consist in the assumption that the enforced separation of the two races stamps the colored race with a badge of inferiority. If this be

so, it is not by reason of anything found in the act, but solely because the colored race chooses to put that construction upon it. The argument necessarily assumes that if, as has been more than once the case and is not unlikely to be so again, the colored race should become the dominant power in the state legislature, and should enact a law in precisely similar terms, it would thereby relegate the white race to an inferior position. We imagine that the white race, at least, would not acquiesce in this assumption. The argument also assumes that social prejudices may be overcome by legislation, and that equal rights cannot be secured to the negro except by an enforced commingling of the two races. We cannot accept this proposition. If the two races are to meet upon terms of social equality, it must be the result of natural affinities, a mutual appreciation of each other's merits, and a voluntary consent of individuals."

24. For excellent histories that cover the period of educational expansion in the United States after the Civil War, see: WATKINS (2001), RAVITCH (2001), and REESE (2011).

25. WILLIAMS (2005).

26. See REESE (2011), 210–211. See also ANDERSON (1988) and DOLLARD (1957).

27. On the history of Native American boarding schools, including first-hand accounts of the experience, see: K. TSIANINA LOMAWAIMA, THEY CALLED IT PRAIRIE LIGHT: THE STORY OF CHILOCCO INDIAN SCHOOL (1995); ADAMS (1997); and KATANSKI (2007). The phrase "Kill the Indian, save the man" is commonly attributed to Richard Pratt, a former officer in the United States Army and one of the founders of the Carlisle Indian Industrial School in Pennsylvania. For Jefferson's views about Native Americans, and for their relationship to subsequent federal policies about Native American removal and incorporation, see ANTHONY WALLACE, JEFFERSON AND THE INDIANS: THE TRAGIC FATE OF THE FIRST AMERICANS (1999); and MILLER (2006).

28. *Chae Chan Ping v. United States*, 130 U.S. 581, on 595 (1889). The reference to "vast hordes" is on 606.

29. NGAI (2010), ch. 2. The quotes are on 20 and 15.

30. *Ward v. Flood*, 48 Cal. 36 (1874). Wallace's citations and analysis of *Roberts* is on 52–55.

31. Wallace said, on 56–57: "In order to prevent possible misapprehension, however, we think proper to add that in our opinion, and as the result of the views here announced, the exclusion of colored children from schools where white children attend as pupils, cannot be supported, except under the conditions appearing in the present case; that is, except where separate schools are actually maintained for the education of colored children; and that, unless such separate schools be in fact maintained, all children of the school district, whether white or colored, have an equal right to become pupils at any common school organized under the laws of the State, and have a right to registration and admission as pupils in the order of their registration, pursuant to the provisions of subdivision fourteen of section 1,617 of the Political Code."

32. *In re Ah Yup*, 1 F. Cas. 223 (C.C.D. 1878).

33. The memorial can be found as "A Petition for Separate Chinese Schools" (1878), retrieved April 7, 2011 from http://www.digitalhistory.uh.edu. For an historical account of early California school law, see: FRANK KREMERER AND PETER SANSOM, CALIFORNIA SCHOOL LAW (2009), ch. 11.

34. *Tape v. Hurley*, 66 Cal. 473, on 473 (1885).

35. Professor Ngai makes this point explicitly: like Homer Plessy, Takao Ozawa, and Bhagat Thind, the Tapes insisted that they were "white" in practically every respect except for skin color or national origin. See NGAI (2010), 52.

36. 66 Cal. 473 (1885).

37. NGAI (2010); for local reactions to and developments from the case, see also YUNG (1995).

38. Mary Tape, quoted in NGAI (2010), 55.

39. See, for example, *Wong Him v. Callahan*, 119 F. 381 (C.C.N.D. Cal. 1902), and *Gong Lum v. Rice*, 275 U.S. 78 (1927).

40. For historical accounts of the Mississippi Chinese, especially in relation to this case, see: Sieglinde Lim de Sanchez, *Crafting a Delta Chinese Community: Education and Acculturation in Twentieth-Century Southern Baptist Mission Schools*, 43 HIST. ED. QUART. 74 (2003); and Joyce Kuo, *Excluded, Segregated and Forgotten: A Historical View of the Discrimination of Chinese Americans in Public Schools*, 5 ASIAN L. J. 181 (1998). For broader social histories of the Mississippi Chinese, including their attempts to define their racial position in sympathy with whites and by distancing themselves from African Americans, see: QUAN (2007) and LOEWEN (1988).

41. *Gong Lum v. Rice*, 275 U.S. 78, 86–87 (1927). For analyses of Taft's opinion, see: *Power to Classify Chinese as Colored Persons*, 16 CAL. L. REV. 346 (1928); and *Separation of Races for Purposes of Education*, 37 YALE L. J. 518 (1928).

42. For a thorough discussion of the legal constructions of whiteness, see HANEY-LOPEZ (1997).

43. For a discussion of these cases and results, especially among Japanese Americans, see: SPICKARD (2009), PARK (2004), and AZUMA (2005).

44. Roosevelt is quoted in TAKAKI (1998), on 202. The quote about the Gentlemen's Agreement is on 203.

45. Here is TAKAKI (1998), on 218–219: "[Between 1925 and 1935,] twenty-five percent [of Nisei] worked in family businesses or trades that did not require a college education, and forty percent had 'blind alley' jobs. University job-placement offices repeatedly reported virtually no employment prospects for Japanese-American graduates. 'Our experience with employment for Japanese and Chinese has been most unsatisfactory,' the University of California at Berkeley stated. 'Many of these students have taken the engineering courses and we have found a distinct prejudice against foreigners existing in the public utilities and manufacturing companies.' Similarly, Stanford University observed: 'It is almost impossible to place a Chinese or Japanese of either the first or the second generation in any kind of position, engineering, manufacturing, or business.'" For additional discussions about Asian American life and economy during the exclusion era, see: CHAN (1991), HSU (2000), and HOSOKAWA (2002).

46. All of these vignettes come from NGAI (2010): Gertrude and Emily at the Le Conte School are on 73; Robert appears on 89–90; Gertrude's education is on 154; and Herbert's is on 155–156.

47. These remarks are from Jack Chow, a Delta Mississippi resident, quoted in Sanchez, supra note 40, 80–81.

48. Sanchez, supra note 40, 84.

49. See: Sanchez, supra note 40, and Robert O'Brien, *Status of Chinese in the Mississippi Delta*, 19 SOC. FORCES 386 (1941).

50. Sanchez, supra note 40, 86–87. Martha Miller, a young teacher at the Cleveland School, had wanted to be a missionary in China, but instead she found this job in Cleveland. In terms of the way she first found her position and conducted her job, Ms. Miller described herself in self-effacing terms, "How stupid I was," and she remembered that no matter how hard her Chinese students and their parents tried to fit into white society, they were kept at a distance. See: *Oral History with Mrs. Martha Sisson Miller*, Center for Oral History and Cultural Heritage at the University of Southern Mississippi (1999).

51. For more about Bhagat Thind and his case, see: Gary Hess, *The 'Hindu' in America: Immigration and Naturalization Policies and India, 1917–1946*, 38 PAC. HIST. REV. 59 (1969); and Deenesh Sohoni, *Unsuitable Suitors: Anti-Miscegenation Laws, Naturalization Laws, and the Construction of Asian Identities*, 41 L. & SOC. REV. 587 (2007). For a discussion of Takao Ozawa and the social history of his case, see: FRANK CHUMAN, THE BAMBOO PEOPLE (1976): and Yuji Ichioka, *The Early Japanese Quest for Citizenship: The Background of the 1922 Ozawa Case*, 4 AMERASIA 1 (1977). Emsen Charr wrote his own autobiography, EASURK EMSEN CHARR, THE GOLDEN MOUNTAIN: THE AUTOBIOGRAPHY OF A KOREAN IMMIGRANT, 1895–1960 (1996), as did Jade Snow Wong, JADE SNOW WONG, FIFTH CHINESE DAUGHTER (1945, 1989). There is an extensive literature on the internment cases, including biographical sketches of all four major plaintiffs, and they appear in the next chapter. For more about Gordon Hirabayshi specifically, see: PETER IRONS, THE COURAGE OF THEIR CONVICTIONS: SIXTEEN AMERICANS WHO FOUGHT THEIR WAY TO THE SUPREME COURT (1988).

52. This account is from Ellen Eisenberg, *'As Truly American as Your Son': Voicing Opposition to Internment in Three West Coast Cities*, 104 OR. HIST. QUART. 542, on 553–555 (2003).

53. Id.; see also GARY OKIHIRO, STORIED LIVES: JAPANESE AMERICAN STUDENTS AND WORLD WAR II (1999). Okihiro estimated that about 5,500 students of Japanese ancestry were allowed to continue their education on college campuses across the country, although the vast majority of these students were released from the camps only after *Ex parte Endo*, 323 U.S. 283 (1944), when the United States Supreme Court required the federal government to release from custody anyone it conceded was "a loyal and law abiding citizen."

54. The quotes are from a Letter from President Ernest Wilkins to L. P. Sieg, Correspondence Series, RG 2/7 Ernest Wilkins, Box 58, Oberlin College Archives (Mar. 19, 1942). For a discussion of how Japanese American students dealt with such disruptions in their education, see: ROBERT O'BRIEN, THE COLLEGE NISEI (1978).

CHAPTER 7: RACE, IMMIGRATION, AND THE PROMISE OF EQUALITY

1. Ellen Eisenberg, *'As Truly American as Your Son': Voicing Opposition to Internment in Three West Coast Cities*, 104 OR. HIST. QUART. 542 (2003).

2. Warren is quoted in Roger Daniels, *Incarcerating Japanese Americans*, 16 OAH MAG. 19, on 20 (2002), and in Mikiso Hise, *Wartime Internment*, 77 J. AMER. HIST. 569, on 571 (1990).

3. See, Hise, supra note 2, on 575.

4. WHITE (1987), on 71. Other biographers have reached similar conclusions; see, for example, JIM NEWTON, JUSTICE FOR ALL: EARL WARREN AND THE NATION HE MADE (2007); and ED CRAY, CHIEF JUSTICE: A BIOGRAPHY OF EARL WARREN (2008). The scholarly literature on Japanese American internment is voluminous. A sample of some of the most important works would include: DANIELS (2004); BRIAN HAYASHI, DEMOCRATIZING THE ENEMY: THE JAPANESE AMERICAN INTERNMENT (2008); and ROBINSON (2009). For first-hand accounts of the experience among the internees themselves, see: LAWSON INADA, ONLY WHAT WE COULD CARRY: THE JAPANESE AMERICAN INTERNMENT EXPERIENCE (2000); LAST WITNESSES: REFLECTIONS ON THE WARTIME INTERNMENT OF JAPANESE AMERICANS (Erica Harth, ed., 2003); and MARY GRUNEWALD, LOOKING LIKE THE ENEMY: MY STORY OF IMPRISONMENT IN JAPANESE AMERICAN INTERNMENT CAMPS (2005).

5. The letter is reprinted in CRAY, supra note 4, on 92.

6. The quote comes from a Letter from Earl Warren to Jerry Enomoto, the President of the Japanese American Citizens League (Mar. 18, 1970), reprinted in Masumi Izumi, *Prohibiting 'American Concentration Camps': Repeal of the Emergency Detention Act and the Public Historical Memory of the Japanese American Internment*, 74 PAC. HIST. REV. 165 (2005).

7. For the first quote, see CRAY, supra note 4, 520; for the second, see: WARREN (1977), on 149, and G. Edward White, *The Unacknowledged Lesson: Earl Warren and the Japanese Relocation Controversy*, 55 VA. Q. REV. 613 (1979).

8. The *Korematsu* case appears as *Korematsu v. United States*, 323 U.S. 214 (1944). The scholarly literature on *Korematsu* is extensive, but for discussions of the origins of strict scrutiny analysis in the federal courts, see: Greg Robinson and Toni Robinson, Korematsu *and Beyond: Japanese Americans and the Origins of Strict Scrutiny*, 68 L. & CONT. PROBLEMS 29 (2005); and Stephen Siegel, *The Origins of the Compelling State Interest Test and Strict Scrutiny*, 48 AMER. J. LEG. HIST. 355 (2006). The landmark cases citing to *Korematsu* include: *Shelley v. Kraemer*, 334 U.S. 1 (1948) [on the constitutionality of enforcing racially restrictive covenants in housing]; *Oyama v. California*, 332 U.S. 633 (1948) [about alien land laws]; and *Loving v. Virginia*, 388 U.S. 1 (1967) [about state miscegenation rules].

9. Two of the more important contributions about *Korematsu* and the other internment cases, *Hirabayashi, Yasui,* and *Endo,* and their aftermath include: IRONS (1993) and YAMAMOTO et al. (2001). The four major internment cases are: *Hirabayashi v. United States*, 320 U.S. 81 (1943); *Yasui v. United States*, 320 U.S. 115 (1943); *Korematsu,* supra note 8; and *Ex parte Endo*, 323 U.S. 283 (1944). For scholarly work on the *Mendez* case, see: Charles Wollenberg, Mendez v. Westminster: *Race, Nationality, and Segregation in California Schools*, 53 CAL. HIST. Q. 317 (1974); Steven Wilson, *Brown over 'Other White': Mexican Americans' Legal Arguments and Litigation Strategy in School Desegregation Lawsuits*, 21 L. & HIST. REV. 145 (2003); Vicki Ruiz, *South by Southwest: Mexican Americans and Segregated Schooling*, 15 OAH MAG. HIST. 23 (2011); and STRUM (2010). In recent years, many scholars have noted that the Mexican American plaintiffs in *Mendez* did not wish to join either the National Association for the Advancement of Colored People or the Japanese American Citizens' League in a coordinated effort against racial segregation in public schools. Instead, they favored pointing out the vagueness of existing statutes as they'd pertained to "Mexicans," noting that Mexicans were neither Asian nor African and thus should not be subject to segre-

gation based on those statutes. In effect, Mexican Americans sought to distance themselves from other racial pariahs. For this historical argument, see: Wilson, *Brown over 'Other White,'* and Toni Robinson and Greg Robinson, *The Limits of Interracial Coalitions: Mendez v. Westminster Re-examined,* in RACIAL TRANSFORMATIONS: LATINOS AND ASIANS REMAKING THE UNITED STATES (Nicholas De Genova, ed., 2006).

10. The opinion appears as *Westminster School District v. Mendez,* 161 F.2d 774 (1947). The quote appears on 781.

11. Of course, the scholarly literature on *Brown* is vast. For discussions that emphasize the position of public schools and the subsequent impact of that decision on public schools, see: BELL (2005) and KOZOL (2005). For an account of how this case and other civil rights cases were related to the Cold War in the postwar years, see: DUDZIAK (2000) and BORSTELMANN (2003).

12. Warren's quotes about education itself come from *Brown v. Board of Education,* 347 U.S. 483, on 492–493 (1954). For scholarly discussions about public schools and public university systems in the early to mid-twentieth century, see: REESE (2011), chs. 5 and 6, and DOUGLASS (2007), ch. 4.

13. For a discussion of race and public education in the South prior to *Brown,* as well as discussions of public financing in public school systems in the postwar years, see: TYACK (1974), NELSON (2005), and FISCHEL (2009).

14. 347 U.S. on 493. The leading social scientists referred to in *Brown* were Kenneth and Mamie Clark; for their role in the desegregation cases, see: MARKOWITZ AND ROSNER (1999). The claim that the Court went too far comes from the *Southern Manifesto,* 102 CONG. REC. 4515–4516 (1956), which was signed by nineteen United States Senators and eighty-one members of the House of Representatives. On the political objections to racial integration in public schools, see: NELSON (2005).

15. For a discussion of the Civil Rights Act of 1964, see: HALPERN (1995); THE CIVIL RIGHTS ACT OF 1964: THE PASSAGE OF THE LAW THAT ENDED RACIAL SEGREGATION· (Robert Loevy, ed., 1997); and KLARMAN (2006). Leading federal cases from this period dealing with school desegregation include: *Green v. New Kent County School Board,* 391 U.S. 430 (1968) [about the constitutionality of a 'free choice' plan that effectively maintained segregated schools]; *Swann v. Charlotte-Mecklenburg Board of Education,* 402 U.S. 1 (1971) [about the constitutionality of a federal judge ordering specific measures to further racial integration within a public district]; and *Pasadena Board of Education v. Spangler,* 427 U.S. 424 (1976) [about the constitutionality of a federal judge modifying district boundaries to achieve racial integration]. For social histories of bussing and other desegregation measures, see: LUKAS (1986); JEFFREY HENIG, RETHINKING SCHOOL CHOICE (1995); and PETER MORAN, RACE, LAW, AND DESEGREGATION OF PUBLIC SCHOOLS (2004). For scholarly discussions of the Immigration Act of 1965, its relationship to the Civil Rights Movement, and the demographic changes it brought to the United States, see: LIGHT AND BONACICH (1991); MASSEY, DURAND, AND MALONE (2002); PARK AND PARK (2005); THE NEW AMERICANS: A GUIDE TO IMMIGRATION SINCE 1965 (Mary Waters et al., eds., 2007); and BRANCH (2007).

16. Many scholarly works have dealt with the demographic, economic, and political aspects of "white flight" over several decades. For some representative works from a range of disciplines, see: Christine Rossell, *School Desegregation and White Flight,* 90 POL. SCI. Q. 675 (1975); Kent Tedin, *Self-Interest, Symbolic Values, and the Financial*

Equalization of the Public Schools, 56 J. Pol. 628 (1994); Franklin Wilson, *The Impact of School Desegregation Programs on White Public School Enrollments, 1968–1976*, 58 Soc. Ed. 137 (1985); John Logan, Deirdre Oakley, and Jacob Stowell, *School Segregation in Metropolitan Regions, 1970–2000: The Impacts of Policy Choices on Public Education*, 113 Amer. J. Soc. 1611 (2008); and Leah Platt Boustan, *Was Postwar Suburbanization 'White Flight'? Evidence From the Black Migration*, 125 Q. J. Econ. 417 (2010). For an interesting cultural history of white flight and the conservative political consciousness it served, see Eric Avila, Popular Culture in the Age of White Flight: Fear and Fantasy in Suburban Los Angeles (2004). For a close study of race, public finance, and resistance to *Brown* at the state level, see Robbins Gates, The Making of Massive Resistance: Virginia's Politics of Public School Desegregation, 1954–1956 (2011).

17. The phrase "all deliberate speed" appeared in *Brown v. Board of Education*, 349 U.S. 294, on 301 (1955), and it was repeated in *Cooper v. Aaron*, 358 U.S. 1, on 7 (1958). Resistance to any and all forms of racial equality emanated from every region long before *Brown*; see, for example, The Myth of Southern Exceptionalism (Matthew Lassiter and Joseph Crespino, eds., 2009), and Ward (2011). *Brown* may have accelerated these trends, but certainly did not originate them. For close examinations of "white flight" in two separate regions, see: Kevin Kruse, White Flight: Atlanta and the Making of Modern Conservatism (2007), and Rachael Woldoff, White Flight/Black Flight: The Dynamics of Racial Change in an American Neighborhood (2011). Other major scholarly works examining the divides between "chocolate cities and vanilla suburbs," between suburban and urban America, include: Wilson (1980); Massey and Denton (1993); and Lipsitz (2011). The leading case involving interdistrict remedies is *Milliken v. Bradley*, 418 U.S. 717 (1974), in which the Supreme Court struck down a federal court order to implement a bussing plan that would encompass white suburban districts and black urban districts in Detroit.

18. Subsequent studies inspired by, or in reference to, *San Antonio* confirm similar findings for spending, educational outcomes, and projected racial disparities: see, for example, Pat Goldsmith, *Schools or Neighborhoods or Both? Racial and Ethnic Segregation and Educational Attainment*, 87 Soc. Forces 1913 (2009); and Eric Hanushek, John Kain, and Steven Rivkin, *New Evidence about* Brown v. Board of Education*: The Complex Effects of School Racial Composition on Achievement*, 27 J. Lab. Econ. 349 (2009).

19. These remarks paraphrase some of the darker critics of American public education, including: Samuel Bowles and Herbert Gintis, Schooling in Capitalist America: Educational Reform and the Contradictions of Economic Life (1976); Jonathan Kozol, Savage Inequalities: Children in America's Schools (1992); and Kozol (2005). Cases similar to *San Antonio* had appeared in other states, the most notable being *Serrano v. Priest*, 487 P.2d 1241 (1971), in which the California Supreme Court ruled that the California state funding system violated the equal protection principles of both the federal and California state constitutions.

20. *San Antonio Independent School District v. Rodriguez*, 411 U.S. 1 (1974). The finding that Texas and its funding scheme do not absolutely deprive any students of a public education is on 25; the phrase about wealth and the equal protection clause appears on 24; that education is a "service" rather than a "right" is on 30; that it's not

the business of the Court to create substantive constitutional rights is on 33; and the reference to education as being closer to "social and economic legislation" is on 35. On the last point, Powell went further, on 43: "The question regarding the most effective relationship between state boards of education and local school boards, in terms of their respective responsibilities and degrees of control, is now undergoing searching re-examination. The ultimate wisdom as to these and related problems of education is not likely to be divined for all time even by the scholars who now so earnestly debate the issues. In such circumstances, the judiciary is well advised to refrain from imposing on the States inflexible constitutional restraints that could circumscribe or handicap the continued research and experimentation so vital to finding even partial solutions to educational problems and to keeping abreast of ever-changing conditions." Some scholars and observers read these phrases as a rebuke against aggressive federal court supervision of urban school districts. See, for example, Mark Yudof and Daniel Morgan, Rodriguez v. San Antonio Independent School District: *The Politics of School Finance Reform*, 38 L. & CONT. PROB. 383 (1974); Ian Millhiser, *What Happens to a Dream Deferred? Cleansing the Taint of* San Antonio Independent School District v. Rodriguez, 55 DUKE L. J. 405 (2005); and Jeffrey Sutton, San Antonio Independent School District v. Rodriguez *and Its Aftermath*, 94 VA. L. REV. 1963 (2008). Justice Marshall insisted that state funding schemes were constitutional, as well as political, matters: "It is an inescapable fact that if one district has more funds available per pupil than another district, the former will have greater choice in educational planning than will the latter. In this regard, I believe the question of discrimination in educational quality must be deemed to be an objective one that looks to what the State provides its children, not to what the children are able to do with what they receive. That a child forced to attend an underfunded school with poorer physical facilities, less experienced teachers, larger classes, and a narrower range of courses than a school with substantially more funds—and thus with greater choice in educational planning—may nevertheless excel is to the credit of the child, not the State. . . . Indeed, who can ever measure for such a child the opportunities lost and the talents wasted for want of a broader, more enriched education? Discrimination in the opportunity to learn that is afforded a child must be our standard." 411 U.S. on 83–84.

21. For a pair of illuminating studies about state funding remedies in light of *San Antonio*, see: Douglas Reed, *Twenty-Five Years After* Rodriguez: *School Finance Litigation and the Impact of the New Judicial Federalism*, 32 L. & SOC. REV. 175 (1998); and Christine Roch and Robert Howard, *State Policy Innovation in Perspective: Courts, Legislatures, and Education Finance*, 6 POL. RES. Q. 333 (2008). For state court opinions in the wake of *San Antonio*, see: *Robinson v. Cahill*, 69 N.J. 133 (1975); *Serrano v. Priest*, 557 P.2d 929 (1976); and *McDuffy v. Secretary of the Executive Office of Education*, 415 Mass. 545 (1993).

22. For broader studies of wealth disparities and public education, see: RICHARD ROTHSTEIN, CLASS AND SCHOOLS: USING SOCIAL, ECONOMIC, AND EDUCATIONAL REFORM TO CLOSE THE BLACK-WHITE ACHIEVEMENT GAP (2004); HEATHER JOHNSON, THE AMERICAN DREAM AND THE POWER OF WEALTH: CHOOSING SCHOOLS AND INHERITING INEQUALITY IN THE LAND OF OPPORTUNITY (2006); and THE STRUCTURE OF SCHOOLING: READINGS IN THE SOCIOLOGY OF EDUCATION (Richard Arum, Irenee Beattie, and Karly Ford, eds., 2010). For discussions of local and state government law and the meaningfulness of political boundaries in terms of race and class,

see: Gerald Neuman, *Territorial Discrimination, Equal Protection, and Self-Determination*, 135 U. Penn. L. Rev. 261 (1987); Richard Ford, *The Boundaries of Race: Political Geography in Legal Analysis*, 107 Harv. L. Rev. 1841 (1994); and Lipsitz (2011). A number of cases have arisen in which parents have used false documents to establish residency within a district for the purposes of enrolling their children in the public schools there. See, for example, *Board of Education of the City of St. Louis v. Elam*, 70 S.W.3d 448 (Mo. Ct. App. E.D. 2000). For popular news accounts of this phenomenon, see: Kristen Noz, *Schools Target Illegal Students; Chesterfield Cracking Down on Outsiders*, Richmond Times Disp. (Apr. 14, 1999); *Parents Shouldn't Have to Lie to Get a Better Education for Their Kids*, S.F. Chron. (Aug. 27, 2006); Timothy Williams, *Jailed for Switching Her Daughters' School District*, N.Y. Times (Sept. 27, 2011); and Tom Howell, *Why Are MD, VA Students in DC Schools?* Wash. Times (Oct. 6, 2011).

23. The quote appears in the plaintiff's complaint, filed in May 1970, and appears also in Ling-chi Wang, Lau v. Nichols: *The Right of Limited-English-Speaking Students*, 2 Amerasia 16 (1974). Wang himself participated in this case, and he wrote, on 17–18: "*Lau v. Nichols* did not develop in a vacuum; it was the last resort after all other strategies had been exhausted. For a number of years, the community had tried meetings, negotiations, studies, demonstrations, and community alternative programs to rectify the rapidly deteriorating situation. While the number of new immigrants entering the school system continued to escalate each year by leaps and bounds, these efforts resulted in token gestures—Band-Aids here and there on different parts of the school district. The school district did not show interest, willingness, competence or commitment to cope with the rising number of non-English-speaking children. . . . Recent influxes of Chinese immigrants . . . aggravated the problem and created the acute crisis situation which now exists in our schools." For legal commentary about the case as it was developing, see: Stephen Sugarman and Ellen Widess, *Equal Protection for Non-English-Speaking Children:* Lau v. Nichols, 62 Cal. L. Rev. 157 (1974).

24. *Lau v. Nichols*, 414 U.S. 563, on 566–567 (1974).

25. For summaries of these contentious issues, both in the United States and elsewhere, see: Kymlicka (2001), Hewitt (2005), Bloemraad (2006), and Song (2007).

26. James Lyons, *The Past and Future Directions of Federal Bilingual Education Policy*, 508 Ann. Amer. Acad. Pol. & Soc. Sci. 66 (1990); Guadalupe San Miguel, Contested Policy: The Rise and Fall of Federal Bilingual Education in the United States, 1960–2001 (2004). For scholarly accounts of the relationship between bilingual education and English-only rules, see: Nancy Hornberger, *Bilingual Education and English-Only: A Language-Planning Framework*, 508 Ann. Amer. Acad. Pol. & Soc. Sci. 12 (1990); Wayne Santoro, *Conventional Politics Takes Center Stage: The Latino Struggle Against English-Only Laws*, 77 Soc. Forces 887 (1999); Donald Macedo, *The Colonialism of the English Only Movement*, 29 Ed. Res. 15 (2000); and Robert Preuhs, *Descriptive Representation, Legislative Leadership, and Direct Democracy: Latino Influence on English Only Laws in the States, 1984–2002*, 5 State Pol. & Pol'y Quart. 203 (2005).

27. Blackmun's concurring opinion appears on 414 U.S. 572.

28. For a discussion of the historical context for *Plyler*, see: Michael Olivas, *The Story of Plyler v. Doe: The Education of Undocumented Children and the Polity*, in Immigration Stories (David Martin and Peter Schuck, eds., 2005).

29. Id. See also, Olivas (2012). The penultimate case itself appears as *Plyler v. Doe*, 457 U.S. 202 (1982).

30. 457 U.S. on 212 and 220.

31. Id., 230. On 229, Brennan said: "There is no evidence in the record suggesting that illegal aliens impose any significant burden on the State's economy. To the contrary, the available evidence suggests that illegal aliens underutilize public services, while contributing their labor to the local economy and tax money to the state fisc." Brennan drew this claim from earlier federal appellate manifestations of *Plyler*, which in turn relied on a set of government and academic studies. See: *Doe v. Plyler*, 458 F.Supp. 569 (E.D. Texas, 1978).

32. Id.

33. Burger's dissenting opinion, joined by Justices White, Rehnquist, and O'Connor, begins on 457 U.S. 242. "Were it our business . . ." and policymaking role" are on 242; the analysis of education with reference to *San Antonio* is on 247; "By definition illegal aliens . . ." and the reference to *De Canas* appear on 250; and "finite resources" is on 251. For economic histories of this period, including discussions of "stagflation" under the Carter administration, see: W. Carl Biven, Jimmy Carter's Economy: Policy in an Age of Limits (2002); Alfred Eckes, The Contemporary Global Economy: A History since 1980 (2011); and Patterson (1997).

34. The interviews with Jim Plyler and the participants from *Plyler v. Doe* appear in Mary Ann Zehr, *Case Touched Many Parts of Community*, Ed. Week (June 6, 2007), and Mary Ann Zehr, *High Court's Access Ruling Endures as a Quiet Fact of Life*, Ed. Week (June 6, 2007). Another article dealing with the litigants is by Paul Feldman, *Texas Case Looms Over Prop 187's Legal Future*, L.A. Times (Oct. 23, 1994), cited in Olivas, supra note 28. Many scholars and commentators have written about *Plyler* since 1982. Some of the best pieces that situate the case within broader themes in race, immigration, and public law would include: Michael Olivas, Plyler v. Doe *and Postsecondary Admissions: Undocumented Adults and 'Enduring Disability,'* 15 J. Higher Ed. 19 (1986); Kevin Johnson, *Public Benefits and Immigration: The Intersection of Immigration Status, Ethnicity, Gender, and Class*, 42 UCLA L. Rev. 159 (1995); Goodwin Liu, *Education, Equality, and National Citizenship*, 116 Yale L. J. 330 (2006); and Hiroshi Motomura, *Immigration Outside the Law*, 108 Columbia L. Rev. 2037 (2008).

35. See: *Toll v. Moreno*, 458 U.S. 1 (1982). A description of the G-4 visa is in *Toll*, on 13–17.

36. Id.

37. *Nyquist v. Mauclet*, 432 U.S. 1 (1977). The following cases were some of the ones that Brennan also cited in *Toll*, in which the Supreme Court had struck down alienage-based classifications: *Examining Board v. Flores de Otero*, 426 U.S. 572 (1976) (this case ruled invalid a Puerto Rico statute that permitted only United States citizens to practice as private civil engineers); *In re Griffiths*, 413 U.S. 717 (1973) (this case overturned rules that limited membership in state bar associations to citizens); *Sugarman v. Dougall*, 413 U.S. 634 (1973) (this case overturned rules that limited participation in a State's competitive civil service to citizens only); *Takahashi v. Fish & Game Commission*, 334 U.S. 410 (1948) (this case overturned a California rule that denied commercial fishing licenses to persons "ineligible to citizenship"); and *Hampton v. Mow Sun Wong*, 426 U.S. 88 (1976) (this case overturned federal rules excluding

noncitizens from certain forms of federal employment). The only other case striking down a classification on the basis of alienage, *Graham v. Richardson*, 403 U.S. 365 (1971), involved the denial of welfare benefits deemed "essential" to sustain life for aliens, while citizens similarly situated were given such benefits. The Court has noted elsewhere the crucial role that such benefits play in providing the poor with "the means to obtain essential food, clothing, housing, and medical care." See, for example, *Goldberg v. Kelly*, 397 U.S. 254, 264 (1970).

38. 458 U.S. on 45, 42, and 25. The emphases in Rehnquist's opinion are from the original. In *Nyquist v. Mauclet*, 432 U.S. on 12, Rehnquist also said: "New York's choice to distribute these limited funds (i.e., financial aid) to resident citizens and to resident aliens who intend to become citizens, while denying them to aliens who have no intention of becoming citizens, is a natural legislative judgment."

39. Van de Kamp's opinion is in 67 Ops. Cal. Atty. Gen. 241 (1984). He said, in part, that "the [California] Legislature did not intend to . . . permit undocumented aliens to establish residence for tuition purposes in California's public institutions of higher education."

40. *Leticia A. v. Board of Regents of the University of California*, No. 588982-4 (May 7, 1985).

41. Bradford's appellate case is reported as *Regents of the University of California v. Superior Court of Los Angeles*, 225 Cal. App. 3d 972 (1990). His lawyers characterized the education of undocumented students as a "waste and misuse of public funds," and they were quoted in *Forced to Enroll Illegals, Man Claims; UCLA Sued*, L.A. TIMES (Jul. 11, 1986). Judge Klein's remarks are on 225 Cal. App. 3d 980–981. She discussed at length the "state's legitimate interests in denying resident tuition to undocumented aliens." "We will name just a few: the state's interests in not subsidizing violations of law; in preferring to educate its own lawful residents; in avoiding enhancing the employment prospects of those to whom employment is forbidden by law; in conserving its fiscal resources for the benefit of its lawful residents; in avoiding accusations that it unlawfully harbors illegal aliens in its classrooms and dormitories; in not subsidizing the university education of those who may be deported; in avoiding discrimination against citizens of sister states and aliens lawfully present; in maintaining respect for government by not subsidizing those who break the law; and in not subsidizing the university education of students whose parents, because of the risk of deportation if detected, are less likely to pay taxes." Subsequently, in 1995, another appellate court upheld Klein's opinion and the rule about undocumented students being ineligible for in-state tuition; that case appears as *American Association for Women v. Board of Trustees of CSU*, 38 Cal. Rptr. 2d 15 (1995).

CHAPTER 8: UNDOCUMENTED AND UNAFRAID

1. For Senator and Governor Wilson's positions on immigration in the 1980s and 1990s, see: Daniel Tichenor, *The Politics of Immigration Reform in the United States, 1981–1990*, 26 POLITY 333 (1994); Philip Martin, *Harvest of Confusion: Immigration Reform and California Agriculture*, 24 INT. MIG. REV. 69 (1990); and Susan Baker, *The 'Amnesty' Aftermath: Current Policy Issues Stemming From the Legalization Programs*, 31 INT. MIG. REV. 5 (1997).

2. The full text of Proposition 187 appears in Appendix A of *League of United Latin American Citizens v. Wilson*, 908 F. Supp. 755 (C.D. Cal 1995).

3. Id. The scholarly literature on Proposition 187 is voluminous, as it has been discussed in over a thousand scholarly articles and books, one or two of which I've written myself. At the time of its passage, one prominent law professor did describe the rule as a political "earthquake"; see Peter Schuck, *The Message of Proposition 187*, 26 PAC. L.J. 989 (1995). Another said that the rule reduced illegal aliens to "outlaws" and would presage similar state and federal rules that would push undocumented aliens to the margins of American society; see Gerald Neuman, *Aliens as Outlaws*, 42 UCLA L. REV. 1425 (1995). And still another insisted that although the rule had race-neutral provisions, it had clear, racist undertones; see Kevin Johnson, *An Essay on Immigration Politics, Popular Democracy, and California's Proposition 187*, 70 WASH. L. REV. 629 (1995). These three articles are cited here because similar themes appear so often in scholarly work about Proposition 187 in sociology, anthropology, communication, and ethnic studies, among other fields. In the elections of 1994 in California, the final tally in favor of the rule was 59 percent. For a key scholarly study published during this period, one that connected fugitive slave rules and early immigration rules, especially in the states, see: NEUMAN (1996); for another study that places Proposition 187 within the broader politics of race and racism in the post–civil rights era, see: DANIEL HOSANG, RACIAL PROPOSITIONS: BALLOT INITIATIVES AND THE MAKING OF POSTWAR CALIFORNIA (2010).

4. 908 F. Supp. 755, on 85–86. The proponents of Proposition 187 did not give up in the federal courts—litigation dragged on for another five years.

5. For an overview of Congress and immigration reform during these years, see GIMPEL AND EDWARDS (1999), chs. 5 and 6.

6. For a longer overview of these rules in 1996, see PARK AND PARK (2005). For a discussion of Jay Kim and other Asian American congressmen during this period, see: James Lai, Wendy Tam Cho, Thomas Kim, and Okiyoshi Takeda, *Asian Pacific-American Campaigns, Elections, and Elected Officials*, 34 PS: POL. SCI. & POL. 611 (2001); and THOMAS KIM, THE RACIAL LOGIC OF POLITICS: ASIAN AMERICANS AND PARTY COMPETITION (2007).

7. *Tuition Benefits to Undocumented Aliens*, 115 HARV. L. REV. 1548, on 1549 (2002). A key supporter of the rule, Professor Kris Kobach of the University of Missouri School of Law, insisted that there was no confusion in IIRIRA with respect to the resident tuition provision: "If a state wished to make resident tuition rates available to illegal aliens, it would have to make the benefit available to all non-resident U.S. citizens and nationals." See: Kris Kobach, *Immigration Nullification: In-State Tuition and Lawmakers Who Disregard the Law*, 10 N.Y.U. J. LEGIS. & PUB. POL'Y 473, on 477 (2006/2007).

8. The provisions of the Illegal Immigration Reform and Illegal Immigrant Responsibility Act dealing with "Higher Education Benefits" for undocumented aliens was codified in 8 U.S.C. §1623. The provisions of the Personal Responsibility and Work Opportunity Reconciliation Act dealing with "Welfare and Public Benefits for Aliens" was codified in 8 U.S.C. § 1621 (2006).

9. For succinct summaries of these debates about Section 505, see: Jessica Salsbury, *Evading 'Residence': Undocumented Students, Higher Education, and the States*, 53

AM. U.L. REV. 459 (2003); and Thomas Ruge and Angela Iza, *Higher Education for Undocumented Students*, 15 IND. INT'L & COMP. L. REV. 257 (2005).

10. These figures were reported through the University of California, and published in the *New York Times* in 1991. See: Robert Reingold, *Budget Cuts Jar University of California*, N.Y. TIMES (Jan. 21, 1991). By 2005, undergraduate tuition and fees in public colleges and universities in states providing tuition subsidies averaged about $4,000 for residents, while out-of-state students were paying about $11,000. See: Washington Higher Education Coordinating Board, *Tuition and Fee: A National Comparison* (2005). For the 1922 figures, see *Bryan v. Regents*, 188 Cal. 559 (1922).

11. See, for instance, Kevin Dougherty, H. Kenny Nienhusser, and Blanca Vega, *Undocumented Immigrants and State Higher Education Policy: The Politics of In-State Tuition Eligibility in Texas and Arizona*, 34 REV. HIGHER ED. 123 (2010).

12. Kobach's complaints about "immigration nullification" are detailed in Kobach, supra note 7; his quote is on 521. For the two cases, see: *Day v. Bond*, 500 F.3d 1127 (10th Cir. 2007), and *Martinez v. Regents*, 50 Cal. 4th 1277 (2010). Elton Gallegly's opposition to in-state tuition benefits also appears in Elton Gallegly, *College for Illegal Immigrants?* N.Y. TIMES (Sep. 10, 2011).

13. Dennis Romboy, *Utah House Amends, Shelves Repeal of In State College Tuition for Illegal Immigrants—For Now*, DESERET NEWS (Feb 24, 2011); see also, *School Daze*, ECONOMIST (Nov. 27, 2010). For an overview of some of the state rules, see: Kobach, supra note 7; Stella Flores, *State Dream Acts: The Effects of In-State Resident Tuition Policies and Undocumented Latino Students*, 33 REV. HIGHER ED. 239 (2010); and Michael McLendon, Christine Mokher, and Stella Flores, *Legislative Agenda Setting for In-State Resident Tuition Policies: Immigration, Representation, and Educational Access*, 117 AMER. J. ED. 563 (2011).

14. Senator Hatch's remarks appear in 147 Cong. Rec. S8, 581 (Aug. 1, 2001).

15. The rule, in part, "[authorized] the Attorney General to cancel the removal of, and adjust to permanent resident status, an alien who: (1) has attained the age of 12 prior to enactment of this Act; (2) files an application before reaching the age of 21; (3) has earned a high school or equivalent diploma; (4) has been physically present in the United States for at least five years immediately preceding the date of enactment of this Act (with certain exceptions); (5) is a person of good moral character; and (6) is not inadmissible or deportable under specified criminal or security grounds of the Immigration and Nationality Act." The bill appeared as S.1291 in the 107th Congress.

16. For an overview of the legislative history of the DREAM Act, see: Elisha Barron, *The Development, Relief, and Education for Alien Minors (DREAM) Act*, 48 HARV. J. LEGIS. 623 (2011).

17. For media accounts of the congressional debate in late 2010, see Kathleen Hennessy, *DREAM Act May Haunt GOP*, L.A. TIMES (Dec. 15, 2010); and Julia Preston, *After a False Dawn, Anxiety for Illegal Immigrant Students*, N.Y. TIMES (Feb. 8, 2011). The undocumented student, a Miss Maricela Aguilar of Wisconsin, was quoted in Preston. For a discussion of the DREAM Act as part of more comprehensive immigration reform, see Michael Olivas, *Problems, Possibilities, and Pragmatic Solutions: The Political Economy of the DREAM Act and the Legislative Process: A Case Study of Comprehensive Immigration Reform*, 55 WAYNE L. REV. 1757 (2009).

18. For the Illinois Dream Act, see: Todd Wilson, *Lawmakers Send Illinois Dream Act Bill to Quinn*, CHIC. TRIB. (May 30, 2011); and Monique Garcia, *For Undocumented Immigrants, One Barrier to College Falls*, CHIC. TRIB. (Aug. 2, 2011).

19. For media accounts of the California Dream Act, see: Jennifer Medina, *Legislature in California Is Set to Pass a Dream Act*, N.Y. TIMES (Sep. 1, 2011); Teresa Watanabe, *More Anxiety Over the Dream Act; Legal Students Wonder if They'll Be Pitted Against Illegal Immigrants for Aid*, L.A. TIMES (Sep. 25, 2011); and *Gov. Brown Signs Part II of California DREAM Act*, ED. WEEK (Oct. 19, 2011). Donnelly's remarks are quoted in Patrick McGreevy and Anthony York, *Brown Signs California Dream Act*, L.A. TIMES (Oct. 9, 2011); his unsuccessful petition drive is discussed in Nicholas Riccardi, *Dream Act Opponents' Petition Drive Fails*, L.A. TIMES (Jan. 7, 2012).

20. See, for example, Flores, supra note 13, on 271: "This study has shown that the availability of an [in-state resident tuition] policy positively and significantly affects the college decisions of students who are likely to be undocumented as measured by an increase in their college enrollment rates."

21. Leisy Abrego, *Legal Consciousness of Undocumented Latinos: Fear and Stigma as Barriers to Claims-Making for First- and 1.5-Generation Immigrants*, 45 L. & SOC. REV. 337 (2011). The quote are on 355 and 356, and on 357, Abrego cites to Cecilia Menjivar and Leisy Abrego, *Parents and Children Across Borders: Legal Instability and Intergenerational Relations in Guatemalan and Salvadoran Families*, in ACROSS GENERATIONS: IMMIGRANT FAMILIES IN AMERICA (Nancy Foner, ed., 2009). For other work about the legal and social consciousness of people who are out of status, see: CHAVEZ (1998); COUTIN (2003); DE GENOVA (2005); and Cecilia Menjivar, *Liminal Legality: Salvadoran and Guatemalan Immigrants' Lives in the United States*, 111 AMER. J. SOC. 999 (2006).

22. Leisy Abrego, *Legitimacy, Social Identity, and the Mobilization of Law: The Effects of Assembly Bill 540 on Undocumented Students in California*, 33 L. & SOC. INQ. 709 (2008). "I'm motivated to speak up . . ." appears on 729, and "Students who are born . . ." appears on 721.

23. For a concise history of IDEAS as a student organization, see: UNDERGROUND UNDERGRADS: UCLA UNDOCUMENTED IMMIGRANT STUDENTS SPEAK OUT (Gabriela Madera et al., eds., 2008), and UNDOCUMENTED STUDENTS: UNFULFILLED DREAMS (2007). Both publications were produced at the UCLA Center for Labor Research and Education. For more about political activism and the overall challenges faced by undocumented students, see: Roberto Gonzalez, *Left Out But Not Shut Down: Political Activism and the Undocumented Student Movement*, 3 Nw. J. L. & SOC. POL'Y 219 (2008); and Lindsay Huber and Maria Malagon, *Silenced Struggles: The Experiences of Latina and Latino Undocumented College Students in California*, 7 NEV. L. J. 841 (2007).

24. For short biographies of Tam Tran, including her congressional testimony, her experiences as a witness before Congress, and the impact that this may have had on her family in California, see: Testimony of Tam Tran before the House Judiciary Committee's Subcommittee Immigration, Citizenship, Refugees, Border Security, and International Law (May 18, 2007); Teresa Watanabe, *Vietnamese Refugee Family Finds Itself in Limbo*, L.A. TIMES (Oct. 19, 2007); and Kent Wong and Matias Ramos, *Undocumented and Unafraid: Tam Tran and Cinthya Felix*, 1 BOOM: J. CAL. (2011).

25. The brief, and the account of the brief and its subjects, appeared in two articles: *Brief of the Amici Curiae, Asian Pacific American Legal Center and 80 Asian Pacific American Organizations in Support of Respondents and Defendants*, 15 UCLA ASIAN PAC. AM. L. J. 43 (2009/2010); and Connie Choi, Carmina Ocampo, and Yungsuhn Park, *Shining a Spotlight on the Invisible: How an Amicus Brief Helped Organize the Asian American Community to Support Undocumented Asian Students*, 15 UCLA ASIAN PAC. AM. L. J. 43 (2009/2010). The report about AB 540 students in the UC system was written by staff in the President's office of the University of California, and it appears as *Annual Report on AB 540 Tuition Exemptions, 2006–2007 Academic Year* (Mar. 5, 2008). The tables showing household income among AB 540 families appears on page 9.

26. For the organization at UC Santa Cruz, see Neidi Dominguez et al., *Constructing a Counternarrative: Students Informing Now (S.I.N.) Reframes Immigration and Education in the United States*, 52 J. ADOLESCENT & ADULT LIT. 439 (2009); for the ones within the City University of New York, see Carolina Bank Munoz, *A Dream Deferred: Undocumented Students at CUNY*, 84 RADICAL TEACHER 8 (2009). For a more general account, see Maggie Jones, *Coming Out Illegal*, N.Y. TIMES (Oct. 24, 2010).

27. "I think losing the shame . . ." appears in Preston, supra note 17; "There are undocumented students . . ." appears in Miranda Sain and Candice Cameron, *Undocumented Students Urge Becker to Ignore Ban*, SIGNAL (Apr. 19, 2011).

28. For examples of news stories about these phenomenon, see: Dana Priest, *Arlington School Policy Entangled Hispanics*, WASH. POST (Mar. 14, 1988); Doreen Carvajal, *Immigrants Fight Residency Rules Blocking Children in Long Island Schools*, N.Y. TIMES (Aug. 7, 1995); Tim Vanderpool, *Southwestern Schools Root Out Illegal Pupils*, CHRIST. SCI. MON. (Mar. 26, 2004); and Nina Bernstein, *Despite Ruling, Many School Districts Ask for Immigration Papers*, N.Y. TIMES (Jul. 23, 2010).

29. The New York Civil Liberties Union protested some of the practices among public school districts in New York and petitioned the Commissioner of the New York State Education Department to stop these practices; see: Letter from Donna Lieberman and Udi Ofer, NYCLU, to Commissioner David Steiner (Jul. 21, 2010). For more about the Alabama rule, see Stacy Khadaroo, *Alabama Immigration Law Leaves Schools Gripped by Uncertainty*, CHRIST. SCI. MON. (Sep. 30, 2011); *Judge Upholds Alabama Law Which Rules Public Schools Must Investigate Legal Residency of Children as Part of Immigration Crackdown*, DAILY MAIL (Sept. 29, 2011); and Stephen Caesar, *Federal Court Blocks Part of Alabama Immigration Law*, L.A. TIMES (Oct. 14, 2011).

30. The Student and Exchange Visitor Information System, or SEVIS, is described briefly in Ruge and Iza, supra note 9, on 263–264, and in Teresa Miller, *Citizenship and Severity: Recent Immigration Reforms and the New Penology*, 17 GEO. IMMIGR. L.J. 611 (2003). For scholarly discussions about privacy, education, and undocumented status historically and since 9/11, see: Linda Bosniak, *Opposing Proposition 187: Undocumented Immigrants and the National Imagination*, 28 CONN. L. REV. 555 (1996); Victor Romero, *Noncitizen Students and Immigration Policy Post 9/11*, 17 GEO. IMMIGR. L.J. 357 (2003); and Laura Khatcheressian, *FERPA and the Immigration and Naturalization Service: A Guide for University Counsel on Federal Rules for Collecting, Maintaining and Releasing Information About Foreign Students*, 29 J.C. & U.L. 457 (2003). For discussions of E-Verify and how the program has changed since 1997, see: Lora Ries,

B-Verify: Transforming E-Verify into a Biometric Employment Verification System, 3 ALB. GOV'T L. REV. 271 (2010), and Peter Asaad, Bruce Morrison, et al., *Panel on E-Verify: Chamber of Commerce v. Whiting*, 1 AM. U. LABOR & EMP. L. F. 301 (2011).

31. For accounts of the protests in Georgia following the Regents' ban, see: *School Daze*, supra note 13; Sain and Cameron, supra note 27; Carla Caldwell, *UGA President Won't Defy Regents' Ban of Undocumented Students*, ATLANTA BUS. CHRON. (Dec. 1, 2011); and Laura Diamond and Kristina Torres, *Senate Votes to Ban Illegal Immigrants from Georgia's Public Colleges*, ATLANTA J. & CONST. (Mar. 5, 2012)

32. Sain and Cameron, supra note 27, and Diamond and Torres, supra note 31. For additional background about the rules in Georgia and similar legislation in other states, see: Laura Hernandez, *Dreams Deferred*, 21 CORNELL J. L. & PUB. POL'Y 525 (2012); and Mariano Willoughby, *Illegal Immigrants Play Tiny Role in Overcrowding Classes*, ATLANTA J. & CONST. (Feb. 28, 2011).

33. Maureen Downey, *Freedom University: College Profs Teach Barred Immigrant Students*, ATLANTA J. & CONST. (Aug. 25, 2011); and Thelma Gutierrez and Traci Tamura, *Freedom University: Studying in Secret*, CNN (Dec. 1, 2011).

34. See: R. I. Brigham, *Negro Education in Ante-Bellum Missouri*, 30 J. NEGRO HIST. 405 (1945).

35. For details of Obama's policy change with respect to students eligible for one or more versions of the DREAM Act, and for the Congressional reaction against it, see: Christopher Goffard, Esmeralda Bermudez, and Melissa Leu, *Elation and Uncertainty: Young Immigrants Rejoice*, L.A. TIMES (June 16, 2012); Christi Parsons, Brian Bennett, and Joseph Tanfani, *Obama Opens New Door: The President Halts Deportation For Some Who Came to the U.S. Illegally as Children*, L.A. TIMES (June 16, 2012); and Julia Preston and John Cushman, *Obama to Permit Young Migrants to Remain in U.S.*, N.Y. TIMES (June 16, 2012). A transcript of Obama's formal statement appears as *Transcript of Obama's Speech on Immigration Policy*, N.Y. TIMES (June 16, 2012).

36. For an overview of Ms. Crandall's later years and the subsequent developments of the place where she lived and taught in Canterbury, see: Kathleen Hunter, *Teaching with Historic Places Lesson Plans: From Canterbury to Little Rock: The Struggle for Educational Equality for African Americans*, 15 OAH MAG. HIST. 37 (2001).

37. For media accounts of this story, see: Larry Gordon, *UC to Award Honorary Degrees to Interned Japanese American Students*, L.A. TIMES (Jul. 17, 2009); Patrick McDonnell, *UCLA Awards Honorary Degrees to Japanese Americans Who Were Interned*, L.A. TIMES (May 16, 2010).

38. For other aspects of this story, I relied on: Robin Hindrey, *Honorary Degree Ceremony Aims to Help Right a 67-Year-Old Wrong*, UCSF NEWSCENTER (Dec. 7, 2009); Cathy Cockrell, *Japanese Americans Receive Honorary Degrees, 67 Years After World War II Internment Cut Their Studies Short at Berkeley*, UC NEWSCENTER (Dec. 16, 2009); and Anne Wolf, *UC Employees Make Honorary Degrees Their Mission*, UC NEWSROOM (Sep. 1, 2009).

39. For accounts of Tam Tran and Cinthya Felix, see: Wong and Ramos, supra note 24; Patrick McDonnell, *UCLA Mourns Two Graduates Killed in Maine Traffic Accident*, L.A. TIMES (May 21, 2010); Suzannah Weiss, *Tran Remembered as Advocate for Immigrants*, BROWN DAILY HER. (May 19, 2010); and *Support Group for Undocumented Students Wins UC's Top Leadership Award*, UCLA TODAY (May 19, 2010). Yudof's remarks appeared in *Support Group*. The Rhode Island resolution appeared

as *Rhode Island Senate Resolution Expressing Profound Sympathy on the Passing of Tam Ngoc Tran* (May 20, 2010).

CHAPTER 9: UTOPIAN VISIONS AND THE UNLAWFUL OTHER

1. For patterns of land acquisition among whites in the decades after the Revolution, see: Stanley Lebergott, *The Demand for Land: The United States, 1820–1860*, 45 J. ECON. HIST. 181 (1985). For prevailing, recurring ideas of how Native Americans needed to be "cleared" for white settlement, especially as an aspect of local sovereignty against British or American federal law, see: Roger Kennedy, *Jefferson and the Indians*, 27 WINTERTHUR PORT. 105 (1992); AMERICAN ENCOUNTERS: NATIVES AND NEWCOMERS FROM EUROPEAN CONTACT TO INDIAN REMOVAL, 1500–1850 (Peter Mancall and James Merrell, eds., 1999); MILLER (2006); and TIM GARRISON, THE LEGAL IDEOLOGY OF REMOVAL: THE SOUTHERN JUDICIARY AND THE SOVEREIGNTY OF NATIVE AMERICAN NATIONS (2009). For an interesting discussion of land claims, past and present, see: Burke Hendrix, *Memory in Native American Land Claims*, 33 POL. THEORY 763 (2005).

2. LITWACK (1965), 72. For discussions of the Naturalization Act of 1790 and how it shaped American citizenship, immigration, and race relations, see: SMITH (1999), DANIELS (2002), KETTNER (2005), and SPICKARD (2007).

3. For a scholarly discussion of African American life in Ohio before the Civil War, see: Joan Cashin, *Black Families in the Old Northwest*, 15 J. EARLY REP. 449 (1995). The quote is on 449.

4. Recent biographies of President Washington that deal with his slaveholding and with the manumission of his own slaves in his will include: JOSEPH ELLIS, HIS EXCELLENCY: GEORGE WASHINGTON (2004); HENRY WIENCEK, AN IMPERFECT GOD: GEORGE WASHINGTON, HIS SLAVES, AND THE CREATION OF AMERICA (2004); and RON CHERNOW, WASHINGTON: A LIFE (2010). For a helpful collection of letters by George Washington about his slaves and about slavery, see: George Washington, *Letters of George Washington Bearing on the Negro*, 2 J. NEGRO HIST. 411 (1917). For a wonderful retelling of the complicated relationship between George Washington and one his slaves, Henry, see: SIMON SCHAMA, ROUGH CROSSINGS: BRITAIN, THE SLAVES, AND THE AMERICAN REVOLUTION (2006).

5. BERWANGER (2002), 31–32.

6. For scholarly discussion of Illinois and its debates about slavery, see SIMEONE (2000). For brief discussions of Indiana's constitution with respect to free blacks, see: Gregory Rose, *The Distribution of Indiana's Ethnic and Racial Minorities in 1850*, 87 IND. MAG. HIST. 224 (1991); Richard Nation, *Violence and the Rights of African Americans in Civil War Era Indiana: The Case of James Hays*, 100 IND. MAG. HIST. 215 (2004); and David Bodenhamer and Randall Shepard, *The Narratives and Counternarratives of Indiana Legal History*, 101 IND. MAG. HIST. 348 (2005). For discussions of free blacks in Oregon before the Civil War, see: Lenwood Davis, *Sources of History of Blacks in Oregon*, 73 OR. HIST. QUART. 196 (1972); Thomas McClintock, *James Saules, Peter Burnett, and the Oregon Black Exclusion Law of June 1844*, 86 PAC. NW. QUART. 121 (1995); and Keith Richard, *Unwelcome Settlers: Black and Mulatto Oregon Pioneers*, 84 OR. HIST. QUART. 29 (1983).

7. See, for example, BERWANGER (2002), 78.

8. Litwack (1965), 119.

9. See, for instance, Cornish (1990) and McPherson (2003).

10. Horton (1993), 57.

11. Id.

12. See, for example: Refugees from Slavery: Autobiographies of Fugitive Slaves in Canada (Benjamin Drew, ed., 1856, 2004); Jacqueline Tobin, From Midnight to Dawn: The Last Tracks of the Underground Railroad (2008); and Hendrick and Hendrick (2010).

13. For responses to the Fugitive Slave Act among African Americans, see: Campbell (2011); Franklin and Schweninger (2000); and Lubet (2010). As many historians have noted, there were substantial regional variations among Americans to the Fugitive Slave Act. See, for example: Emmett Preston, *The Fugitive Slave Acts in Ohio*, 28 J. Negro Hist. 422 (1943); Julius Yanuck, *The Garner Fugitive Slave Case*, 40 Miss. Va. Hist. Rev. 47 (1953); Harold Schwartz, *Fugitive Slave Days in Boston*, 27 New Eng. Quart. 191 (1954); and Anthony Sebok, *Judging the Fugitive Slave Acts*, 100 Yale L. J. 1835 (1991).

14. Berwanger (2002), 63–64. Berwanger continued: "Because he had left the slave states to escape competition with slave labor and association with Negroes, the editor announced that he strongly opposed the presence of Negroes, free or slave. Agreeing with the *Californian*, Samuel Brannan of the *California Star* wrote than any type of Negro labor would drive away the 'sober and industrious middle class' because it was not respectable for white men to work with Negroes. Inasmuch as the majority of the people opposed the presence of Negroes, Brannan predicted that both slavery and free Negroes would be excluded from the future state."

15. Shirley Moore, *"We Feel the Want of Protection": The Politics of Law and Race in California, 1848–1878*, 81 Cal. Hist. 96, 109 (2003).

16. Berwanger (2002), 74–75, and 111.

17. Almaguer (2008), 29.

18. The scholarly literature on the Chinese Exclusion Act and its political origins is extensive, but for accounts of Chinese Exclusion as it emanated from and was enforced in California, see: Almaguer (2008); Entry Denied: Exclusion and the Chinese Community in America, 1882–1943 (Sucheng Chan, ed., 1994); Salyer (1995); and Lee (2007). The phrase "gatekeeping nation" is from Lee (2007).

19. See, for example, Takaki (1998); Ngai (2005); and Chinese American Transnationalism: The Flow of People, Resources, and Ideas between China and America during the Exclusion Era (Sucheng Chan, ed., 2005).

20. All of these strategies are discussed in Lee (2007). The figures about women giving birth are in Takaki (1998), 235–236. *Wong Kim Ark* appeared as *United States v. Wong Kim Ark*, 169 U.S. 649 (1898). For a discussion of federal court responses to Chinese petitioners, including people claiming to be merchants or members of other exempt classes, see: Salyer (1995) and Anna Law, The Immigration Battle in American Courts (2010). For scholarly discussions that discuss the consequences of this case on Chinese American migrations and identities, see: Claiming America: Constructing Chinese American Identities during the Exclusion Era (K. Scott Wong and Sucheng Chan, eds., 1998).

21. Helpful pictures of the peanut shells, banana peels, and the immigration prison on Angel Island are in Lee (2007), 214–215, and 219. Many of the representative

poems carved into the prison walls are in HIM MARK LAI, GENNY LIM, AND JUDY YUNG, ISLAND: POETRY AND HISTORY OF CHINESE IMMIGRANTS ON ANGEL ISLAND, 1910–1940 (1991).

22. For social histories of Chinese Americans, especially with respect to ethnic media and other important social institutions through which Chinese Americans interacted with one another in the early twentieth century, see: HSU (2000); ZHAO (2002); LAI (2004); and GLORIA CHUN, OF ORPHANS AND WARRIORS: INVENTING CHINESE AMERICAN CULTURE AND IDENTITY (1999).

23. PFAELZER (2008), 252–253.

24. For an excellent discussion of public health institutions and Chinese immigrants in the late 19th and early 20th centuries in San Francisco, see: NAYAN SHAH, CONTAGIOUS DIVIDES: EPIDEMICS AND RACE IN SAN FRANCISCO'S CHINATOWN (2001). For comparative accounts that examine race and public health in other American settings and periods, see: J. H. POWELL, BRING OUT YOUR DEAD: THE GREAT PLAGUE OF YELLOW FEVER IN PHILADELPHIA IN 1793 (1993); MARGARET HUMPHREYS, YELLOW FEVER AND THE SOUTH (1999); JOHN PIERCE, YELLOW JACK: HOW YELLOW FEVER RAVAGED AMERICA AND WALTER REED DISCOVERED ITS DEADLY SECRETS (2005); BENJAMIN TRASK, FEARFUL RAVAGES: YELLOW FEVER IN NEW ORLEANS, 1796–1905 (2005); and MOLLY CROSBY, THE AMERICAN PLAGUE (2007).

25. *Wong Wing v. United States*, 163 U.S. 228 (1896).

26. *United States v. Ju Toy*, 198 U.S. 252 (1905). For lengthier discussions of both *Wong Wing* and *Ju Toy*, see: PARK (2004).

27. As one might imagine, the scholarly discussions about aspects of the rule of law and about the rule of law as a concept in legal theory, both in contemporary discourse and in Western legal history, are extensive. For purposes of this discussion, I've relied heavily on the following texts: RAZ (1980); HART (1997); TAMANAHA (2004); RAWLS (2005); Andrei Marmor, *The Rule of Law and Its Limits*, 23 L. & PHIL. 1 (2004); CONSTABLE (2007); and Jeremy Waldron, *The Concept and the Rule of Law*, 43 GA. L. REV. 1 (2008). For an excellent discussion of contemporary societies ruled *through* law, as a way of better understanding that concept, see: TOM GINSBURG AND TAMIR MOUSTAFA, RULE BY LAW: THE POLITICS OF COURTS IN AUTHORITARIAN REGIMES (2008).

28. The phrase "full dominion of the owner of the slave" comes from *State v. Mann*, 13 N.C. 263 (1829), on 265. This is one of the most important cases to examine the nature of slavery, and so it has drawn significant scholarly attention. See, for example, TUSHNET (2003).

29. In political and legal theory, many scholars have examined the moral underpinnings of national sovereignty and pointed also to the arbitrary nature of political membership. For outstanding representative works, see: BENHABIB (2004), BOSNIAK (2008), SHACHAR (2009), DAUVERGNE (2009), JOHNSON (2009), BROWN (2010), and STEVENS (2009). For an elegant argument about how American immigration law wasn't always so unwelcoming, nor needn't continue in that vein, see: MOTOMURA (2007). For an amazing story about two children switched at birth, one into slavery and the other out of it, see MARK TWAIN, THE TRAGEDY OF PUDD'NHEAD WILSON (1894).

30. The sheriff to whom I'm referring is Joe Arpaio of Maricopa County, Arizona, and for more about him, see: Tanya Golash-Boza, *A Confluence of Interests in Immigration Enforcement: How Politicians, the Media, and Corporations Profit from Immigra-*

tion Policies Destined to Fail, 3 Soc. Compass 1 (2009); and Meghan McDowell and Nancy Wonders, *Keeping Migrants in Their Place: Technologies of Control and Racialized Public Space in Arizona*, 36 Soc. Just. 54 (2009–2010).

31. I am indebted to Professor Pratheepan Gulasekaram, whose most excellent presentation at the UC Irvine School of Law in 2011 inspired the ideas in this paragraph. For the essay upon which his presentation was based, see: Pratheepan Gulasekaram, *Why a Wall?* 2 UC Irvine L. Rev. 147 (2012).

32. Senator Sessions was quoted in Carl Hulse and Jim Rutenberg, *Senate Votes to Extend Fence Along Border*, N.Y. Times (May 17, 2006). The figures for nonimmigrant admissions were taken from U.S. Department of Homeland Security, Statistical Yearbook (2010), Table 25.

33. Dolores Ines Casillas, *Sounds of Surveillance: U.S. Spanish-Language Radio Patrols La Migra*, 63 Amer. Quart. 807, on 807 (2011). Casillas continued: "As one radio host shared with me, 'The lines light up like a Christmas tree well before we say, 'OK, we welcome your calls.' Depending on the particulars of the radio show, listeners receive an hour or two of current and free legal updates as they sympathetically listen to the legal plight of others. Together, listeners make sense of revisions to already intricate legal forms, complain about periodic increases in filing fees, share their frustrations with long bureaucratic waits or, as with the caller above, ask with apparent worry whether to report to a Department of Homeland Security regional office on the U.S. or Mexico side of the border." Patterns of internet use among Spanish-speaking immigrants and Latino Americans also have similar qualities; see, for example, Sasha Costanza-Chock, *The Immigrant Rights Movement on the Net: Between 'Web 2.0' and Comunicacion Popular*, 60 Amer. Quart. 851 (2008).

34. The scholarly literature about immigration law and policy after 1990 has been extensive. Some of the best scholarly books that capture the new legal regimes of enforcement include: Mark Dow, American Gulag: Inside U.S. Immigration Prisons (2004); Hing (2006); Daniel Kanstroom, Deportation Nation: Outsiders in American History (2007); Keeping Out the Other: A Critical Introduction to Immigration Enforcement Today (David Brotherton and Philip Kretsedemas, eds., 2008); Tanya Golash-Boza, Immigration Nation: Raids, Detentions, and Deportations in Post 9/11 America (2012); and Daniel Kanstroom, Aftermath: Deportation Law and the New American Diaspora (2012). For a discussion of the REAL ID Act of 2005, see: Brian Murphy, *The REAL ID Act of 2005*, 19 Geo. Immigr. L. J. 191 (2004); and Gerald Neuman, *On the Adequacy of Direct Review after the REAL ID Act of 2005*, 51 N.Y.L. Sch. L. Rev. 133 (2006). On Secure Communities, its origins in the War on Terror, and its subsequent development, see: Bill Ong Hing, *Misusing Immigration Policies in the Name of Homeland Security*, 6 CR: New Cent. Rev. 195 (2006); Rachel Ray, *Insecure Communities: Examining Local Government Participation in U.S. Immigration and Customs Enforcement's 'Secure Communities' Program*, 10 Seattle J. Soc. Just. 327 (2011); Karen Hacker, Jocelyn Chu, Lisa Arsenault, and Robert Marlin, *Provider's Perspectives on the Impact of Immigration and Customs Enforcement (ICE) Activity on Immigrant Health*, 23 J. Health Care Poor & Underserved 651 (2012); and Stephanie Kang, *A Rose By Any Other Name: The Chilling Effect of ICE's Secure Communities Program*, 9 Hastings Race & Poverty L. J. 83 (2012). For the figures on formal removals, see U.S. Department of Homeland Security, supra note 32, Table 36.

35. Excellent discussions of "immigration federalism," including lengthy discussions of the federal rules governing local and state collaborations, have been published and summarized within a special issue of LAW AND POLICY. See: Doris Marie Provine and Monica Varsanyi, *Scaled Down: Perspectives on State and Local Creation and Enforcement of Immigration Law*, 34 L. & POL'Y 105 (2011). For the figures about state legislatures, their immigration rules, and their relationship to federal immigration law, see: Lina Newton, *Policy Innovation or Vertical Integration? A View of Immigration Federalism from the States*, 34 L. & POL'Y 113 (2012); Keith Cunningham-Parmeter, *Forced Federalism: States as Laboratories of Immigration Reform*, 62 HASTINGS L.J. 1673 (2011); and Rick Su, *Police Discretion and Local Immigration Policymaking*, 79 UMKC L. REV. 901 (2011).

36. Casillas, supra note 33, 808–809. "*Limones verdes*" appears in Lizette Alvarez, *Fear and Hope in Immigrant's Furtive Existence*, N.Y. TIMES (Dec. 20, 2006). Jimmy Carter Boulevard appeared in Joe Johnson, *Climate of Fear*, ATHENS BANNER-HERALD (Mar. 27, 2006); the laundromats of Escondido appeared in Rachel Uranga, *Afraid to Go Outside: Illegals Frightened of Immigration Sweeps and Arrests*, DAILY NEWS L.A. (June 17, 2004); and the flea markets of San Jose appeared in Edwin Garcia, *Rumor Hurts Flea Market*, SAN JOSE MERCURY NEWS (May 30, 1997).

37. The poster from Boston is reprinted in JUNIUS RODRIGUEZ, THE HISTORICAL ENCYCLOPEDIA OF WORLD SLAVERY 501 (2001). For the warnings in Chinese, see CHANG (2003), 141. Chang was quoting Ng Poon Chew, the founder of the *Chung Sai Yat Po*, one of the first Chinese-language newspapers in the United States with a national circulation.

Selected Books Cited

Adams, David Wallace. *Education for Extinction*. Lawrence: University Press of Kansas, 1997.

Almaguer, Tomas. *Racial Fault Lines: The Historical Origins of White Supremacy in California*. Berkeley: University of California Press, 2008.

Anderson, James D. *The Education of Blacks in the South, 1860–1935*. Chapel Hill: University of North Carolina Press, 1988.

Andreas, Peter. *Border Games: Policing the U.S.-Mexico Divide*. Ithaca, NY: Cornell University Press, 2009.

Arac, Jonathon. *Huckleberry Finn as Idol and Target: The Functions of Criticism in Our Time*. Madison: University of Wisconsin Press, 1997.

Arnesen, Eric. *Brotherhoods of Color: Black Railroad Workers and the Struggle for Equality*. Cambridge, MA: Harvard University Press, 2002.

Azuma, Eiichiro. *Between Two Empires: Race, History, and Transnationalism in Japanese America*. New York: Oxford University Press, 2005.

Bain, David Haward. *Empire Express: Building the First Transcontinental Railroad*. New York: Penguin, 2000.

Bates, Beth Tompkins. *Pullman Porters and the Rise of Protest Politics in Black America, 1925–1945*. Chapel Hill: University of North Carolina Press, 2000.

Bell, Derrick. *Silent Covenants:* Brown v. Board of Education *and the Unfulfilled Hopes for Racial Reform*. New York: Oxford University Press, 2005.

Benhabib, Seyla. *The Rights of Others: Aliens, Residents, and Citizens*. Cambridge: Cambridge University Press, 2004.

Berlin, Ira. *Many Thousands Gone: The First Two Centuries of Slavery in North America*. Cambridge, MA: Harvard University Press, 2000.

———. *Slaves without Masters: The Free Negro in the Antebellum South*. New York: New Press, 2007.

Berwanger, Eugene H. *The Frontier against Slavery: Western Anti-Negro Prejudice and the Slavery Extension Controversy.* Champaign: University of Illinois Press, 2002.

Bingham, Tom. *The Rule of Law.* New York: Penguin Global, 2011.

Bloemraad, Irene. *Becoming a Citizen: Incorporating Immigrants and Refugees in the United States and Canada.* Berkeley: University of California Press, 2006.

Borjas, George J. *Friends or Strangers: The Impact of Immigrants on the U.S. Economy.* New York: Basic Books, 1991.

———. *Heaven's Door: Immigration Policy and the American Economy.* Princeton, NJ: Princeton University Press, 2001.

Borstelmann, Thomas. *The Cold War and the Color Line: American Race Relations in the Global Arena.* Cambridge, MA: Harvard University Press, 2003.

Bosniak, Linda. *The Citizen and the Alien: Dilemmas of Contemporary Membership.* Princeton, NJ: Princeton University Press, 2008.

Branch, Taylor. *At Canaan's Edge: America in the King Years, 1965–68.* New York: Simon and Schuster, 2007.

Brands, H.W. *Traitor to His Class: The Privileged Life and Radical Presidency of Franklin Delano Roosevelt.* New York: Anchor, 2009.

Briggs, Vernon M. *Immigration and American Unionism.* Ithaca, NY: Cornell University Press, 2001.

Brooks, James F. *Captives and Cousins: Slavery, Kinship, and Community in the Southwest Borderlands.* Chapel Hill: University of North Carolina Press, 2001.

Brown, Dee. *Bury My Heart at Wounded Knee: An Indian History of the American West.* New York: Holt, 2007.

Brown, Wendy. *Walled States, Waning Sovereignty.* Cambridge, MA: MIT Press, 2010.

Calavita, Kitty. *Inside the State: The Bracero Program, Immigration, and the I.N.S.* New York: Routledge, 1992.

Campbell, Stanley W. *Slave Catchers: Enforcement of the Fugitive Slave Law, 1850–1860.* Chapel Hill: University of North Carolina Press, 2011.

Carens, Joseph H. *Culture, Citizenship, and Community: A Contextual Exploration of Justice as Evenhandedness.* New York: Oxford University Press, 2000.

Chadwick-Joshua, Jocelyn. *The Jim Dilemma: Reading Race in Huckleberry Finn.* Jackson: University Press of Mississippi, 1998.

Chan, Sucheng. *Asian Americans: An Interpretative History.* Boston: Twayne, 1991.

Chang, Iris. *The Chinese in America: A Narrative History.* New York: Viking, 2003.

Chavez, Leo R. *Shadowed Lives: Undocumented Immigrants in American Society.* Independence, KY: Wadsworth, 1998.

Chun, Jennifer Jihye. *Organizing at the Margins: The Symbolic Politics of Labor in South Korea and the United States.* Ithaca, NY: Cornell University Press, 2011.

Chung, Angie Y. *Legacies of Struggle: Conflict and Cooperation in Korean American Politics.* Stanford, CA: Stanford University Press, 2007.

Cohen, Arthur M., and Carrie B. Kisker. *The Shaping of American Higher Education: Emergence and Growth of the Contemporary System.* San Francisco: Jossey-Bass, 2010.

Cohen, Deborah. *Braceros: Migrant Citizens and Transnational Subjects in the Postwar United States and Mexico.* Chapel Hill: University of North Carolina Press, 2011.

Cohen, Lizabeth. *A Consumers' Republic: The Politics of Mass Consumption in Postwar America.* New York: Vintage, 2003.

————. *Making a New Deal: Industrial Workers in Chicago, 1919–1939*. Cambridge: Cambridge University Press, 2008.

Constable, Marianne. *Just Silences: The Limits and Possibilities of Modern Law*. Princeton, NJ: Princeton University Press, 2007.

Cornish, Dudley Taylor. *The Sable Arm: Black Troops in the Union Army, 1861–1865*. Lawrence: University Press of Kansas, 1990.

Coutin, Susan Bibler. *The Culture of Protest: Religious Activism and the U.S. Sanctuary Movement*. Boulder, CO: Westview Press, 1993.

————. *Legalizing Moves: Salvadoran Immigrants' Struggle for U.S. Residency*. Ann Arbor: University of Michigan Press, 2003.

Cushman, Barry. *Rethinking the New Deal Court: The Structure of a Constitutional Revolution*. New York: Oxford University Press, 1998.

Daniels, Roger. *Coming to America: A History of Immigration and Ethnicity in American Life*. New York: Harper, 2002.

————. *Prisoners without Trial: Japanese Americans in World War II*. New York: Hill and Wang, 2004.

Das Gupta, Monisha. *Unruly Immigrants: Rights, Activism, and Transnational South Asian Politics in the United States*. Durham, NC: Duke University Press, 2006.

Dauvergne, Catherine. *Making People Illegal: What Globalization Means for Migration and Law*. Cambridge: Cambridge University Press, 2009.

Davis, David Brion. *Inhuman Bondage: The Rise and Fall of Slavery in the New World*. New York: Oxford University Press, 2008.

De Genova, Nicholas. *Working the Boundaries: Race, Space, and 'Illegality' in Mexican Chicago*. Durham, NC: Duke University Press, 2005.

Delano, Alexandra. *Mexico and Its Diaspora in the United States: Policies of Emigration since 1948*. Cambridge: Cambridge University Press, 2011.

Delgado, Hector L. *New Immigrants, Old Unions: Organizing Undocumented Workers in Los Angeles*. Philadelphia: Temple University Press, 1994.

Deyle, Steven. *Carry Me Back: The Domestic Slave Trade in American Life*. New York: Oxford University Press, 2006.

Dollard, John. *Caste and Class in a Small Southern Town*. New York: Doubleday Anchor, 1957.

Douglass, Frederick. *Autobiographies*. New York: Library of America, 1994.

Douglass, John Aubrey. *The California Idea and American Higher Education: 1850 to the 1960 Master Plan*. Stanford, CA: Stanford University Press, 2007.

Dudziak, Mary L. *Cold War Civil Rights: Race and the Image of American Democracy*. Princeton, NJ: Princeton University Press, 2000.

Dworkin, Ronald. *Sovereign Virtue: The Theory and Practice of Equality*. Cambridge, MA: Harvard University Press, 2002.

Einhorn, Robin L. *American Taxation, American Slavery*. Chicago: University of Chicago Press, 2008.

Ellis, Joseph. *American Sphinx: The Character of Thomas Jefferson*. New York: Vintage, 1998.

Ellison, Ralph. *Shadow and Act*. New York: Vintage, 1995.

Fantasia, Rick, and Kim Voss. *Hard Work: Remaking the American Labor Movement*. Berkeley: University of California Press, 2004.

Faust, Drew Gilpin. *This Republic of Suffering: Death and the American Civil War*. New York: Vintage, 2009.

Fehrenbacher, Don E., and Ward McAfee. *The Slaveholding Republic: An Account of the United States Government's Relation to Slavery*. New York: Oxford University Press, 2002.

Fine, Janice. *Workers Centers: Organizing Communities at the Edge of the Dream*. Ithaca, NY: Cornell University Press, 2006.

Fischel, William A. *Making the Grade: The Economic Evolution of American School Districts*. Chicago: University of Chicago Press, 2009.

Fishback, Price V., and Shawn Everett Kantor. *A Prelude to the Welfare State: The Origins of Workers' Compensation*. Chicago: University of Chicago Press, 2006.

Fishkin, Shelley Fisher. *Lighting Out for the Territory: Reflections on Mark Twain and American Culture*. New York: Oxford University Press, 1998.

———. *Was Huck Black? Mark Twain and African American Voices*. New York: Oxford University Press, 1994.

Fogel, Robert William, and Stanley L. Engerman. *Time on the Cross: The Economics of American Slavery*. New York: W.W. Norton, 1995.

Foley, Neil. *The White Scourge: Mexicans, Blacks, and Poor Whites in Texas Cotton Culture*. Berkeley: University of California Press, 1999.

Foner, Eric. *Free Soil, Free Labor, Free Men: The Ideology of the Republican Party Before the Civil War*. New York: Oxford University Press, 1995.

Foote, Shelby. *The Civil War: A Narrative, Vols. 1–3*. New York: Vintage, 1986.

Forbath, William E. *Law and the Shaping of the American Labor Movement*. Cambridge, MA: Harvard University Press, 1991.

Franklin, John Hope, and Loren Schweninger, *Runaway Slaves: Rebels on the Plantation*. New York: Oxford University Press, 2000.

Friedman, Lawrence M. *A History of American Law*. New York: Touchstone, 2005.

Frymer, Paul. *Black and Blue: African Americans, the Labor Movement, and the Decline of the Democratic Party*. Princeton, NJ: Princeton University Press, 2007.

Gaddis, John Lewis. *The United States and the Origins of the Cold War*. New York: Columbia University Press, 2000.

Galarza, Ernesto. *Merchants of Labor: The Mexican Bracero Story*. Charlotte, NC: McNally and Loftin, 1964.

Gamboa, Erasmo. *Mexican Labor and World War II: Braceros in the Pacific Northwest, 1942–1947*. Seattle: University of Washington Press, 2000.

Garcia, Juan Ramon. *Operation Wetback: The Mass Deportation of Mexican Undocumented Workers in 1954*. New York: Praeger, 1980.

Genovese, Eugene D. *Roll, Jordan, Roll: The World the Slaves Made*. New York: Vintage, 1976.

Gillman, Howard. *The Constitution Besieged: The Rise and Demise of the Lochner Era Police Powers Jurisprudence*. Durham, NC: Duke University Press, 1992.

Gimpel, James G., and James R. Edwards. *The Congressional Politics of Immigration Reform*. Boston: Allyn and Bacon, 1999.

Gleeson, Shannon. *Conflicting Commitments: The Politics of Enforcing Immigrant Worker Rights in San Jose and Houston*. Ithaca, NY: Cornell University Press, 2012.

Go, Julian. *American Empire and the Politics of Meaning: Elite Political Cultures in the Philippines and Puerto Rico during U.S. Colonialism*. Durham, NC: Duke University Press, 2008.

Gomez, Laura E. *Manifest Destinies: The Making of the Mexican American Race*. New York: New York University Press, 2008.

Gordon, Jennifer. *Suburban Sweatshops: The Fight for Immigrants Rights*. Cambridge, MA: Harvard University Press, 2007.

Gordon, Linda. *Pitied But Not Entitled: Single Mothers and the History of Welfare, 1890–1935*. Cambridge, MA: Harvard University Press, 1998.

Guevarra, Anna R. *Marketing Dreams, Manufacturing Heroes: The Transnational Labor Brokering of Filipino Workers*. New Brunswick, NJ: Rutgers University Press, 2009.

Gutierrez, David G. *Walls and Mirrors: Mexican Americans, Mexican Immigrants, and the Politics of Ethnicity*. Berkeley: University of California Press, 1995.

Gutierrez, Ramon A. *When Jesus Came, the Corn Mothers Went Away: Marriage, Sexuality, and Power in New Mexico, 1500–1846*. Stanford, CA: Stanford University Press, 1991.

Halpern, Stephen C. *On the Limits of the Law: The Ironic Legacy of Title VI of the 1964 Civil Rights Act*. Baltimore: Johns Hopkins University Press, 1995.

Hamalainen, Pekka. *The Comanche Empire*. New Haven, CT: Yale University Press, 2009.

Haney-Lopez, Ian. *White by Law: The Legal Construction of Race*. New York: New York University Press, 1997.

Hart, H.L.A. *The Concept of Law*. New York: Oxford University Press, 1997.

Hayes, Kevin J. *The Road to Monticello: The Life and Mind of Thomas Jefferson*. New York: Oxford University Press, 2008.

Heidegger, Martin. *Basic Writings*. New York: Harper, 2008.

———. *Being and Time*. New York: Harper, 2008.

Hendrick, George, and Willene Hendrick. *Black Refugees in Canada: Accounts of Escape During the Era of Slavery*. Jefferson, NC: McFarland, 2010.

Hernandez, Kelly Lytle. *Migra! A History of the U.S. Border Patrol*. Berkeley: University of California Press, 2010.

Hewitt, Roger. *White Backlash and the Politics of Multiculturalism*. Cambridge: Cambridge University Press, 2005.

Higginbotham, A. Leon. *In the Matter of Color: Race and American Legal Process: The Colonial Period*. New York: Oxford University Press, 1980.

Higham, John. *Send These to Me: Immigrants in Urban America*. Baltimore: Johns Hopkins University Press, 1984.

———. *Strangers in the Land: Patterns of American Nativism, 1860–1925*. New Brunswick, NJ: Rutgers University Press, 2002.

Hing, Bill Ong. *Deporting Our Souls: Values, Morality, and Immigration Policy*. Cambridge: Cambridge University Press, 2006.

Hondagneu-Sotelo, Pierrette. *Domestica: Immigrant Workers Cleaning and Caring in the Shadows of Affluence*. Berkeley: University of California Press, 2007.

Honey, Michael K. *Black Workers Remember: An Oral History of Segregation, Unionism, and the Freedom Struggle*. Berkeley: University of California Press, 2002.

Horton, James Oliver. *Free People of Color: Inside the African American Community*. Washington, DC: Smithsonian Institution Scholarly Press, 1993.

———, and Lois E. Horton. *In Hope of Liberty: Culture, Community and Protest among Northern Free Blacks, 1700–1860*. New York: Oxford University Press, 1998.

Hosokawa, Bill. *Nisei: The Quiet Americans*. Boulder: University Press of Colorado, 2002.

Hsu, Madeline Y. *Dreaming of Gold, Dreaming of Home: Transnationalism and Migration Between the United States and South China, 1882–1943*. Stanford: Stanford University Press, 2000.

Huck Finn. Edited by Harold Bloom. New York: Chelsea House, 1990.

Irons, Peter H. *Justice at War: The Story of the Japanese-American Internment Cases*. Berkeley: University of California Press, 1993.

Jacobson, Matthew Frye. *Whiteness of a Different Color: European Immigrants and the Alchemy of Race*. Cambridge, MA: Harvard University Press, 1999.

Johnson, Kevin R. *Opening the Floodgates: Why America Needs to Rethink Its Borders and Immigration Laws*. New York: New York University Press, 2009.

Jones, Jacqueline. *Labor of Love, Labor of Sorrow: Black Women, Work, and the Family, From Slavery to the Present*. New York: Basic Books, 2009.

Jung, Moon-Ho. *Coolies and Cane: Race, Labor, and Sugar in the Age of Emancipation*. Baltimore: Johns Hopkins University Press, 2008.

Jung, Moon-Kie. *Reworking Race: The Making of Hawaii's Interracial Labor Movement*. New York: Columbia University Press, 2010.

Kashima, Tetsuden. *Judgment without Trial: Japanese American Imprisonment during World War II*. Seattle: University of Washington Press, 2004.

Katanski, Amelia V. *Learning to Write 'Indian': The Boarding School Experience and American Indian Literature*. Norman: University of Oklahoma Press, 2007.

Katz, Michael B. *In the Shadow of the Poorhouse: A Social History of Welfare in America*. New York: Basic Books, 1996.

Kennedy, David M. *Freedom from Fear: The American People in Depression and War, 1929–1945*. New York: Oxford University Press, 1999.

Kettner, James H. *The Development of American Citizenship, 1608–1870*. Chapel Hill: University of North Carolina Press, 2005.

Klarman, Michael J. Brown v. Board of Education *and the Civil Rights Movement*. New York: Oxford University Press, 2007.

———. *From Jim Crow to Civil Rights: The Supreme Court and the Struggle for Racial Equality*. New York: Oxford University Press, 2006.

Kluger, Richard. *Simple Justice: The History of* Brown v. Board of Education *and Black America's Struggle for Equality*. New York: Vintage, 2004.

Kolchin, Peter. *American Slavery: 1619–1877*. New York: Hill and Wang, 2003.

Kozol, Jonathan. *The Shame of the Nation: The Restoration of Apartheid Schooling in America*. New York: Crown, 2005.

Kramer, Paul A. *The Blood of Government: Race, Empire, the United States, and the Philippines*. Chapel Hill: University of North Carolina Press, 2006.

Kryder, Daniel. *Divided Arsenal: Race and the American State During World War II*. Cambridge: Cambridge University Press, 2001.

Kwong, Peter, and Dusanka Miscevic. *Chinese America: The Untold Story of America's Oldest New Community*. New York: New Press, 2007.

Kymlicka, Will. *Politics in the Vernacular: Nationalism, Multiculturalism, and Citizenship*. New York: Oxford University Press, 2001.

Lai, Him Mark. *Becoming Chinese American: A History of Communities and Institutions*. Walnut Creek, CA: Altamira Press, 2004.

Lee, Erika. *At America's Gates: Chinese Immigration during the Exclusion Era, 1882–1943*. Chapel Hill: University of North Carolina Press, 2007.

Lepore, Jill. *New York Burning: Liberty, Slavery, and Conspiracy in Eighteenth-Century Manhattan*. New York: Vintage, 2006.

Levy, Jacques E. *Cesar Chavez: Autobiography of La Causa*. Minneapolis: University of Minnesota Press, 2007.

Lichtenstein, Nelson. *State of the Union: A Century of American Labor*. Princeton, NJ: Princeton University Press, 2003.

Light, Ivan, and Edna Bonacich. *Immigrant Entrepreneurs: Koreans in Los Angeles, 1965–1982*. Berkeley: University of California Press, 1991.

Lipsitz, George. *How Racism Takes Place*. Philadelphia: Temple University Press, 2011.

Litwack, Leon F. *Been in the Storm So Long: The Aftermath of Slavery*. New York: Vintage, 1980.

———. *North of Slavery: The Negro in the Free States, 1790–1860*. Chicago: University of Chicago Press, 1965.

Locke, John. *Two Treatises of Government*. Cambridge: Cambridge University Press, 1988.

Loewen, James W. *The Mississippi Chinese: Between Black and White*. Long Grove, IL: Waveland Press, 1988.

Lubet, Stephen. *Fugitive Justice: Runaways, Rescuers, and Slavery on Trial*. Cambridge, MA: Harvard University Press, 2010.

Lukas, J. Anthony. *Common Ground: A Turbulent Decade in the Lives of Three American Families*. New York: Vintage, 1986.

Maltz, Earl M. *Fugitive Slave on Trial: The Anthony Burns Case and Abolitionist Outrage*. Lawrence: University Press of Kansas, 2010.

Mark Twain's Humor: Critical Essays. Edited by David E.E. Sloane. New York: Taylor and Francis, 1995.

Markowitz, Gerald, and David Rosner. *Children, Race, and Power: Kenneth and Mamie Clark's Northside Center*. New York: Routledge, 1999.

Massey, Douglas S., and Nancy A. Denton. *American Apartheid: Segregation and the Making of the Underclass*. Cambridge, MA: Harvard University Press, 1993.

———, Jorge Durand, and Nolan J. Malone. *Beyond Smoke and Mirrors: Mexican Immigration in an Era of Economic Integration*. New York: Russell Sage Foundation Press, 2002.

McAfee, Ward M. *Religion, Race, and Reconstruction: The Public School in the Politics of the 1870s*. Albany: State University of New York Press, 1998.

McPherson, James M. *The Negro's Civil War: How American Blacks Felt and Acted during the War for the Union*. New York: Vintage, 2003.

McWilliams, Carey. *Factories in the Fields: The Story of Migratory Farm Labor in California*. Berkeley: University of California Press, 2000.

Meeks, Eric V. *Border Citizens: The Making of Indians, Mexicans, and Anglos in Arizona*. Austin: University of Texas Press, 2007.

Merry, Robert W. *A Country of Vast Designs: James K. Polk, the Mexican War and the Conquest of the American Continent*. New York: Simon and Schuster, 2009.

Messent, Peter B. *The Cambridge Introduction to Mark Twain*. Cambridge: Cambridge University Press, 2007.

Milkman, Ruth. *L.A. Story: Immigrant Workers and the Future of the U.S. Labor Movement*. New York: Russell Sage Foundation Press, 2006.

Mill, John Stuart. *On Liberty and Other Writings*. New York: Classic Books, 2010.

Miller, Robert J. *Native America, Discovered and Conquered: Thomas Jefferson, Lewis and Clark, and Manifest Destiny*. Westport, CT: Praeger, 2006.

Montejano, David. *Anglos and Mexicans in the Making of Texas, 1836–1986*. Austin: University of Texas Press, 1987.

Morgan, Edmund S. *American Slavery, American Freedom*. New York: W.W. Norton, 2003.

Motomura, Hiroshi. *Americans in Waiting: The Lost Story of Immigration and Citizenship in the United States*. New York: Oxford University Press, 2007.

Nelson, Adam R. *The Elusive Ideal: Equal Educational Opportunity and the Federal Role in Boston's Public Schools, 1950–1985*. Chicago: University of Chicago Press, 2005.

Neuman, Gerald L. *Strangers to the Constitution: Immigrants, Borders, and Fundamental Law*. Princeton, NJ: Princeton University Press, 1996.

Nevins, Joseph. *Operation Gatekeeper: The Rise of the 'Illegal Alien' and the Remaking of the U.S.-Mexico Boundary*. New York: Routledge, 2001.

Newton, Lina. *Illegal, Alien, or Immigrant: The Politics of Immigration Reform*. New York: New York University Press, 2008.

Ngai, Mae M. *Impossible Subjects: Illegal Aliens and the Making of Modern America*. Princeton, NJ: Princeton University Press, 2005.

———. *The Lucky Ones: One Family and the Extraordinary Invention of Chinese America*. New York: Houghton Mifflin Harcourt, 2010.

Okihiro, Gary Y. *Cane Fires: The Anti-Japanese Movement in Hawaii, 1865–1945*. Philadelphia: Temple University Press, 1992.

———. *Margins and Mainstreams: Asians in American History and Culture*. Seattle: University of Washington Press, 1994.

Olivas, Michael A. *No Undocumented Child Left Behind: Plyler v. Doe and the Education of Undocumented Schoolchildren*. New York: New York University Press, 2012.

Oshinsky, David M. *Worse than Slavery: Parchman Farm and the Ordeal of Jim Crow Justice*. New York: Free Press, 1997.

Park, Edward J.W., and John S.W. Park. *Probationary Americans: Contemporary Immigration Policies and the Shaping of Asian American Communities*. New York: Routledge, 2005.

Park, John S.W. *Elusive Citizenship: Immigration, Asian Americans, and the Paradox of Civil Rights*. New York: New York University Press, 2004.

Patterson, James T. *Brown v. Board of Education: A Civil Rights Milestone and Its Troubled Legacy*. New York: Oxford University Press, 2002.

————. *Grand Expectations: The United States, 1945–1974*. New York: Oxford University Press, 1997.

Pfaelzer, Jean. *Driven Out: The Forgotten War Against Chinese Americans*. Berkeley: University of California Press, 2008.

Quan, Robert Seto. *Lotus among the Magnolias: The Mississippi Chinese*. Jackson: University Press of Mississippi, 2007.

Quirk, Tom. *Coming to Grips with Huckleberry Finn: Essays on a Book, a Boy, and a Man*. Columbia: University of Missouri Press, 1995.

Ravitch, Diane. *Left Back: A Century of Battles Over School Reform*. New York: Simon and Schuster, 2001.

Rawls, John. *A Theory of Justice*. Cambridge, MA: Harvard University Press, 2005.

Raz, Joseph. *The Concept of a Legal System: An Introduction to the Theory of the Legal System*. New York: Oxford University Press, 1980.

Reese, William J. *America's Public Schools: From Common School to "No Child Left Behind."* Baltimore: Johns Hopkins University Press, 2011.

Robinson, Forrest. *In Bad Faith: The Dynamics of Deception in Mark Twain's America*. Cambridge, MA: Harvard University Press, 1992.

Robinson, Greg. *A Tragedy of Democracy: Japanese Confinement in North America*. New York: Columbia University Press, 2009.

Rockman, Seth. *Scraping By: Wage Labor, Slavery, and Survival in Early Baltimore*. Baltimore: Johns Hopkins University Press, 2008.

Roediger, David R. *The Wages of Whiteness: Race and the Making of the American Working Class*. New York: Verso, 2007.

————. *Working Towards Whiteness: How America's Immigrants Became White*. New York: Basic Books, 2006.

Romero, Mary. *Maid in the USA*. New York: Routledge, 2002.

Rosenberg, Samuel. *American Economic Development since 1945: Growth, Decline and Rejuvenation*. New York: Palgrave Macmillan, 2003.

Rousseau, Jean-Jacques. *'The Social Contract' and Other Later Political Writings*. Cambridge: Cambridge University Press, 1997.

Salyer, Lucy E. *Laws Harsh as Tigers: Chinese Immigrants and the Shaping of Modern Immigration Law*. Chapel Hill: University of North Carolina Press, 1995.

Satire or Evasion? Black Perspectives on Huckleberry Finn. Edited by James S. Leonard, Thomas A. Tenney, and Thadious M. Davis. Durham, NC: Duke University Press, 1991.

Saxton, Alexander. *The Indispensible Enemy: Labor and the Anti-Chinese Movement in California*. Berkeley: University of California Press, 1975.

Seidman, Joel I. *The Yellow Dog Contract*. Baltimore: Johns Hopkins University Press, 1932.

Shachar, Ayelet. *The Birthright Lottery: Citizenship and Global Inequality*. Cambridge, MA: Harvard University Press, 2009.

Shaw, Randy. *Beyond the Fields: Cesar Chavez, the UFW, and the Struggle for Justice in the 21st Century*. Berkeley: University of California Press, 2008.

Simeone, James. *Democracy and Slavery in Frontier Illinois: The Bottomland Republic*. DeKalb: Northern Illinois University Press, 2000.

Skocpol, Theda. *Protecting Soldiers and Mothers: The Political Origins of Social Policy in the United States.* Cambridge, MA: Harvard University Press, 1995.

Slater, Joseph E. *Public Workers: Government Employee Unions, the Law, and the State, 1900–1962.* Ithaca, NY: Cornell University Press, 2004.

Smith, Rogers M. *Civic Ideals: Conflicting Visions of Citizenship in U.S. History.* New Haven, CT: Yale University Press, 1999.

Song, Sarah. *Justice, Gender, and the Politics of Multiculturalism.* Cambridge: Cambridge University Press, 2007.

Spickard, Paul R. *Almost All Aliens: Immigration, Race, and Colonialism in American History and Identity.* New York, Routledge, 2007.

———. *Japanese Americans: The Formation and Transformation of an Ethnic Group.* New Brunswick, NJ: Rutgers University Press, 2009.

Stampp, Kenneth M. *The Peculiar Institution: Slavery in the Ante-Bellum South.* New York: Vintage, 1989.

Stanley, Amy Dru. *From Bondage to Contract: Wage Labor, Marriage, and the Market in the Age of Slave Emancipation.* Cambridge: Cambridge University Press, 1998.

Stevens, Jacqueline. *States without Nations: Citizenship for Mortals.* New York: Columbia University Press, 2009.

Strum, Philippa. Mendez v. Westminster: *School Desegregation and Mexican American Rights.* Lawrence: University Press of Kansas, 2010.

Takaki, Ronald. *Strangers from a Different Shore: A History of Asian Americans.* New York: Little, Brown, 1998.

Tamanaha, Brian Z. *On the Rule of Law: History, Politics, Theory.* Cambridge: Cambridge University Press, 2004.

Thelin, John R. *A History of American Higher Education.* Baltimore: Johns Hopkins University Press, 2011.

Tichenor, Daniel J. *Dividing Lines: The Politics of Immigration Control in America.* Princeton, NJ: Princeton University Press, 2002.

Trattner, Walter I. *From Poor Law to Welfare State: A History of Social Welfare in America.* New York: Free Press, 1998.

Trotter, Joe W., and Jared N. Day. *Race and Renaissance: African Americans in Pittsburgh since World War II.* Pittsburgh: University of Pittsburgh Press, 2010.

Tushnet, Mark V. *Slave Law in the American South.* Lawrence: University Press of Kansas, 2003.

Twain, Mark. *Adventures of Huckleberry Finn.* Berkeley: University of California Press, 2001.

Tyack, David B. *The One Best System: A History of American Urban Education.* Cambridge, MA: Harvard University Press, 1974.

Urban, Wayne J., and Jennings L. Wagoner. *American Education: A History.* New York: Routledge, 2008.

Van Cleve, George. *A Slaveholder's Union: Slavery, Politics, and the Constitution in Early American Republic.* Chicago: University of Chicago Press, 2010.

Wahl, Jenny Bourne. *The Bondman's Burden: An Economic Analysis of the Common Law of Southern Slavery.* Cambridge: Cambridge University Press, 1998.

Ward, Jason Morgan. *Defending White Democracy: The Making of a Segregationist Movement and the Remaking of Racial Politics, 1936–1965.* Chapel Hill: University of North Carolina Press, 2011.

Warren, Earl. *The Memoirs of Chief Justice Earl Warren.* New York: Doubleday, 1977.

Watkins, William H. *The White Architects of Black Education: Ideology and Power in America, 1865–1954.* New York: Teachers College Press, 2001.

Westad, Odd Arne. *The Global Cold War: Third World Interventions and the Making of Our Times.* Cambridge: Cambridge University Press, 2007.

White, G. Edward. *Earl Warren: A Public Life.* New York: Oxford University Press, 1987.

Whitman, T. Stephen. *The Price of Freedom: Slavery and Freedom in Baltimore and Early National Maryland.* Lexington: University Press of Kentucky, 1997.

Wiecek, William M. *The Lost World of Classical Legal Thought, 1886–1937.* New York: Oxford University Press, 2001.

Wieck, Carl F. *Reconfiguring Huckleberry Finn.* Athens: University of Georgia Press, 2004.

Wilkerson, Isabel. *The Warmth of Other Suns: The Epic Story of America's Great Migration.* New York: Vintage, 2011.

Williams, Heather Andrea. *Self-Taught: African American Education in Slavery and Freedom.* Chapel Hill: University of North Carolina Press, 2005.

Wilson, William J. *The Declining Significance of Race: Blacks and Changing American Institutions.* Chicago: University of Chicago Press, 1980.

Witt, John Fabian. *The Accidental Republic: Crippled Workingmen, Destitute Widows, and the Remaking of American Law.* Cambridge, MA: Harvard University Press, 2006.

Woodson, Carter G. *The Mis-Education of the Negro.* Washington, DC: Associated Publishers, 1972.

Wright, Gavin. *The Political Economy of the Cotton South: Households, Markets, and Wealth in the Nineteenth Century.* New York: W.W. Norton, 1978.

Yamamoto, Eric K., Margaret Chon, Carol L. Izumi, Jerry Kang, and Frank H. Wu. *Race, Rights, and Reparation: Law of the Japanese American Internment.* New York: Aspen, 2001.

Yoshino, Kenji. *Covering: The Hidden Assault on Our Civil Rights.* New York: Random House, 2007.

Young, Iris Marion. *Justice and the Politics of Difference.* Princeton, NJ: Princeton University Press, 2011.

Yung, Judy. *Unbound Feet: A Social History of Chinese Women in San Francisco.* Berkeley: University of California Press, 1995.

Zhao, Xiaojian. *Remaking Chinese America: Immigration, Family, and Community, 1940–1965.* New Brunswick, NJ: Rutgers University Press, 2002.

———. *The New Chinese America: Class, Economy, and Social Hierarchy.* New Brunswick, NJ: Rutgers University Press, 2010.

Zieger, Robert H. *American Workers, American Unions: The Twentieth Century.* Baltimore: Johns Hopkins University Press, 1986.

John S. W. Park is Professor of Asian American Studies at the University of California at Santa Barbara. He also serves as the Associate Director of the University of California Center for New Racial Studies.